LITERARY ENCOUNTERS
WITH THE
REIGN OF GOD

LITERARY
ENCOUNTERS
——— WITH THE ———
REIGN OF GOD

Edited by
Sharon H. Ringe and **H. C. Paul Kim**

T&T CLARK INTERNATIONAL
A Continuum imprint
NEW YORK • LONDON

T & T Clark International, Madison Square Park, 15 East 26th Street, New York, NY 10010

T & T Clark International, The Tower Building, 11 York Road, London SE1 7NX

T & T Clark International is a Continuum imprint.

Cover design: Wesley Hoke

Library of Congress Cataloging-in-Publication Data

Literary encounters with the reign of God / edited by Sharon H. Ringe and H. C. Paul Kim.
    p. cm.
  Includes bibliographical references.
  ISBN 0-567-02590-X (hardcover)
  1. Bible – Criticism, interpretation, etc. I. Ringe, Sharon H. II. Kim, H. C. Paul.
BS511.3.L58 2004
220.6 – dc22

              2003020880

Printed in the United States of America

04   05   06   07   08   09   10   9   8   7   6   5   4   3   2   1

Contents

Abbreviations

ABD	*Anchor Bible Dictionary.* Edited by D. N. Freedman. 6 vols. New York, 1992
ABR	*Australian Biblical Review*
ABRL	Anchor Bible Reference Library
ACNT	Augsburg Commentaries on the New Testament
ANRW	*Aufstieg und Niedergang der römischen Welt: Geschichte und Kultur Roms im Spiegel der neueren Forschung.* Edited by H. Temporini and W. Haase. Berlin, 1972–
ANTC	Abingdon New Testament Commentaries
AThR	*Anglican Theological Review*
BDAG	Bauer, W., F. W. Danker, W. F. Arndt, and F. W. Gingrich. *A Greek-English Lexicon of the New Testament and Other Early Christian Literature.* 3d ed. Chicago, 1999
BECNT	Baker Exegetical Commentaries on the New Testament
BETL	Bibliotheca ephemeridum theologicarum lovaniensium
Bib	*Biblica*
BibInt	*Biblical Interpretation*
BRev	*Bible Review*
BT	*The Bible Translator*
BTB	*Biblical Theology Bulletin*
BZ	*Biblische Zeitschrift*
CBQ	*Catholic Biblical Quarterly*
CEV	Contemporary English Version
CL	*Classical Quarterly*
CNT	Commentaire du Noveau Testament

CRBR   *Critical Review of Books in Religion*

CurBS   *Currents in Research: Biblical Studies*

CurTM   *Currents in Theology and Mission*

Enc   *Encounter*

ET   English translation/version

ETL   *Ephemerides theologicae lovanienses*

EvT   *Evangelische Theologie*

FCNTECW   Feminist Companion to the New Testament and Early Christian Writings

HNTC   Harper's New Testament Commentaries

HTR   *Harvard Theological Review*

IBC   Interpretation: A Bible Commentary for Teaching and Preaching

ICC   International Critical Commentary

IDBSup   *Interpreter's Dictionary of the Bible: Supplementary Volume.* Edited by K. Crim. Nashville, 1976

Int   *Interpretation*

JB   Jerusalem Bible

JAAR   *Journal of the American Academy of Religion*

JBL   *Journal of Biblical Literature*

JETS   *Journal of the Evangelical Theological Society*

JFSR   *Journal of Feminist Studies in Religion*

JJS   *Journal of Jewish Studies*

JR   *Journal of Religion*

JSNT   *Journal for the Study of the New Testament*

JSNTSup   Journal for the Study of the New Testament: Supplement Series

JTS   *Journal of Theological Studies*

KJV   King James Version

LBC   Layman's Bible Commentary

LCL	Loeb Classical Library
LSJ	Liddell, H. G., R. Scott, H. S. Jones. *A Greek-English Lexicon.* 9th ed. with revised supplement. Oxford, 1996
LXX	Septuagint Greek version of Hebrew Bible
NAB	New American Bible
NASB	New American Standard Bible
NCB	New Century Bible
NEB	New English Bible
Neot	*Neotestamentica*
NIB	*New Interpreter's Bible*
NIBCNT	New International Biblical Commentary on the New Testament
NICNT	New International Commentary on the New Testament
NIGTC	New International Greek Testament Commentary
NIV	New International Version
NJB	New Jerusalem Bible
NovT	*Novum Testamentum*
NRSV	New Revised Standard Version
NT	New Testament
NTG	New Testament Guides
NTL	New Testament Library
NTS	*New Testament Studies*
NZSTh	*Neue Zeitschrift für systematische Theologie und Religionsphilosophie*
OTL	Old Testament Library
OTP	*Old Testament Pseudepigrapha.* Edited by J. H. Charlesworth. 2 vols. New York, 1983–1985
PG	Patrologia graeci [= Patrologiae cursus completus: Series graeca]. Edited by J.-P. Migne. 162 vols. Paris, 1857–1886
PL	Patrologia latina [= Patrologia cursus completus: Series latina]. Edited by J.-P. Migne. 217 vols. Paris, 1844–1864

PNTC	Pelikan New Testament Commentaries
PRSt	*Perspectives in Religious Studies*
PRStSS	Perspectives in Religious Studies Special Studies
QR	*Quarterly Review*
RB	*Revue biblique*
REB	Revised English Bible
RGG	*Religion in Geschichte und Gegenwart*. Edited by K. Galling. 7 vols. 3d ed. Tübingen, 1957–1965.
RSV	Revised Standard Version
SBL	Society of Biblical Literature
SBLSP	*Society of Biblical Literature Seminar Papers*
SBLSymS	Society of Biblical Literature Symposium Series
SE	*Studia evangelica I* (= Texte und Untersuchungen 73 [1959])
SNTSMS	Society for New Testament Studies Monograph Series
SP	Sacra pagina
ST	*Studia theologica*
STK	*Svensk teologisk kvartalskrift*
TBei	*Theologische Beiträge*
TDNT	*Theological Dictionary of the New Testament*. Edited by G. Kittel and G. Friedrich. Translated by G. W. Bromiley. 10 vols. Grand Rapids, 1964–1976
TEV	Today's English Version (= Good News Bible)
THNT	Theologischer Handkommentar zum Neuen Testament
TNTC	Tyndale New Testament Commentaries
TPINTC	TPI New Testament Commentaries
TS	*Theological Studies*
TynBul	*Tyndale Bulletin*
USQR	*Union Seminary Quarterly Review*
WBC	Word Biblical Commentary

WD	*Wort und Dienst: Jahrbuch der Theologischen Schule Bethel*
WTJ	*Westminster Theological Journal*
WW	*Word and World*
ZEE	*Zeitschrift für evangelische Ethik*
ZNW	*Zeitschrift für die neutestamentliche Wissenschaft und die Kunde der älteren Kirche*
ZTK	*Zeitschrift für Theologie und Kirche*

Preface

"It's time for the 'Lilies of the Field' lecture!" Professor Robert Tannehill would have been spotted crossing the campus of the Methodist Theological School in Ohio, carrying a bouquet of wild flowers from the nearby meadows. Knowing smiles from senior colleagues would assure new students studying the Gospels with him that they were in for a special treat. His meticulous precision as an interpreter of Scripture and his passion for the beauty and integrity of nature as a reflection and model for the justice and peace of the divine reign would come together in a lecture on the Sermon on the Mount — a lecture that lingered in the memory of mind and heart alike.

During his three years on the faculty of the Oberlin School of Theology and his twenty-nine years as professor and, eventually, Academic Dean at the Methodist Theological School in Ohio, Bob Tannehill influenced countless students, alumni/ae, and members of congregations whom he taught and led in the study of the New Testament. He always brought the best and latest of his work into the classroom or Sunday school class. Often it was only later that students realized that they had been present at the beginning of ground-breaking work in literary criticism of the Synoptic "sayings" material, for example, or in narrative-critical study of Luke-Acts. Academic skills that Bob honed at Hamline, Yale, and Tübingen Universities acquired unaccustomed grace under the tutelage of wrens, cardinals, and bluebirds, and of the flowers of the field and garden.

Not only his faculty colleagues and the students who have studied directly with Bob Tannehill, but also friends and scholars near and far recognize how much they have learned from him and enjoyed his companionship in professional meetings and common projects. A number of the authors whose work is represented in this volume spoke of waiting eagerly, when they were still in graduate school, for Bob's latest articles and books, and of their excitement at finding themselves his colleagues and collaborators as members of the Society of Biblical Literature. This volume collects some of those testimonies in the form of articles that demonstrate the variety of critical avenues to which Bob has provided leadership. The articles begin with a look at historical Jesus studies and the role of new criticisms in changing that pursuit (McKnight, Parsons). They pursue the ethical concerns related to the New Testament, to which Bob's life as well as his writings have borne witness (Talbert, Rhoads), and the roots of those concerns in the Hebrew Bible (De Vries). They follow Bob's leads and break new ground in the study of individual pericopes and of overall narrative projects on the Gospels of Matthew (Capel Anderson, Brawley, Thomas, Burnett), Mark (Struthers Malbon, Shiner, Dowd, Ringe), and Luke (Robbins, Powell, O'Day, Moessner). The collection concludes with a look forward into such new movements and challenges as postcolonial criticism (Staley) and the change brought by the electronic media to what we mean by "Scripture" (Fowler).

As editors we have been moved by the tributes to Professor Tannehill that have accompanied the articles, and by praise that came with regrets when circumstances prevented the writers' participation in this volume. We add our voices as well to the acclamation and celebration of the career of our dear friend and colleague in whose honor this volume is offered.

SHARON H. RINGE   H. C. PAUL KIM
Wesley Theological Seminary   Methodist Theological School in Ohio
Washington, D.C.   Delaware, Ohio

1

The Historical Shaping
of a Heroic Jesus

Theological Implications

Edgar V. McKnight

The construction of the "historical Jesus" is a task that has proceeded with "modern" (secular, historical-critical) assumptions and approaches. By their very nature, the results of these modern approaches challenge traditional dogmatic presentations of Jesus. They even seek to supplant dogmatic understandings of the life of Jesus; the "heroic" Jesus of critical scholarship offers an alternative to the Jesus of Christian faith. It is the thesis of this essay that research into Jesus in his own time and place may contribute to Christian faith and practice today. The first part of the essay explores the major kinds of decisions that have guided critical study of Jesus; the second part explores the thesis that twentieth-century attempts to rediscover Jesus involve hermeneutical and not just scientific-historical assumptions and decisions; and the third part examines the christological and theological implications of Jesus research.

The Shaping of a Method of Study:
From Albert Schweitzer to N. T. Wright

Schweitzer's (1875–1965) story begins with Hermann Samuel Reimarus's (1694–1768) challenge of traditional accounts of Jesus' story — accounts that grow out of, and support, the orthodox truth of Christianity. And it ends with a thoroughly eschatological Jesus —

1

a mistaken apocalyptist who, as a figure of history, is irrelevant for the truth of Christianity. The "modern" approach that allowed Schweitzer to discover the Jesus of history is one that is uncompromisingly rigorous, that does not succumb to the "law of mental inertia" that Schweitzer saw manifesting itself in the majority of scholars, a law that results in a "mediating stance."[1]

With the work of Johannes Weiss (1863–1914) — and the view that the preaching of Jesus was purely eschatological — came the beginning of the end to mediating views concerning Jesus' eschatology. In movement from the mediating efforts of Wilhelm Weiffenbach (b. 1842) and Wilhelm Baldensperger (1856–1936) to the work of Johannes Weiss,

> the reader feels like an explorer who after weary wanderings through billowy seas of reed-grass at length reaches a wooded tract, and instead of swamp feels firm ground beneath his feet, instead of yielding rushes sees around him the steadfast trees. At last there is an end of "qualifying clause" theology, of the "and yet," the "on the other hand," the "not withstanding"![2]

The alternative between "eschatological *or* noneschatological" was the third of three major alternatives in the study of Jesus. But the first two alternatives were vital for arriving at that alternative. The first alternative was "*either* purely historical *or* purely supernatural." David Friedrich Strauss (1808–1874) was the scholar who laid down this alternative. The work of Strauss is understood against the background of an orthodox supernaturalistic explanation of the events of the life of Jesus (primarily the miracles) and a rationalistic explanation that made the events intelligible as natural occurrences. Both explanations proceeded from the assumption that we have always in the Gospels testimony to fact. Strauss, however, had been influenced by philosophical concepts and had come to value the Christ-idea rather than the Christ-event. Strauss, therefore, found that we often

---

1. Albert Schweitzer, *The Quest of the Historical Jesus: A Critical Study of Its Progress from Reimarus to Wrede* (trans. W. Montgomery; New York: Macmillan, 1968), 238–39.
2. Ibid., 238.

have in the Gospels profound apprehension of truth not in historical narrative directed to outward facts but in poetic narrative directed to spiritual truth (myth).

Schweitzer declares that for Strauss's contemporaries his work "made an end of miracle as a matter of historical belief, and gave the mythological explanation its due." Schweitzer adds, "We, however, find in it also an historical aspect of a positive character, inasmuch as the historic personality which emerges from the mist of myth is a Jewish claimant of the Messiahship, whose world of thought is purely eschatological."[3]

The second "either-or" was "*either* Synoptic *or* Johannine." Strauss saw that John represented a more advanced stage of the mythopoeic process. John was more theological, the Synoptics more historical. Strauss's position did not win the day immediately, however. It was the Tübingen School and Schweitzer's teacher Heinrich Julius Holtzmann (1832–1910) who are credited by Schweitzer with overcoming the mediating approach and establishing the choice of the Synoptics over the Gospel of John.

In fact, the Tübingen School and Holtzmann are part of a history that not only saw the Synoptic Gospels as historically more primary than the Gospel of John, but also proposed the two-source theory of synoptic relationships. The almost complete elimination of the Gospel of John as a historical source *was* accepted by Schweitzer, but the two-source hypothesis of Synoptic relationships was not.

Schweitzer found the Gospel of Mark adequate for his presentation of the eschatological Jesus *only* with contributions by Matthew. Mark alone was not sufficient even for understanding Mark. Mark was invaluable, however, for giving reliable information about the last month of Jesus' career. A central problem is the reconciliation of the assertion of the sources that Jesus felt himself to be Messiah and the conduct of Jesus that implies that he did not feel himself to be Messiah. The key to understanding the life of Jesus, Schweitzer

3. Ibid., 95.

suggested, is the fact that Jesus took himself to be the Messiah but did not feel obliged to make this a factor in his public ministry.

The three parables of Mark 4 provide evidence for Schweitzer of the "dogmatic idea" that dominated Jesus' life. They reveal the "mystery of the kingdom of God." This mystery is more than the general fact that the kingdom is near. This fact had been openly proclaimed by John the Baptist and Jesus. The parable of the Sower in Mark 4 relates the coming of the kingdom symbolically and temporally to the *harvest at hand*. "The harvest ripening upon earth is the last! With it comes also the Kingdom of God which brings in the new age. When the reapers are sent into the fields, the Lord in Heaven will cause His harvest to be reaped by the holy angels."[4]

The beginning took place when Jesus was going to Jerusalem for Passover. He came in contact with John the Baptist, was baptized by John, and became aware that he was the one whom God destined to be Messiah. Following his baptism, Jesus, as John before him, proclaimed the near approach of the kingdom. He did not proclaim himself as Messiah — that remained a secret to be revealed only at the dawning of the new eon — but the secret controlled all of his preaching. In spite of the lack of success in this initial period, Jesus recognized that the time was near. Jesus sent forth his apostles as he and his disciples were returning to Nazareth from an excursion to the region of the Decapolis, for now he recognized that it was harvesttime, the time of success.

Jesus' sending out of the Twelve was the last effort for bringing about the kingdom. Jesus expected the dawn of the kingdom in the most immediate future, claimed Schweitzer. As the disciples returned and announced to him their success, reporting the power they had over the evil spirits, it signified to Jesus that all was ready. The kingdom expected in the near future, however, failed to make its appearance. Jesus' prediction did not take place. The failure of the coming of the kingdom at harvesttime clarifies what is explained by other scholars as the result of the desertion of the multitudes: the

—————————————

4. Ibid., 357.

alteration in the conduct of Jesus, his withdrawal from public life, and his resolve to die. The reconceptualization of the coming of the kingdom was enabled by the prophecies of Isaiah that spoke of the Suffering Servant of the Lord. Jesus saw the description of the one who bears the guilt of others as pointing to himself.

The journey to Jerusalem, then, was the funeral march to victory. Schweitzer concluded his summary of the life of Jesus by recounting the passion story from the perspective of Jesus' secret. He describes the Last Supper:

> In the neighbourhood of death Jesus draws himself up to the same triumphant stature as in the days by the seaside, — for with death comes the Kingdom. On that occasion he had celebrated with the believers a mystic feast as an anticipation of the messianic banquet; so now he rises at the end of the last earthly supper and distributes to the Disciples hallowed food and drink, intimating to them with a solemn voice that this is the last earthly meal, for they are soon to be united at the banquet in the Father's Kingdom.[5]

The authorities arrest Jesus and condemn him to death. On the cross Jesus expects God to intervene and bring in the kingdom of God. Jesus was mistaken. Jesus' final cry was "My God, my God, why hast thou forsaken me?"

It would seem that Schweitzer's understanding of Jesus as a mistaken apocalyptic would mean the end of Christian belief. Yet this was not even true for Schweitzer. The Jesus Christ discovered by Schweitzer, indeed, is not one who supports the thoughts and ideas of conventional theology or of popular Christianity. The historical Jesus is "a stranger and an enigma." Yet Jesus does mean something to the world "because a mighty spiritual force streams forth from Him and flows through our time also. This fact can neither be shaken nor confirmed by any historical discovery. It is the solid foundation of

---

5. Albert Schweitzer, *The Mystery of the Kingdom of God: The Secret of Jesus' Messiahship and Passion* (trans. Walter Lowrie; Amherst, N.Y.: Prometheus Books, 1985), 172.

Christianity."[6] Schweitzer's historical study leads to the conclusion that historical study cannot uncover a Jesus who supports conventional religious ideas. It is the discovery of the apocalyptic Jesus that allows a different sort of relevance.

In his "Preface to the Sixth Edition (1950)," Schweitzer addresses directly the question of the relationship of Christian faith to the historical truth. Once Schweitzer had established the historical truth of the apocalyptic Jesus, Schweitzer was willing to engage in what he had earlier called "mediating" theology. He first of all distinguishes between the essence and the form of religious truth. "The ideas through which it finds expression may change as time goes on, without destroying its essence. Its brightness is not dimmed by what happens to it. Changing seems to make the ideas more transparent as a means whereby the truth is revealed."[7]

Schweitzer suggests that the spiritualized view of the kingdom was not entirely foreign to the historical Jesus. When the kingdom failed to appear in supernatural fashion, believers took a more and more spiritual view of the kingdom of God and the messiahship of Jesus. This view was so obvious that it was attributed to Jesus himself. Schweitzer does not bemoan this development. He suggests that the spiritualizing of the kingdom of God took place under the influence of the Spirit of Jesus and that indeed "it was Jesus who began to spiritualize the ideas of the Kingdom of God and the Messiah."[8]

Jesus introduced his strong ethical emphasis on love into the late-Jewish conception of the kingdom, according to Schweitzer. He made love and the consistent practice of love the indispensable condition of belonging to the kingdom. By this means the late-Jewish idea of the kingdom of God was charged with ethical energy that transformed it into the spiritual and ethical reality that it now is. Later believers could regard their own notion of the kingdom of God as identical

---

6. Schweitzer, *Quest*, 399.

7. Albert Schweitzer, *The Quest of the Historical Jesus* (ed. John Bowden: Minneapolis: Fortress, 2001), xliv.

8. Ibid., xliv.

with that of Jesus and leave out of account those sayings in which the otherness of the kingdom appeared.

In the closing decade of the twentieth century, N. T. Wright makes central the spiritual aspect of the kingdom. But this is not set in opposition to the apocalyptic aspect. Schweitzer had concluded his quest with the declaration that Jesus "comes to us as one unknown." But Wright concludes his study of the historical Jesus with words reflecting a different conclusion:

> We come to him as ones unknown, crawling back from the far country, where we have wasted our substance on riotous but ruinous historicism. But the swinehusks — the "assured results of modern criticism" — reminded us of that knowledge which arrogance had all but obliterated, and we began the journey home. But when we approached, as we have tried to do in this book, we found him running to us as one well known, whom we had spurned in the name of scholarship or even of faith, but who was still patiently waiting to be sought and found once more.[9]

The ambiguous attitude that Schweitzer had about the results of historical research in his day is also held by Wright. Wright's negative remarks ("swinehusks") are directed to the skeptical brand of study carried out in the twentieth century and influenced particularly by Rudolf Bultmann (1884–1976). Wright himself finds that a sympathetic historical study uncovers a Jesus worth following in a direct fashion. Wright's reconstruction parallels that of Schweitzer with one exception — Jesus was not mistaken, Jesus was right. Jesus as a figure of history, therefore, is not irrelevant to the truth of Christianity.

The concept of "story" gives Wright access to the three branches of knowledge (literature, history, and theology) involved in his enterprise. Instead of a positivistic construction of small-scale hypotheses on the basis of sense-data that are confirmed (or modified or de-

---

9. N. T. Wright, *Jesus and the Victory of God* (vol. 2 of *Christian Origins and the Question of God*; Minneapolis: Fortress, 1996), 662.

stroyed) by additional sense-evidence, Wright sees the necessity of postulating large-scale historical hypotheses and the verification of those hypotheses. When his hypotheses work — when they are logical, supported by the historical data, and help make sense of additional data — they are acceptable. This nonskeptical approach to the history of Jesus involves hypotheses about the sources (the Synoptic Gospels are reflections not simply of the early church but of the historical figure of Jesus), about Jesus as a theologian (the Gospel writers were creative theologians dependent upon Jesus as a yet greater, more original, and creative theologian), as well as the way that the sources correlate with the historical situation of Jesus.

Wright begins by postulating exile and restoration as the metanarrative for Israel. The story of a prodigal son who goes off into a far country and returns to find his welcome challenged by another son who has stayed put is the story of Israel's exile and restoration. At a deep level it is the story of the exilic prophets, the books of Ezra and Nehemiah, and a good deal of subsequent Jewish literature. The story of the prodigal says that the hope of Israel is now being fulfilled. But Jesus' retelling of the story is subversive. Israel went into exile because of her own folly and disobedience, and the return is the result of the fantastically generous love of her God. Moreover, the real return from exile is taking place in Jesus' own ministry.

The way that Jesus is related to Judaism in both a positive and negative fashion provides Wright with his major criteria for authenticity. To make historical sense Jesus' proclamation of the kingdom must be clearly understood within its Jewish context *and* it must challenge some prevailing assumptions within that Jewish context. In addition, Jesus' proclamation must be clearly understood as the presupposition for the very different resonance of "kingdom" in the early church *and* retain a focus characteristic of Jesus' career and not simply the work of Jesus' post-Easter followers. Wright calls this the criteria of double similarity and double dissimilarity.

Wright does not apply these criteria to individual sayings and actions but to the Gospels' story line about Jesus in light of other prevailing Jewish narratives concerning the end of the exile. In fact, no tradition of the Synoptic Gospels is called into question with the use of the criteria used by Wright. The criteria validate the agenda of a "Third Quest" that fits Jesus into first-century Judaism. And the criteria allow the synoptic traditions to be accepted as historical: Wright fits them comfortably within the ministry of Jesus as apocalyptic prophet. The criteria are useful as they are used to show how the data of the Synoptic Gospels fit into the large-scale narrative Wright constructs.

For Wright, Jesus was a first-century apocalyptic prophet who understood himself to be Israel's Messiah and, in some sense, the very embodiment of Yahweh. Jesus received the call to act as Israel's Messiah (or confirmation of such a call) at his baptism by John the Baptist. Jesus announced that the long-awaited kingdom of Israel's God was coming to birth. This involved the return from exile, the defeat of evil, and the return of Yahweh to Zion. Israel was warned, however, that her present ways of advancing the kingdom were counterproductive and would result in a great national disaster. Indeed, Satan had made its home in Israel's national institutions and aspirations. The agenda of Jesus involved not a military victory of God over evil but a victory involving turning the other cheek, going the second mile, taking up the cross.

Jesus not only engaged in an itinerant prophetic ministry, calling twelve disciples and announcing the kingdom in praxis, story, and symbol; he also drew matters to a head in one particular trip to Jerusalem. Prophecies detailing the return from Babylonian exile (Isa 40–55 in general and 52:13–53:12 in particular) shed light on that trip — events in the temple, the upper room, and the hill outside the city gate. And Mark 13 sheds light on Jesus' understanding of the significance of the fall of Jerusalem in 70 C.E. Jesus interpreted his death and vindication after death as the defeat of evil; this was the way that Yahweh would return to Zion. The destruction of Jerusalem demonstrates that Jesus was right and the nation wrong.

Jesus, however, knew that his followers would be muddled and ambiguous — as he also knew that the nation as a whole would not repent. It was, therefore, within Jesus' intention that his followers would return to Jesus' summons after failing to heed his summons during his lifetime. They would reuse Jesus' teachings, his challenge to Israel, as a basis for their understanding of themselves as the renewed community of Yahweh's people.

To understand the historical Jesus, however, the Gospels must be studied from the context of the life of Jesus, not from the setting in the life of the later church. When this is done, Wright finds a close fit between Jesus and first-century Judaism, with Jesus understanding himself and his work in terms of Judaism. Along with his affirmation of the basic Jewish paradigm that offered a long-awaited renewal and restoration, however, Jesus provided new terms and new goals — as other Jewish sects had done (including the followers of John and the Essenes).

The work of Wright may be compared with the work of Schweitzer and Schweitzer's presuppositions about critical study. Wright and Schweitzer are amazingly close in their view of the sources to be used. The Synoptic Gospels are the basic sources used by Wright in his volume on Jesus, but they are used in quite different ways than New Testament specialists used them in the twentieth century. In *The New Testament and the People of God*, Wright applauds the fact that "biblical specialists are at last following their classical colleagues in abandoning the endless and torturous search for exactly reconstructed sources."[10]

In a certain sense, Wright is replicating the position of Schweitzer. But because work since Schweitzer has emphasized exactly reconstructed sources, Wright's work is a conscious rejection of the procedure and results of the source analysis of critical scholars. He does assume the use of Mark by Luke and Matthew, but he does not support the view that Luke and Matthew also used the source generally called Q. Wright's procedure is the positing of a scenario and the fitting of data into that construction. Wright, then, is not interested in analysis of literary relationships between the sources. The materials

---

10. N. T. Wright, *The New Testament and the People of God* (vol. 1 of *Christian Origins and the Question of God*; Minneapolis: Fortress, 1992), 26.

are not seen as the results of literary shaping but as accurate historical records. They result from Jesus' performance of the basic script provided in the Old Testament.

The first either-or decision that Schweitzer saw in the study of the historical Jesus was "either purely historical or purely supernatural." For Schweitzer this choice was made in the context of the insistence of rationalism that the biblical narrative is historical and can be understood in light of normal human experiences, and the insistence of supernaturalism that the text must be understood in light of experiences that transcend normal human life. The eschatological explanation of Jesus' history is for Schweitzer the proper synthesis of these alternatives. Wright seeks to maintain the tension between a naturalistic worldview and a supernaturalistic worldview by positing alternatives to the "premodern" and the "modern" worldviews.

In *The New Testament and the People of God*, Wright proposes a worldview and ontology that is not based on a nature/supernature distinction, and he tells a story about reality that takes the Creator God seriously:

> Reality as we know it is the result of a creator god bringing into being a world that is other than himself, and yet which is full of his glory. It was always the intention of this god that creation should one day be flooded with his own life, in a way for which it was prepared from the beginning. As part of the means to this end, the creator brought into being a creature which, by bearing the creator's image, would bring his wise and loving care to bear upon the creation. By a tragic irony, the creature in question has rebelled against this intention. But the creator has solved this problem in principle in an entirely appropriate way, and as a result is now moving the creation once more toward its originally intended goal. The implementation of this solution now involves the indwelling of this god within his human creatures and ultimately within the whole creation, transforming it into that for which it was made in the beginning.[11]

---

11. Ibid., 97–98.

Wright suggests that the similarity of this story to the parable of the Wicked Tenants is no accident, that it fits with more of the real world than usual post-Enlightenment stories. He declares: "To abandon this story in favour of reducing everything to 'mere history', just when that Enlightenment-style project is collapsing like the Berlin Wall . . . would be as dishonest as it would be foolish."[12]

But Wright stresses the necessity of the Christian story being subject to historical scrutiny. Christians believe that

> the creator of the universe is also the lord of history, . . . that he has acted climactically, *and not merely paradigmatically*, in Jesus of Nazareth; that he has implemented that climactic act in the gift of his own spirit to his people; and that he will complete this work in the final renewal of all things.

This belief drives the Christian to history, "not simply in the search for legitimization, but in the search for the modifications and adaptations necessary if the hypothesis is to stand the test of reality."[13]

The historical study that Wright engages in faces in two directions at the same time. It acknowledges the Christian worldview *and* it seeks to be recognized as genuine historical research. Wright, however, distances himself from a naive precritical supernaturalism. For example, Wright interprets the miracles of Jesus within the historical framework developed by contemporary scholars and concludes that it is historical fact that Jesus' contemporaries (followers and opponents) regarded him as possessing remarkable powers. Wright sees the miracles not as proof of Jesus' "divinity," but as indication of his prophetic vocation.

Comments Wright makes on Jesus' statement about the future and on Jesus' own self-understanding show that Wright wants to present Jesus' life in a way more consistent with conventional historiography than with a supernaturalism. A central passage is Mark 13 — a passage seen by Schweitzer as evidence that Jesus believed that the

---

12. Ibid., 98.
13. Ibid., 136.

end of history was shortly to occur, and seen by many Christians as referring to the second coming of Jesus. Wright sees the sayings that speak of coming destruction and vindication as originating with Jesus and referring to the future overthrow of Jerusalem. According to Wright, Jesus did not need supernatural aid to understand that the Jewish people were moving toward revolt against Rome and that such revolt would prove disastrous. The coming of false messiahs, for example, "did not take much guessing."[14] Wright says that in the context of first-century Jewish thought and language, passages such as Mark 13:24–25, 27 can be understood as neither bizarre nor fantastic.

Jesus' self-understanding is expressly distanced from a naive supernatural understanding by Wright:

> Jesus did not . . . "know that he was God" in the same way that one knows one is male or female, hungry and thirsty, or that one ate an orange an hour ago. His "knowledge" was of a more risky, but perhaps more significant, sort: like knowing one is loved. One cannot "prove" it except by living by it. Jesus' prophetic vocation thus included within it the vocation to enact, symbolically, the return of YHWH to Zion. His messianic vocation included within it the vocation to attempt certain tasks which, according to scripture, YHWH had reserved for himself. . . . He was Israel's Messiah; but there would, in the end, be "no king but God."[15]

The third either-or choice, according to Schweitzer, was "either noneschatological or eschatological." It has become clear that the decisions about sources and their use, the supernatural, and eschatology are closely interrelated. Wright's view of Jesus as an apocalyptic prophet is the capstone to his views on sources and the supernatural. The counterposed eschatological or noneschatological is usually seen as an opposition between a view of the kingdom in spiritual terms and a view of the kingdom in apocalyptic end-of-the-space-time-universe

---

14. Wright, *Jesus and Victory*, 360.
15. Ibid., 653.

terms. Wright sees that this way of viewing the question is too simplistic — that apocalyptic is not synonymous with the end of the
space-time universe.

A redefinition of Jewish eschatology and, therefore, an alternative
historical reconstruction is necessary.

> The attempt to follow Schweitzer has resulted in a major re-
> finement of what precisely Jewish eschatology and apocalyptic
> really was. One of the things for which Schweitzer has become
> most famous is now increasingly questioned: "apocalyptic" was
> for him, and for the ninety years since he wrote, almost synony-
> mous with the end of the space-time universe, but it is now clear
> that this is a bizarre literalistic reading of what the first century
> knew to be thoroughly metaphorical.[16]

By means of a metaphorical reading of apocalyptic eschatology,
Wright is able to make sense of Jesus as an apocalyptic prophet who
would have been understood in thoroughly historical terms.

Albert Schweitzer at the beginning of the twentieth century and
N. T. Wright at the close of the century presented historical Jesuses that formally satisfy the drive for critical historical knowledge.
These scholars are very creative and use their imagination liberally
in their reconstructions of the historical Jesus. But the demands of a
severely historical approach are evident throughout their work. Ernst
Troeltsch's treatment of the significance of Jesus presents a way of
combining critical study and imagination that was not persuasive
in his day but that may be helpful in our postmodern epoch. Ernst
Troeltsch (1865–1923) was a German Protestant theologian and cultural philosopher whose theology is described by Friedrich Wilhelm
Graf as one of "cultural modesty."

Troeltsch encountered intensive criticism from the German Protestant theology of the 1920s that was antiliberal and mostly antidemo-
cratic, but today Troeltsch's thought is important because it "permits

---

16. Ibid., 81.

central problems of contemporary theological and philosophical discussion — for instance, the pluralism of religious traditions, the dependency of theology upon contexts, the relationship of Christianity to cultural modernity — to be grasped outside of all claims of dogmatic absolutism."[17]

In his 1911 essay on "The Significance of the Historical Existence of Jesus for Faith," Troeltsch declares that "one of the main questions for Christian religious thought today is . . . the effect of historical criticism upon faith in Christ."[18] Troeltsch questions what a picture of Jesus subject to and shaped by historical criticism could mean for faith that is concerned with the suprahistorical, with the eternal, timeless, and unconditioned. The position of Troeltsch combines two elements. First, it accepts "the wholehearted historical criticism of, and research into, the gospel narratives." At the same time, however, it wishes "to preserve Christianity as redemption through faith's constantly renewed personal knowledge of God." These two presuppositions apply for people who "recognize modern thought and at the same time see in Christianity religious powers which should not be given up." And Troeltsch adds: "The writer of these lines gladly and resolutely includes himself in this group."[19]

Troeltsch finds a "foundation" for the study of the historical Jesus in "laws" from the realm of social-psychology, because if one wishes a "sure and powerful redeeming knowledge of God," one will find that in community and cult.

> A cult illuminated by the Christian idea must . . . always centre upon gathering the congregation around its head, nourishing and strengthening it by immersion in the revelation of God contained in the image of Christ, spreading it not by dogmas, doctrines and philosophies but by handing on and keeping alive the image of Christ, the adoration of God in Christ. So long

---

17. Friedrich Wilhelm Graf, "Troeltsch, Ernst," *Encyclopedia of Religion* (ed. Mircea Eliade et al.; New York: Macmillan, 1987), 15:61.

18. Ernst Troeltsch, "The Significance of the Historical Existence of Jesus for Faith," in his *Writings on Theology and Religion* (trans. and ed. Robert Morgan and Michael Pye; Atlanta: John Knox, 1977), 182.

19. Ibid., 191.

as Christianity survives in any form it will always be connected
with the central position of Christ in the cult. It will either exist
in this form or not at all.[20]

Because we need a cult and community and we need Christ as the
head and rallying point of the congregation, it is not possible to be
indifferent to historical-critical questions. If the "symbol of Christ"
is to have a basis in the "fact" of Jesus, the basic information about
Jesus and his teaching must be established by means of historical criticism as historical reality. At one point Troeltsch acknowledges the
"difficulties, distress, and uncertainty" involved in the accommoda-
tion of faith to learning. He even speaks of "a dependence upon the
general feeling of historical reliability produced by the impression
of scientific research." The historical-critical method is relativized.
It is valuable as a way of providing support in an epoch that values historical-critical method as "scientific." In other epochs ancient
philosophy supplied reliability, and yet later natural science did so.
"Today the historicising and psychologising of our whole view of
man [*sic*] and his earthly existence must be added."[21]

A pragmatic element is involved — what is sufficient for properly
religious purposes. Troeltsch sees the fact that the historical person of
Jesus is set in "a wide context of historical preparation and effects"
as very important in achieving this pragmatic goal. This fact makes
necessary only a "basic overall picture." Jesus' religious ideas exist in
the center of a history of development that begins with the prophets
of Israel, and his ideas are further developed by Paul and other great
theologians. The personality of Jesus, then, is not to be grasped as
an isolated fact. Since Jesus is the completion of the prophets, the
prophets' faith in God and ethical teachings play their role in interpreting Jesus. But Jesus must also be seen as the object of apostolic
belief. A dialectical relationship exists between the interpretation of
the historical Jesus and the preparation and effects of the person of

---

20. Ibid., 196.
21. Ibid., 199.

Jesus. Once Jesus is seen "in all truth and honesty" as the center, concern that one is composing a myth without object or basis in reality disappears and the picture of Christ can be interpreted "in practical proclamation very freely and flexibly, using everything that flowed into him and everything which in the course of thousands of years has been accommodated and loved in him."[22]

Troeltsch understands the image of Jesus in light of his view of the medium of religious consciousness. Human consciousness is finally dependent upon material objects. Divine revelation, then, requires objects of mediation. The medium that is most appropriate for a spiritual religion is the image of the founder recalled by followers. For Christianity, then, the personality of Jesus is the lasting medium, and for Troeltsch imagination is one of the most important factors involved in the construction of this medium. The factor of imagination allows a plurality of valid images of Jesus. According to Troeltsch, however, "symbolizing imagination" is not to be understood as a completely free capacity. It is based on an objective reality that bears a definite profile in terms of content and yet can be interpreted in line with individual creativity and needs. In spite of the possibility of a free creation, the image of Jesus must remain historically oriented. The central point of Christian worship is not an unhistorical, contentless point of escape but is a focus of reality whose contour is due to an individual person.[23]

Different images of Jesus are legitimate and necessary because of differences among religious subjects — individual life histories, ethical options, aesthetic preferences, gender-specific experience, emotional constraints are manifested in different images of Jesus. Different images of Jesus are also legitimate and necessary because of different expressions of the Christian principle in different Christian communities. As is well-known, influenced by Max Weber, Troeltsch

---

22. Ibid., 200–201.

23. Ernst Troeltsch, "Die Selbständigkeit der Religion," *ZTK* 6 (1896): 102–5; idem, "On the Possibility of a Liberal Christianity," in his *Religion in History* (trans. James Luther Adams and Walter F. Bense; Minneapolis: Fortress, 1991), 347–51; see Johann Hinrich Claussen, *Die Jesus-Deutung von Ernst Troeltsch im Kontext der liberalen Theologie* (Tübingen: Mohr/Siebeck, 1997), 259–79.

differentiated between church, sect, and mystical types. The Christ of the church is the Redeemer whose work of salvation is presented in the established church and its sacraments. The Christ of the sect is the Lord, the model and lawgiver of divine worth and authority whose redemption will be completed in the future. The sects radicalize the tensions between religion and society to the place where there is absolute opposition between the norms of culture and the law of Christ. The Christ of the mystical type is an inner spiritual principle that is realized in the arousal of religious feeling. These three images of Jesus possess a relationship to the historical message of Jesus, and no one of the images expresses that message in its entirety.[24]

Troeltsch held that the plurality of images of Jesus did not mean an infinite number of images. Limits existed in terms of creative possibilities and the constraints of the different types of religious structure. Norms or criteria exist for judgment of the validity of the images of Jesus. The effect of the image is one criterion. Does the image of Jesus serve the needs of authentic religious experience, or does it serve interests that are foreign to authentic religion? This is a subjective matter, and Troeltsch suggests historical evidence as a simpler, more useful criterion. The historical reconstruction of the person and preaching of Jesus is an important criterion of judgment for all subjectively created images of Jesus. Troeltsch lists critical consensus on a number of points. An image of Jesus is not authentically Christian if it does not express such things as Jesus' personal belief in God; his ethical transcendence; the unconditioned evaluation of the individual irrespective of the individual's national, social, or cultural membership; and Jesus' religious universalism.[25]

Hermeneutics and History in Twentieth-Century Studies

Major studies of Jesus in the twentieth century show that scientific and historical scholarship and imagination are related in different

---

24. Ernst Troeltsch, "The Social Philosophy of Christianity," in his *Religion in History,* 210–34; Claussen, *Jesus-Deutung,* 274–79.
25. Claussen, *Jesus-Deutung,* 276–77.

ways to religious and theological scholarship and imagination. The correlation between the historical figure of Jesus and Christian faith is not simply a fact that is to be discovered by the proper religious and scholarly approaches and tools. The correlation is something to be negotiated. The challenge of criticism to the orthodox faith makes this negotiation a test of faith and learning. In America in the first half of the twentieth century, accounts of Jesus' life continued in the liberal perspective, influenced by the optimistic cultural mood and written to serve the social gospel and to combat fundamentalist ideas. In the second half of the twentieth century, the center of critical scholarship moved to the universities and graduate schools in America, and this has presented a new academic context and new challenges that must be negotiated.

The following emphases may be seen in the study of Jesus in the last century: (1) Orthodox images of Jesus with traditional christo-logical doctrines remained in the background either as images to be challenged, images to be correlated with new knowledge, or images to cling to in spite of the challenges of historical research. (2) Following Schweitzer, liberal lives of Jesus were able to integrate liberal portraits of Jesus with apocalyptic understandings. Liberal studies emphasized Jesus' teachings and show his heroic qualities. Liberal studies attempted to show that Jesus was a credible founder of Christianity and the continuing object of devotion. (3) Challenges to the historical existence of Jesus — such as that of Arthur Drews — took the position that the historical Jesus of the liberals could not serve contemporary religious life.[26] Humankind can itself become divine through moral activity. (4) Rudolf Bultmann's approach to Jesus was part of the challenge to liberal optimism on the part of dialectical theology. The study of the historical Jesus was impossible, illegitimate, and unnecessary. In Bultmann the solid foundation of existential interpretation is contrasted with the shifting sands of historical research.

Then (5) the "new·quest" of the historical Jesus by students of Bultmann proceeded with the conviction that Jesus' appearance and

---

26. Arthur Drews, *The Christ Myth* (trans. C. Delisle Burns; Amherst, N.Y.: Prometheus Books, 1998).

his preaching imply a Christology, and that anyone failing to follow up on the historical questions implied in this ends with a mythological Lord. (6) The renewed liberal quest of the historical Jesus, with its origins in a new American setting, acknowledged the limitations of historical-critical method and supplemented historical method with sociological analysis. (7) A "third quest" of the historical Jesus that is basically anti-Bultmannian has proceeded with a higher valuation of the authenticity of the sources. (8) To be differentiated from the "third quest" is an emphasis upon the historic biblical Christ mediated through the Gospel texts. The result of the ever-shifting sands of historical research was distanced from the presence of the risen Christ in the Christian community. (9) Jewish and Roman Catholic studies of the historical Jesus in the twentieth century may be seen partly in light of developments in the Roman Catholic Church and its scholarship and in developments in the larger cultural world. Influential work on the historical Jesus has been done by the Roman Catholic scholar John P. Meier, who seeks to base his study on purely historical sources and arguments.

A variety of Jesuses have resulted from twentieth-century study. Among the most popular in the final decades of the century were the social prophet (Richard A. Horsley), the charismatic Jew (Geza Vermes), the Jewish sage (Ben Witherington III), the Cynic philosopher (F. Gerald Downing), the social revolutionary (John Dominic Crossan), the religious mystic (Marcus J. Borg), the prophet of the end time (E. P. Sanders), the marginal Jew (John P. Meier), and the true Messiah (N. T. Wright).

Although critical scholarship is vital for any of the images to be given more than passing attention, it is clear that more is involved than purely objective scholarship. Scholars have made decisions that do not grow out of the data themselves. Klaus Haacker says, "The changing and competing images of Jesus would be understood better as the result of an *interaction* between the historical data and the assumptions of the researchers and their time."[27] He sees

---

27. Klaus Haacker, "Die Moderne Historische Jesus-Forschung als Hermeneutisches Problem," *TBei* 31 (2000): 62.

three interrelated factors at work in the hermeneutical problem that constitutes modern historical Jesus study: evidence, relevance, and emergence. Evidence is related to the fact that the study of Jesus involves objective material data. Relevance has to do with the judgment of value for the historians personally and especially for social significance. Emergence is the constructive interplay of the evidence and relevance in the process of perception.

The emergence Haacker has in mind is similar to the way a picture gradually emerges when a photograph is developed. There is an objective, material element that insures the outline of the whole. But there is a variability of light and darkness insofar as the parts of the picture are concerned. "So the textual foundation for Jesus study remains stable to a large extent. But the interpretation can expose certain parts of the tradition in a stronger fashion (through frequent citations, for example) and underexpose other parts of the tradition so as to allow them to remain faint."[28] The process is summarized by Haacker: "On the foundation of a definite data base (especially textual data) certain aspects are judged to be especially relevant; they stimulate the organization of available information into a harmonious totality."[29]

When we examine the major moves in the study of Jesus, we may find some correlation with major cultural and theological movements (or paradigms). Geert Hallbäck has attempted to explain the major moves in the study of the historical Jesus as related to the broader history of theology and culture. The liberal theologians at the close of the nineteenth century sought to harmonize Christianity and modern civilization, and the Jesus uncovered was one who proclaimed "a moral message aiming at the perfection of man's civil and personal behavior."[30] The apocalyptic Jesus of Johannes Weiss and Albert Schweitzer at the turn of the century — while not a simple projection of the imagination of Weiss and Schweitzer — was a Jesus who fit into the "changing of the times."

---

28. Ibid., 63.
29. Ibid., 73.
30. Geert Hallbäck, "From Apocalyptic to Sage: Paradigms of Jesus in the 20th Century," *STK* 77 (2001): 118.

Now, nearly a hundred years later, we can see that this apocalyptic Jesus had more in common with the new period than his partisans could have been aware of. They were experiencing not only a *fin de siècle,* but the end of a whole epoch based on a long period of peace and progress; the epoch of industrial optimism was being met with spleen and nihilism by the more sensitive artists and scholars. The decadence of symbolistic poetry was almost as apocalyptic as the Jewish apocalypses of antiquity, although it knew nothing of the hopes of ancient apocalypticism. The First World War came not only as a sudden interruption of continuous progress: it came as the logical culmination of a culture that had exhausted its potentialities, so that the melting down in collective bloodshed was almost felt like a relief.[31]

Hallbäck sees a similarity between the cultural situation of the late nineteenth century that supported the liberal Jesus and the contemporary cultural situation.

We too have experienced a long period of peace and prosperity; especially after the downfall of Communism we are no longer confronted with serious military or political threats: we are confident in our abilities and most of the time we are satisfied with our lives — although they may be a bit stressed. Life could of course be even better, if we were not such slaves of conventions and social censorship or if we were more open to spiritual perspectives.[32]

Hallbäck sees that the new cultural situation supports what he calls a "wisdom Jesus," but he also sees that the detour of eschatology and apocalypticism had an impact on contemporary Jesus-images. "Since hardly any scholar would be able to deny the existence of eschatological material in the New Testament," the significance of this material is open for discussion in the understanding of Christian origins. One important impact on the new Jesus-images "will be the

---

31. Ibid., 119.
32. Ibid., 124–25.

inclination to see Jesus as a representative of an anti-Establishment attitude — be it political or personal." [33]

Theological Implications

Historical study uncovers a figure understandable in terms of first-century Palestine. This figure may be understood through historical treatment as an individual tied to his environment and yet one who was historic in his heroism. To move knowledge and appreciation of Jesus Christ as Lord *within* a recognizable scholarly framework, we must carefully examine our ways of knowing and ways of situating the objects of our knowledge. The "modern" ways of knowing may be compared with the "postmodern." The "modern" approach involved a drive to discover the history of Jesus as that history actually took place and not as the story was told and retold in the history of the church or as that story impinges upon contemporary readers. The identification and evaluation of written sources, the isolation of forms, and the development of criteria of authenticity — all were fed by the assumption that we would eventually get back to Jesus as he actually existed. Larger worldviews within which the modern critical methods made sense were self-evident and not subject to investigation.

In a postmodern epoch, we are aware of the "modern" paradigm that has guided critical study of the historical Jesus. And we are aware that the data uncovered by contemporary historical-critical methods are always completed by frameworks for understanding that do not arise in the data themselves. Imaginative operations of the scholar remain necessary.

The fact that the study of Jesus is a "poetic" study and each of the different Jesuses created is satisfying as it "fits" the critical data and the cultural and theological worldview of their creator, does not mean that the historical Jesus is simply an imaginative figure. The

---

33. Ibid., 125.

pictures of Jesus differ widely, but they present a Jesus who is genuinely human, one whose mind and will were affected by his finite
social location in history. The figure of Jesus is not so subject to the
background, motives, and activities of researchers that the Jesuses of
historical imagination are merely self-portraits of their authors. They
are not totally dependent upon the reigning theological and cultural
paradigms. There is a wide range of images, to be sure, as all the
accounts of Jesus go beyond the sources to make sense of the sources
and the data in the sources. Just as religious symbols, images, and
stories of Jesus have been continually reinterpreted in the church, so
historical hypotheses have been continually transformed and rede-
fined. But there is a clear identification — the same sources are used,
the same basic sayings of Jesus are quoted, the same individuals and
groups of persons around Jesus are found.

Perhaps the most important contribution for the church made by
historical Jesus research is the way that religious imagination is influenced by the process and results of historical imagination. Christology
and theology (as language about Christ and language about God) are
being revised by contemporary Jesus research. Roman Catholic scholars especially have noted a paradigm shift in Christology resulting in
part from Jesus research that has provided the Christian imagination
with more realistic and human pictures of Jesus. In the first two-thirds
of the twentieth century the focus was upon the humanity of Christ,
with attention given particularly to the content and implications of
statements of the early church councils. Then a paradigm shift began
with a movement in the 1950s and 1960s to correct docetic tendencies
by retrieving previously neglected features of Jesus' humanity from
the New Testament portraits of Christ. Philosophical developments
were utilized to reconcile those features with Christ's divine status. In
the early 1970s, Christology began to draw upon the results of Jesus
research, and the earlier boundaries of the corrective move "began
to burst," resulting in a new paradigm.[34]

---

34. William P. Loewe, "From the Humanity of Christ to the Historical Jesus," *TS* 61 (2000):
315–16. See Elizabeth A. Johnson, *Consider Jesus: Waves of Renewal in Christology* (New
York: Crossroad, 1990).

John P. Galvin has described "twin interests" of Roman Catholic theologians in the paradigm shift — the examination of the christological dimensions of the grounds for believing and the investigation of the actual content of central christological affirmations. These twin interests determine the precise questions concerning Jesus to which systematic theologians typically turn their attention.[35] Galvin has delineated five issues where historical information about Jesus is "of pivotal significance" for Christology:

> (1) the presuppositions in Jesus' own person for his preaching and public activity, (2) Jesus' understanding of his own salvific significance, (3) the coexistence of present and future dimensions in Jesus' proclamation of the kingdom of God, (4) Jesus' stance toward the approach of his own death, and (5) reference points in Jesus' public life and death for the emergence of the Church and the origin of the sacraments.[36]

Elizabeth A. Johnson, a Roman Catholic scholar, is less concerned with correlating historical data with dogmatic issues than with showing how Jesus research is changing Christian imagination. This changing of Christian imagination is important because it is the "memory image" of Jesus that has functioned in the life of Christian faith. Especially for churches that have lived by a "high Christology" and a literal reading of the Gospels, Jesus research is changing this memory image.[37]

Johnson speaks of the various profiles constructed by contemporary scholars (Jesus the Jew; a marginal Jew; a prophet of Israel's restoration; a Spirit-filled leader, compassionate healer, subversive sage, and founder of a revitalization movement within Judaism; a Mediterranean Jewish peasant; an eschatological prophet proclaiming the dawning of the reign of God and paying the price with his life)

---

35. John P. Galvin, "From the Humanity of Jesus to the Jesus of History: A Paradigm Shift in Catholic Christology," *TS* 55 (1994): 260.

36. Ibid., 262.

37. Elizabeth A. Johnson, "The Word Was Made Flesh and Dwelt Among Us: Jesus Research and Christian Faith," in *Jesus: A Colloquium in the Holy Land* (ed. Doris Donnelly; New York and London: Continuum, 2001), 150.

as providing new categories by which Jesus can be understood. But she argues that this changed imagination may actually approximate aspects of the earliest disciples' memory more closely than has the memory of images of the church for generations.

In the contemporary contributions to Jesus research, the genuine starting point for a renewal in Christology is the presentation of Jesus of Nazareth as a specific human being.

> His human nature is not an abstraction but a concrete human life shaped by a real history in the world. He is situated in time and place, namely, first-century Palestine. Like everyone else, he de-scends from a line of ancestors — in his case the people of Israel. He is Jewish, both culturally and religiously, and his worldview is fed by that stream of human tradition. His human identity is shaped by his relationship to a quite specific family, soci-ety, and God. He is no stranger to the passions of red-blooded humanity but experiences the vagaries of the flesh in his own circumstances. Despite his many gifts he is limited in knowledge and needs to grow in self-awareness and discernment of his vo-cation. His career is not pre-programmed but is the result of free decisions, not always easily made, about his ministry and its focus.[38]

Roger Haight is most daring in his presentation of Jesus as "symbol of God" in a postmodern world.[39] For the most part, imaginative perceptions of Jesus Christ and his relationship to God have been fashioned by the language of the liturgy, the catechism, and general church devotion. Today, however,

> the Jesus literature most forcefully influences Christology by bringing the imagination back to an historical personage, and in so doing reinforces the conviction that at one point had to be

---

38. Ibid., 152.

39. Roger Haight, *Jesus: Symbol of God* (Maryknoll, N.Y.: Orbis, 1999). In a faculty colloquium lecture of the Boston Theological Society on November 18, 1999, Haight pre-sented "The Logic of Christology from Below." This lecture is available on the web at http://bostontheological.org/colloquium/bts/haight.htm.

doctrinally affirmed: Jesus was a human being like us. In short, Jesus research is reschooling our image of Jesus.[40]

Jesus research and the reschooling of our image of Jesus becomes a way of recovering aspects of the mystery of God that were obscured by classical doctrines. Haight speaks of Jesus as a powerful and dialogical "symbol of God" for Christian faith. Symbols may transcend other ordinary ways of knowing. They may open up the way of participatory knowledge. "Conceiving of Jesus as a symbol of God...opens up a form of participatory knowledge that exceeds what is communicated by univocal and literal speech." Symbols may operate in an "ontological mediation" — an example would be "mediation of human personal presence to another through bodily gesture."[41]

Haight's understanding of Jesus as symbol of God is made clearer in his four-part characterization of what Jesus did for human salvation:

First, Christian faith in God mediated by Jesus is at the same time an opening up of imagination in a way that allows Jesus to be the parable of God. Second, in existential terms this means that Christians encounter God in Jesus. This phrase represents the absolute foundation and point of departure for a Christology from below. Third, within this encounter Jesus reveals God, that is, mediates God and makes God present. Fourth, Christian salvation consists in the encounter with the saving God in and through Jesus, so that Jesus saves by revealing and making God present.[42]

Johnson speaks of a "revolution" taking place in the concept of God resulting from Jesus research. The revolution that recombines history and the really real is in a sense a return to Jewish and Christian tradition. In that tradition, God was viewed as revealed through

---

40. Haight, "Logic of Christology," 6.
41. Ibid., 7–8.
42. Ibid., 9.

the actual events of human history. The God of Jesus Christ is the God
of Israel who had been nurturing God's people for past centuries, and
God was expressed by Jesus in the ordinariness in life — above all in
caring concern for people. The earliest generations of Christians had
a sense of God's presence such that the division between the sacred
and the ordinary tended to disappear. Roman Catholic theology was
provided with a useful model for revising thought about the transcen-
dence/immanence of God by Karl Rahner — a scholar who initiated
consideration of a "Jesus from below." Rahner stressed that ordinary human experience is unintelligible apart from the transcendent
mystery called "God," and that this mystery is to be encountered
and known in and through the historical environment that people
experience daily.[43]

Jesus research puts specific content into the image of God when
Jesus is seen as a symbol or parable of God. According to Johnson, insights now on the table in part through Jesus research present
"the being of God as triune self-relation, truly related to the world,
able in freedom to self-empty and become, able in love to suffer
with beloved creation, powerfully compassionate over the pain of
the world, willing to be its liberator from evil."[44]

The logic of Leander Keck is called into play. Keck insists that
"whom God vindicates discloses the character of God."[45] Johnson
applies the logic:

> In Jesus, God vindicates a prophet who proclaims the compas-
> sionate rule of the living God, who is coming to overturn evil
> and set the world free from powers that enslave; God vindicates
> a preacher and teacher who liberates people from a constricting
> view of this God, understanding that divine mystery draws near
> to seek the lost; God vindicates a lively Spirit-filled human being
> who in gracious acts of inclusive table community, forgiveness,
> and healing lives out his own message in the concrete. In this

43. Karl Rahner, *Grundkurs des Glaubens. Einführung in den Begriff des Christentums*
(Freiburg im Breisgau: Herder, 1976).
44. Johnson, "Word Made Flesh," 163.
45. Leander E. Keck, *A Future for the Historical Jesus* (Nashville: Abingdon, 1971), 234.

way of thinking, Jesus not only teaches parables about God. He is concretely the parable God is telling in this historical world.[46]

The Jesus research highlighted in this essay is not essential for Christian faith. As the Roman Catholic scholar William P. Loewe has cautioned, the historical Jesus cannot be conceived of as the foundation or primary norm of Christology.[47] But as Christians who have experienced the revolution of historical consciousness, Jesus research enables us to avoid the alternative of literalism or skepticism in relation to Jesus and the Gospels. Marcus J. Borg claims that the Jesus research he has experienced as a historian "has made it possible to be a Christian again."[48] "To the extent that historical study provides us with glimpses of Jesus (of what he was like, what he taught and did, and what his own passion and vision were), it is an epiphany of an epiphany. As such, it can provide content for our vision of what it means to take Jesus seriously as an epiphany of God."

For Borg, "as a historian who is also a Christian," this means

to see God as an experiential reality, not simply an article of belief. It means to live by an alternative wisdom, whose primary content is a relationship with the same Spirit Jesus knew. It means to actualize compassion in the world, both as an individual virtue and as the core value of the alternative social vision of Jesus. And it means to be a part of a community of memory that celebrates, nourishes, and embodies the new way of being that we see in Jesus.[49]

---

46. Johnson, "Word Made Flesh," 163.
47. Loewe, "From the Humanity of Christ," 331.
48. Marcus J. Borg, "The Historian, The Christian and Jesus," *ThTo* 52 (1995): 16.
49. Ibid., 16.

2

The Quest of
the "Rhetorical" Jesus

Mikeal C. Parsons *

Introduction

In 1910, Albert Schweitzer published the English translation of his
survey of nineteenth-century liberal lives of Jesus under the title *The
Quest of the Historical Jesus.*[1] Since that time, historical Jesus research has flooded the religious market in what one scholar has
called a "Renaissance in Jesus research,"[2] and John Dominic Crossan,
Robert Funk, John Meier, Marcus Borg, and Tom Wright, among
others, are almost household names — a rather remarkable feat for
religious academic scholars. We are even accustomed to speaking
of the reference to twentieth-century quests for the historical Jesus
as the "Second or New Quest" followed by the "Third Quest."[3]

---

*I am pleased to contribute to a Festschrift honoring Dr. Robert Tannehill. I first met Bob
at a professional conference at St. Meinrad's Seminary, while I was a graduate student in
Louisville, Kentucky. I mentioned to him that I had just completed my dissertation on the
ascension narratives, which included a literary-critical treatment of the texts, and he asked to
see a copy. Not only did he cite me in the first volume of *The Narrative Unity of Luke-Acts*
(Philadelphia: Fortress, 1986) — my first citation! — he also generously offered to write a letter
supporting publication of my manuscript to the editors of JSNTSup, on whose editorial board
he served. Such stories of Bob's benefaction could be repeated countless times by our colleagues
in the guild. Thus, although Robert Tannehill may never have had doctoral students per se,
the number of NT scholars owing him a huge debt are no doubt legion. I am happy to count
myself in that number.

 1. Albert Schweitzer, *The Quest of the Historical Jesus* (New York: Macmillan, 1968).
 2. Marcus J. Borg, *Jesus in Contemporary Scholarship* (Valley Forge, Pa.: Trinity Press
International, 1994), 18.
 3. Stephen Neill, Tom Wright, and N. T. Wright, *The Interpretation of the New Testament
1861–1986* (2d ed.; New York: Oxford University Press, 1988), 379–403.

This interest in the historical Jesus has also driven much of contemporary parable research from Joachim Jeremias to C. H. Dodd to, more recently, Brandon Scott, since the parables, properly recovered, constitute the "bedrock" of the historical Jesus tradition.

While I would not wish to denigrate the importance of this rigorous historical research, I submit that one of the casualties of this intense focus on things historical has been an adequate understanding of the parables in their final canonical form and within their larger Greco-Roman context. In this essay, I develop the thesis that, however important is inquiry into the historical Jesus, understanding the way the first Greco-Roman audiences would have responded to the parables of Jesus, as they were set down in their Gospels contexts, is no less crucial for both the academy and the church. And I contend further that specifically the tradition of Greek fables and the *progymnasmata* (schoolboy rhetorical exercises) shed considerable light on the early reception of Jesus' parables.[4]

We will look at three parables in Luke, the (so-called) Prodigal Son, the Vengeful King, and the Dishonest Steward, in light of their larger Greco-Roman context.[5] In so doing, perhaps we will understand a bit better the "rhetorical" Jesus whom Luke presents to us in his narrative. At the end, I will return briefly to the issue of the relationship between the rhetorical Jesus we have been considering and the historical Jesus of modern scholarship.

---

4. Robert Tannehill has contributed to both enterprises, although his contribution to historical Jesus research has been largely cautionary. For example, in *The Sword of His Mouth* (Philadelphia: Fortress, 1975), 2, Tannehill offers this caveat to those interested in the historical Jesus: "The argument that the poetic form of some synoptic material is evidence that these are authentic words of the historical Jesus appears dubious to me." Of course, his contributions to reading the literary and aesthetic dimensions of Luke-Acts are well-known; see the two volumes of *The Narrative Unity of Luke-Acts* (2 vols.; Philadelphia: Fortress, 1986–90), cited throughout this collection.

5. The extant *progymnasmata* have been collected and translated by George A. Kennedy, *Progymnasmata: Greek Textbooks of Prose Composition and Rhetoric* (Atlanta: Society of Biblical Literature, 2003). For a review of Kennedy's work, see Michael Martin and Mikeal Parsons, "Review of *Progymnasmata: Greek Textbooks of Prose Composition and Rhetoric*, Review of Biblical Literature [http://www.bookreviews.org]." For the Greek text of Theon, I have consulted the critical edition of Michel Patillon and Giancarlo Bolognesi, eds., *Aelius Théon: Progymnasmata* (Paris: Les Belles Lettres, 1997).

First, a preliminary comment is in order. Since George Kennedy's brief chapter on Acts in *New Testament Interpretation through Rhetorical Criticism,* a flurry of rhetorical analyses of the speeches in Acts have appeared.[6] Though these works have marked differences in detail, the cumulative effect of these studies (noting in various speeches, especially by Paul, the use of major components of rhetorical speech, especially judicial), has been to demonstrate that the author of Luke and Acts was familiar with the devices and strategies of ancient rhetoric as practiced during the Hellenistic period.[7] This is especially evident in Luke's characterization of Paul in Acts as a Hellene of virtue who is capable of making a rhetorically appropriate speech whenever the context demands it.[8] Thus, one might rightly explore whether or not Jesus in the Gospel is also depicted as a man versed in various forms of Hellenistic rhetoric.

---

6. George Kennedy, "The Speeches in Acts," in *New Testament Interpretation through Rhetorical Criticism* (Chapel Hill: University of North Carolina Press, 1984), 114–40. See also Clifton C. Black II, "The Rhetorical Form of the Hellenistic Jewish and Early Christian Sermon: A Response to Lawrence Wills," *HTR* 81 (1988): 1–8; Jerome Neyrey, "The Forensic Defense Speech and Paul's Trial Speeches in Acts 22–26: Form and Function," in *Luke-Acts: New Perspectives from the Society of Biblical Literature Seminar* (ed. C. H. Talbert; New York: Crossroad, 1984), 210–24; Philip E. Satterthwaite, "Acts against the Background of Classical Rhetoric," in *The Book of Acts in Its Ancient Literary Setting* (ed. Bruce W. Winter and Andrew D. Clarke; vol. 1 of *The Book of Acts in Its First Century Setting,* ed. Bruce W. Winter; Grand Rapids: Eerdmans, 1993), 337–79; Marion L. Soards, "The Speeches in Acts in Relation to Other Pertinent Ancient Literature," *ETL* 70 (1994):65–90; idem, *The Speeches in Acts: Their Content, Context, and Concerns* (Louisville: Westminster John Knox, 1994); F. Veltman, "The Defense Speeches of Paul in Acts," in *Perspectives on Luke-Acts* (ed. C. H. Talbert; PRStSS 5; Macon, Ga.: Mercer University, 1978), 243–56; D. F. Watson, "Paul's Speech to the Ephesian Elders (Acts 20.17–38): Epideictic Rhetoric of Farewell," in *Persuasive Artistry: Studies in New Testament Rhetoric in Honor of George A. Kennedy* (ed. D. F. Watson; JSNTSup 50; Sheffield: Sheffield Academic, 1990), 184–208; Bruce W. Winter, "The Importance of the *Captatio Benevolentiae* in the Speeches of Tertullus and Paul in Acts 24:1–21," *JTS* 42 (1991): 505–31; idem, "Official Proceedings and the Forensic Speeches in Acts 24–26," in *The Book of Acts in Its Ancient Literary Setting* (ed. Bruce W. Winter and Andrew D. Clarke; vol. 1 of *The Book of Acts in Its First Century Setting;* Grand Rapids: Eerdmans, 1993), 305–36; D. Zweck, "The *Exordium* of the Areopagus Speech, Acts 17.22, 23," *NTS* (1989): 94–103; and now also, Derek Hogan, "Paul's Defense: A Comparison of the Forensic Speeches in Acts, *Callirhoe,* and *Leucippe and Clitophon,*" *PRS* 29 (2002): 73–87.

7. Philip Satterthwaite, "Acts against the Background," 378, concludes: "At point after point Acts can be shown to operate according to conventions similar to those outlined in classical rhetorical treatises." Furthermore, I suggest that, given the "rhetoric in the air" of antiquity, Luke's authorial audience, while no doubt unable themselves to reproduce these rhetorical devices in composition, were nevertheless able to respond to their effects.

8. See John Lentz, *Luke's Portrait of Paul* (SNTSMS 77; Cambridge: Cambridge University Press, 1993).

Parsing the Parables:
The So-Called Parable of the Prodigal Son

Every beginning language student is aware that Greek is a highly inflected language, but in light of the *progymnasmata,* the significance
of that fact for interpretation has not been fully appreciated. Inflecting the main subject or topic (*klisis*) was one of the first exercises
taught to beginning students of elementary rhetoric and provided a
transition from the study of grammar to the study of rhetoric since
the exercise focused on the rhetorical function of inflection.[9] Theon
gives a rather full description of how such inflection is to take place
in his discussion of *chreia* (maxim) and fable and refers back to it in
his discussion of narrative (85.29–31; Patillon [Budé ed., 1997], 48).
In his chapter on "Fables," Theon asserts:

> Fables should be inflected, like chreia, in different grammatical
> numbers and oblique cases.... The original grammatical con-
> struction must not always be maintained as though by some
> necessary law, but one should introduce some things and use
> a mixture (of constructions); for example, start with one case
> and change in what follows to another, for this variety is
> very pleasing. (74.24–35, passim 74–75; Patillon, 33; cf. also
> 101.10–103.2)

Quintilian (*Institutio oratoria* 9.1.34) also comments briefly on the
use of inflection as a rhetorical device.[10] Following a discussion of
the effects of repetition, he suggests: "Other effects may be obtained
by the graduation or contrast of clauses, by the elegant inversion of
words, by arguments drawn from opposites, asyndeton, paraleipsis,

---

9. Nicolaus, *Progymnasmata* 4.18–19 suggests that more advanced students could skip
the exercise of grammatical inflection and move on to elaborating, condensing, refuting, or
confirming.

10. Aristotle had also commented briefly on *ptōsis,* as he called it (cf. *Poetics* 20.10; *Rhetoric*
1.7.27; 2.23.2; and esp. 3.9.9), but he used the term generally to refer to similar forms of words
whether nouns, verbs, adjectives, or adverbs. See also *Ad Herennium* 4.22.30–31, which like
Quintilian views *poluptoton* as a form of paronomasia.

correction, exclamation, meiosis, the employment of a word in different cases (*in multis casibus*), moods and tenses." And again, at 9.3.37:

> At times the cases and genders of the words repeated may be varied, as in "Great is the goal of speaking, and great the task, etc."; a similar instance is found in Rutilius, but in a long period. I therefore merely cite the beginnings of the clauses. *Pater hic tuus? Patrem nunc appellas? Patris tui filius es?* [Is this your father? Do you still call him father? Are you your father's son?] This figure may also be effected solely by change of cases, a proceeding that the Greeks call *poluptoton*.

What Theon calls *klisis*, Quintilian refers to as *poluptoton;* but the phenomenon is the same. Inflection was more than just an ornamental figure of style designed to please the esthetic tastes of the audience. In fact, Quintilian included inflection in his discussion of figures of thought, a "class of figure, which does not merely depend on the form of the language for its effect, but lends both charm and force to the thought as well" (*Inst.* 9.3.28 [LCL]).[11] And the function of inflection was for emphasis (*Inst.* 9.3.67) and to attract the audience's attention to the subject under discussion (*Inst.* 9.3.27).

Any student of elementary rhetoric then would have been accustomed to inflecting the main topic or subject of a *chreia,* fable, or narrative, and presumably an ancient audience would have been naturally, almost instinctively, able to identify the main subject by hearing the topic inflected in the various cases of the Greek noun. If true and if Luke were the student of rhetoric that I think he was, then we might expect our rhetorical Jesus to have used this inflection convention to provide rhetorical markers as to the topic or subject of various parables.

Among the parables in Luke, the last parable in chapter 15 proves a fascinating case. The parable in Luke 15:11–32 has long been known in English as the parable of the Prodigal Son, and this is probably

---

11. The Latin text reads: "...genus, quod non tantum in ratione positum est loquendi, sed ipsi sensibus cum gratiam tum etiam vires accommodat."

still the most popular title of the parable. No less prominent a figure than Joachim Jeremias, however, in his classic study of the parables, suggested that this parable is more aptly described as a "parable of the Father's Love."[12] But even Jeremias's judgment could not derail the tide of subsequent interpreters, many of whom still see the parable as predominately about the prodigal younger brother. Joel Green's comments are characteristic: "As important as the father is to this parable, center stage belongs to the younger son."[13]

Does the grammar of inflection help us understand better how the authorial audience may have heard this parable? The term "son" occurs eight times in Luke 15:11–32, once in the accusative case (and plural, v. 11) and seven times in the nominative singular, in reference to the prodigal (15:13, 19, 21 [2x], 24, 25, 30). We might reasonably expect that the subject of a parable or story would occur most frequently in the nominative case; however, if we take seriously the role of grammatical inflection in the educational system of late antiquity, then we might not be surprised to learn that not only does the word "father" occurs twelve times in the parable, it appears in all five cases at least once, and in four cases, including the vocative (a rarity in Luke) at least twice: nominative, vv. 20, 22, 27, 28; genitive, 17; dative, 12, 29; accusative, 18, 20; vocative, 12, 18, 21.

The conclusion seems irresistible that an ancient audience hearing Luke 15, who were conditioned, even unconsciously, upon "hearing" a word inflected to identify that term as the subject of the story at hand, would have naturally understood that the subject of the parable was the Father and his love.

We should not be alarmed that Luke does not use inflection to mark the subject of every story. Quintilian rightly warned that these figures are only effective "if the figures are not excessive in number nor all of the same type or combined or closely packed, since economy in their use, no less than variety, will prevent the hearer from being surfeited" (9.3.27 [LCL]).

---

12. Joachim Jeremias, *The Parables of Jesus* (2d rev. ed.; trans. S. H. Hooke; New York: Charles Scribner's Sons, 1972), 128.

13. Joel B. Green, *The Gospel of Luke* (Grand Rapids: Eerdmans, 1997), 578.

Nor should we view the use of inflection as a particularly elegant rhetorical device. Remember that it was one of the first exercises practiced by the beginning student of rhetoric, who quickly passed on to more challenging exercises.[14] In fact, Quintilian recognized that inflection and other figures like it "derive something of their charm from their very resemblance to blemishes, just as a trace of bitterness in food will sometimes tickle the palate" (9.3.27 [LCL]).[15] But its "ordinary" nature might argue for its effectiveness as a rhetorical device in signaling the importance of the inflected term for the understanding of the narrative in which it is couched. Theon certainly hoped for that. In one of the chapters on "Listening to What Is Read," preserved only in the Armenian versions, Theon comments: "In listening, the most important thing is to give frank and friendly attention to the speaker. Then the student should recall the subject of the writing, identify the main points and the arrangement, [and] finally recall also the better passages" (Patillon, 105–6).[16] At the least the practice of inflection deserves further reflection, both as it was practiced in the ancient world, and as it may have been employed by the rhetorical Jesus in Luke.

The Parable and the Rhetorical Topos
of the Vengeful King

Alan Culpepper has labeled the Lukan version of the parable of the Ten Pounds (Luke 19:11–27) as a "cultural type scene" about evil tyrants.[17] While Culpepper is right in placing this story in its larger

---

14. Nicolaus, *Progymnasmata* 4.18–19, for example, suggests that more advanced students could skip the exercise of grammatical inflection and move on to elaborating, condensing, refuting, or confirming.

15. The author of *Ad Herennium*, who also cautions that poluptoton is to be used sparingly, considers poluptoton to be merely an ornament of style, more appropriate for entertainment (or at best epideictic speech) than for juridical speech; the author is less charitable than Quintilian about its aesthetic value (see 4.22.32).

16. At this point, I am relying on Kennedy's English translation of Patillon's French translation of the Armenian version of a lost Greek text. Nonetheless, my general conclusion seems warranted.

17. R. Alan Culpepper, "Luke," in *NIB* 9 (1995): 362–64. Culpepper is here extending Robert Alter's observation about literary type scenes (discussed in *The Art of Biblical Narrative* [San Francisco: HarperCollins, 1981], 47–62) to include social conventions as well. As

cultural context, it might be better to view the story in light of the discussion of the "Commonplace" in the *progymnasmata* tradition. According to Theon, a topos "is speech amplifying something that is acknowledged to be either a fault or a brave deed; it is of two kinds; one is an attack on those who have done evil deeds, for example, a tyrant (!), traitor, murderer, profligate; the other in favor of those who have done something good; for example, a tyrannicide, a hero, a lawgiver (Theon 106.1). Apthonius even gives as his examples of commonplace a speech against evil tyrants (18R–21R; Kennedy, 82–84).

As a commonplace against tyrants, the actions in Jesus' parable of the Evil Tyrant, who orders the execution of those who object to his unjust treatment of the third servant, are not to be seen as reflecting the impending eschatological judgments of a righteous God.[18] Thus, the parable in Luke 19 sets the stage for Luke to depict Jesus in the following story, the triumphal entry, as a benevolent ruler ("Blessed is the King who comes in the name of the Lord!" [19:38 RSV]).[19] Jesus as benevolent ruler stands in contrast to the evil tyrant of the parable in Luke 19, a point reinforced by the fact that only in Luke, contra Matt 25:14–30, does the absentee landlord assume the role of a *basileus,* a king (Luke 19:12, 27).

Further, Luke is the only writer who prefaces the parable with the note that Jesus told the parable of the Pounds because the crowds "supposed that the kingdom of God was to appear immediately" (19:11). By employing the rhetorical device of the commonplace, Luke is able to contrast the tyranny of earthly kings with the humility and benefaction of king Jesus. Jesus' humility is seen in the

---

Culpepper notes (362 n. 212), he and I had discussed this nomenclature while he was writing his commentary. (What he doesn't tell you is that we were taking a break from playing tennis when the discussion occurred!) We might also note in passing that Alter's notion of a literary "type scene" (so effectively applied to Luke/Acts by Robert Tannehill), might rather have been heard by the authorial audience as an example of "paraphrase" (saying the same thing well a second time or more), which Theon discusses extensively in his introduction (62.10–64.25) and in chapter 15 in the Armenian version (Patillon, 107–8).

18. Though this does not this rule out this particular interpretation for the Matthean version of the story.

19. This point is highlighted by the fact that in the Matthean and Markan versions of the triumphal entry, reference to "the *King*" who "comes in the name of the Lord" is missing (see Matt 21:9//Mark 11:9; but cf. John 12:15).

so-called triumphal entry in the fact that he chooses to enter the city riding on a colt (19:34).[20] Jesus makes a similar point later in Luke at the Last Supper: "The kings of the Gentiles exercise lordship over them; and those in authority over them are called benefactors. But not so with you; rather let the greatest among you become as the youngest, and the leader as one who serves. For which is the greater, one who sits at table, or one who serves? Is it not the one who sits at table? But I am among you as one who serves" (Luke 22:25–27 RSV). This strategy of comparison, *synkrisis*, is a common one in the rhetorical *progymnasmata* and not unknown elsewhere in Luke.

The Dishonest Steward and the Slave-as-Trickster Tradition

The parable of the Unjust Steward has been deemed "the most difficult of all the synoptic parables."[21] C. C. Torrey has succinctly stated the problem:

> This passage brings before us a new Jesus, one who seems inclined to compromise with evil. He approves a program of canny self-interest, recommending to his disciples a standard of life which is generally recognized as inferior: "I say to you, gain friends by means of money." This is not the worst of it; he bases the teaching on the story of a shrewd scoundrel who feathered his own nest at the expense of the man who had trusted him; and then appears to say to his disciples, "Let this be your model!"[22]

"The seeming incongruity of a story that praises a scoundrel has been an embarrassment to the Church at least since Julian the Apostate

---

20. This tradition is common to all four Gospels. Jesus' humility in this scene is a point widely recognized in the commentaries. His humility and pacifism (in contrast to the militaristic pomp and circumstance of the Roman *adventus*, which celebrated the return home of the victorious warring emperor) is reflected in some early Christian sarcophagus art where Jesus is shown riding the donkey sidesaddle (for a discussion, see Thomas F. Mathews, *The Clash of the Gods: A Reinterpretation of Early Christian Art* [rev. ed.; Princeton: Princeton University Press, 1999]).

21. Kenneth E. Bailey, *Poet and Peasant* (Grand Rapids: Eerdmans, 1976), 86.

22. Charles C. Torrey, *Our Translated Gospels* (New York: Harper, 1936), 59.

used the parable to assert the inferiority of the Christian faith and its founder."[23]

The parable raises several sets of interpretive questions. First, what was the nature of the dismissal? Second, what was the nature of the steward's actions? Finally, there is the question of the literary integrity of the parable: what is the relationship of the parable proper to its various interpretations? We shall appeal to the slave-as-trickster tradition to address the first two stories and Theon's *Progymnasmata* to answer the third.

What Was the Nature of the Dismissal?

To understand the nature of the dismissal, we must first ponder the relationship of the master to the steward. Many commentators assume that we have here an employer-employee relationship, in which the employer has fired the untrustworthy employee. In the ancient world, however, the term "steward" more often than not referred to a slave who had been placed in charge of his master's household or estate.[24] If the steward here is a slave, then this parable is one of nine synoptic parables in which servants or slaves figure prominently.[25]

Assuming that the ancient audience would have presumed a master-slave relationship as the parable's context, we are in a position to ask about the nature of the dismissal. We may infer that the master has decided to demote the slave to outside labor or expel him from the premises altogether. But what is the master's motive? Again, we are faced with two alternatives. Most commentators assume that the master acts on reliable information and justifiably dismisses the steward. But it is possible and, I will argue, even probable that the ancient audience would have imagined that the slave was falsely accused and that the master has summarily dismissed him without a proper hearing. Several features internal to the text suggest this reading. First, the master is

---

23. Bailey, *Poet and Peasant*, 86.

24. See Mary Ann Beavis, "Slavery as an Interpretive Context for the New Testament Servant Parables with Special Reference to the Unjust Steward (Luke 16:1–8)," *JBL* 111 (1992): 45; W. G. Rollins, "Slavery in the NT," *IDBSup* (1976): 830.

25. For a list, see John Dominic Crossan, "The Servant Parables of Jesus," *Semeia* 1 (1974): 17–32.

described as a "rich man." Throughout the Gospel of Luke, the "rich" were understood negatively. Jesus includes the rich in the list of "woes" in chapter 6, "Woe to you who are rich, for you have already received your consolation" (6:24 RSV; cf. 12:16–21; 14:12; 16:1–13, 19–31; 18:25; 21:1–4). The audience (despite their own socioeconomic status) would be inclined immediately to side against the "rich man."[26]

Second, the accusers are anonymous and have made their accusation offstage, raising questions as to their credibility. Finally, the text gives no indication that the rich master made any attempts to verify the veracity of their claims. He dismisses the steward before he submits his records for review, presumably strictly on the basis of hearsay. As such, this story fits nicely into the larger category of "slave-as-trickster" stories, which circulated widely in the Greco-Roman world. In these stories, a slave, most often falsely accused by his master, resorts to cunning and trickery to vindicate himself and outsmart his master. Consider the following story from the *Life of Aesop* (Appendix 1).

Here Aesop, falsely accused of eating his master's figs, is able both to outsmart his master and vindicate himself by exposing the lies of his fellow slaves. In the synoptic tradition, relations between masters and slaves are often hostile (wicked tenants, talents/pounds; laborers in the vineyard), and Aesop material "amply illustrates the motif of harsh, foolish, or vain masters who are quick to punish slaves for real or imagined faults."[27]

What Was the Nature of the Steward's Actions?

This brings us to our second question, "What was the nature of the steward's actions?" Before addressing this question, we should note that the size of the debtors' indebtedness indicates that the rich master was engaged in a commercial business. One hundred baths of oil was approximately nine hundred gallons, a quantity only reasonable for a business enterprise.[28]

---

26. See also Brandon Scott, "A Master's Praise: Luke 16,1–8a," *Bib* 64 (1983): 187.
27. Beavis, "Slavery," 48.
28. Culpepper, "Luke," 308.

What then can we say about the steward's action? First, his action was not dishonest at all. Either he was foregoing his own commission on the deal (thus using what was properly his own quite legitimately and to good effect), or he was canceling out a part of the debt that was interest on the loan and thus bringing his master into line with Old Testament prohibitions on charging interest (Lev 25:36). The problems with this interpretation are multiple: it is doubtful that the steward's own commission would have been included in the statement of amount owed to master. Also, there is no reason to imagine the "dishonest" manager now acting honestly.

Second, the steward's action effectively puts the master into a corner. The relieved debtors will have been so full of gratitude and praise for the master for his unexpected generosity that the master either had to risk great bitterness by disowning the steward's action, or he was forced to take credit for the action himself and, no matter what he really felt privately, to praise the steward for his action. In this sense, the story is again part of the larger stock of slave-as-trickster stories (as in the *Life of Aesop*), in which the shrewd slave outwits the master. These stories found their way into Jewish tradition as well.[29]

What Is the Relation of the Parable Proper to the Subsequent Interpretations?

The relation of the parable proper, in Luke 16:1–8a, to the material that immediately follows, 16:8b–13, has long vexed interpreters. C. H. Dodd called verses 8–13 "notes for three separate sermons on the parable as text."[30] Joseph Fitzmyer concludes that the applications of the parable found in verses 8–9, 10–12, and 13 "undoubtedly stem from different settings."[31] Viewing from the perspective of Theon's *Progymnasmata*, however, provides an alternative angle on the interpretation.

---

29. See the story cited from the Talmud in Culpepper, "Luke," 310.

30. C. H. Dodd, *Parables of the Kingdom* (1935; repr., New York: Scribner, 1961), 17.

31. Joseph A. Fitzmyer, *The Gospel According to Luke: Introduction, Translation, and Notes* (AB 28A; Garden City, N.Y.: Doubleday, 1985), 1105. Charles H. Talbert, *Reading Luke: A Literary and Theological Commentary on the Third Gospel* (New York: Crossroad, 1982), 153, comes closer to acknowledging the unity of the interpretations by noting that they are held together by a "complex web of interlocking devices."

Theon devotes an entire chapter to the "fable," and his definition of the fable as "a fictitious story which depicts or images truth"
(72.28; Patillon, 30) sounds like a typical, rough-and-ready definition
many would use to describe Jesus' parables.

Theon later notes, "It may be possible for one fable to have several
conclusions (or morals), if we take a start from each of the matters
in the fable" (75.28–31). Thus, if Luke and his audience were accustomed to a fable or parable having more than one conclusion or
interpretation or "moral," then it is unlikely that anything about the
literary shape of this parable would have given the authorial audience
any reason to question its rhetorical unity.[32] Far from a clear sign of
redactional disruption and separate social settings, according to the
Progymnasmata, a conclusion with multiple interpretations or applications was a conventional and acceptable way to end a fictitious
story imaging truth. The text itself bears out this suggestion.

Verses 8–9 correspond remarkably to the three episodes and three
main characters of the story. This fits what Theon says elsewhere
about attending to the perspective of the characters/speakers (63–
64). Verse 8a addresses the parable from the *master's* perspective:
he praises the steward. All of God's people will be called to give a
reckoning concerning the nature of their service to him. Verse 8b is
from the perspective of the *steward* and comments on his shrewd-
ness. Preparation for that reckoning should involve a prudent use of
all our resources, especially in the area of finances. Making friends
of "unrighteous mammon" is stock phrase for all money (cf. Qumran). Verse 9 is from the point of view of the *debtors* and describes
the grace that the debtors experience. Such prudence, demonstrat-
ing a life of true discipleship, will be rewarded with eternal life
and joy.

Finally, verses 10–13 represent a form of the lesser-to-greater argument. One who is faithful in little is also faithful in much (v. 10).

---

32. In that sense, Craig Blomberg's attempt to see each of the interpretations as reflecting the
point of view of one of the characters in the parables is closer to Theon's account than most
modern interpreters (see *Interpreting the Parables* [Downers Grove, Ill.: InterVarsity, 1990]).

Verses 11 and 12 replace "little" with "earthly riches" and "another's" (what is loaned from God) and replace "much" with "true (heavenly) riches" and "one's own" (what will last into eternity).

Conclusion

In the Third Gospel, Jesus is seen employing the practice of inflection to signal to his audience the subject of his parable of the Loving Father. He employs the rhetorical topos of the vengeful king to contrast with his own actions in the triumphal entry. His parable of the Dishonest Steward takes on new meaning when read in light of slave-as-trickster fables, and the integrity of Luke 16:1–13 is no longer in question when illumined by Theon's comments on "fable."

Our observations have been limited to the presentation of the words and deeds of Jesus in the final form of the Lukan writings. Nevertheless, one cannot help but wonder if the historical Jesus could not also have been also a rhetorical Jesus, whether or not such elaborate rhetorical strategies finally find their origins in the historical Jesus himself. If that were so, then much of the form-critical work upon which historical reconstructions of Jesus now rest would be severely compromised. But that question is for another day. For whatever may be the state of historical Jesus research, let the quest for the rhetorical Jesus continue!

Appendix 1

[Aesop is falsely accused by his fellow slaves of having stolen some figs. At this point in the story, Aesop is unable to speak.]

At the appointed hour the master came from his bath and dinner with his mouth all set for figs. He said, "Agathopous, give me the figs." The master, seeing that he was cheated for all his pains and learning that Aesop had eaten the figs, said, "Somebody call Aesop." He was called, and when he came, the master said to him, "You scoundrel, do you have so little respect for me that you would go to the storeroom and eat the figs that were set aside for me?" Aesop heard but couldn't talk because of the impediment in his speech, and seeing his accusers face-to-face, and knowing he would get a beating, he threw himself at his master's knees and begged him to wait a bit. When the master acceded, he took a pitcher that he saw at hand and by gestures asked for some warm water. Then, putting a basin before him, he drank the water, put his fingers into the throat, retched, and threw up the water he had drunk. He hadn't eaten a thing. Then having proved his point through his resourcefulness, he asked that his fellow slaves do the same thing so that they might find out who had eaten the figs. The master was pleased with this idea and ordered the others to drink and vomit. The other slaves said to themselves: "What shall we do, Hermas? Let's drink and not put our fingers down our throat but only in our cheek." But as soon as they drank the warm water, the figs, now mixed with bile, rose up, and they no sooner removed their fingers than out came the figs. The master said, "Look how you've lied against a man who can't speak. Strip them." They got their beating and learned a good lesson to the effect that when you scheme up trouble for someone else, the first thing you know, you are bringing the trouble on yourself (*Life of Aesop* 3).[33]

---

33. Cited by Beavis, "Slavery," 46.

3

Is It with Ethics That the Sermon on the Mount Is Concerned?

Charles H. Talbert

Is it with ethics that the Sermon on the Mount is concerned? To ask this question is to evoke a nearly unanimous response: Yes, of course. Consider a recent claim by a leading New Testament scholar. The Sermon on the Mount is a "call to Christian ethics." Its aim is the morality of the individual.[1] This assertion is no innovation. It is representative. Virtually all secondary literature on the Sermon on the Mount assumes that Matthew 5–7 is an ethical text, aiming to provide guidance for decision-making.[2] Is this assumption about the nature of Matthew 5–7 an appropriate one? Is the Sermon on the

---

1. Donald A. Hagner, "Ethics and the Sermon on the Mount," *ST* 51 (1997): 45, 53.

2. Tom Deidun, "The Bible and Christian Ethics," in *Christian Ethics: An Introduction* (ed. Bernard Hoose; Collegeville, Minn.: Liturgical Press, 1998), 33, says, "Nearly all of them regard the 'Sermon' as a source of law (binding on some or all)." Note the surveys in E. Fascher, "Bergpredigt II: Auslegungsgeschichte," *RGG* (3d ed.) 1:1050–53; Harvey K. McArthur, *Understanding the Sermon on the Mount* (New York: Harper & Brothers, 1960), 105–48; Warren S. Kissinger, *The Sermon on the Mount: A History of Interpretation* (Metuchen, N.J.: Scarecrow, 1975); Clarence Bauman, *The Sermon on the Mount: The Modern Quest for Its Meaning* (Macon, Ga.: Mercer University Press, 1985); Ursula Berner, *Die Bergpredigt: Rezeption und Auslegung im 20. Jahrhundert* (3d ed.; Göttingen: Vandenhoeck & Ruprecht, 1985); and Marcel Dumais, *Le Sermon sur la Montagne: État de la recherche, interpretation, bibliographie* (Sainte-Foy, Quebec: Letouzey et Ané, 1995). This way of reading apparently began early. Cf. R. M. Grant, "The Sermon on the Mount in Early Christianity," *Semeia* 12 (1978): 215–31. Alternate ways of reading are occasionally suggested. Leander Keck, "Ethics in the Gospel according to Matthew," *Iliff Review* 40 (1984): 51, says: "The entire SM [Sermon on the Mount] is to be understood, not as Jesus' legislation for morality, but as a series of concretions of what a proper response to the news of the Kingdom entails." That is, the SM tells what repentance looks like. Even here, the focus is on actions, actions that constitute repentance. Ernest Ligon, *The Psychology of Christian Personality* (New York: Macmillan, 1953), reads the SM as psychological advice. Richard Lischer, "The Sermon on the Mount as Radical Pastoral Care," *Int* 41 (1987): 157–69, takes the SM as pastoral care. Martin Thornton, *English Spirituality* (Cambridge, Mass.: Cowley, 1985), chap 3; and William F. Warren Jr., "Focuses on Spirituality in the Sermon on the Mount," *Theological Educator* 46 (1992): 115–24, advocate a reading of the SM as spirituality.

Mount's aim to provide guidance for ethical decision-making? I think not. Why not? For two reasons.

First, note that "there is not just ethical instruction in the Sermon but instruction in worship and prayer"[3] as well. Matthew 5–7 is concerned with the vertical (Matt 5:3, 4, 5, 6, 33; 6:1–18, 24, 33; 7:7–11) as well as the horizontal (e.g., Matt 5:21–26, 27–30, 38–42, etc.) relations of life. In this the Sermon on the Mount is like biblical law (vertical — Exod 20:3, 4–6, 7; horizontal — Exod 20:13–17), prophecy (vertical — Jer 4:1–2; Hos 14:1–8; horizontal — Hos 4:1–3; Amos 6:4–7), and wisdom (vertical — Prov 3:9–10, 11–12; horizontal — Prov 15:1; 16:32), which also address both vertical and horizontal dimensions of life.

The teaching of the Sermon on the Mount, like that of biblical law, prophecy, and wisdom, cannot be reduced to ethics (the horizontal). In all these streams of biblical material, the ethical is but one dimension of the larger concern for "covenant faithfulness," which includes the vertical as well. The Sermon on the Mount contains material focused on piety as well as that concerned with ethical behavior. Is it with ethics that the Sermon on the Mount is concerned? Yes and no! Yes, the Sermon is concerned with ethics. No, that is not all about which it is concerned.

Second, the Sermon of the Mount functions primarily as a *catalyst* for the formation of identity or character. Only in a secondary way can it serve as a *contributor* to the task of decision-making. The ethical material contained in the Sermon on the Mount is directed not in the first instance to decision-making but rather to the formation of moral character,[4] just as the material focused on the vertical dimension is aimed at the formation of character in one's relation with God. There is a need to clarify these categories before proceeding further.

---

3. John Riches, *Matthew* (NTG; Sheffield: Sheffield Academic, 1996), 68.

4. James Gustafson, "The Relation of the Gospels to the Moral Life," in *Jesus and Man's Hope* (ed. Donald G. Miller and D. Y. Hadidian; Pittsburgh: Pittsburgh Theological Seminary, 1971), 2:103–17, in his quest for the Gospels' influence on one's moral character, focuses on paradigms of Jesus' action that inform one's dispositions, intentions, and manner of life. He recognizes the need for further work to be done on such paradigms in Jesus' teaching. It is this latter task that this essay attempts to undertake, at least for the Sermon on the Mount.

What exactly is meant by *decision-making?* Suppose a person is confronted with a problem and must make a decision about what is the right thing to do under the circumstances. The question arises: is there a norm, a principle, a rule, a law that will inform the person's decision? If the Sermon on the Mount is designed to assist in decision-making, it will provide norms, rules, laws to guide the person's decision about what is the right thing to do in this or that circumstance. Dilemma-based ethics are, then, reactive.

What exactly is meant by *character formation?*[5] Character and identity may be regarded as interchangeable terms. The chief elements in character or identity are perceptions (how one sees things), dispositions (persisting attitudes that flow from the overarching orientation or vision), and intentions (deliberately chosen or self-conscious activity, motivation). If the Sermon on the Mount is designed for character formation, it will facilitate a new way of seeing life ("viewing the world with eyes that are . . . Christlike"),[6] issuing in new dispositions and intentions/motivations toward life. Character ethics are, then, proactive.

There are, then, two questions to distinguish.[7] First, what is a disciple of Jesus to *be* (virtue ethics)? Second, what is a disciple of Jesus to *do* (dilemma-based ethics)? The first is a question of character or identity; the second is a question of decision-making to enable proper action. The First Evangelist reflects this distinction between being and doing. Matthew distinguishes between tree and fruit (7:16–18; 12:33), heart and mouth (12:34; 15:18–19), being and speaking (12:34), and person and things (12:35). These distinctions are what

---

5. Bruce C. Birch and Larry L. Rasmussen, *Bible and Ethics in the Christian Life* (Minneapolis: Augsburg, 1976), 81–93, provide the following insights about character/identity.

6. Deidun, "The Bible and Christian Ethics," 37.

7. James F. Keenan, "Virtue Ethics," in *Christian Ethics: An Introduction* (ed. Bernard Hoose; Collegeville, Minn.: Liturgical Press, 1998), 84–94, clarifies the differences. He further indicates that virtue ethicists expand the question of being into three key, related questions: Who am I? Who ought I to become? How am I to get there? In the Sermon on the Mount, the Matthean Jesus deals with each of these questions. I do not think, however, that because one works with moral character one is thereby obligated to employ the Aristotelian or Thomistic categories of the four cardinal virtues: prudence, justice, temperance, and fortitude. The Matthean Jesus did not. Keenan himself develops his own four cardinal virtues: justice, fidelity, self-care, and prudence.

we would refer to as character or identity on the one side, and behavior or actions on the other. In Matt 5:14–16 one finds the distinction expressed as "You are the light of the world" (character/identity) and "Let your light shine" (behavior/actions) — that is, act in accordance with your nature; let your actions reflect your character.

In light of this distinction between *being* and *doing*, let me repeat my contention. The Sermon on the Mount functions primarily as a *catalyst* to enable an auditor to become a person whose identity or character is appropriate to the life of one who follows Jesus. Only secondarily does the Sermon function as a *contributor* to the task of decision-making that is appropriate to a disciple of Jesus.

The Sermon on the Mount as a Catalyst for Character Formation

The contention of this chapter is that the Sermon on the Mount is aimed at character formation rather than decision-making. Its primary concern is with the kind of person the decision-maker is. Of course, this claim can only be confirmed or contradicted by the text of Matthew 5–7. To that material we now turn. We begin with the Beatitudes.

The Opening of the Sermon on the Mount

The Sermon on the Mount opens with a unit, 5:3–12, that includes material about vertical and horizontal relationships in which disciples find themselves and that functions in the interests of character formation. How so? Matt 5:3–12 is a poem composed of nine beatitudes that give a portrait of, and promises to, disciples. What is the portrait of disciples that is given? Of the nine beatitudes, the first four deal with the disciples' vertical relationships, the last five with horizontal relations. Among the final five, the first three focus on relationships in which the disciples have the initiative, the last two on relations in which the disciples are acted upon in negative ways. These first eight beatitudes are all in the third person. They sketch the outlines of a good person, a person of piety toward God and of right behavior toward other humans.

This answers the question: Who does Jesus want me to become? Such a portrait would affect the auditors. Plutarch (*Quomodo quis suos in virtute sentiat profectus* 84d) tells how. He says that one's being in the presence of a good person has the effect: "Great is his craving all but to merge his own identity in that of the good man." The ninth beatitude then shifts to the second person, thereby drawing its auditors into an identification with the portrait given. This is who *we* are or aspire to become! A new way of seeing themselves occurs with the shift from third to second person. Participation in the dispositions and intentions reflected in the portrait is effected. Jesus sees us this way. This is really who we are! We want to become who we really are! In its portrait of disciples, then, the poem functions to form the character of the auditors in their vertical and horizontal relationships.

What about the promises contained in the poem? They constitute eschatological judgment proleptically given, on the basis of Jesus' assumed knowledge of the end times and his authority at the Last Judgment. They promise fullness of eschatological blessing to those who participate in the portrait sketched, namely, the disciples who are auditors. It is assumed that Jesus' disciples are attached to him (4:18–22) and that they resemble the portrait given in 5:3–12 (this is implied in 5:13–16: "You are salt," and "You are light"). Like any promise, these promises are "performative language," which is not just a saying of something but is the doing of an action.[8]

These promises oblige the speaker, putting him on record as assuming a responsibility for the disciples' ultimate destiny. The disciples now are enabled to see their destiny differently. This is the way Jesus sees us! He is the one who by his promises has now undertaken responsibility to enable the fulfillment of the Beatitudes. This answers

---

8. I am indebted to J. L. Austin, *How to Do Things With Words* (Cambridge: Harvard University Press, 1962). Cf. also *Semeia* 41 (1988), which is concerned with speech act theory, especially Hugh C. White, "Introduction: Speech Act Theory and Literary Criticism," *Semeia* 41 (1988): 1–24. Thanks to Mikeal Parsons for directing me to this material.

the question: How am I to get there? The disposition of the auditor that flows from this insight is to trust Jesus. In the new perception and its resulting change of disposition, character is being formed. From the first of the Sermon on the Mount, the Beatitudes of Matt 5:3–12, this is how the language functions.

An objection to this assertion must be faced from the first. Does not the very *form* of much of the material in the Sermon on the Mount raise questions about the contention that the Sermon on the Mount's *content* is focused on character formation? True, the Beatitudes seem directed, in some respects, to character: for example, poor in spirit, merciful, pure in heart. But in most places in the Sermon on the Mount, attention is directed, on first glance at least, not to one's being but to one's doing: for example, insulting a brother, looking lustfully, divorcing a wife, swearing, retaliating, hating enemies, judging others before having judged oneself. Does not the focus on doing mean that the Sermon on the Mount aims to provide guidance for ethical decision-making?

Both Robert C. Tannehill and John Dominic Crossan have attempted to address this issue. Both contend that the material is not to be taken as casuistic law. Tannehill's alternative category is "focal instance,"[9] Crossan's is "case law parody."[10] Both sense that in spite of the Sermon on the Mount's apparent focus on actions, the language functions very differently. I agree. Furthermore, a consideration of Mediterranean ways of thinking about acting and being deflects the claim that the focus in the Sermon is on decision-making.

Proper appreciation of the texts in the Sermon on the Mount that seem focused on actions is enabled by a recognition that the Sermon comes from a culture that thinks in terms of actions and assumes that one's character is produced by, and is a reflection of, what one repeatedly does. For example, 1 John 3:7–8a says: "The one who habitually does right is righteous;... the one who habitually does sin

---

9. Robert C. Tannehill, *The Sword of His Mouth* (Semeia Supplements 1; Missoula, Mont.: Scholars, 1975), esp. 67–77.

10. John Dominic Crossan, "Jesus and Pacifism," in *No Famine in the Land* (ed. James W. Flanagan and Anita Weisbrod Robinson; Missoula, Mont.: Scholars, 1975), 195–208.

is of the devil." If so, then the language of doing does not, of necessity, exclude a focus on character. This mind-set is reflected in Matt 6:19–21. In this logion an action is prohibited (do not continually act greedily, v. 19); an action is commanded (continually act generously, v. 20); the command and prohibition are issued because how one acts will determine one's character (v. 21). One's character is determined by, and reflects, what one habitually does. The Sermon on the Mount, then, shares the general cultural assumptions about the relations between actions and character. A focus on actions, then, does not detract from the Sermon's emphasis on character.[11]

Ultimately, examination of specific texts must show that the focus on actions leads to a concern for the formation of character at both the horizontal and vertical levels.

Two Texts with a Horizontal Focus

We may begin with two examples that show how the Sermon on the Mount's *ethical material* is oriented to character formation.

The first example, Matt 5:38–42, offers a *series* of four examples in which nonretaliation is advocated.[12] These examples are *specific* and *extreme:* (1) "If anyone strikes you on the right cheek, turn the other also." (2) "If anyone wants to sue you and take your inner garment, give your outer garment as well."[13] (3) "If anyone forces you to go one mile, go also the second mile." (4) "Do not refuse anyone who wants to borrow from you" (even if that one has refused you earlier).[14] The examples are specific! How often is one struck

---

11. This insight defuses Dale Allison's claim that the Sermon on the Mount cannot be limited to the shaping of the moral imagination; rather, both virtue and rules are present; the SM integrates the two (Dale C. Allison Jr., *The Sermon on the Mount* [Companions to the New Testament; New York: Crossroad, 1999], 80). In the Sermon on the Mount, this essay contends, what appear to be rules function to shape the imagination, morally (horizontal relationships) and spiritually (vertical relationship).

12. I am indebted in what follows to Robert C. Tannehill, *Sword of His Mouth*, 67–77.

13. Deut 24:10, 12–13 did not allow the suer to demand the outer garment that was used as a blanket by night. According to law, the outer garment belonged as one's inalienable possession and could only to be taken until sunset (Exod 22:25–26; Deut 24:12–13). Hence, the suer in Matt 5:40 demands the inner garment.

14. The fourth command also fits into the pattern of nonretaliation if it is read against the background of discussions like that in *b. Yoma* 23a. Lev 19:18 is cited: You shall not take vengeance nor bear any grudge. A comment is made: This refers to monetary matters. An example follows: Suppose a neighbor asks to borrow his fellow's sickle and the fellow says no.

on the right cheek? They are extreme. If the advice of the second one is followed, the disciple will be left standing in court naked! These examples reverse our natural tendency; they are the opposite of what we normally do. They appear in a series. The series, moreover, establishes a pattern that can be extended to other instances. It is open-ended. Much more is at stake, therefore, than behavior in the situations explicitly mentioned. The series suggests an alternative to what we normally do. Verse 39 offers it: "Do not retaliate against an evildoer."[15]

The pericope causes the auditor to *see* life in a new way! Non-retaliation is that new way. The effect, then, is to enable the auditor to see nonretaliation as the pattern for relating, to be disposed toward nonretaliation, and to intend nonretaliation. If so, then this text would be aiming at the formation of character.

Is not this statement, "Do not retaliate against an evildoer," rather a norm or rule or law to cover a general area of human behavior? Is not this the obvious reading? No. To take it as a norm/principle/rule/law providing guidance for decision-making would contradict the Matthean Jesus' priorities. How? Jesus in Matthew sets love (Matt 22:37–40) and mercy (Matt 12:7) and the Golden Rule (Matt 7:12) at the center of God's intention for human behavior. All of Scripture must be read in this light (22:40; 7:12); all of Jesus' teachings must be heard in these terms.[16]

Then the next day the fellow comes to the neighbor and asks to borrow the neighbor's axe. If the neighbor replies, "I will not lend it to you, just as you would not lend me your sickle" — that is revenge/retaliation.

15. Hans Dieter Betz, *The Sermon on the Mount* (Hermeneia; Minneapolis: Fortress, 1995), 280–81, argues persuasively for a translation of *antistenai* not as "resist" but as "retaliate." Unfortunately, in the discussion that follows, he assumes the saying about nonretaliation is a rule offering guidance for decision-making, thus treating it as law.

16. That the double love command expresses the purpose and unity of Scripture and, in so doing, constitutes the hermeneutical norm in terms of which all Scripture should be interpreted, is supported by: Günther Bornkamm, "Das Doppelgebot der Liebe," in *Neutestamentliche Studien für Rudolf Bultmann* (2d ed.; Berlin: Alfred Töpelmann, 1957), 85–93; Birger Gerhardsson, "The Hermeneutical Program in Matthew 22:37–40," in *Jews, Greeks, and Christians* (ed. R. Hammerton-Kelly and Robin Scroggs; Leiden: Brill, 1976), 129–50; Wolfgang Schrage, *The Ethics of the New Testament* (Philadelphia: Fortress, 1988), 148–50; Terence Donaldson, "The Law That Hangs (Matthew 22:40): Rabbinic Formulation and Matthean Social World," *CBQ* 57 (1995): 689–709. Augustine identified the purpose of Scripture as love for God and neighbor (*De doctrina christiana* 1.84–85). The right approach to

If "Do not retaliate" is taken as a general rule, however, when the neighbor is violated by another, the disciple will be obligated to abstain from defending, protecting, or vindicating the neighbor because of obedience to the rule "Do not retaliate." In so acting, the disciple will sacrifice loving the neighbor (Matt 22:39) to the rule "Do not retaliate against evil." This contradicts the Matthean Jesus' stated priorities. Assuming that the Matthean Jesus' teaching represents a rationally coherent stance,[17] "Do not retaliate against evil" cannot be taken as a general rule for an area of life.

If, however, it is understood as a provocation that arouses the hearers' moral imagination so that they are enabled to *see* their situation in a new way with a resultant change of disposition and intention, it is a catalyst for the creation of a nonretaliatory character. If so, then one should envision the hierarchy of values making up the selfhood of the disciple as incorporating both love of the neighbor and nonretaliation against evildoers, with the former being more basic. If so, then when confronted by an evildoer, the disciple with such a character would likely retaliate if necessary to defend, protect, and vindicate the neighbor.

Variations on the Good Samaritan story illustrate the two options (Luke 10:29–37). Suppose on the one hand the Good Samaritan had come upon robbers attacking a fellow traveler on the road to Jericho, and suppose he had earlier heard Jesus' words "Do not retaliate against an evildoer" and had taken them as a norm/rule/law. Then he would likely have waited until the attack was over, the robbers were gone, and before making his way to the victim, binding up his wounds with oil and wine, setting him on his animal, and taking him to the inn to provide care for him. He would have thereby satisfied the two commands: "Do not retaliate" and "Love the neighbor," in that order. Judged by the Matthean Jesus' value system, however, he would have acted improperly because love of the neighbor was not central to his behavior.

Scripture, he therefore thought, is to make one's understanding of it aim toward love (1.95–96; 3.54).

17. Trimming with Occam's razor.

If on the other hand the Good Samaritan, with a character shaped by the Matthean Jesus' priorities, had come along when robbers were attacking someone else on the road to Jericho, he would likely have taken his staff, cuffed the robbers about their ears, driven them off, and then gone to the man with oil and wine, binding up his wounds before setting him on his donkey to take him to the inn for further care. In so doing he would have made his ethical decision out of a character that gave mercy and love for the neighbor the priority. He remained a nonretaliatory person but he was a loving person above all.

The second example, Matt 5:33–37, is spoken in the context of a culture in which oaths were widely used, ostensibly to guarantee the truthfulness of what was said. In this culture, however, distinctions came to be made between oaths that were binding and those that were not. For example, if people swore "by heaven and earth," they were not bound (*m. Sebu'ot* 4:13); if they swore "by Jerusalem," it was not binding (*m. Nedarim* 1:3); if they swore "by one's head," they were not bound (*m. Sanhedrin* 3:2). In this context oaths came to be used rather to conceal dishonesty. As Philo put it, "From much swearing springs false swearing" (*De decalogo* 92). The Matthean Jesus says the intent of Scripture ("do not swear falsely" — Lev 19:12; cf. Deut 6:13; "perform what you have sworn" — Ps 50:14b; Deut 23:21, 23; Num 30:2) is truthfulness in relations among humans and with God.

Sweeping aside the nonbinding oaths, Jesus says simply, "Do not swear at all" (v. 34). Instead of looking for loopholes in the demand for truthfulness, act in line with God's intention. "Let what you say be simply 'Yes' or 'No' " (v. 37). Be truthful! The pericope functions as a lens to enable a new way of *seeing* human communications: in terms of honesty. From this perception flows a disposition to tell the truth and the intent to be truthful, not deceptive. Character is being formed.

Should not this teaching rather be understood as a general rule: always tell the truth? Does not this seem the obvious way to read it? No. To do so would once again contradict the primacy of love and mercy in the Matthean Jesus' teaching. This is best grasped from an illustration. The example comes from a story told to me in my youth.[18]

Suppose you were in your house and heard a frantic knocking on your door. You opened it to find a young woman, blood-smeared, eyes wild with fright, who said: "Let me in, hide me; I am being chased by a maniac who wants to kill me." You hurriedly let her in and motion her to the back room, where she can hide. Then there is more pounding on your door. You open it and see a wild-eyed man, breathing heavily, with a huge knife in his hand. He asks: "Did you see a young woman run this way?" Now the question: is Jesus' disciple obligated to tell the truth regardless of the circumstances? If the pericope is understood as setting forth a rule or law to govern human decision-making, then the answer is, Yes. If, however, the text aims at character formation, and if the disciple acts out of a hierarchy of values in which what is central to Jesus' teaching, love and mercy, is primary, then No. The disciple replies, "Why, no, I have not seen any such person," then closes and locks the door.

One cannot take 5:33–37 as a general rule without violating the coherence of the Matthean Jesus' teaching. If, however, the pericope is understood to provide a new way of seeing human communication, it functions as a catalyst enabling one to be a truthful person. Then the problem is solved. A truthful person does not always tell the truth no matter what the circumstances. Sometimes love and mercy trump truthfulness. The unit, then, is designed to form the character of the disciple in the direction of being a truthful person.

These two examples show clearly how the ethical material in the Sermon on the Mount does not function adequately as norms, rules, laws to be used in decision-making. Rather, the contents that address the horizontal level of life function to provoke the auditor into a new way of seeing life, a way of perceiving that will issue in changed dispositions and intentions. Can the same be said for the material in

---

18. The story may be rooted in the comments of Hilary of Poitiers (*Homilies on Psalms* 10): "There is a lie that is most necessary, and sometimes falsehood is useful, when we lie to a murderer about someone's hiding place or falsify testimony for a person in danger."

the Sermon on the Mount that focuses on the vertical dimension? To that matter we now turn.

Two Texts with a Vertical Focus

Two examples show how the material in the Sermon on the Mount that is focused on the *vertical relation* is also directed to the formation of character.

The first example, Matt 6:2–4, 5–6, 16–18, offers three *specific* illustrations of how to relate to God properly in the areas of almsgiving,[19] prayer, and fasting. The specific cases are *extreme* (sounding a trumpet as one contributes, praying on street corners, disfiguring one's face when fasting). They are part of a *series* establishing a *pattern* that causes the auditor to see beyond these three specific instances. The series is open-ended. In each case the emphasis is on the worshiper's motivation in the performance of these acts of piety. A different kind of person is being called for.

That the Evangelist intended the admonitions about these three specific acts to be something more than case law[20] may also be seen from verse 1, the introduction to the series: "Beware of practicing your righteousness [= covenant faithfulness] before others in order to be seen by them; for then you have no reward from your Father in heaven" (cf. Matt 23:5–7, 28). A consequentialist argument is used to enable the reader to *see* an orientation toward God in which a person relates to God for God's sake and not merely to enhance one's status among other humans.[21] The unit introduces the auditor into an alternative world of relating to God.

---

19. That almsgiving would be understood by the Matthean Jesus as a part of the vertical dimension may be seen from *Avot de Rabbi Nathan* 4, which contains the story of R. Johanan ben Zakkai and the destruction of the Herodian temple by the Romans in 70 C.E. Rabbi Joshua cried out: "Woe unto us that this, the place where the iniquities of Israel were atoned for, is laid waste." To which R. Johanan replied: "Do not fret. We have another atonement as effective as this. It is acts of loving-kindness."

20. Kari Syreeni, "Separation and Identity: Aspects of the Symbolic World of Matthew 6:1–18," *NTS* 40 (1994): 522–41, contends that the aim of Matt 6:1–18 is not to give practical rules for cultic activities. It is not a cultic didache (as H. D. Betz has claimed). It aims to affect perceptions.

21. Tannehill, *Sword of His Mouth*, 78–88.

Should not the injunction in verse 1 be taken rather as a rule that one's piety be kept private? No. To take it this way would violate other teachings of the Matthean Jesus. In 5:16 Jesus exhorts his disciples: "Let your light so shine before others that they may see your good works and glorify your Father who is in heaven." Matt 10:32–33 has Jesus say that one's ultimate destiny depends upon acknowledging him publicly. It is clear that the Matthean Jesus does not advocate a "private piety" in texts such as these. Again, assuming a rational coherence for the teaching of the Matthean Jesus, 6:1–18 cannot be understood as a rule that one's piety be kept private. Understood as the formation of character in a way that relates to God for himself, not for the status it gives one among other humans, however, Matt 6:1–18 makes sense.

The second example that focuses on the vertical dimension requires some justification for its being so classified. Matt 6:25–34 has sometimes been read as an ethical text. Live like the birds and flowers! Make no provision for the future. To do so, however, would lead to the divestment of one's savings, retirement plans, and insurance policies. This is a misreading. "The image (of the birds) is meant to evoke an awareness of God's pervasive care and provision, not to give encouragement to be as careless as the ravens."[22] Rather than being an ethical text with a horizontal focus, 6:25–34 focuses on the vertical dimension. In Matt 6:25–34 the threefold "Do not be debilitatingly anxious" (vv. 25, 31, 34) involves one in an alternative world of birds and flowers where anxiety is absent, and it activates one's imagination so that one can begin to *see* self and world from a new perspective. It does not simply command but seeks to make possible what it commands, shaping the character of the auditor.[23] It functions to facilitate one's being a person who trusts God's providential care.

Should not this material rather be read as a rule prohibiting anxiety or worry? Note the threefold repetition of "Do not be anxious." If it is understood as a rule, its message is futile. One does not stop

---

22. John Nolland, *Luke 9:21–18:34* (ed. David A. Hubbard; WBC 35B; Dallas: Word, 1993), 692.

23. Tannehill, *Sword of His Mouth,* 60–67.

worrying or being anxious by obeying a command to do so. Indeed, such a command would further complicate the situation. From my youth I remember a ditty that makes the point:

> I've joined the new "don't worry club,"
> In fear I hold my breath,
> I'm so afraid I'll worry,
> I'm worried half to death.

It takes more than a rule or law to deal with human anxiety. Only divine enablement makes trust in God possible. That, it seems to me, is how Matt 6:25–34 functions: as a catalyst enabling trust in God's providence.

From the argument thus far, it ought to be possible to see first that the Sermon on the Mount is not to be reduced to ethics (= horizontal relationships) and second that the ethical material in the Sermon is not to be restricted to a decision-making function. Rather, the material with a horizontal focus, just as the texts with a vertical orientation, is aimed at the formation of character, a character of covenant faithfulness. This is what is properly called spiritual formation.[24] Such a conclusion, however, inevitably raises a further question. Can the Sermon on the Mount be used at all in decision-making?

The Sermon on the Mount as a Contributor to Decision-Making

The Sermon can most definitely contribute to decision-making, but for it to make its contribution, the interpreter must take a further step. One must read in context! To read in context means (1) in the context of the whole Gospel of Matthew,[25] (2) in the context of the

---

24. William C. Spohn, "Spirituality and Ethics: Exploring the Connections," *TS* 58 (1997): 114, says: "Perception, motivation, and identity are three regions of moral experience where concerns and practices of spirituality are supplementing, if not supplanting, formal ethical approaches."

25. Dale C. Allison Jr., *The Sermon on the Mount*, 9, says: "The Sermon on the Mount belongs to a book apart from which it was never intended to be read. This matters because so often interpretation has gone astray by ignoring the Sermon's context."

whole of the New Testament,[26] and sometimes (3) in the context of the entire biblical plot.[27] Examples are in order for both texts that deal with the horizontal relationships and those that focus on the vertical dimension. Because of the previous analysis, some repetition may be expected. We begin with the two texts with an *ethical* focus.

Two Texts with a Horizontal Focus

We begin with Matt 5:38–42, a text aiming to shape a disciple's character in the direction of nonretaliation. This text raises a question for decision-making: if one is a nonretaliatory person, does this mean one never resists evil people? Let us read in context. (1) *In the context of Matthew as a whole,* Matt 22:39–40 gives the commandments to love God and to love the neighbor the highest priority, alongside the Golden Rule (Matt 7:12) and mercy (Matt 12:7). Matt 5:39 must be read in connection with these texts. Love of the neighbor may demand retaliation against an evildoer. (2) *In the context of the New Testament as a whole,* Rom 12:17, 19; 1 Thess 5:15; and 1 Pet 3:9 speak on behalf of nonretaliation. Rom 13:1–7, however, relegates vengeance against, and retaliation for, evildoing to the state in this present evil age. Matt 5:39 must be read in connection with Rom 13:1–7. (3) *In the context of the Bible as a whole,* Lev 19:18 and Prov 20:22 speak against vengeance and for leaving it to God. Ps 72:1–2 is representative when it assumes that the king judges evildoers and vindicates the vulnerable.

Examined in light of these three contexts, one may say (a) that there may be occasions when the love of the neighbor trumps one's commitment to nonretaliation, and (b) that a Christian who works for the state may find it necessary to retaliate/resist in his/her role. Being a nonretaliatory person does not relieve one of the responsibility of defending the neighbor and does not negate the state's role as

---

26. Hagner, "Ethics and the Sermon," 55, contends that an adequate hermeneutic must take into consideration the whole of the NT with the love command as its guide.

27. H. K. McArthur, *Understanding the Sermon on the Mount,* 120–22, critiques the "analogy of Scripture view" because it reduces all of Scripture to the same level and undermines the radical character of Jesus' demands. Appeal to the biblical plot avoids this criticism because within the overall plot of the Bible are different levels of authority.

bearer of the sword. At this point, Matt 5:38–42 is ready to make a contribution to ethical decision-making.

Let us return now to Matt 5:33–37, a call for Jesus' disciple to be a truthful person, given in the form of a prohibition of oaths. This text raises a question for ethical decision-making: does being a truthful person mean that one always tells the truth no matter what the circumstances? Let us read in context. (1) *In the context of Matthew as a whole*, Matt 7:12; 12:7; and 22:36–40 have the Matthean Jesus setting up the Golden Rule, mercy, and love as primary values. In the First Gospel, Jesus follows "a generally accepted juridical axiom: that fundamental law takes precedence over all other law; that each individual statute and paragraph must give expression to the demand and spirit of that fundamental law."[28] According to Matthew, Jesus has adopted this principle and carried it out in a radical way. Everything is seen in light of the Golden Rule, mercy, and love. If so, then the call to be a truthful person is conditioned by mercy and love of the neighbor. This perspective comes from reading 5:33–37 in the context of the entire First Gospel.

Then (2) *in the context of the New Testament as a whole*, God does not lie (Titus 1:2; Heb 6:18), though the devil does (John 8:44); Christians are exhorted to speak the truth to their neighbors (Eph 4:25); Christians are not to lie to God (Acts 5:3–4). Nevertheless, Matt 26:64a//Luke 22:70b; Luke 23:3; and John 18:37a show Jesus, while on trial, being evasive in his answers to questions from the authorities. This was a mainline Jewish value. When one is facing the possibility of death at the hands of the authorities, one is not obligated to speak the absolute truth; one may be evasive.[29] To do otherwise is to manifest a lust for martyrdom. Such a lust for death was frowned upon by pagans (Seneca, *Epistulae morales* 24:25), the rabbis (*Genesis Rabbah* 82), and early Christians (*Martyrdom of Polycarp* 4) alike. From the New Testament at large, the example of

---

28. Birger Gerhardsson, *The Ethos of the Bible* (Philadelphia: Fortress, 1981), 41.

29. David Daube, *Civil Disobedience in Antiquity* (Edinburgh: Edinburgh University Press, 1972), 112–14.

Jesus conditions the call for truthfulness in a certain context. A reading of Matt 5:33–37 in the context of the First Gospel as a whole and in the context of the New Testament as a whole leads to the conclusion that truthfulness in every situation is not an ethical imperative for Jesus' disciples. Other priorities may sometimes overrule the demand for honesty.

Finally, (3) *in the context of the Bible as a whole,* God's people in the Old Testament are exhorted not to lie in court (Prov 6:19; Isa 59:3–4), to a neighbor/to one another (Lev 6:2–3), or to God (Ps 78:36). Nevertheless, the obligation to speak the truth may be qualified by the need to protect someone's life (Exod 1:19; Josh 2:4–6; 1 Sam 16:2–3; 2 Sam 17:14, 20; Jer 38:27). Again we see that truthfulness is sometimes subordinated to other values.

From this reading of Matt 5:33–37 in context, one concludes that (1) truthfulness is a value because it is fundamental to the establishment and continuance of relationships; lying is a vice because it undermines relationships; but (2) truthfulness is not an absolute/fundamental value; love and mercy are more important because they are more basic to maintenance of relationships. At this point one is ready to properly use the contribution of Matt 5:33–37 in one's decision-making.

Two Texts with a Vertical Focus

Turning now to two texts with a focus on the *vertical relationship,* we may look first at Matt 6:2–4, 5–6, 16–18 whose aim is to shape persons whose piety before God is done for God alone, and not for themselves or to enhance their standing before other humans. This text raises a question for decision-making: must Christian piety be totally private and never public? Let us read in terms of three contexts. (1) *In the context of Matthew as a whole,* Matt 5:16 encourages Jesus' disciples to let their light shine before others so that the others may see the disciples' good works. Matt 10:32–33 calls for disciples' public acknowledgment of Jesus. Matt 11:25–27 shows Jesus praying before his disciples.

Then (2) *in the context of the New Testament as a whole,* Luke 11:1 has Jesus praying before his disciples and 1 Thess 1:8 says recognition of the readers' faith is spread abroad. Second Corinthians 9:2 says the readers' zeal has stirred up many others. Colossians 4:5–6 calls the readers to conduct themselves wisely before outsiders, making the most of the time. First Peter 2:12 likewise calls the readers to conduct themselves honorably among the Gentiles, so that, "though they malign you as evildoers, they may see your honorable deeds and glorify God" (NRSV here and throughout).

Finally, (3) *in the context of the Bible as a whole,* Genesis 41 reports that Joseph's actions are witnessed by Pharaoh; in Dan 6:11, Daniel's enemies see him at his prayers. The conclusion reached is inevitable. The aim of Matt 6:2–4, 5–6, 16–18 is not the privatization of piety but the purification of motive in one's relating to God. Piety may be public, but when it is, it should be for God's sake.

We turn now to Matt 6:25–34. Does this passage encourage idleness? Is there a difference between not being anxious and being irresponsible? Reading 6:25–34 in three contexts enables one to understand how it should be used in a disciple's decision-making. (1) *In the context of Matthew as a whole,* Matt 25:14–30, the parable of the Talents, encourages both work and forethought. (2) *In the context of the New Testament as a whole,* on the one hand, the New Testament encourages work: Acts 20:34–35, Paul works with his own hands; Eph 4:28, Christians are admonished to work honestly with their own hands; 1 Thess 5:14 says to warn the idlers; 2 Thess 3:6–13 commands the believers to keep away from other believers who are living in idleness. On the other hand, the New Testament encourages forethought: Luke 14:28–32 says one should count the cost of an action; 2 Cor 12:14 expects parents to lay up for their children; 1 Tim 5:8, 16 states that whoever does not provide for family members is worse than an unbeliever. (3) *In the context of the biblical plot as a whole,* on the one hand, passages like Prov 6:6 ("Go to the ant, you lazybones; consider its ways, and be wise") encourage work. On the other hand, passages like Gen 50:20–21 (I "will provide for you and your little ones" what you need) speak of forethought and its advantages.

Reading Matt 6:25–34 in these three contexts leads to a dual conclusion. First, there is a difference between being anxious and being idle. To trust God's goodness does not relieve one of the responsibility of work. Second, there is a difference between being anxious and being irresponsible. To trust God's goodness does not relieve one of the responsibility of providing for others in one's care (parents, children, family). At this point, one is ready to use Matt 6:25–34 in one's decision-making.[30]

We began this essay with the thesis that the Sermon on the Mount functions first of all as a *catalyst* for the formation of character/identity but that it can be a *contributor* to a disciple's decision-making if it is read in context. I hope that by this point enough evidence has been provided to enable the reader's assent to the legitimacy of this thesis. Is it with ethics that the Sermon on the Mount is concerned? Yes and no. Yes, the Sermon contains material that must be considered ethical. No, the Sermon cannot be reduced to ethics. It is concerned with piety as well. Furthermore, both the material with an ethical focus and that devoted to piety aim first of all at the shaping of character. Only after being read in the three contexts mentioned above can either type of material be used in Christian decision-making.[31]

---

30. Does this use of material in the SM return the Christian disciple to a casuistry that enables the interpreter to delimit one's responsibility, leaving life outside these parameters unaccountable to God? That, unfortunately, is a possible perversion of the position, one that must be resisted. Properly used, however, this "reading in context" provides balance and protects against eccentric readings and inappropriate applications of the material.

31. But the Sermon can be used! I do not wish my argument to contribute to what James M. Gustafson, "The Use of Scripture in Christian Ethics," *ST* 51 (1997): 15–29, has called the "erosion of confidence in using the Bible for ethics." My aim is to clarify how it should be used so as to inspire confidence in the use of the Bible for ethics.

4

Who Will Speak for the Sparrow?

Eco-Justice Criticism of the New Testament

David M. Rhoads*

Giving Voice to Nature in Biblical Interpretation

In recent decades, there has been a revolution in biblical studies due in part to the many new voices that have entered the academic arena of interpretation — Jewish scholars, European-American women, women of color, diverse cultural groups within the United States, and voices of men and women from virtually every continent, nation, and culture in the world.[1] These new voices are speaking out of their respective "social locations," offering not only new perspectives on biblical texts but also fresh insights about the appropriation of biblical texts for a diversity of modern contexts. They have initiated a dialogue with the biblical materials that invites transformation and at the same time calls for critique of, and resistance to, the Bible. These voices often speak from circumstances of oppression and exploitation

---

*It is a pleasure for me to contribute an essay in honor of Robert Tannehill. Robert is one of the most thoughtful people I know, not only in terms of personal kindness but also in terms of the way he does scholarship. He listens well. He responds only after reflection. He speaks carefully. What he says is full of insight and wisdom. He writes only after rigorous analysis of his subject matter, and he writes in ways that are engaging and illuminating. I have learned so much from him. I am deeply grateful to be his colleague and his friend. And I am delighted to share some reflections that might further in some modest way his love of nature.

1. Some ideas for this chapter appeared in an earlier article, "Reading the New Testament in an Environmental Age," *Currents in Theology and Mission* 24 (1997): 259–66. On new voices, see, for example, Fernando Segovia and Mary Ann Tolbert, eds., *Reading from This Place: Social Location and Biblical Interpretation in the United States* (Minneapolis: Fortress, 1995); and *Reading from This Place: Social Location and Biblical Interpretation in Global Perspective* (Minneapolis: Fortress, 1995).

in colonial or postcolonial situations, and they expose the ways in which the Bible has been used in the service of oppression.

Yet even with these many voices, there is a perspective that is seldom spoken for: the natural world. As much as any group of humans, nature requires a voice in biblical interpretation. Given the exploitation, domination, and degradation of creation at human hands, we desperately need to expose the role of the Bible in the human (mis)treatment of nature and to explore the role that the Bible might take in fostering a renewing and sustaining approach to nature. Of course, we cannot separate human beings from the rest of nature. We are inextricably formed by, dependent upon, and bound up with all of nature. What we humans do affects the rest of nature, and what happens to the rest of nature affects the well-being of humans. Therefore, concern for nature should inform our reading of the Bible. In a sense, because we are so integrally related to the rest of nature, those who interpret the Bible with nature in mind will be giving voice to creation, both human and nonhuman. So who will speak for creation? If it is true that "not one sparrow is forgotten in God's sight" (Luke 12:6), who will speak for the sparrow?

Eco-Justice Criticism of the New Testament

I believe we are entering an environmental age in which the devastating changes to the environment and our consequent preoccupation with the environment will alter every aspect of our personal and communal lives. Therefore, as Christians we need to explore the Bible for what it says about creation and the role of human beings as part of that creation. Of course, we will not find in the Hebrew Bible or the New Testament our modern concerns over the human degradation of creation — the deterioration of the ozone layer, threats to life from global warming, the effects of massive garbage and toxic waste disposal, the problems of deforestation and desertification, or the loss of biological diversity. Nevertheless, there is much in the New Testament that has implications for the environmental crisis and that undergirds a commitment to care for God's creation. Some seminal books and articles in eco-justice interpretation have appeared in Old Testament studies, but only a few such articles have appeared in New Testament studies.[2]

This essay seeks to offer some systematic reflection on reading the New Testament in an environmental age by proposing what we might call eco-justice criticism. Such a methodological approach would be similar to feminist criticism. Just as feminist criticism recovered the presence of women in the text and in the early church as a means to change our picture of early Christianity, so eco-justice criticism would seek to recover New Testament images and attitudes toward nature as a means to change our understanding of biblical texts. Eco-justice criticism would use traditional historical-critical methods, along with literary and social-science methods, as ways to construct the possible meanings of biblical writings in their first-century contexts. At the same time, eco-justice criticism would offer ways to appropriate biblical texts for our time in light of modern concerns for ecology and justice.

I lift up various elements as potentially important dimensions of eco-justice criticism:

1. A hermeneutic of suspicion
2. A hermeneutic of recovery
3. Constructing New Testament understandings of nature and cosmology
4. Interpreting each biblical writing with nature and cosmology in the picture
5. New Testament models of diagnosis and transformation
6. Reframing biblical concepts in eco-justice terms
7. The New Testament as a manual for facing a possible end to the world

---

2. The most ambitious project for reading the Bible with ecology in mind is *The Earth Bible* (Sheffield: Sheffield Academic, 2000–), a series of volumes edited by Norman C. Habel (et al.) and composed of articles on different parts of the Bible that deal with issues bearing ecological implications. For further information, see www.webofcreation.org/earthbible/earthbible.html, which also presents the aims and eco-justice principles of The Earth Bible Project. This site contains an extensive bibliography of books and articles on the Bible that are of ecological interest.

What follows is a brief explication and illustration of each of these areas as a way to project possible methods and procedures for an eco-justice criticism.

1. A Hermeneutic of Suspicion

We need to embrace a hermeneutic of suspicion that ferrets out the negative and destructive dynamics of the human relationship to creation as portrayed in the New Testament. Some of the problems in reading the New Testament from an eco-justice perspective clearly lie with the New Testament itself. Egregious examples of disparaging attitudes toward nature in the New Testament include the drowning of a herd of two thousand pigs in the Sea of Galilee (Mark 5:1–20), the cursing of a fig tree (Mark 11:12–14, 20–25), an aside by Paul that God has no interest in oxen for their own sake (1 Cor 9:9–10), and the destruction of nature by God as punishment for idolatry in the Book of Revelation. More difficult than these passages are some of the assumptions and worldviews of the New Testament writings, such as anthropocentrism, dualism, other-worldly apocalyptic expectations, an absence of connection to the "land" of Israel, and the tendency to see this world simply as a pilgrimage to heaven.

Other problems lie with our interpretations of the New Testament rather than with the writings themselves. When we look at the secondary literature on the Bible, we can see that we have not tended to integrate nature and cosmology into the overall interpretations of biblical texts. In fact, cosmology and nature may be the most neglected factors in New Testament interpretation today. North America European-American Christians have tended to read the New Testament on the basis of our detachment from nature. We have failed to see the assumptions of the early Christians that all life is communal and that all human communities are embedded in the natural world. Thus, in the New Testament, there is no salvation apart from community, and there is no community apart from the whole (re-)creation.

We need to rectify our neglect and begin to restore nature and the cosmology of creation to our interpretations of the New Testament views of the world.

One way to rectify our blindness is for interpreters of the Bible to be conscious of reading not only from our "social location" but also from our "natural location." That is, we can interpret and appropriate the biblical materials in light of our human relationship to the natural world — personal, regional, and global. If we keep before us the dynamic, interactive relationship between humans and the rest of nature, we will surely begin to see aspects of the biblical materials we have long neglected. And in so doing, we will be able to integrate our commitment to care for creation into our whole interpretive process.

2. A Hermeneutic of Recovery

Despite some "texts of terror" in relation to nature, there is much in the New Testament that is also promising from an eco-justice perspective, and we need to recover it from its embeddedness in the texts. In this regard, there has been somewhat of a revolution in the interpretation of the Hebrew Bible in recent years. Biblical theology of the Hebrew Bible used to emphasize salvation history as human history only, predicated on the idea that the Hebrews focused on a human, historical covenant with God in contrast to a relationship with nature that was typical of the nature religions of the time. Now, however, scholars have realized that nature was always an integral part of the Hebrew view of the world and that we need to speak of salvation history as the history of the whole created order.

When we come to reading the New Testament, we see that the amount of material on creation is much smaller, even proportionally, than what we find in the Hebrew Bible. Views of nature and cosmology are embedded in texts almost as incidental matters. So we have to do somewhat of a rescue operation. What follows are examples of four areas of contrast between the Hebrew Bible and the New

Testament and some suggestions about what we can recover from the New Testament for our study of nature and cosmology.

First, unlike the Hebrew Bible, there are no stories that explicitly describe the act of creation and the place of humans in creation. Nevertheless, there is more material in the New Testament than we might expect. For example, we can infer a great deal about creatures and creation from the New Testament, because the writers tend to assume Hebrew Bible views about creation. Further, several New Testament writings, such as the Gospel of John and the Letter to the Hebrews, assign a role for Christ in creation. In addition, the New Testament tells many re-creation stories — stories about the restoration of creation (for example, the Letter to the Colossians) and stories of people who recover their proper place in creation (such as we find in the Gospel of Mark). These stories affirm that God does not abandon creation but instead redeems and fulfills it. Finally, while there are no "creation" stories in the New Testament, there are indeed "consummation" stories about the fulfillment of creation, such as the vision of the new Jerusalem in the Book of Revelation (21:1–22:5) — apocalyptic stories that have many implications for our view of humans in relation to nature.

Second, unlike the Hebrew Bible, there are no extended passages in the New Testament that describe the larger natural world, treating it with awe and with delight for its own sake, descriptions such as we find in some Psalms and in certain passages in the Prophets and in the Book of Job. Nevertheless, there are views of nature embedded in, or implied throughout, the New Testament writings in a line here or a brief passage there. For example, Jesus used many parables and sayings about nature in his teaching. Also, there are numerous incidental descriptions of nature, such as the reference to the heavens being ripped open in the description of Jesus' baptism (Mark 1:10). And we find several acclamations of God as Creator, such as the portrayal of God as "the Lord of the heaven and the earth" (Acts 17:22–28). When we treat these brief passages as windows through which to discern the larger affirmations and assumptions about nature behind them, then the whole writing in which they are embedded may look quite different.

Third, the Hebrew Bible offers explicitly integrated histories of humans in relation to the rest of nature. As we have just indicated, recent scholarship has made it clear that salvation in the Hebrew Bible sees both human history and natural history as one unified story.[3] Salvation histories in the Hebrew Bible are creation histories. By contrast, salvation in the New Testament is predominantly anthropocentric, focusing almost exclusively on the salvation of humans; it is centered on human beings rather than on the redemption of nature or of creation as a whole. In the New Testament there is no covenant that includes animals, no promises connected with the land, and the metaphors for salvation are overwhelmingly human — as if redemption existed for humans alone and not for all of creation. Nevertheless, the New Testament writers often imply and suggest a great deal about cosmology and nature as an integral part of human salvation. For example, despite the neglect of nature in the New Testament, events of human salvation and judgment are never really completely divorced from the rest of the natural world. For instance, a star appears at Jesus' birth (Matt 2:2), the arrival of the kingdom involves the calming of storms at sea (e.g., Mark 4:35–41), the oppression of humans will be accompanied by signs in the sun and stars (Luke 21:25–26), Jesus will return on the clouds (Luke 21:27–28), and at the end time the trees will produce fruit all year round (Rev 22:2). Thus, in the New Testament, as in the Hebrew Bible, the human world, the natural world, and the spirit world comprise one world with one integrated history.

Finally, the Hebrew Bible does not seem to have major ontological dualisms. By contrast, dualisms pervade most of the New Testament writings, such as God's Spirit and the life of the flesh, heaven and earth, this age and the age to come, and so on. Such dualisms tend to denigrate this world as an age passing away or simply as a place of pilgrimage on the way to heaven. However, even the dualistic aspects

---

3. See especially Theodore Hiebert, *The Yahwist's Landscape: Nature and Religion in Early Israel* (New York: Oxford University Press, 1996).

of New Testament thought are not totally negative toward creation. In the New Testament, Spirit fulfills the matter; it does not do away with it. The New Testament condemns an orientation to the flesh as an object of trust and an opening for sin, not flesh or body as such. After all, as John testifies, the Word became flesh. Also, the coming apocalyptic age focuses not on heaven, but on a transformed earth (or a new heaven and a new earth), for the expectation was that Jesus was coming back to the earth — a view that supports the vision of the new creation as an affirmation of the world rather than as a rejection or abandonment of it.

3. Constructing New Testament Understandings of Nature and Cosmology

We will benefit from efforts to describe the first-century views of nature and the cosmos, ferreting out some of the distinctive religious attitudes and prescientific understandings of the world. What may be significant here is the way in which the construction of the cosmos informs social attitudes and behavior.

For the most part, the New Testament writers shared the Hebrew view of the world. The earth was flat, with land and sea bounded by the four corners of the earth, from whence came the four earthly winds. The earth was covered by a canopy, on which the sun, moon, and stars were affixed and moved as the whole canopy circulated. There was an underworld of some murky reality. And there was water over the canopy (whence rain) and water under the earth (whence springs and wells).

One factor that stands out in the Hebrew conception of the world is that the cosmos was bounded on all sides. It was a closed system. As large and awesome as the world seemed to ancient peoples, it had limits on every side. There was no such notion as infinite or expanding space. The cosmos was finite. The image of the cosmos as a closed system reinforced the experience people had that all of life was limited. There was only so much land on which to live, only so much fruit could grow on any given plant, and a woman could have only so many children. Such a view of the world as finite extended to the life experiences of people: the land around a village could only support so many people to live in that village. There was only so much wealth to go around, only so much power, and only so much honor. This typical perception of peasant cultures that "all goods were limited and in short supply" affected the economic, social, and political system: people were discouraged from accumulating wealth because it meant that others were deprived. There was always a struggle to maintain one's honor and not to seek honor beyond one's place, and only so many people could wield power.[4]

A moment's consideration will enable us to realize that our modern Western attitudes and behaviors are likewise reflected in our view of the cosmos. In our view, the universe is infinite. There are no perceived boundaries or limits to things. This view of the cosmos parallels our economic, social, and political attitudes. Our economic system is predicated on unlimited resources. The unlimited accumulation of wealth is not treated as greed or considered to diminish any one else's capacity to become wealthy. In the words of a brokerage firm, "Your world should know no boundaries." Conventional wisdom says that "profit profits everyone." Socially, we believe we can do anything if we set our minds to it. Politically, there is enough power for everyone, and anyone can be president. These attitudes and behaviors form a coherent mentality and are informed by our view of the universe as unlimited.

However, we are learning from ecology that the earth is, in fact, finite. We are a closed system (spaceship earth). The earth is bounded by an ozone layer. There are limited natural resources in the earth. The land can only support so large a population. There is only so much space to dump waste. Carbon dioxide released by human activities does not disappear into some endless space but heats the globe. There is a limit to the diversity of plants and animals we can drive to

---

4. See Bruce Malina, *New Testament World: Insights from Cultural Anthropology* (3d rev. ed.; Louisville: Westminster John Knox, 2002). For an application of this insight to the Letter of James, see my "The Letter of James: Friend of God," *Currents in Theology and Mission* 25 (1998): 473–86.

extinction before we threaten regional ecosystems and global life in general. Perhaps we could learn from the biblical materials how the authors addressed the human problems that come from living in such a closed system — such as greed, envy, arrogance, and conflicts over limited goods. And we could learn from them how they understood that God acted in and through Jesus to enable people to overcome these human problems.

4. Interpreting Each Biblical Writing with Nature and Cosmology in the Picture

One approach to reading the New Testament through "green lenses" is to take each writing as a whole and interpret it with a sensitivity to its views of all creation. Here, briefly, are four such probes.

The Gospel of Mark

> And the Spirit immediately drove him out into the wilderness. He was in the wilderness forty days, tempted by Satan; and he was with the wild beasts; and the angels waited on him. (Mark 1:12–13 NRSV here and throughout)

Traditional treatments of the kingdom of God view it as an establishment of God's rulership over people and society. However, it is clear from a closer look at the Gospels, Mark in particular, that the kingdom of God involves a restoration of all creation, nature included.

Mark's view of the rule of God focuses on power from God to liberate people from all forms of oppression, including oppression from nature. For Mark, the arrival of the kingdom of God restores people to their proper place in creation. With access to power from God, agents of the kingdom — Jesus and the disciples — have authority over demons, illness, and natural phenomena but not over other people. Through faith (which, for Mark, provides access to God's power), humans can stop destructive winds, calm seas, provide bread in the desert, and, if appropriate, move mountains (11:23). Like people, nature is to serve rather than to destroy. Hence, the Gospel of Mark portrays the arrival of the kingdom of God as a restoration of human society in the context of all creation.

We get a glimpse into Mark's view from his depiction of the temptation of Jesus. The words "and he was with the wild beasts" are an aperture into the overall view of nature in Mark's Gospel. Wild beasts are examples of nondomesticated creation, which pose a threat to humans. In Mark's depiction of the world, the threats posed by nature are signs of a created order gone awry. According to Richard Bauckham, the temptation scene in the desert depicts the ideal restoration.[5] Jesus is with the wild beasts, but they are no threat to him. In Mark's view, Jesus has come in part to bring harmony between humans and the rest of the created order — exercising an authority (dominion) in which animals are not a threat to humans. In anticipation of such a realm, Hosea predicted a time when God will abolish war from the land and make a covenant "with the wild animals, the birds of the air, and the creeping things of the ground; and . . . make you lie down in safety" (2:18).

We get another glimpse into Mark's view of nature with the cursing of the fig tree (11:12–25). Distressing as this image is of a tree "withered to its roots," the episode reveals a positive relationship between humans and nature. Jesus curses the fig tree because of his hope, as he enters Jerusalem, that the fig tree might be bearing fruit, even though "it is not the season for figs." The expectation Mark implies here is that when the rule of God comes fully, trees will flourish and bear fruit all year long (even out of season) — as the author of Revelation imagines it in his vision of the new Jerusalem (22:2). Jesus hoped that a fig tree bearing fruit out of season would signal that Israel was ready for the end to come now. When the tree was not bearing fruit out of season, this could only mean that Israel was not bearing fruit and was therefore not ready for the final establishment of the rule of

---

5. Richard Bauckham, "Jesus and the Wild Animals (Mark 1:13): A Christological Image for an Ecological Age," in *Jesus of Nazareth: Christ and Lord* (ed. Joel Green and Max Turner; Grand Rapids: Eerdmans, 1994).

God — and, as a consequence, Jesus would have to endure opposition and death in Jerusalem.

When we look at the whole of Mark, a consistent picture emerges: nature is potentially threatening. The arrival of the kingdom of God restores human beings to their proper place and role in creation. By faith, followers participate in the restoration of creation — either coming into harmony with nature or by having authority to overcome its threat. When the rule of God is finally consummated, all life — animals, plants, humans — will flourish together, and there will be no threats or deprivations for humans.

The Letter to the Romans

> For the creation waits with eager longing for the revealing of the children of God; for the creation was subjected to futility, not of its own will but by the will of the one who subjected it, in hope that the creation itself will be set free from its bondage to decay and will obtain the freedom of the glory of the children of God. We know the whole creation has been groaning in labor pains until now; and not only the creation, but we ourselves, who have the first fruits of the Spirit, groan inwardly while we wait for adoption, the redemption of our bodies. (Rom 8:19–23)

In commenting on this passage, Robert Jewett notes that the creation is here personified as it awaits with eager expectation and groans inwardly in labor pains.[6] This, Jewett notes, is similar to the modern ecological movement that sees the fate of the creation as intimately tied to the fate of the children of God. In Paul's view, creation fell when the first people in the garden of Eden sinned and overstepped their limits in arrogance. Through Christ and the Spirit, God is re-creating people capable of righteousness who will treat one another and all of creation with justice and care. When the new creation arrives and true human beings are revealed and liberated, then all nonhuman creation will also be set free from its bondage to decay

---

6. Robert Jewett, "Romans 8:18–30" (unpublished draft of his Hermeneia commentary on Romans [Minneapolis: Fortress], by permission), 15.

and experience the freedom of the glory of the children of God. This will begin to "restore a rightful balance to creation once again, overcoming the corruption and disorder that resulted from the curse on Adam."[7] In other words, all creation is eager, because when human beings become righteous they will treat the rest of creation in such a way that all creation will thrive.

Thus, there is a clear connection between the righteousness of human beings and the state of creation. The issue is whether humans will express true dominion or idolatrous dominion. The basic idea, Jewett writes, is that "by acting out idolatrous desires to have unlimited dominion over the garden, the original purpose of creation — to express goodness and to reflect divine glory — was emptied."[8] The phrase "the glory of the children of God" is thus understood in terms of humans regaining their proper dominion over creation and participating in the righteousness and justice of God, whose scope is cosmic.

The Letter to the Colossians

> He [Christ] is the image of the invisible God, the firstborn of all creation; for in him all things in heaven and on earth were created. . . . He himself is before all things, and in him all things hold together. . . . For in him all the fullness of God was pleased to dwell, and through him God was pleased to reconcile to himself all things, whether on earth or in heaven, by making peace through the blood of his cross. (Col 1:15–20)

We are used to thinking of the Christ as a figure who saves humans. The astounding acclamation of this letter is that Christ is redeeming not just human beings but the whole created order. This is the New Testament image of a cosmic Christ. In analyzing this post-Pauline

---

7. Ibid., 17.
8. Ibid., 19. For another treatment of Paul's holistic approach to redemption, see Brendan Byrne, *Inheriting the Earth: A Pauline Basis for Spirituality for Our Time* (New York: Alba House, 1990).

letter, Joseph Sittler was acutely aware of the anthropocentric nature of most metaphors of redemption.[9] When he thought about the environmental degradation of creation, he was led to conclude that our view of the work of Christ is too small. Now that we are aware how much *all* of nature needs to be redeemed, he reasoned, we need a Christology that is as large as the size of the problems we face, a Christology that addresses not just human fallenness but the fallenness of all creation — a fallenness caused in large part by human actions.

Sittler pointed to this passage from Colossians as an adequate Christology. Here is an understanding of the cross of Jesus that extends to the whole created order. Jesus did not die for humans alone to be reconciled to God. Instead, Jesus' death is a reconciliation of all things in the whole of creation. The consequence is that humans too are reconciled with "all things" and therefore placed in a new and responsible relationship with the whole created order. The work of Christ as the cosmic Redeemer catches the hearer up in a drama of redemption that includes the whole cosmos and is therefore able to address our environmental crisis.[10]

The Book of Revelation

> Then I saw a new heaven and a new earth, for the first heaven and the first earth had passed away. And the sea was no more. (Rev 21:1)

The Book of Revelation was written to counter the evil and idolatry of the Roman Empire. In the author's view, Rome acclaims itself eternal by virtue of its wealth and power and the extent of its imperial reach (18:7). By its wealth, it has seduced people into an allegiance to Rome that belongs only to God (18:3). By its power, it has coerced

---

9. See Joseph Sittler, "Called to Unity," *Ecumenical Review* 14 (1962): 177–87.

10. Larry Rasmussen, ethics professor at Union Theological Seminary in New York, tells the story of a congregation in Africa. The leader chants: "What did we used to believe?" And the congregation responds, "That Jesus died for our sins." The leader then continues, "And what do we believe now?" And the congregation announces, "That Jesus died for all creation!"

tribes, tongues, people, nations, and kings into cooperation (13:4). By its religion, it demands worship from people and cities, and threatens death to those who refuse to submit (13:15). Rome gets drunk on the blood of God's people (17:6). Not only does Rome exploit and enslave and dominate and kill people, it also dominates the sea with its shipping (18:11–13, 19), and it rapes the earth with its military conquests and its greed.

The author of Revelation counters the idolatrous arrogance and tyranny of Rome over creation with a call to worship the one God who "created the heavens and the earth, the sea and the fresh water springs" (14:7). This is a God whose throne in heaven, whose power, and whose promised wealth in the new Jerusalem are so great that the Roman Empire looks like a pale imitation, a pathetic effort to imitate the true God. This is a God of justice who will give to people as they deserve (2:23). So, when God unleashes wrath against Rome and its idolaters, God does so by doing the very kinds of things that the Romans did when they conquered: people are killed by famine and sword, the land and grass are burned, trees are destroyed, crops are overrun, the rivers and springs are turned to blood or poisoned, rivers dry up, even the sun and moon and stars are compromised so as to plunge people into darkness. Rome is burned to the ground, and the kings and merchants and sailors who benefited from her power and wealth watch from afar the smoke from her burning in terror and agony (18:9–19).

Yet there is mercy. This devastation is carried out in incremental stages so as to give people an opportunity to repent of their idolatry and immorality (9:20–21; 16:9, 11). But in the end, because they refuse to repent, justice is meted out by God. As an angel says to God, "You are right in pronouncing this sentence, Holy One, you who are and were. Because they shed the blood of prophets and saints, you have given them blood to drink. They have their just reward" (16:4–6).

This destruction eventually leads to a new heaven and a new earth represented in the vision of the new Jerusalem (21:1–22:5).

As Barbara Rossing has shown,[11] this vision is compelling because it integrates all creation — humans and the rest of nature — in a harmony of mutual thriving: there is no more sea, which the Romans dominated to exploit the earth economically. The wealth of the new city is enjoyed by all. The river of life is crystal clear, and the water of life is given free of charge. Trees line the river of life and are nourished by it. The tree of life bears fruit for humans every month of the year, and the leaves of the trees are a cure for the nations. The glory of God and Jesus will give light to the city, and the nations will walk by this light (of justice). The nations who have been freed from Roman domination will voluntarily bring into the city their treasures and wealth. God will dwell with people; the Lamb will shepherd them. And God will wipe away every tear from their eyes so that there will be no more grief and crying and pain. The description of the new heaven and new earth is a marvelous depiction of the integration of all creation: nature is enabled to thrive and bring healing and nourishment to human beings, who in turn live together in justice.

We could illustrate the distinctive views of other New Testament writings as well. As with those portrayed above, the task of eco-justice criticism would be to construct a holistic interpretation of each writing so as to include the place of the entire created order in our understanding of that writing.

5. New Testament Models of Diagnosis and Transformation

A different way we can look at the New Testament in relation to the environment is less direct. We might seek to understand in what ways the New Testament writings diagnose the human condition and offer redemption through transformation. The various writings of the New Testament address the different ways people are sinful, ways that may today be contributing to our present ecological predicament.

---

11. Barbara Rossing, "Rivers of Life in God's New Jerusalem: An Eschatological Vision of Earth's Future" in *Christianity and Ecology: Seeking the Well-Being of Earth and Humans* (ed. Dieter Hessel and Rosemary Radford Ruether; Cambridge: Harvard University Press, 2000), 205–24.

Do we exploit the earth because of greed? Because we need to gain honor or justify our existence? Because we have blinded ourselves, by the good things we do, from seeing the harm we do to creation? Because we are afraid to sacrifice our present security with choices made for the good of future generations? Because we are alienated from the Creator and from the rest of creation? The New Testament writings address these differing forms of human sinfulness and offer some resources to liberate people for a transformed existence that will foster sustainable lifestyles.[12]

In a world where people are poor and marginalized, for example, Luke condemns the accumulation of wealth as an abomination to God (16:14–15). He invites everyone into a new reality of God's rule, where wealth and power and honor are shared. His message of social repentance and divine forgiveness evokes compassion for a transformed life lived for others. Luke's condemnation of wealth and vision of justice could call us to a more equitable sharing of the world's goods and a more sustainable lifestyle.

Paul addresses the exploitation of people (and, by implication, nature) that occurs when we humans try to justify ourselves (Gal 6:11–12). When we seek to justify ourselves, we see other people as pawns in our effort to prove our own significance or worth. Paul's announcement of good news that we are already justified by grace liberates us to love others (and nature) for *their own* sake (rather than love them for *our* sake) without the need to use them in our project to prove something about ourselves.[13] Paul's gospel could free us from our personal and national drive to be number one and empower us to make decisions that benefit the larger good, even if it means less for ourselves.

Matthew condemns our blind hypocrisy that prevents us from acknowledging the destructive aspects of our behavior. As the Sermon on the Mount shows, Jesus seeks to confront us with our hypocrisy

---

12. For a more extended discussion of the ideas that follow, see my book *The Challenge of Diversity: The Witness of Paul and the Gospels* (Minneapolis: Fortress, 1996).
13. For this analysis of Paul, see especially Robin Scroggs, *Paul for a New Day* (Philadelphia: Fortress, 1977).

and to reveal it to us. At the same time, Jesus dies for people's sins and promises to be with them. With these spiritual resources, we have no need to be defensive or to hide our failures and sins. Instead, we now have the capacity to look honestly at ourselves, to repent, and to change our behavior. Matthew can help us to take an unblinking look at what we are doing to the environment as a basis for assessing the ways we need to change.

John's Gospel lifts up our alienation from the Creator as the root of the human condition. He proclaims a gospel in which Jesus acts to bring people back into spiritual relationship with God. In the process, the whole created order (bread, water, light, vines and branches, doors, and so on) is sanctified by its capacity metaphorically to bear the reality of the One through whom all things were created. John's Gospel could enliven in us a renewed love of creation as the basis for our relationship to it and our use of it.

As we come to a clearer understanding of the ways we contribute to the ecological crisis and discover our resistances to change, the different gospels in the New Testament can enable us to address our human sinfulness and empower us for transformation. If we seek to overcome our environmental problems out of guilt or fear or anxiety about ourselves or a sense of hopelessness, we will probably only make matters worse. But if we address the environmental crisis out of the good news of God's promise of redemption and liberation, then we will be fed by the hope and the grace and the compassion and the joy of God. Such resources will better prepare us for the choices and changes that may be required of us as we face the crises that environmental degradation is bringing upon us.

6. Reframing Biblical Concepts in Eco-Justice Terms

New Testament texts clearly do not deal with modern ecological issues, just as they do not deal with so many contemporary issues. Nevertheless, when appropriated, certain central theological ideas can be extended or reframed to address our contemporary environmental situation.

For example, the biblical motif of identification with the least and the oppressed could be extended to encompass nature. Matthew declares, "Insofar as you have done it unto the least of these my brothers and sisters, you have done it to me" (25:40). Mark declares, "Whoever receives one such little child receives me" (9:37). Luke states that Jesus "came to seek and to save the lost" (19:10). Luke's overarching theme is about God's "preferential option for the poor." Why not include trees, animals, air, and water as oppressed, exploited, dominated, and marginalized creatures with whom God identifies? What would it mean to live with nature in such a way as to serve nature? What would it mean to care for the most vulnerable and endangered species in creation? How would our humane treatment of the least in nature redound to our care for the least of our brothers and sisters? Can we even think about the liberation of humans without also thinking about the liberation of the whole creation in which we are embedded?

Another motif that might be extended is Paul's concept of justification. Justification by grace means that human beings do not justify themselves by their works, by their usefulness. Rather, they are justified by God's gracious act of acceptance in Christ. They are valued for their own sake. And it is living out of such free acceptance by God that human beings can live up to their own nature as beings who act righteously toward others. Similarly, could we not ask what it would mean that other creatures and plants of the earth and the earth itself do not justify themselves by their usefulness to humans? Instead, they are valuable in their own right and should be delighted in for their own sake. As such, delight would be the right basis for our use of them. Such an acceptance of nature "for its own sake" on the part of humans would in turn lead humans to treat nature in such a way that the earth and its creatures would be able to thrive by living up to their natures as well.

Finally, we may consider a concept that could be reframed for relevance. The Gospel of John and 1 John make much of the incarnational theology that Jesus became flesh. First John places it as a theological test: "Every spirit that confesses that Jesus Christ has come in the flesh is from God" (4:2). Here is a biblical affirmation of the full humanity of Jesus. Yet when we read and interpret this, we generally think of the divine becoming a human being in isolation from the rest of nature. However, when we reframe this in our contemporary environmental context, we have a different understanding of being fully human. To be human is to be a biological creature, to be counted among the animals as Homo sapiens, a higher primate, a mammal. It is to recognize that we are all emergent from, and dependent upon, the web of nature. To say this of Jesus, then, is to place him squarely in the context of the whole natural world. To say "Jesus was a mammal" changes the way we think about Jesus and how we think about incarnational theology. God now not only takes the form of a human; God is also at the same time taking the form of creatures of the earth, thus making Jesus an integral part of nature. God's incarnation and solidarity are now not just with humans but with all of creation. In 1 John, the test of whether one believes Jesus came in the flesh is directly related to the capacity to love other people who are in the flesh (4:2, 7–12). In the same way, a test today declaring Jesus to be fully human leads us to measure our love for all creatures of the earth and, indeed, all of nature.

Other theological views and ethical values in Scripture may lend themselves to similar reframing.

7. The New Testament as a Manual for Facing a Possible End to the World

What do we do with apocalyptic expectations of the New Testament? Most early Christians believed that the end of the world as they knew it was imminent and that soon Christ would return for final judgment and salvation. Perhaps, instead of thinking of apocalyptic as otherworldly and irrelevant to our time, we can see it as analogous to our situation. We too are facing a possible end of the world as we humans know it because of drastic changes that may take place in the earth's environment. Parallels between New Testament apocalyptic expectations and the crises of our own time become obvious and may require a radical response from us.

In the face of a vision of a new world before them, the early Christians did not abandon the present age, nor did they (like we may) expect God to come and clean up their mess. On the contrary, they prepared for the salvation of the new age as a means to enjoy the full blessings of God in the present and as a means to avoid God's judgment. We are in a similar position. On the one hand, if we are not able to repent and change our destruction of the very ecosystems that sustain human life, the consequences will be a judgment upon us. On the other hand, if we are able to repent and create a sustainable life together for future generations on the earth, the results will constitute a transformation that in some sense would represent salvation for all creation.

So, how did the early Christians act in the face of their expectation of the possible end of the world? What can we learn from them? Here are several characteristic behaviors of some early Christians that were shaped by their expectation of the end of the world:

• There was a deep *sense of mission*, illustrated best by the life of the apostle Paul and the mission charges in the Gospels (Mark 13:10; Matt 28:19–20; Luke 24:47). The early Christians had a tremendous urgency to spread the message from village to village, from city to city — to call people and cities and nations to repentance and change of behavior.

• Like Jesus, the early Christians were *truth-tellers*. They made penetrating analyses of the human condition, not just in terms of obvious evil, but in terms of the dark side of our goodness and our compromises. The Sermon on the Mount and the Letter of James illustrate how they sought to discern their own hypocrisy and to face it. They saw evil in themselves and sought to change it. They identified many of the destructive dynamics of their culture (such as the avoidance of people ritually defiled) and transformed or replaced them with life-giving stories.

• Many early Christians *withdrew* and dissociated themselves from the behavior and lifestyles and beliefs of the culture. Mark, for example, urged people to break with cultural values and institutions that were destructive — for example, narrow family loyalties, the quest for wealth, the desire for positions of honor, certain interpretations of the law, the use of power to control people (see especially Mark 8:27–10:45). The author of Revelation admonishes people to withdraw from participation in the social and economic life of idolatrous Rome (Rev 18:4). In place of participation in the cultures of destruction, the early Christians identified with the values and behavior of the emerging new world of God's kingdom.

• The early Christians *confronted the destructive powers,* fearlessly challenging their idolatry and hypocrisy. Early Christians, such as those represented in the first three Gospels, the Acts of the Apostles, and the Book of Revelation, showed their willingness to risk loss, persecution, and death in order to break with narrow allegiances of survival. They condemned the rulers, embraced a larger allegiance to God's whole world, and were in some cases willing to suffer and die for their convictions.

• They *created alternative communities,* quite different from the culture around them, such as those reflected in the Johannine writings, the Acts of the Apostles (2:43–47), and 1 Peter (2:9–10). They did not just make a negative break from the culture; they also created a positive participation in kingdom. They had a vision of the future and sought to live it now, in the present. Insofar as they lived that vision in the present, the kingdom had come! In this way, the early Christians sought to be a light for the world.

• Like Jesus, they *did prophetic acts.* In a sense, their lives were prophetic symbols, for every act is a prophetic act when done out of a vision of the future. So, healing the sick, feeding the hungry, eating with outcasts, forgiving sinners — these all were prophetic symbols of a new age impinging on the present.

• In all of this, they were willing to *act unilaterally,* as far as they were able, to create a new world without waiting for the leaders of the nation or the rest of the populace to lead the way or even to agree with them.

Thus, we can study the behavior of the early Christians facing what they believed to be the end of the world as a means to discover alternative behaviors — some of which may be appropriate for us as we face ultimate choices for avoiding ecological disaster and for creating a sustainable life on earth.

Conclusion

The Bible is a powerful force in our culture. It has been for centuries and will be for a long time to come. People look to the Bible for guidance and for strength. Each generation of Christians must renew its understanding of the Bible in order to face the issues of their time and place. This is acutely true for our generation in relation to our treatment of the environment. Eco-justice criticism of the Bible can help us address the environmental crisis.

With regard to eco-justice issues, there is much in the New Testament to resist and there is much to celebrate. There is much to be cautious about and there is much that can guide us and empower us for the decisions that lie ahead. To learn from the Bible and to be transformed by what we read is not a matter of some wooden imitation. We live in a world quite different from the biblical world. Our problems take a similar but also a quite dissimilar shape. We are called to discern how the various gospels proclaimed by the early church can now address us in the circumstances in which we live, can help us see what God is calling us to do in *our* time. The New Testament is a resource book for such a vocation, a collection of powerful testimonies to the work of God, authorizing us to be creative and empowering us to address our problems in the environmental age with courage and with hope.[14]

---

14. To find extensive bibliographical resources on the Bible relevant to eco-justice criticism, see footnote 2 (above) for information about the Internet site for The Earth Bible series.

5

God's Provision for the Well-Being of Living Creatures in Genesis 9

Simon J. De Vries*

The account in this chapter of Genesis is not narrative in the usual sense of the word. It has no plot, no character development, and no story line. Nor is it anything like lyrical poetry, apart from the aphorism in verse 6 and the recital in verses 12–16 (v. 6 is a wisdom saying in rhythmical form, and the recital shows the style of a theological liturgy).

The priestly writer (P), though not creating beautiful verses in the high style of the psalmists and prophets, characteristically expresses hymns in series of rhythmical utterances having less the structure of synonymous parallelism than that of the heaping up item upon item in order to create a whole. The general effect upon the reader may be to occasion monotony, yet in great theological texts such as the creation story in Gen 1:1–2:4a and the account of a new creation in Gen 9:1–17, this style conveys a sense of solemnity and gravity. In both these passages it displays an acerbic and disciplined minimalism, rather than fulsome expansiveness or aimless repetition. The careful reader realizes that each word, each phrase, and each clause must be treasured and carefully evaluated.[1]

---

*This is my tribute to a beloved former colleague at the Methodist Theological School in Ohio, known both as a lover of nature and as a lover of God's word in Scripture. He will certainly rejoice in, and agree with, what I say here regarding God's desires for animals and for humankind.

1. This question is treated extensively in Sean E. McEvenue, *The Narrative Style of the Priestly Writer* (Analecta biblica 50; Rome: Biblical Institute Press, 1971).

Text and Structure of Genesis 9:1–17

1. A blessing on Noah and his sons   1–7
   a. Narrative introduction   1a
   b. Encouragement to abundant proliferation   1b
   c. Nonhuman flesh appointed as food for humankind   2–3
      (1) All animals placed in subjugation   2
      (2) Nonplant food made equal to plant food   3
   d. Restrictions relating to the shedding of blood   4–6
      (1) Prohibition against eating blood with living flesh   4
      (2) Prohibition against the shedding of human blood   5
   e. Aphorism about shedding human blood   6
   f. Encouragement to abundant proliferation[2]   7

2. God sets up a covenant to preserve all flesh   8–16
   a. Narrative introduction   8
   b. Decree of protection   9–11
      (1) The parties   9–10
         (a) God over against Noah and his descendants   9
         (b) God over against the animal world[3]   10
      (2) Benefits   11
   c. Appointment of a binding sign   12–16
      (1) Strophe I: Divine designation of the sign   12
      (2) Strophe II: The rainbow in the clouds   13–15
         (a) A sign of the bond between Creator and creation   13
         (b) The sight: Out of clouds the rainbow appears   14
         (c) A reminder of the covenant with humankind and animals   15
      (3) Strophe III: A reminder of a perpetual covenant   16

3. Concluding summary[4]   17

    The overall structure of this passage is governed by four statements of God's act of speaking (vv. 1, 8, 12, 17), which define a beginning and an ending with two internal breaks, creating three separate sections. Two details show, however, that the three sections are not equal. The first detail is that verse 12 creates an inclusio with 17 regarding the sign of the covenant. The second is that verses 12–17, thus defined, are closely attached to 8–11, where God promises never to bring another flood. Thus verses 8–11 and 12–17 are closely attached to each

---

    2. Since *ûrᵉbû* has already appeared as the second verb in the first stich of Gen 9:7, it seems probable that its second use is a dittograph supplanting an original *ûrᵉdû*, found at this position in the verse being quoted, Gen 1:28.

    3. LXX omits this clause, followed by the RSV.

    4. The translator and the exegete should accept the responsibility of thoroughly dissecting the Hebrew text of Gen 9:1–17.

other. Verses 1–7 concern God's blessing of abundant proliferation, together with the conditions and restrictions defining it. The term "covenant" (*bᵉrît*) is not found here, yet it stands clearly defined over against verses 8–17 by the counterbalancing *wᵉʾattem,* "as for you," in verse 7, juxtaposed with *waʾᵃnî,* "now I on my part," in verse 9.

One further formal detail deserving attention is the presence of links back to the P creation account in chapters 1–2 and to the beginning of the P flood story in chap. 6. The encouragement to be abundantly prolific in verses 1 and 7, the arrangement of living beings into three or four orders in verses 2 and 10, and the mention of God's previous provision of human food in verse 4 — these are direct references to the creation story, in effect requiring that details of this account be interpreted in the light of what is stated there. Also, the mention in verses 11 and 15 of devastation through the flood echoes God's decision to bring the flood in 6:13 as well as the reason for it: the earth was corrupt and "all flesh" had corrupted its/their "way (*derek*)," their order and manner of life. Thus the passage we are studying has been composed both as a conclusion to the divine act of destroying corrupt life and as a continuation or renewal of the original divine act of creating life. The blessing, the covenant, and the sign mentioned in chapter 9 are designed to put an end to all devastation, past, present, and future, while providing a beginning to a new life that God has designed.

The Animal Creatures

It is apparent that P conceives of animal life and human life as inseparable. True, the subordination of animals to human beings has already been made evident in humankind's creation as a second phase of the fourth-day act of creation, Gen 1:24–25, 26ff., as well as in the statement in 9:2 that the various types or orders of animals had been delivered into the hand of Noah and his sons and placed under the fear and dread of them. This is in fact the first part of the blessing that was bestowed on Noah and his posterity, 9:1ff. An essential part of the subordination of the animals to human beings was, furthermore, that human beings might now benefit from the flesh of animals as food, alongside the plants that had previously been approved, according to 1:29. Access to plant food had not, in matter of fact, been human beings' exclusive privilege, for it had been assigned to every order of animal life as well (1:30). In any case, nothing is said about the animals being given human flesh to eat; in fact, if an animal eats a human being, the shedding of blood must be punished in the same way, and to the same measure, as if it had been done by another human being (9:5).

In spite of this subordination, the two orders of being, human and animal, are treated as alike in their guilt, in their punishment through the flood, in their preservation by the ark, and in the life and fecundity which they were to share in the new creation envisaged in this chapter. Even though the encouragement to abundant fruitfulness is spoken only to the human survivors of the deluge (but cf. Gen 1:22), and in spite of the fact that the animals preserved in the ark are now put under the fear and dread of humanity, part of the new covenant is that not only the human beings but also the animals shall never again be "cut off" in another flood. According to P, not humankind alone but "all flesh" are both needed and valued within God's new world.

It is worthwhile to pay close attention to the references to animals within the priestly narrative of the flood. "Flesh" (*bāśār*) is something specific in 9:4, where it means "meat" — an important ingredient in whatever is covered by the word "food," something in addition to the previously authorized green plants. "All flesh" (*kol bāśār*) occurs in Gen 6:12, 13, 17; 7:15, 16, 21; 9:11, 15–17 (also "from among [= some of] all flesh" in 6:19; 7:15–16; 8:17); this expansion is modified by the phrase, "in which is the spirit of life" in 6:17 and 7:15. Another modifier, "every living thing of all flesh," occurs in 6:19 and 8:17. The distinction intended in Gen 8:1 between "all that was alive and every beast" is not clear; nor is that of the phrase "every living thing of all flesh," both in 8:1 and 8:17; nor is that of the phrase "every living creature" in 9:10, nor that of "all life on earth" in 9:2.

In distinction from *kol bāśār*, the terms *kol haḥayyâ* and *kol nepeš haḥayyâ* refer exclusively to animals. In 9:5 the phrases "at the hand of every animal" (*miyyad kol-ḥayyâ*) and "at the hand of the human being" (*miyyad hā'ādām*) make this distinction certain. The expressions "and between every living animal that may be with you unto perpetual generations" (*ûbên kol-nepeš ḥayyâ 'ᵃšer'ittkem lᵉdōrôt 'ôlām*) in 9:12 and "and between every living animal out of all flesh" (*ûbên kol-nepeš ḥayyâ bᵉkol-bāśār*) in 9:15–16 are inclusive expressions pertaining to all varieties of animal life in distinction from human life. In any event, "all flesh" represents the wider category to which "every living being" belongs.

The same term may, however, be given a more precise definition when it is applied to the distinct orders of animals. Thus in Gen 1:20 God, on the third day, causes the seas to bring forth *šereṣ nepeš ḥayyâ*, "a swarm of living animals." This is explicated in 1:21, where it is said that God also creates from the sea (1) great monsters, (2) "every kind of living animal that moves" (*kol-nepeš haḥayyâ hārōmeśet*), and (3) winged birds. According to 1:24, God, on the fourth day, commands the earth to bring forth another order of *nepeš ḥayyâ*, one that includes the three kinds, cattle (*bᵉhēmâ*), creeping things (*remeś*), and wild animals of the earth (*ḥaytô 'ereṣ*); but it is remarkable that in the report of compliance that follows in 1:25, these three are presented in a different order, *ḥayyat hā'āreṣ, habbᵉhēmâ*, and *kol-remeś hā'ādāmâ*. This listing of three orders has not acquired the status of a stereotype and is less schematic than the Deuteronomist formulation found in Deut 4:16–18, which lists four orders: the beasts on the earth, the bird in the air, that which creeps on the ground, and the fish in the water under the earth. The apocalyptic passage Ezek 38:20 has the same four orders, though in a different sequence: fish of the sea, birds of the air, beasts of the field, and all *hāremeś hārōmēś 'al-hā'ᵃdāmâ*.

What Are *Remeś* and *Rōmēś*?

The foregoing discussion places details of the account in Genesis 9 within a preliminary framework of understanding, but questions remain concerning two crucial identifications, that of the group with the name *remeś*, and that of an overarching category known as *kol-bāśār*. The first is of crucial exegetical importance for an understanding of this passage because it pertains to the animal food that humankind is permitted to eat. Are Noah and his family permitted to eat only lizards and beetles and other creeping sorts of things? Most of us would be inclined to think that not much of a privilege!

In Gen 9:2 P agrees with Deut 4:16–19 and Ezek 38:20 in mentioning four rather than three orders — though this may not be original. The four are (1) the group known as *kol-ḥayyat hā'areṣ*, (2) the group known as *kol-'ôp haššamāyim*, (3) the group verbally designated as *kol 'ašer tirmōś hā'adāmâ*, and (4) the group called *kol-deĝê hayyām* (v. 2). Usually the word *behēmâ* is in first place, though "every living being" is sometimes substituted for it, as here, and may be intended as its synonym, or at least its equivalent. The birds and the fish are readily identified with the proper habitats, the sky and the sea, which they claim as their own, with neither humans nor beasts to supplant them. It is the third group, referred to in a participial phrase, that remains out of focus.

The noun *remeś* and the participle, *rōmēś*, have been translated as "creeping thing," "moving thing," "that which slithers," "worms," "maggots," and the like, but these are vague, generalized, and generally misleading. They are mostly guesses based on rabbinical tradition and do little or nothing to clarify the archaic Hebrew term. For definitions, dictionaries and lexicons have relied on the context, but this is often doubtful or even contradictory. There is an Akkadian cognate, but it is as ill-defined as the Hebrew. The Hebrew word occurs in the Damascus Code (CD 12.12), but merely as a copy of the biblical phrase upon which it depends.

The Hebrew text of Sir 10:11 has four terms (*rmh wtw' knym wrmś*) that have been reduced to three in the LXX and the RSV based upon it: "For when a man is dead, he will inherit creeping things, wild beasts and worms." It is apparently Greek *herpeta*, "snakes, worms," that translates *rmś*, but apparently in the wrong order. The LXX translator probably gave up trying to render all of these words, leaving us in the dark as to which Hebrew word *herpeta* is translating.

Thus, this passage is of little help to the lexicographer, and all that can be deduced with confidence is that *rmś* as such is in Sirach's Hebrew text and has come to mean something defiling, stinking, or draining from a corpse.[5] The word seems to have this meaning in Middle Hebrew (*Niddah* 3:2; *Sanhedrin* 8:2): "creeping thing," "worm," "snake" — in any case, definitely something defiling in a ritual sense.

In an effort to avoid futility and confusion, along with the fallacy of defining something by itself, we should observe the following data:

1. From the P creation account in Gen 1–2: It designates one of three orders, usually but not always with this mysterious word as the third in sequence. The order may live and swarm in the sea, but usually occupies the earth or ground.[6]

2. From Gen 6:20: The P order of animals entering the ark is: "some" (*min*) of the birds, "some" of the beasts (*habbᵉhēmâ*), "some" of all the *remeś ʿal hāʾᵃdāmâ.*[7]

3. From Gen 7:21: The "all flesh" that die in the flood, according to P, is further defined as *hārōmeśet ʿal hāʾāreṣ*, which is further described as consisting of five orders: birds, cattle (*bᵉhēmâ*), wild animals (*ḥayyâ*), "that which swarms (*haššōrēṣ*)[8] on the earth," and humankind.

4. From Gen 7:23: God wipes out "all that exists (*yᵉqûm*)[9] on the face of the ground." This entity is comprised of two inclusive groups of two each: (1) "those from human to beast" (*bᵉhēmâ*) and (2) "those from *remeś* to the birds of the sky."

5. From Gen 8:17: "Every animal" (*haḥayyâ*) emerging from the ark is said to belong to the wider category "all flesh," which in turn consists of three orders: birds, beasts (*bᵉhēmâ*), and "every sort of

---

5. Patrick W. Skehan and Alexander A. Di Lella, *The Wisdom of Ben Sira: A New Translation with Notes* (AB 39; New York: Doubleday, 1987), 225, suggest that, in this diatribe against vain rulers, the language is deliberately vague.

6. The two terms *ʾereṣ* and *ʾādāmâ* are virtual synonyms in spite of the fact that the latter is the most distinctive and therefore the most probable setting for the *remeś*.

7. Cf. J at Gen 7:9.

8. Cf. Gen 1:20.

9. Cf. Deut 11:6.

ḥāremeś"; the last is further defined and limited by the participial phrase *ḥārōmēś ʿal-hā'āreṣ*.[10]

6. From Gen 8:18–19: Here the *remeś/rōmēś* comes first, but the report of Noah's compliance with the divine command seems to be garbled, and the LXX may represent a secondary restoration.

7. From Gen 9:2: Our four orders as "every animal of the earth," "every bird of the sky," "everything that *rmś* [the verb] the ground," and "every fish of the sea" are subjected to human beings. All except the third — a participial phrase — are in nominal form. We should raise the question whether the fourth order may constitute an afterthought in this text because "the fish" are generally not included in P's tabulations. If P's syntactical shift to the verbal clause is to be interpreted as more than a stylistic flourish, there must be a special reason for this variation. What this reason may be is suggested by the fact that the following verse (9:3) commences with a parallel participial phrase, *kol-remeś ᵃšer hû'-ḥay*, "every *remeś* that lives." Unless verse 3 comes from a separate literary source, it is to be assumed that its function is to define something important about the contents of the verbal phrase in verse 2.[11]

8. The Psalms and prophetic literature have references to this order in the following passages: Ps 69:35 [ET 69:34], in which the order of the *rōmēś* is said to live in the sea, adding there to God's praise; Ps 104:20, which speaks of some of the same who live in the forest doing their thing — whatever that is — at night; Ps 104:25, which speaks of the *remeś* inhabiting the sea in great numbers; Ps 148:10, which simply mentions them in parallelism with beasts, cattle, and birds (*haḥayyâ wᵉkol-bᵉhēmâ, remeś wᵉṣippôr kānāp*), without suggesting what they are or what they do; 1 Kgs 5:13 [ET 4:33], in which Solomon is said to have encyclopedic knowledge of beasts, birds, *ḥāremeś* and the fish; Hos 2:20 [ET 2:18], which speaks of an eschatological covenant with the wild beasts, the birds, and the *remeś hā'ᵃdāmâ*; Hab 1:14, which states that YHWH makes human beings like fish of the sea, who are without a ruler like the *remeś*; Ezek 8:10,

---

10. According to Gen 1:21, the last mentioned may also live in the sea.
11. As suggested by R. Smend, Holzinger, and McEvenue, among others.

which describes abominable images of this particular order of animals; Ezek 38:20, exhibiting the familiar four orders, but in another sequence, while defining it by itself in the expression *kol ḥāremeś ḥārōmēś ʿal-hāʾᵃdāmâ*.[12]

9. In the cult-legislative literature this changes. Lev 11:46–47 reads, *zōʾt tôrat habbᵉhēmâ wᵉhāʿôp wᵉkol nepeš haḥayyâ hārōmeśet bammāyim*, "This is the law of beast and bird and every living being that is *rōmeśet* in the waters." The clause that is added to this does nothing to clarify it: *ûlᵉkol-nepeś haśśōreśet ʿal-hāʾāreṣ*, "and every living being that swarms upon the earth." The parallelism seems to be largely stylistic in view of the artificiality of the phrase "any swarming thing that swarms" occurring in verse 44; yet it is strange to hear of this order of animals doing their thing in the waters, while the defiling creatures that "swarm" do so on earth.

10. Leviticus 20:25 definitively states that "everything that *rmś* the ground is an abomination that makes a person unclean." With Lev 11:46–47, it may have been influential in turning the order of the *rōmeś* into something that defiles, as reflected in the literature of postbiblical Judaism.

Three important conclusions arising from this analysis are the following: (1) The living beings belonging to this order may exist on the land or on the sea. (2) Their order is distinct from the *bᵉhēmâ* and the *ḥayyâ*, though often confused with them. (3) That, except in very late passages, they are certainly not something odious or defiling in themselves. Else, how could *remeś* serve as food (= meat) for humankind in God's new era of blessedness?

But we still do not know who or what they are, and precisely what they do. They are not a species or even a biological class or order. Perhaps Ps 104:25 may give us the clue we need: "Yonder is the sea, great and wide, where there is *remeś* beyond counting, living things (*ḥayyôt*) both small and great." We cannot dismiss this as mere metaphorical language. It is the language of classical Hebrew and Near Eastern wisdom that we are hearing. We realize that the

---

12. Cf. Gen 8:17.

remeś belongs mainly on the earth or ground; we know also that it is found in the sea and even in a forest (Ps 104:20). It can consist of large or small creatures; but out in nature, not in a stable or a barnyard.

Thus the individual beings belonging to *remeś* may "swarm" in the sea or they may prowl the jungle. The main thing is that they are too many for anyone to count and are beyond human control or manipulation. They seem to vary so much among themselves that they bring wonder and amazement to those who try to understand them and describe them. This is why P speaks of them with apparent inconsistency. They are all of the things described; they may do any of things assigned to them.

From the observation that the third order appearing in the list in Gen 9:2 is not given a name like the other three, but is designated by a relative clause, *kol ʾᵃšer tirmōś hāʾᵃdāmâ*, I draw the conclusion that P recognizes that there are animal beings that do not fit readily within any of the other categories mentioned: "beast of the earth," "bird of the air," or "fish of the sea"; P therefore speaks of what they do rather than of what they are. Still, God included them among the creatures given into the power of human beings.

A reasonable explanation for the vagueness and variegation with which this order is depicted might be that the root *rmś* is primarily verbal, normally appearing in inflected or participial forms even though the simple noun is also employed. It is understandably the verbal/participial constructions that tell where (on the earth/ground or in the sea) and when (even at night) they do their special thing.[13] Among passages having the nominal form,[14] only Gen 1:25; 6:20; Hos 2:20 (ET 2:18); and Ezek 38:20 tell where they are to be found. An additional reason is that the entity *remeś* appears to be a category larger and more extensive than any other order, and therefore cannot

---

13. Gen 1:21, 26, 28, 30; 7:8; 8:17, 19; 9:2; Lev 11:44, 46; 20:25; Deut 4:18; Ezek 38:20; Pss 69:35; 104:20.

14. Gen 1:24, 25, 26; 6:7, 20; 7:14, 23; 8:17, 19; 9:3; 1 Kgs 5:13 (ET 4:33); Hos 2:20 (ET 2:18); Ezek 8:10; 38:20; Hab 1:14; Pss 104:25; 148:10.

be subsumed under, or coordinated with, a specific group of living beings.

This perhaps explains why it usually appears as third in sequence when a tabulation is being made, following the mention of more cohesive and recognizable groups — those well-known, those frequently seen, those who can be managed to human advantage through the skills of animal husbandry. *Remeś* is added apparently as a catchall term for all orders and may include some or all, but it refers especially to those that lurk in obscure places and out of sight.

One passage expressing this perspective reveals this rather clearly. In Gen 7:21 we read, "And all flesh (*hārōmēś*) upon the earth died, both bird and beast, both animal life (*ûbaḥayyâ*) and that which swarms upon the earth, as well as human beings." *Kol-bāśār* is the main subject but is qualified immediately by *hārōmēś 'al-hā'āreṣ*, a term that qualifies and limits this term as used because the flood had killed only the land creatures. Nevertheless, it will be seen that the second term coordinates with the first. *Kol-bāśār* — at least that which exists on the earth — is tantamount to, if not equivalent with, *hārōmēś!* This compound expression is in turn broken down into the smaller groups, the first two of which appear as pairs: (1) birds and (domestic) cattle, (2) wild animals and creatures that swarm, and (3) humankind.

Certain verses in this passage seem to confuse this distinction, but it is easy to understand why, for P's description remains vague and complex. It is best simply to ask, What do the *remeś* and *rōmēś* do? The *remeś* or *rōmēś* do something different from what the other various species do, and yet the *remeś* or *rōmēś* also do what all species do: live, breathe, and move about.

Since we need an English equivalent, no matter how imperfect, if we wish to translate this biblical passage, we may have to resort to an equivalent that we cannot prove, such as "moving thing," but certainly we must avoid prejudicial terms such as "creeping thing." The term "moving animal," though perhaps a redundancy, may be more appropriate because Gen 9:2–3 clearly does intend to make a sharp distinction between the plants that stay unmoved in their places (and are therefore easy to gather for food) and (now) these animals that move about on the ground or in the sea, and therefore must be caught.

God Punishes and Blesses "All Flesh"

It seems strange to read in Gen 9:9 that God makes a covenant with Noah and his descendants, and then in verse 10 that God includes animals, both those that are with Noah in the ark and — presumably — those that are not.[15] If verse 10 is retained, the meaning would be that God saves animals both from the ark and from the dry land. Though this might disturb the logic of claiming that all animals still living had been in the ark, the author may intend to say that the covenant is to extend not only to those that had actually been in the ark, but to all those who eventually inhabit the earth.

Verse 15 repeats that the covenant is extended to "every living creature of all flesh." The content of the covenant is a promise never again to send a flood to destroy all living beings. It is not actually a covenant like the one in Gen 17:2–17, but an agreement or arrangement[16] like that of Gen 6:18,[17] to save Noah's family and representative individuals of all creaturely orders from the coming flood by bringing them all into the ark.[18] This has to stand as an exemplar of the most perfect kind of divine grace bestowed upon the animals — that for which the beneficiaries would do nothing whatsoever in order to deserve, or reciprocate for, what God was doing on their behalf.

Noah and his family did labor to build the ark, gather the animals, and perform the chores of feeding and watering. Especially to do so

---

15. Because the LXX omits the final phrase in verse 10, l'kol ḥayyat hā'āreṣ, the RSV places it in a footnote and does not include it in the translation proper.

16. This does not deny that the full weight of divine self-giving stands behind the two promises. It is full of solemnity and authority. Nevertheless, the old theologians went far astray in speaking of a "Noachian covenant" as an agreement on God's part to accept humankind's good works as a satisfaction to God for his blessing.

17. "But I will establish my covenant with you; and you shall come into the ark [and so on]."

18. Martin Luther's Genesis commentary makes great sport at speculating about where so many animals had to be kept and how much labor needed to be expended in shoveling out all the manure that accumulated over many days.

in the face of what would have been a jeering, persecuting crowd of onlookers would certainly demand significant participation in working toward their own salvation, thus making themselves available and accessible for the working of divine grace. What needs to be said is that yes, certainly, the animals also needed a covenant with God! God had appointed humankind to have dominion over the wild creatures (Gen 1:28), but clearly this excluded exploitation of the animals, demanding rather their diligent care. God valued them highly enough to provide the means of rescuing the animals from the flood and to preserve them alive unto perpetuity!

In this light it should not surprise us that, according to the Priestly writer of Genesis, God deliberately included the animals in God's covenant of restoration guaranteed by the sign of the rainbow. There are Old Testament passages that give special recognition to the essential role that animals may play in human well-being. Deut 11:15 mentions God's provision of grass for the cattle in order that humankind might have plenty. Ps 104:21 states that the young lions seek their food from God. Ps 145:15–16 says that the Lord upholds, raises up, gives food to all — apparently not just all human beings — opening the Lord's hand to satisfy the desire of every living being (*maśbîa' lᵉkol-ḥay rāṣôn*). Ps 147:9 mentions that the Lord "gives to the beasts their food, and to the young ravens that cry."

Sometimes the animals participate in the ritual contrition of their human masters. So do the beasts, herds, and flocks who wore the Ninevites' sackcloth (Jonah 3:7–9) to induce YHWH to change YHWH's mind about destroying their city, and in the end YHWH expresses the divine intent to save "many cattle" along with innumerable innocent humans (4:11). There are times, too, when an animal, such as the donkey of Balaam, speaks out in good Hebrew to protest the impiety as well as the cruelty of his master (cf. Num 22:28–30). In addition, there are occasions when erring animals need to be haled before the court of justice, as regulated by Lev 20:15–16:

> If a man lies with a beast, he shall be put to death and you shall kill the beast. If a woman approaches any beast and lies with

it, you shall kill the woman and the beast; they shall be put to death, their blood is on them.

Or again, according to Exod 21:28–29, 32:

When an ox gores a man or a woman to death, the ox shall be stoned and its flesh shall not be eaten. . . . If the ox gores a slave, male or female, the owner shall give to their master thirty shekels of silver, and the ox shall be stoned.

In accordance with the principle of mutual responsibility governing both animals and humans, Gen 9:5 specifies, "For your blood I will surely require a reckoning; of every beast I shall require it and of humanity." In the new order that God is creating, P speaks of animals as though they were ethical and responsible agents. If they transgress the standards laid down in God's creation, they must be punished for it — punished not as one punishes a stubborn mule or a wayward horse in order to make them obey, but punished for a moral wrong. This is to be a rule in God's covenant with the "all flesh" who survive the flood.

Thus we see why, according to P, there had to be a flood. As says Gen 6:12, this was because "all flesh" had "corrupted their way upon the earth." The first question to raise here is, Who is or are "all flesh"? In Gen 6:19; 7:15–16; 8:17; and 9:15 it refers explicitly to animals, and to animals alone. But in Gen 6:12–13, 17; 9:11, 15–17, it probably refers both to human beings and to animals. In Gen 7:21 it cannot exclude human beings, who are mentioned last in a sequence governed by this expression. The explanation for this interesting variation is that it is determined by the contexts' demands: in one passage "all flesh" may be limited to animals alone because it is concerned with them alone; in another passage it may include both animals and human beings because they are dealt with according to a common principle. An important question is whether this expression ever refers exclusively to human beings, because that is what most interpreters have assumed about Gen 6:12–13, which is usually taken to refer to all humanity, all nations. But this is an unwarranted assumption drawn from the introductory material in the J account beginning in 6:5–7, which does refer exclusively to the delinquency of humankind, and of it alone.

The P flood account is introduced in Gen 6:11 with a summary statement, "And the earth was corrupt in God's sight, so that the earth was filled with violence." This is immediately followed by the narrative statement of a declaratory judgment: "And God saw the earth, and behold, it was corrupt, for all flesh had corrupted their way upon the earth" (6:12). The account has next a narrative introduction with God's explanation to Noah that God had determined to make an end of "all flesh" because the earth was filled with violence through "all flesh." God was resolved to destroy all who were included in this category along with the earth that they had corrupted (6:13). The earth had been made corrupt because "all flesh" had corrupted its way upon earth (*darkô ʿal-hā'āreṣ*; 6:12).

Mention of a "way" gives us a clue that the problem is ethical and behavioral, rather than theological and spiritual, as in the J account.[19] Accordingly, there is no good reason for excluding a delinquency on the part of the animals from P's complaint. In view of what has been said about the personification of animals in this account, there should be no hesitation about animals along with humankind in this, the very first, use of "all flesh" within the P flood account.[20]

What in particular the corruption is that has occurred among human beings and animals is neither explained nor described by P. The "violence" that results from this corruption is likewise left un-clarified. There are numerous instances of corruption and violence within the Old Testament, to which we might turn for illustrations. But we do not need them because it is safe to assume that P is think-ing these as the opposites of the harmony, wholeness, and peace that God had created in Paradise. Keeping in mind that it is "their way,"

---

19. In Gen 6:5–6 YHWH observes that it is the great wickedness of humankind that must bring the flood because "every imagination of the thoughts of their heart was only evil contin-ually." This description makes perfectly clear that human beings alone are the cause, and that the created animals must suffer solely on their account.

20. In view of the fact that every other instance of this expression in the P account includes the animals, with or without human beings, it would be difficult to understand why only here it should mean human alone in this introductory verse.

their pattern of behavior, that has become corrupt and violent, we may assume that primarily includes all the shedding of blood, abuse of animals, and human injustice that causes the flood. Only a deluge would be sufficient to stifle the violence and to cleanse the corruption so that a new creation might begin.

This is the point at which our discussion will benefit from an illustrative comparison with parallel material from another ancient Near Eastern culture, in this instance, the Epic of Atrahasis, with its fragments of a flood story.[21] Here are some poignant lines from this remarkable document:[22]

> The land became wide, the peop[le became nu]merous,
> The land *bellowed* like wild oxen.
> The god was disturbed by their uproar.
> [*Enlil*] heard their clamor
> (And) said to the great gods:
> "Oppressive has become the clamor of mankind.
> By their uproar they prevent sleep."
> ∙∙∙∙∙∙∙∙∙∙∙∙∙∙∙∙∙∙∙∙∙∙∙∙∙∙∙∙∙∙∙
> "In the morning let him cause . . . to pour [down],
> Let it extend through the night [. . .]."
> ∙∙∙∙∙∙∙∙∙∙∙∙∙∙∙∙∙∙∙∙∙∙∙∙∙∙∙∙∙∙∙
> Enki [opened] his mouth,
> Saying to En [*lil*]:
> "Why hast thou sworn [. . .]?
> I will stretch out my hand at the [. . .]
> The flood which thou commandest [. . .]."
> ∙∙∙∙∙∙∙∙∙∙∙∙∙∙∙∙∙∙∙∙∙∙∙∙∙∙∙∙∙∙∙
> [Atramhasis] opened his mouth,
> [Saying] to his lord:
> "[. . . make known unto me its content
> [. . .] that I may *seek* its . . . "

---

21. More elaborate is the flood account in the better-known Epic of Gilgamesh.

22. James B. Pritchard, ed., *Ancient Near Eastern Texts Relating to the Old Testament* (2d ed.; Princeton: Princeton University Press, 1955), 104–6.

[E.a] opened his mouth,
[Say]ing to his servant:
"Thou sayest 'Let me seek . . .'
The task which I am about to tell thee
Guard thou well:
'Wall, hearken to me,
Reed-hut, guard well all my words!
Destroy the house, build a ship,
Renounce (worldly) goods,
Keep the soul alive!
The ship that thou shalt build.' "
. . . .
"[. . .] I will loosen.
[. . .] he will seize all the people together,
[. . .], before the flood appears.
[. . .], as many as there are,
I will cause overthrow, affliction, . . .
[. . .] build a large ship.
[. . .] of good . . . shall be its structure.
That [ship] shall be an ark, and its name
Shall be 'Preserver of Life.'
[. . .] ceil (it) with a mighty cover.
[Into the ship which] thou shalt make,
[Thou shalt take] the beasts of the field,
The fowl of the heavens." . . . .
"[. . .] at the stated time of which I will inform t[hee],
Enter [the ship] and close the door of the ship.
Aboard her [bring] thy grain, thy possessions, thy goods,
Thy [wife], thy family, thy relations, and the craftsmen.
Beasts of the field, creatures of the field, as many as eat herbs,
I will send to thee and they shall guard thy door."

The people's rowdiness and clamor is identified as the cause of the flood in this remarkable parallel, and that does not fit the biblical account from the ideological point of view. It is, however, the raucous behavior of humankind as a formal equivalent to the "corruption" and "violence" that causes the flood, according to P. Again, the problem is not depicted as a deeply spiritual matter, but as a matter of behavior. The things of the heart may remain hidden, and so long as they are, they are unlikely to bring a flood. But if wild disturbance and disruption occurs in the world and in society, nothing less than a flood can remedy the situation. This rioting and misbehavior is bad enough when only humanity is at fault, but when even the beasts burst their bonds, all hell breaks loose![23]

Thus a covenant must be made with both Noah and his descendants, and with the animals, comprising "all flesh" together. The rainbow is for them all. I leave room for additional exposition of Genesis 9. Suffice it to say that every individual item referred to in chapter 9 of Genesis must be explained in terms of a new possibility of salvation and a new creation, or creation renewed. Definitely, this includes the special rules about the shedding of blood. If even the wild animals are to be held indictable for the shedding of human blood, how much more human beings who shed each other's blood!

Let it not be left unsaid, however, that this passage is protective also of the rights and needs of the animal world, and in equal measure with those of humankind. They are put in fear and dread of human beings — obvious enough! Their flesh may be utilized as food, but humanely and respectfully,[24] as P says; but few seem to listen anymore. The sad truth of our day is that humankind is harrowing and raping nature; animals that escape being shot with rifles are often deprived of the habitat necessary for living as God intended them to live — under a wise and protective management on the part of those under whose hand they must now live.

No, there will never be another deluge to destroy the world. God has promised that. When the world is destroyed, it will be because the land has been eroded away, the trees have been cut down, the

---

23. On this theme, we may think of the calculated horror created in films like *Jurassic Park* and *Godzilla*.

24. And why not? Is it better to leave their carcasses rotting in the field? Humans may as well benefit from them as to consign them to the vultures and the maggots!

waters have been fished out, and the animals who remain alive are consigned to zoos!

The animals that remain on the earth, in the sea, and in the air would welcome being dealt with in strict accord with the covenant of Genesis 9, but in the main, humankind daily disregards it. Has the earth been again corrupted by human beings? Has a violence far worse than in Noah's time taken over the earth?

I think the God of Noah still desires his *remeś* to prowl the forest, cavort in the lakes and seas, and fly through the air. This God still desires luxurious plant growth, full of nourishment for animals and for humankind, beautiful enough to lift human spirits and give joy and comfort both to the beasts and to humankind.

6

What Are We Teaching about Matthew?

Janice Capel Anderson *

Introduction

As teachers we are or should be accustomed to asking ourselves what we want students to know and what we want them to be able to do as a result of a course unit.[1] We want them to not only be able to name the parts of a bicycle, but also to be able to ride it. Frequently, especially in the first years of teaching, we are guided by our choice of texts for the course. I would venture to guess that those of us who teach New Testament Introduction or Introduction to Early Christian Texts assign readings from the New Testament and other first- or second-century primary sources. Some stop there, but most go on to use an introductory textbook as well. These introductory texts shape how students come to view the primary sources. I know I can

---

*In asking the questions, I pay homage to Bob Tannehill, who first was an inspiration to me through his article "The Disciples in Mark: The Function of a Narrative Role," *JR* 57 (Oct. 1977): 386–405. This article excited young graduate students about the possibilities that literary methods had for interpretation of the Gospels and Acts. Later, I joined Bob and a talented group of colleagues as together we explored literary criticism in the Society of Biblical Literature's Group on the Literary Aspects of the Gospels and Acts (1981–1999). In that group Bob was gentle but firm and insightful in his comments and generous in his contributions. It was clear that he really liked to grapple with texts and explore new methods. He was never patronizing to less-experienced colleagues. For a time I was privileged to serve with him as cochair of the group. Over the years I also learned of our mutual connections to North Dakota and of his interest in birding. I hope that Bob, like myself, will be interested to see how far the newer methods of gospel interpretation, especially the literary methods he pioneered, have penetrated the current textbooks as well as how much is left to be done.

1. I write this chapter with thanks to Paulist Press's WATSA (What Are They Saying About?) series for inspiring my title: "What Are We Teaching about Matthew?" An earlier version of this chapter was presented as a paper in the Matthew Section of the Society of Biblical Literature's Annual Meeting in Toronto, Canada, in November 2002.

never read the Hebrew Bible without having been influenced by B. W. Anderson's *Understanding the Old Testament,* or read the New Testament without hearing the words of Calvin J. Roetzel's *The Letters of Paul: Conversations in Context* or the first edition of Norman Perrin's *The New Testament* echoing in the background.

Textbooks also influence the views of teachers who cannot be up to the latest scholarly speed on all the early Christian texts. In some sense, unless they are very idiosyncratic and therefore unlikely to sell many copies, introductions represent a scholarly consensus on the books that are their subject matter. So in approaching this topic, I asked the question, What do recent popular secondary texts teach us, both students and teachers, about Matthew? I also wanted to know what methods they employ and urge readers to adopt as well as what assumptions they make. What sorts of methods do their chapters model? Finally, I wanted to see whether these texts incorporated literary, social scientific, feminist, or other scholarly approaches developed over the last twenty-five years. To what extent had the textbooks that teach students embraced these newer methods? To what extent do they remain strangers whose hands are yet to be clasped?

In engaging in this task I used seven recent American New Testament introductions. These included the following:

David L. Barr, *New Testament Story: An Introduction* (3d ed.; Belmont, Calif.: Wadsworth/Thomson Learning, 2002).

Raymond E. Brown, *An Introduction to the New Testament* (ABRL; New York: Doubleday, 1997).

Dennis C. Duling and Norman Perrin, *The New Testament: Proclamation and Parenesis, Myth and History* (3d ed.; Fort Worth: Harcourt Brace, 1994).

Bart D. Ehrman, *The New Testament: A Historical Introduction to the Early Christian Writings* (2d ed.; New York: Oxford University Press, 2000).

Stephen L. Harris, *The New Testament: A Student's Introduction* (4th ed.; Boston: McGraw-Hill, 2002).

Luke Timothy Johnson, *The Writings of the New Testament: An Interpretation* (2d ed.; Minneapolis: Augsburg Fortress, 1999).

Russell Pregeant, *Engaging the New Testament: An Inter-disciplinary Introduction* (Minneapolis: Augsburg Fortress, 1995).

As controls I also read the chapters on Matthew in two pre-World War II English introductions:

Rev. Marcus Dods, D.D., *An Introduction to the New Testament* (9th ed.; New York: Thomas Whittaker, 1900).

Edgar J. Goodspeed, *An Introduction to the New Testament* (1937; 14th impression, Chicago: University of Chicago Press, 1958).

Matthew in a First-Century Context: "Standard" Introductory Questions

All of the textbooks focus on the meaning of Matthew in its first-century context, either in terms of the author's intent and/or the likely reading of its first audiences. They also largely assume that Matthew was written to address a specific community with specific issues and problems. None of the chapters on Matthew tackle the methodological question of how one justifies reconstructing a community from the Gospel and then turning around and using the reconstruction to interpret the Gospel — treating the Gospel as an allegory. The analogy to Paul's letters as occasional documents is not mentioned or questioned. The Gospel is looked at as transparent to the community — with the words of Jesus addressing the disciples and crowds as words to a Matthean community or its leaders. Brown does point to some of the difficulties in a footnote. It is, he writes, "difficult to know whether the evidence pertains to where the Gospel was written from or written to, or both if the author lived among the addressees, as is normally supposed."[2]

---

2. Raymond E. Brown, *An Introduction to the New Testament* (ABRL; New York: Doubleday, 1997), 212 n. 90.

None of the chapters on Matthew that post-date it take up the suggestion *The Gospels for All Christians* makes that each of the Gospels was not addressed to one particular community, but rather to multiple communities, and that as codices, the Gospels traveled throughout the eastern Mediterranean world like the paperbacks today.[3] I must hasten to add that introductory textbooks may or may not yet be the place to challenge the reigning model.

The practice of establishing information about the author, the setting in life, and going behind the text to examine its likely sources and their editing shows the ongoing legacy of source and redaction criticism. Pregeant, however, with his reader-response reading of the Gospel, places the least emphasis on this. Several authors explicitly state that they are taking a redaction-critical approach. Ehrman, for example, says that he is using a redaction-critical approach to Matthew, whereas he modeled a literary-historical method in the previous chapter on Mark. Perhaps focusing on how Matthew edits Mark is almost inevitable, given both the history of Gospel scholarship and the fact that in all but Dods, the textbooks' chapters on Matthew follow their chapters on Mark. It is natural for authors and students to compare Matthew with the previous Gospel they have studied.

When we look at the picture of the author and process of composition presented, we find a number of remarkable areas of agreement between all of the textbooks going back to Dods's 1900 introduction. All except Dods, who holds out in favor of the apostle Matthew, agree that the author is unknown. All agree that the canonical Gospel was originally written in Greek and is not a translation. They all refer to, but discount, the Papias tradition as speaking of the canonical Matthew. All date the Gospel circa 80–90 C.E., some allowing for a margin slightly before or after those dates. The similarity in dating is largely because they all agree that the evangelist used Mark as one of his sources. Many also hold that the Gospel mentions the fall of

---

3. Richard Bauckham, ed., *The Gospels for All Christians: Rethinking the Gospel Audiences* (Grand Rapids: Eerdmans, 1998). Bauckham writes, "It is probable that the Gospels were written for general circulation around the churches and so envisaged a very general Christian audience" (1).

Jerusalem in 70 C.E. Barr is a good example. He dates Matthew to circa 85 C.E. due to its use of Mark and what he sees as references to the fall of Jerusalem in 21:43; 23:34–39; and 27:35.

As to location or place of composition and reception, again assuming that these are the same, most of the textbooks hold that Matthew was written in and for an urban center where there was a large population of Jewish Christians. Often Antioch is suggested as a likely site, with varying degrees of certainty expressed. Brown, Duling, Harris, and Goodspeed indicate that it may have been Antioch.[4] Ehrman holds that it was "presumably for a Greek-speaking community" and that Matthew "was probably located somewhere outside of Palestine (since most early Christians in Palestine would have spoken Aramaic as their native tongue)."[5]

In terms of sources, the recent introductions hold that Matthew used Mark and Q along with "special M." Harris hedges his bets about Q, describing it as an hypothesis.[6] There is less agreement about special M, including whether it was oral or written or both, or whether it actually represents a number of sources. Some argue that Matthew composed at least some of M. There is no support for the argument for Matthean priority. Even the earlier Goodspeed and Dods concur with Marcan priority.

Accepting Marcan priority is particularly useful in textbook presentations of Matthew because the authors can proceed by means not only of comparing and contrasting Matthew and Mark, but they can also indicate where they think Matthew has added to or changed Mark and why. Harris, for example, has a section entitled "Matthew's Editing of Mark" and has a mini-"Gospel parallels" box comparing

---

4. Brown, *Introduction*, 211–12; Stephen L. Harris, *The New Testament: A Student's Introduction* (4th ed.; Boston: McGraw-Hill, 2002), 148, 153, 175. Because of Ignatius's citation of Matthew circa 110–115 and the prominence given Peter, Harris suggests Antioch as a likely locale (153). He sees "a historical movement away from exclusively Jewish Christianity and toward a ministry that focuses on Gentiles" (153). Edgar J. Goodspeed, in *An Introduction to the New Testament* (Chicago: University of Chicago Press, 1937), 175, writes: "As Ignatius was bishop of Antioch in Syria, it seems probable that it was there the Gospel was written. Antioch was, in Harnack's phrase, the first great fulcrum of Christianity." Goodspeed also notes that Matthew emphasizes Peter, who is associated with Antioch as well (176).

5. Bart D. Ehrman, *The New Testament: A Historical Introduction to the Early Christian Writings* (2d ed.; New York: Oxford University Press, 2000), 84.

6. Harris, *Student's Introduction*, 154.

four instances of pericopes that appear in Matthew and Mark for the student to try out, but he also comments on how Matthew has edited Mark.[7] Having the parallels, if not telling the students how to interpret them, strikes me as a very useful pedagogical device, especially if the students have not been required to purchase a volume that presents the Synoptic Gospels in parallel arrangement. It also offers a way into redaction criticism from source criticism, albeit omitting form criticism, which is the bridge between them in the history of scholarship.

Concerning redaction criticism, Ehrman tells students to pay attention to what an author adds to his source and *even more* to what he changes.[8] He opines that the editor "probably would not have changed his sources unless he had a reason."[9] "Matthew's changes highlight the contrast between Jesus and the Jewish leaders," Ehrman writes, and in comparison to Mark, "Jesus' identity was public, not secret."[10] In terms of a redactional approach, Brown notes that he will focus on comparing and contrasting Matthew with Mark and Luke, but cautions, "We cannot afford to lose sight of Matt's highly effective narrative because of attention to comparative details."[11] (A warning with great appeal for narrative critics!)

An interesting pedagogical point related to the use of redaction criticism is where the textbooks place the majority of their discussion of authorship, sources, and setting, that is, before or after an exposition of the Gospel itself. This is significant because it helps to determine whether, at least on the first reading, students read Matthew against the reconstructed setting, against their reading of Mark (which usually is the previous chapter in the textbook, with the exception of Dods), or both. In college classes many students will not have read Matthew before, especially not as a narrative whole rather than isolated pericopes. Whether the author leads with an exposition of Matthew from which the discussion of author, setting, and sources

---

7. Ibid., 155–57, Box 8.2, "Examples of Matthew's Editing of Marcan Material."
8. Ehrman, *Historical Introduction*, 90.
9. Ibid., 91.
10. Ibid.
11. Brown, *Introduction*, 171.

is presented as arising or the reverse, and whether there is an emphasis on Matthew's editing of sources, makes a difference. In each case the context in which the Gospel is read helps to shape interpretation.

Matthew's Structure and Matthew's Story

Turning to the reading of Matthew as a whole and its structure, most authors do not stray far from a redactional approach. In confronting the issue of the structure of Matthew, the recent textbook authors often reference how Matthew uses and incorporates Mark and Q as important to understanding the Gospel's structure. Three structural proposals are frequently mentioned. The first is the bookend addition of the genealogy/birth story and the resurrection appearance stories to Mark's portrayal of Jesus' ministry with its geographical referents. The second is B. W. Bacon's five-discourse structure, which relies on the insertion of five major discourses into Mark's account and on the concluding/transitional phrases that end the discourses.[12] The third is a model that relies on 4:17 and 16:21 as major structural markers, often following Jack Dean Kingsbury's division into "The Person of Jesus Messiah (1:1–4:16)," "The Proclamation of Jesus Messiah (4:17–16:20)," and "The Suffering, Death, and Resurrection of Jesus Messiah (16:21–28:20)."[13]

---

12. B. W. Bacon's oft-repeated and sometimes modified structural hypothesis appeared in "The 'Five Books' of Moses against the Jews," *The Expositor* 15 (1918): 56–66; and in *Studies in Matthew* (New York: Henry Holt, 1930).

13. Jack Dean Kingsbury, *Matthew: Structure, Christology, and Kingdom* (Philadelphia: Fortress, 1975), 9. For discussion of various structural proposals see David R. Bauer, *The Structure of Matthew's Gospel: A Study in Literary Design* (JSNTSup 31; Sheffield: Sheffield Academic, 1988. Interestingly enough, Dods's textbook, which precedes B. W. Bacon's "The 'Five Books' of Moses against the Jews," points to the importance of 4:17 and 16:21. Marcus Dods, in *An Introduction to the New Testament* (9th ed.; New York: Thomas Whittaker, 1900), 22, writes: "The body of the book falls into two parts, iv.17–xvi.20 and xvi.21–end, each part opening with the words, 'From that time Jesus began.' These two main divisions correspond on the whole to the two chief aspects of the Messiah as the righteous beneficent King, 'God with us,' and as the Man of sorrows. Though not mutually exclusive, the first part exhibits Jesus as bringing fulness of life and righteousness, while the second part exhibits Him preparing His disciples for His death, warning the people against rejecting Him, entering Jerusalem as king, and therefore led to His throne on the cross. The Gospel culminates in the transfiguration, when the representatives of the Old Testament resign to Him their mediatorial functions. Or the turning point may be found in the preceding chapter (xvi), when through unbelief, doubt, rejection, spiteful usage at the hands of rulers and people, Peter's confession rises clear and decided."

David Barr and Dennis Duling also refer to the importance of chiasm for discerning the structure of Matthew.[14] In addition, Barr has two large charts indicating verbal and thematic correlations within Matthew's Gospel, "interlocking quotes and interlocking ideas."[15] These interlocking elements weave the Gospel together. Duling discusses several structural proposals and describes the strengths and weaknesses of each. Acknowledging the difficulties, he offers his own outline that tries to "recognize the story quality of the Gospel and at the same time its stress on Jesus as teaching the new revelation, indeed, as being the new revelation."[16]

Luke Timothy Johnson also mentions story, holding that "the story line of Mark . . . gives Matthew its basic structure."[17] He goes on to note, however, additional structural elements, including the summary transitions between the discourses and narrative; the two temporal transitions of 4:17 and 16:21; the formula citations, which he sees as "offering authorial commentary on the narrative"; and inclusio, citing 1:23 and 28:20 — "Emmanuel" and "Lo, I am with you always."[18] The references to story and authorial commentary indicate the influence of narrative criticism. However, because of the insertion of teaching, Johnson argues, "Matthew's Gospel lacks Mark's dramatic force. . . . The result is a much slower and sometimes less than dramatic plot development."[19] This statement is likely to annoy critics who want to treat Matthew as a narrative on its own terms. Johnson then proceeds to discuss two major structural proposals, one essentially Baconian and the other Kingsburian, offering comments on the strengths and weaknesses of each and choosing neither.

---

14. David L. Barr, *New Testament Story: An Introduction* (3d ed.; Belmont, Calif.: Wadsworth/Thomson Learning, 2002), 312–13. Dennis C. Duling and Norman Perrin, *The New Testament: Proclamation and Parenesis, Myth and History* (3d ed.; Fort Worth: Harcourt Brace, 1994).

15. Barr, *Story,* 302–3, Table 10.1 and Table 10.2.

16. Duling and Perrin, *Proclamation and Parenesis,* 343.

17. Luke Timothy Johnson, *The Writings of the New Testament: An Interpretation* (2d ed.; Minneapolis: Fortress, 1999), 188.

18. Ibid., 188–89.

19. Ibid., 189.

In terms of structure, the textbooks do not reach a consensus except perhaps in presenting alternatives. Ehrman appears to have given up on the search for a structure altogether, not offering one and indeed only discussing portions of the Gospel where there are additions or differences from Mark. This is in tune with his emphasis on redaction criticism in his Matthean chapter. This presentation, however, flies in the face of those who would read Matthew as a narrative whole and argue that what Matthew chooses to include from his sources is as important to understanding the Gospel as what he adds to them. In Ehrman's discussion of the Sermon on the Mount, he does mention in passing that some suggest that the collection of Jesus' teaching into "five major blocks of material is meant to recall the five books of the law of Moses."[20] This is, however, discussed not primarily in terms of its importance for structure or plotting, but in terms of Ehrman's presentation of the Matthean Jesus as "The New Moses." Some recent textbooks offer intriguing hints that Matthew is to be understood as a story complete with characters, plot, and point of view, but an old-fashioned understanding of structure still predominates.

Ehrman does, however, compare the Gospel to Greco-Roman biography, as does Duling. This attention to genre moves in the direction of a literary-social approach. It involves the expectations of a first-century audience as important in thinking about a Gospel's design. Ehrman indicates that the audience would have viewed Matthew as a Greco-Roman biography and thus would have expected conventions such as the presentation of Jesus' life in chronological order and a "highlighting [of] those sayings, actions, and experiences that revealed his essential character."[21]

Few of the textbook authors stress plot by detailing items such as kernels, satellites, retrospection, and other elements discussed by scholars such as Janice Capel Anderson, Warren Carter, Jack Dean Kingsbury, Frank J. Matera, and Mark Allan Powell.[22] Barr's is one

---

20. Ehrman, *Historical Introduction*, 93.
21. Ibid., 85.
22. See, for example, Janice Capel Anderson, *Matthew's Narrative Web: Over, and Over, and Over Again* (JSNTSup 91; Sheffield: Sheffield Academic, 1994), 133–91; Warren Carter,

of the most literary of all the textbooks in presenting "the movement of the plot" and "the shape of the narrative," although his outline remains centered on the alternation between narrative and discourse.[23] Barr's special narrative critical focus in his chapter on Matthew is "character." For example, he has a major subsection entitled "Understanding the Characters." Under that rubric there are subdivisions including "The Matthean Portrayal of Jesus," "The Matthean Portrayal of the Disciples," and "The Matthean Portrayal of Other Characters." This focus on characters as well as other elements of his presentation, including attention to the evaluative point of view of the narrator, is salutary from a narrative-critical perspective.

In the textbooks structural decisions are far more likely to be connected to an author's overall interpretation of the Gospel, the Gospel's Christology, and its view of the community — than to the Gospel's character as a narrative. Historical and redactional concerns are often to the fore. The disciples are often viewed as transparent to the Matthean community or its leaders.[24] Jesus is understood to speak directly to them, especially in the so-called "community discourse" in chapter 18. Typically, the textbook authors situate the Matthean Jesus and the evangelist's community in terms of Judaism. Redaction criticism is concerned with reconstructing the theology of each evangelist as well as the community he addressed, the Gospel's setting-in-life. These elements are important to our authors, although extensive discussion of concerns important to form criticism, redaction criticism's predecessor, are not. Discussion of the Gospel's view of Jesus and the nature of the community it addresses is, however, related to source criticism and questions of the Gospel's unity.

"Kernels and Narrative Blocks: The Structure of Matthew's Gospel," *CBQ* 54 (1992): 463–81; Jack Dean Kingsbury, "The Plot of Matthew's Story," *Int* 46 (1992): 347–56; Frank W. Matera, "The Plot of Matthew's Gospel," *CBQ* 49 (1987): 233–53; and Mark Allan Powell, "The Plot and Subplots of Matthew's Gospel," *NTS* 38 (1992): 187–204.

23. Barr, *Story*, 299–301, 300, 308.

24. For a discussion of the importance of transparency in Matthean interpretation, see Janice Capel Anderson, "Life on the Mississippi: New Currents in Matthaean Scholarship, 1983–1993," *CurBS* 3 (1995): 169–218, especially 178, 185–89, 201.

Matthean Christology and the Portrait of Jesus

As to theology, if we turn to the textbooks' focus on Christology, or as I would prefer, the portrayal of Jesus, we see a great deal of agreement. All the recent writers see Jesus as Messiah, Son of Abraham, and Son of David, as indicated at the very beginning of the Gospel. All point to Jesus as the fulfillment of the Hebrew Scriptures, particularly in the fulfillment quotations. They differ over whether he is to be considered a New Moses or is merely portrayed with some Mosaic overtones. As to Jesus and the Law, especially as seen in the Sermon on the Mount, all express in some way the notion that Jesus offers a deep, penetrating interpretation of the Torah rather than a whole new Torah. Brown, for example, conveys the idea as follows: "The Matthean Jesus presents God's demand not by dispensing with the Law but by asking for a deeper observance that gets to the reason why its demands were formulated, i.e., to be 'perfect as your heavenly Father is perfect' (5:48)."[25]

No author except Dods (in 1900) stresses Jesus as the suffering Son of Man, or as Dods puts it, the "Man of Sorrows."[26] As for the title Son of God, no one accents it as much as Kingsbury has done.[27] Brown does highlight the confession of Peter connecting Messiah and Son of God as a key passage along with the Trinitarian baptismal formula at the end of the Gospel.[28] Johnson notes that the frame of 1:23 and 28:20 makes God present. He sees Jesus as the authentic interpreter of the Torah, the fulfiller of Torah, and as the personification of Torah. He relates the latter to the personification of Wisdom and Torah in various Jewish traditions. Brown and Harris also mention the importance of wisdom in Matthew;[29] the relation of Jesus to

---

25. Brown, *Introduction*, 179. Interestingly enough Dods, *Introduction*, 21, already in 1900 offers a similar opinion although he stresses fulfillment: "The law which had seemed too high for human weakness is re-issued in a more penetrating form and is also fulfilled."

26. Dods, *Introduction*, 22.

27. Jack Dean Kingsbury, *Matthew's Story of Jesus* (Philadelphia: Fortress, 1986), 47–55, especially 55: "Preeminently, however, Jesus is the Son of God"; and idem, *Matthew: Structure, Christology, Kingdom* (Philadelphia: Fortress, 1975), 41, where he states, " 'Son of God' is the central christological title of Matthew."

28. Brown, *Introduction*, 218.

29. Ibid., 218; and Harris, *Student's Introduction*, 175.

Wisdom is also significant for Pregeant, who mentions the work of Jack Suggs and Fred Burnett.[30]

Barr, who is more of an advocate of narrative criticism, describes the portrayal of Jesus involving the use of titles, the responses of other characters, the evaluative point of view of the narrator, and the actions portrayed.[31] He writes: "If we focus our attention on what Jesus does and says, two characteristics seem to predominate: Jesus is the one endowed with great authority, and conversely he is the supremely obedient one."[32] Jesus' miracles show him as "the coming one, bearing the infirmities of his people."[33] Surprisingly, none of the recent authors focus much on Jesus as the coming Son of Man and on his Parousia as central to Jesus' identity. Some focus on this more than others, especially those who point to a Matthean introduction of a period of delay before the Parousia.

Author and Community Redux: Judaism and Anti-Judaism

With this comment, I return to the issue of author and community, which is of much concern in the textbooks' discussion of Matthew. The portrait of Jesus as Jewish Messiah and authoritative interpreter of the Law is closely related to questions about reconstruction of historical background, to determination of the Gospel's structure (with the Baconian hypothesis emphasizing Jewish connections), and to questions of the Gospel's unity or disunity due to the alleged inclusion of incompatible sources. The alleged incompatibilities are located in

---

30. Russell Pregeant, *Engaging the New Testament: An Interdisciplinary Introduction* (Minneapolis: Fortress, 1995), 228. He refers to M. Jack Suggs, *Wisdom, Christology, and Law in Matthew's Gospel* (Cambridge: Harvard University Press, 1970); and Fred W. Burnett, *The Testament of Jesus-Sophia: A Redaction-Critical Study of the Eschatological Discourse in Matthew* (Washington, D.C.: University Press of America, 1981); to which could be added Celia Deutsch, *Hidden Wisdom and the Easy Yoke: Wisdom, Torah and Discipleship in Matthew 11:25–30* (JSNTSup 18; Sheffield: Sheffield Academic, 1987); and idem, *Lady Wisdom, Jesus, and the Sages* (Valley Forge, Pa.: Trinity Press International, 1996).

31. Barr, *Story,* 322.

32. Ibid.

33. Ibid., 323.

contrasts between passages such as those that designate some synagogues as "their synagogues" (4:23; 9:35; 10:17) and others such
as 5:17–19, which holds that "not one iota or one point will pass
away from the law" and that whoever keeps and teaches the law
will be called great in the kingdom of the heavens. Authors struggle
with what Barr quotes Claude G. Montefiore as having expressed
in 1927[34]: "The Gospel seems to contain so many contradictions,
and to wear a double face. It is at once 'Jewish' and anti-Jewish, 'legal', and anti-legal, narrow and anti-Gentile and also catholic and
universalist."[35] These words seem to echo in Ehrman's words:

> When Jesus' strong affirmation of the Torah of Moses is set over
> against his strong opposition to the Jewish leadership, perhaps
> the most striking aspect of Matthew's Gospel emerges. On the
> one hand, Jesus is portrayed as altogether Jewish. He is the
> Jewish messiah sent by the Jewish god to the Jewish people in
> fulfillment of the Jewish Scriptures. He is also the new Moses
> who gives the true interpretation of the Mosaic Law. On the other
> hand, he violently opposes Judaism as it is configured in this
> Gospel among the Jewish leadership. Somewhat paradoxically,
> then, in this Gospel Jesus commands his followers to adhere to
> the Jewish religion as it should be (i.e., as he himself interprets
> it), while urging them to reject the Jewish authorities, who are
> portrayed as evil hypocrites, opposed to God and his people.[36]

I suspect the sometimes hidden and sometimes openly expressed
struggle with these real or seeming contradictions comes from the
fact that the recent textbook authors are writing in the shadow of the
Shoah. Is Matthew anti-Semitic or anti-Judaic? And, if the audience
members are Christian Jews[37] or Jewish Christians, does this get
Matthew at least partly off the hook?

---

34. Claude G. Montefiore, *The Synoptic Gospels* (2 vols.; 2d ed.; New York: KTAV, 1927),
1:lxxiii.
35. Barr, *Story*, 325.
36. Ehrman, *Historical Introduction*, 97.
37. The phrase "Christian Jews" is one of the legacies that Anthony J. Saldarini has left us.
The notion is particularly spelled out in his *Matthew's Christian-Jewish Community* (Chicago:
University of Chicago Press, 1994).

In contrast, Goodspeed, writing in 1937, appears not to have had a similar problem. He holds that the author probably was a Hellenistic Diaspora Jewish Christian, but that the Gospel was not written for Jews.[38] Why? Because, he holds that "the Gospel steadily depreciates the practices and ethics of Judaism." He continues:

> It lays the responsibility for the death of Jesus at the door of the Jewish people with terrible solemnity. It gives the impression that the church and the synagogue are growing more and more hostile. It nowhere has the appearance of seeking to win or to conciliate Jews. Its purpose is rather to explain their refusal of the gospel and to establish the Jewish Scriptures as a possession of the church.... The attitude of the Gospel of Matthew is rather that the Jewish mission is definitely and finally over. It is the Greek mission that is now before the church.[39]

For Goodspeed at least, there seems to be no paradox or contradictions, and thus no issue of the unity of the Gospel. He does not have to decide whether to read the "contradictions" as due to the use of various and sometimes undigested sources, to a gradually developing community, or as part of a narrative whole within which the "contradictions" make sense.[40]

Most of the modern writers solve the problem in part by focusing on Jewish leaders as a character group or as only a subset of the Jews that appear in the Gospels. It is the Jewish leaders in Matthew who are evil hypocrites, and not Jews in general, since Jesus, the disciples, and most of the other characters are themselves Jews. But, if those Jewish leaders are transparent to the leaders of a nascent rabbinic Judaism, then they are representative of what becomes normative

---

38. Goodspeed, *Introduction*, 178–79.
39. Ibid., 178.
40. Dods's approach in 1900 seems to be captured in his quote from F. W. Farrar: "The answer is simple. The asserted discrepancy lay in facts which found their synthesis in wider truths. Jesus was both the Messiah of the Jews and Saviour of the world. He came to the Jew first, and afterwards to the Gentile. The Evangelist was a Jewish Christian, but he could not suppress, nor did he desire to suppress, facts and words which belonged to an order of thoughts infinitely wider than that in which he had been trained" (23–24, quoting Frederic W. Farrar, *The Messages of the Books: Being Discourses and Notes on the Books of the New Testament* [London: Macmillan, 1884], 51).

Judaism. As to whether Matthew's church (again the idea of one community, and even one group of early Christians in one community) had separated from the synagogue, opinions differ.

Barr sees a Christian Jewish context: "Matthew may have lived in a large city, a city with many synagogues. Some were messianic; others were Pharisaic; still others were probably neither. Matthew wrote for his own people, showing them what he saw as their real heritage and differentiating them from the Pharisees."[41] Ehrman agrees with Barr that a separation has not yet taken place: "Matthew's insistence that Jesus continued to adhere to traditional forms of Jewish piety, and that he advanced the true interpretation of the law of Moses, suggests that the author himself and some, perhaps most, of his audience were themselves Jewish."[42] Matthew's community "continued to experience opposition from non-Christian Jews, especially influential scribes and rabbis of the local synagogue(s), who accused them of abandoning Moses and the Law, of becoming apostate from the Jewish religion through their ill-advised faith in Jesus."[43]

In contrast to Barr and Ehrman, who see continuity, Duling, Brown, and Johnson see a separation, while Harris presents the situation as ambiguous. Johnson writes that Matthew's community was "a community that was in contact with, and sought to define itself over against, a developing Pharisaic tradition within Judaism."[44] He also asserts that "the Christian sect not only was aware of the older and better-established Jewish tradition but also found itself required to explain and understand — first of all for itself — why it came to worship here and not in the synagogue down the street."[45] For Johnson, the Matthean "church" is "a church that must define itself in terms of a more-dominant Jewish movement. This accounts both for the thoroughly Jewish (i.e., rabbinic) tone of the Gospel and for its intense hostility toward those who 'sit on the seat of Moses' (23:2)."[46]

---

41. Barr, *Story*, 333.
42. Ehrman, *Historical Introduction*, 101.
43. Ibid., 102.
44. Johnson, *Writings*, 191.
45. Ibid.
46. Ibid., 192.

So has the evangelist or his community(ies) made a decisive break with Judaism? Our textbooks and Matthean scholarship in general remain at an impasse. This impasse leads me to wonder if we have been asking an answerable question, or perhaps not asking the right questions. If the evangelist, as Norman Perrin used to say, was a man of the Hellenistic Jewish Christian mission, if Mark and Q as well as Matthew were written in Greek, and if the consensus is correct that Matthew used Mark and Q, shouldn't we focus more on Matthew as a Greco-Roman text? Since the current textbooks read the Gospel so strongly against a Jewish backdrop — especially against Yavneh (Yabneh, Jamnia) and/or Qumran — whether they perceive that a decisive break was in the past or future for the evangelist seems less significant than the possibility of reading the Gospel against other backdrops.

Empire, Social Change, and Classics

Although there are occasional references to the Jewish War and the Fall of Jerusalem, the textbooks do not read the Gospel very much against the backdrop of life in the Roman Empire, either in Palestine or the Diaspora. None of them has taken up to any great extent (some because they predate it) the kind of interpretation of Matthew and empire recently offered by scholars such as Warren Carter, Mary Rose D'Angelo, Jennifer Glancy, and Musa W. Dube (Shomanah), who offers a feminist postcolonial approach.[47] In addition to taking more seriously the Hellenistic and imperial context of the evangelist and his first audiences, much of the new work relating Matthew to empire employs social-scientific as well as literary approaches and exploits a rich mine of classical scholarship. If much of Matthean scholarship

---

47. Warren Carter, *Matthew and Empire: Initial Explorations* (Harrisburg, Pa.: Trinity Press International, 2001); and idem, *Matthew and the Margins: A Socio-political and Religious Reading* (Maryknoll, N.Y.: Orbis, 2000). Mary Rose D'Angelo, " 'Abba and Father': Imperial Theology and the Jesus Tradition," *JBL* 111 (1992): 611–30. Jennifer A. Glancy, "Slaves and Slavery in the Matthean Parables," *JBL* 119 (2000): 67–90. Musa W. Dube [Shomanah], *Postcolonial Feminist Interpretation of the Bible* (St. Louis: Chalice Press, 2000), who takes to task a number of interpreters of Matthew 15:21–28 (including this author) for failing to consider the context of empire.

since World War II was written in the shadow of the Shoah and with great concerns to read Matthew in the light of rabbinic Judaism, much of the recent work reads Matthew with one eye to our own postcolonial (or perhaps colonial) context.

In the textbooks I reviewed, only Barr, Duling, and Pregeant take up to any great degree social-scientific perspectives, although comparisons to Qumran and particularly the Manual of Discipline are sometimes made. Pregeant points to Saldarini's use of the concept of deviance and his understanding of "Matthew's group as a marginalized sect within the larger community that has its own identity but does not think of itself as beyond the bounds of Judaism, whatever others might have thought of it. In this view, the author still has hopes that other Jews will join the messianic movement."[48] Pregeant continues quoting from Saldarini: "However . . . the orientation of the Matthean community is changing from reformist to isolationist (vis-à-vis Jewish society), and it is beginning to create a new community withdrawn from Judaism and the empire as well."[49]

Pregeant also picks up Malina and Neyrey's contentions, in *Calling Jesus Names,* that at the pre-Matthean level of tradition, when Jesus' followers were still part of Judaism, the followers were a deviant group "with strong internal solidarity but weak influence on the larger society."[50] As such a group, they leveled what anthropologists would label "witchcraft" accusations against their fellow Jews, demonizing their opposition.[51] This accounts for the vituperative tone of material attacking the Jewish leaders in Matthew, and Pregeant argues that it should not be used as a license for modern anti-Semitism or anti-Judaism.

In a discussion of Zealots, Sadducees, Essenes, and Pharisees that serves as a backdrop for his discussion of the situation of the Matthean community, Barr labels the Sadducees as members of a

---

48. Pregeant, *Engaging,* 225.

49. Ibid., 225, quoting from Anthony J. Saldarini, "The Gospel of Matthew and Jewish-Christian Conflict," in *Social History of the Matthean Community: Cross-Disciplinary Approaches* (ed. David L. Balch; Minneapolis: Fortress, 1991), 38–61.

50. Pregeant, *Engaging,* 231, relying on Bruce J. Malina and Jerome H. Neyrey, *Calling Jesus Names: The Social Value of Labels in Matthew* (Sonoma, Calif.: Polebridge Press, 1988).

51. Pregeant, *Engaging,* 231, again speaking about Malina and Neyrey's interpretation.

"ruling elite, the one to two percent of the urban population that ran the affairs of the people."[52] The Essenes are classified as a sectarian group and the Pharisees as coming largely "from the social class we label retainers, people who serve the needs of the ruling elite and mediate their services (and demands) to the masses. Most would have been artisans, shopkeepers, or landowners."[53]

Duling integrates concerns similar to those of Barr. He also writes of Matthew as a sort of foundation myth or a myth of origins, building on the work of Perrin. He discusses an "embryonic" order for regulating church life with certain leadership positions as well.[54] One can recognize here the beginnings of the analysis Duling later developed concerning the Matthean "brotherhood" and marginality.[55]

Literary Criticism: Reception History

In terms of literary criticism, which has often vied for attention with social-scientific work, some influence can be seen in the recent textbook authors. Barr and Pregeant have pursued it most fully. As I noted earlier, Barr employs narrative criticism especially in terms of the portrayal of characters. Pregeant opens his Matthean chapter with an extended reader-response commentary on the Gospel. It is somewhat surprising, nonetheless, given the strong emphasis on reception history by Ulrich Luz in his multivolume commentary and elsewhere, that most of these textbooks pay little if any attention to reception history — something my college students find quite interesting.[56]

---

52. Barr, *Story,* 328.

53. Ibid., 329.

54. Duling and Perrin, *Proclamation and Parenesis,* 336–38.

55. Dennis C. Duling, "Matthew 18:15–17: Conflict, Confrontation, and Conflict Resolution in a 'Fictive Kin' Association," *BTB* 29 (1999): 4–22; idem, " 'Egalitarian' Ideology, Leadership, and Factional Conflict within the Matthean Group," *BTB* 27 (1997): 124–37; idem, "The Matthean Brotherhood and Marginal Scribal Leadership," in *Modeling Early Christianity: Social Scientific Studies of the New Testament in Its Context* (ed. Philip F. Esler; New York: Routledge, 1995), 159–82.

56. Two volumes of Ulrich Luz's commentary have been published in English thus far: *Matthew 1–7: A Commentary* (vol. 1; trans. Wilhelm C. Linss; Hermeneia; Minneapolis: Augsburg, 1989); and *Matthew 8–20: A Commentary* (vol. 2; trans. James E. Crouch; Hermeneia; Minneapolis: Fortress, 2001). Another example of Luz's use of reception history is "The Final

Although not labeled as such, partial exceptions to this occur in Brown and Pregeant. They raise theological questions that modern readers may have. Brown, for example, raises the question of Protestant and Catholic differences in the recitation of the Lord's Prayer. He also comments on the use of Peter's confession as support for the papacy. Pregeant also mentions the Peter controversy, as well as discussing the relationship of Matthew's theology to Jewish-Christian relations. In addition, most authors, aware of the pernicious uses of the verse, at least touch on questions raised by Matt 27:25: "His blood be on us and on our children."

Feminist Criticism and Matthew

Finally, I will consider feminist criticism, an approach to the Gospel which has grown in the last several decades. Only Barr appears in any great degree to have absorbed feminist work on the Gospel of Matthew such as that produced by Emily Cheney, Musa Dube (Shomanah), Amy-Jill Levine, Marla Selvidge, Elaine M. Wainright, Antoinette Clark Wire, myself, and others.[57] Barr discusses important women characters as models:

Judgment (Matt 25:31–46): An Exercise in 'History of Influence' Exegesis," in *Treasures New and Old: Contributions to Matthean Studies* (ed. Mark Allan Powell and David R. Bauer; Atlanta: Scholars, 1996), 271–310.

57. Janice Capel Anderson, "Matthew: Gender and Reading," *Semeia* 28 (1983): 3–27; idem, reprinted in *A Feminist Companion to Matthew* (ed. Amy-Jill Levine with M. Blickenstaff; FCNTECW; Sheffield: Sheffield Academic, 2001), 25–51; idem, reprinted as "Mary's Difference: Gender and Patriarchy in the Birth Narratives," *JR* 67 (1987): 183–202; Emily Cheney, *She Can Read: Feminist Reading Strategies for Biblical Narrative* (Valley Forge, Pa.: Trinity Press International, 1996); Musa W. Dube [Shomanah], *Postcolonial Feminist Interpretation;* Amy-Jill Levine, "Matthew," in *The Women's Bible Commentary* (ed. C. A. Newsom and S. H. Ringe; Louisville: Westminster John Knox, 1992), 252–62; all the essays in Amy-Jill Levine with Marianne Blickenstaff, eds., *A Feminist Companion to Matthew* (FCNTECW; Sheffield: Sheffield Academic, 2001); Jane Schaberg, *The Illegitimacy of Jesus: A Feminist Theological Interpretation of the Infancy Narratives* (San Francisco: Harper & Row, 1987); idem, "Feminist Interpretations of the Infancy Narrative of Matthew," *JFSR* 13 (1997): 35–62; Marla J. Selvidge, "Violence, Woman, and the Future of the Matthean Community: A Redaction Critical Essay," *USQR* 39 (1984): 213–23; idem, *Daughters of Jerusalem* (Scottdale, Pa.: Herald Press, 1987); Elaine M. Wainright, *Towards a Feminist Critical Reading of the Gospel according to Matthew* (New York: de Gruyter, 1991); idem, "The Gospel of Matthew," in *A Feminist Commentary* (vol. 2 of *Searching the Scriptures;* ed. E. Schüssler Fiorenza and Shelly Matthews; New York: Crossroad/Continuum, 1994), 635–77; idem, *Shall We Look for Another? A Feminist Rereading of the Matthean Jesus* (Maryknoll, N.Y.: Orbis, 1998); and Antoinette Clark Wire, "Gender Roles in a Scribal Community," in *Social History of the Matthean Community* (ed. David L. Balch; Minneapolis: Fortress, 1991), 87–121.

Women characters are almost always portrayed positively in this Gospel. Two stand out. The bleeding woman (9:20–22) displays remarkable faith, even more noteworthy when contrasted with the men in the surrounding story who laugh at Jesus (9:24). The Canaanite woman is portrayed even more impressively: she convinces Jesus to change his mind about healing her daughter (15:22–28). And the women at the tomb are portrayed as obedient.[58]

Neither he nor the other authors employs biblical criticism as an essential tool in interpreting the gospels as a whole. Thus, of the three new general approaches to Matthew introduced in the past twenty-five years — literary, social scientific, and feminist — feminist criticism of Matthew is least integrated into the textbooks that are shaping our students' views of the Gospel. Similarly, postcolonial criticism emerging quite recently has yet to make a splash.

Conclusion

In many ways the concentration on author, place of composition, date, and sources that one finds in the pre-World War II textbooks of Dods and Goodspeed remains a sine qua non for New Testament introduction. Redaction criticism, which emerged in the 1950s with Günther Bornkamm's "The Stilling of the Storm" as a prime example, however, has now found a firm foothold.[59] Social-scientific and literary approaches at least have a foot in the door, although they have not crossed the threshold and found a place in the center of the room. Feminist criticism still remains outside, as do new possibilities suggested by even more recent work such as postcolonial interpretation. Just as Matthew has to contend with Mark for serious attention in

---

58. Barr, *Story*, 324. Ehrman, *Historical Introduction*, does have a chapter entitled "From Paul's Female Colleagues to the Pastor's Intimidated Women: The Oppression of Women in Early Christianity."

59. Günther Bornkamm, "Die Sturmstillung im Matthäusevangelium," *WD* (1948): 49–54; idem, ET, "The Stilling of the Storm in Matthew," in *Tradition and Interpretation in Matthew* (ed. G. Bornkamm, G. Barth, and H. J. Held; trans. Percy Scott; NTL; Philadelphia: Westminster Press, 1963), 52–57.

modern New Testament introductions, so also these new approaches must contend with older approaches for space. The interpretive possibilities that they open may yet help them to find an appropriate place in the books that we require our students to read. Perhaps soon what introductions are teaching about Matthew will reflect more fully what scholars have been writing about Matthew with so much passion.

7

Evocative Allusions in Matthew

Matthew 5:5 as a Test Case

Robert L. Brawley

When coach Mike Davis's Indiana University team beat the University of Oklahoma in a semifinal game of the National Collegiate Athletic Association's basketball tournament in 2002, an Indiana fan held up a sign: DAVIS AND GOLIATH. The poster evokes the biblical account of David and Goliath, without explicitly mentioning the story from Scripture. But to what degree does the placard resonate with the story? To what degree does it ignore or reject details of the story, and to what degree does it cast them in new light? The Philistine Goliath curses David by his gods (1 Sam 17:43), whereas David comes in the name of YHWH Sabbaoth (17:45). The "Davis and Goliath" placard abandons the ethnic war and theology of the story of David and Goliath only to reiterate them in terms of cultural loyalties. An athletic contest supersedes war. But do questions of theological allegiance remain on the screen, given that players and fans at times assumed postures of prayer? After Indiana player Tom Coverdale injured his ankle, one supporter sent some water blessed by the Pope to help heal the injury. In sum, "Davis and Goliath" teases the mind beyond a simplistic, defined correlation.

In another case, Clifton Black critiques devotion to method in biblical studies and drops the line "Dr. Strangeuse: Or, How I Learned to Stop Enjoying and Love the Skill."[1] Black alludes to a classic movie title that is unformulated in his text: *Dr. Strangelove, Or: How I*

---

1. C. Black, *The Rhetoric of the Gospel: Theological Artistry in the Gospels and Acts* (St. Louis: Chalice, 2001), 144.

Learned to Stop Worrying and Love the Bomb. Were it not for TV reruns of this satire on the Cold War, Black's allusion might sail over his readers' heads. The movie depicts a conflagration instigated when a U.S. airplane drops a nuclear bomb on the Soviet Union. When the bomb doors open, the berserk commander of the flight crew rides the bomb as if he were a cowboy on a bronco.

To what degree does Black's play on the title cast the values of the movie in a new light? Am I going down the wrong road when I juxtapose Black's line with the film's title, and then suppose that (1) the setting of competitive methods in biblical studies is as ludicrous as the Cold War in the movie, (2) fascination with method is a matter of misdirected affection — *strange love* indeed — and (3) dogmatic devotion to method in biblical studies is crazy?[2] Anticipating a later discussion, I point out that Black's title forms a figuration (trope) on a movie that as satire is already figurative.

In another case Black writes about preaching: "God's parabolic wisdom will unfailingly prosper — perhaps never more evidently so than when revealed to prophets whose persuasiveness irritates the life out of them, whose most memorable performance is a beachhead in fish-vomit."[3] Black again evokes a text that is unformulated — the story of Jonah whose resistance to his prophetic task results in his dire distress in the belly of a fish, but whose prayer for deliverance results in an act of God in which the fish vomits Jonah onto dry land. When Jonah preaches to the Ninevites, their situation replicates his distress in the belly of the fish. Like Jonah, they cry to God. God delivers the Ninevites from their distress just as God delivered Jonah. Prophetic preaching in Nineveh prospers. That is not all. Upon his success, Jonah reveals that the motivation of his initial reluctance

---

2. In a telephone conversation, Black confirmed only my second conclusion as fitting his authorial intent. But he found my interpretations plausible and suggested that authorial activity both constrains and opens up interpretive possibilities. Unconscious aspects of writing can enable interpreters to uncover dimensions that escape authorial intent. See E. Finkelpearl, "Pagan Traditions of Intertextuality in the Roman World," in *Mimesis and Intertextuality in Antiquity and Christianity* (ed. D. MacDonald; Harrisburg, Pa.: Trinity Press International, 2001), 79–81.

3. Black, *Rhetoric*, 149.

is eminently but perversely theocentric. He knows that God is merciful — a central confession of Israel: "For I knew that you are a gracious God and merciful, slow to anger, and abounding in steadfast love, and ready to relent from punishing" (Jonah 4:2 NRSV). But in ethnic jealousy, he does not want God to show mercy upon the Ninevites. He would rather see his prophecy of divine destruction fulfilled. Thus, Black's sentence points to divine accomplishments that reach their goal through prophetic agents in spite of motivations that may be at cross-purposes with God. Again, Black plays figuratively on a text that as parable is already figurative.

Intertextuality

In spite of advances in theories of intertextuality, investigations of Matthew's use of Scripture continue to perpetuate methods of determining sources and models that influence Matthew's composition. In a volume whose dust cover promotes "an up-to-date picture of the most recent research," Maarten Menken searches conventionally for sources of Matthew's use of Scripture in the massacre of the innocents.[4] Intertextuality has also been construed as *mimesis,* not in the sense of the representation of reality (E. Auerbach) but in the sense of Greek school exercises in which students write compositions that imitate classical authors. The premise of this approach is that Matthew duplicated scriptural models as an aspect of composition. Thomas Brodie has produced a number of studies that draw especially on the Elijah and Elisha cycles as literary models.[5]

Martin Rese's investigation of the use of Scripture in Luke-Acts initiated a shift beyond identification of sources and compositional

---

4. M. Menken, "The Quotation from Jeremiah 31 (38).15 in Matthew 2.18; A Study of Matthew's Scriptural Text" [Jer 31:15 = 38:15 LXX], in *The Old Testament in the New Testament: Essays in Honour of J. L. North* (ed. S. Moyise; Sheffield: Sheffield Academic, 2000), 106–25. Because intertextuality includes tensive relationships between texts, Menken's reliance on tension between the citation and the Matthean context lacks theoretical sophistication.

5. T. Brodie, *The Crucial Bridge: The Elijah-Elisha Narrative as an Interpretive Synthesis of Genesis-Kings and a Literary Model for the Gospels* (Collegeville, Minn.: Liturgical Press, 2000); idem, "Fish, Temple, Tithe, and Remission: The God-Based Generosity of Deuteronomy 14–15 as One Component of Matt 17:22–18:35," *RB* 99 (1992): 697–718.

devices.[6] He proposed a hermeneutical function in which Scripture provides a lens through which the New Testament attempts to make sense of the Christ event. Reciprocally, the Christ event provides a lens through which to understand Scripture. This suggests a key for interpreting citation formulas that introduce no citations. For example, Matt 26:54 asks, "How therefore will the scriptures be fulfilled that it is necessary to happen thus," without citing a single text. This implies (1) that Scripture as a whole provides a framework for understanding the Christ event, and (2) that there are patterns in Scripture, such as people who suffer for fidelity to God, that help readers of the Gospel understand the Christ event.

In 1996 at the Colloquium Biblicum at the University of Leuven, Belgium, Donald Senior presented a study of Matthew's use of the Old Testament in the passion narrative. He rehearsed the conventional question of sources but also categorized the functions of quotations and allusions as (1) providing an aura of biblical authority, (2) conferring a new understanding on God's voice in Scripture (similar to Rese's hermeneutical function), (3) serving as the structure for Matthean composition (mimesis), and (4) making a fundamental affirmation of the fulfillment of God's plans and promises.[7] Only the second category moves beyond the conventional attempts to determine sources and models for composition. Emerson Powery produced a similar study but with emphasis on the function of formula citations in the narrative. In particular, he made a distinction between the citation practices of the narrator and of Jesus as a character in the narrative. His narrative functions, however, are conventional — defending, predicting, instructing, correcting.[8]

For Julia Kristeva, intertextuality has little to do with sources or models of composition. It has to do rather with how texts affect society and culture according to the way they make utterances by

---

6. M. Rese, *Alttestamentliche Motive in der Christologie des Lukas* (Gütersloh: Mohn, 1969).

7. D. Senior, "The Lure of the Formula Quotations: Re-assessing Matthew's Use of the Old Testament with the Passion Narrative as a Test Case," *Scripture in the Gospels* (BETL 131; ed. C. Tuckett; Leuven: Leuven University Press, 1997), 89–115.

8. E. Powery, "Jesus Reads Scripture: The Function of Jesus' Use of Scripture in the Synoptic Gospels" (Ph.D. diss., Duke University, 1999), 113–251.

(1) incorporating textual systems (anonymous cultural conventions that are larger than any one text) or (2) referring to textual patterns that they do not themselves contain. In Matt 26:54 Jesus refers to a textual system that Matthew does not contain: "How therefore will the scriptures be fulfilled that it is necessary to happen thus?" "The scriptures" are a textual system that Matthew cannot and does not contain. The incorporation of, or reference to, textual systems produces a shift in values, and Kristeva focuses on the shift in value within the new text.[9] The issue for her is the transformation of the function of the textual pattern or reference.

If I write my own thoughts, my thinking is different from my writing, with a corresponding distinction in values. But to *claim* to write *my own thoughts* implies that the two activities of thinking and writing are equivalent, with the result that the implied equivalence must be figurative. In a related way, Matt 26:54 implies equivalence between the arrest of Jesus and Scriptures, whereas the Scriptures are chronologically independent of the arrest of Jesus. Matthew's claim thus recasts diachrony into synchrony, a move that Harold Bloom calls "a lie against time."[10] Matthew's text makes two distinct discourses equivalent and "admits the existence of an *other* (discourse) only to the extent that it makes it *its own*."[11] Fulfillment is, therefore, figurative: incorporating textual patterns or referring to them in a new writing inevitably forms a figure of speech, a trope, in which differences parade as coherent. The "troping" confers a new voice on textual patterns incorporated or references elicited from outside the new text; at the same time the incorporation or references still speak with voices they already possess.[12] The interplay between old and new texts reconfigures the social construction of reality against the culture of both texts.[13] This figurative aspect of intertextuality

---

9. J. Kristeva, *Desire in Language: A Semiotic Approach to Literature and Art* (New York: Columbia University Press, 1980), 36–63.

10. Kristeva, *Desire*, 65; H. Bloom, *The Breaking of the Vessels* (Chicago: University of Chicago Press, 1982); H. Bloom, *Kabbalah and Criticism* (New York: Seabury, 1975), 112.

11. Kristeva, *Desire*, 46 (emphasis original).

12. Ibid., 73, in dependence upon Bakhtin.

13. See Finkelpearl, "Pagan Traditions," 82.

has largely gone unnoticed in interpretations of Matthew's use of Scripture as source criticism or literary imitation.

Kristeva advocates intertextuality on a large scale, far beyond recognizable textual patterns relating with each other. To illustrate, Kristeva argues that Western society recognizes differences between males and females but then fallaciously takes the differences to mean that one gender ranks above the other. She then argues that social constructs that rank males over females find expression in literature as the heroic idealization of woman.[14] Kristeva's interests lie, therefore, in large issues of value involved in the move from conventional utterances that males and females are different, to a textual expression (the idealization of woman) that produces a shift in values (from nonhierarchical difference to patriarchy).

Though Kristeva reflects on citations, she allows little place for analysis of citations and allusions as intertexts.[15] This, however, is precisely the interest of many interpreters of Matthew. Daniel Boyarin has helped to define a level of intertextuality that is both distinct from, and in continuity with, Kristeva. He distinguishes between influences on composition as a *diachronic* approach, and mutual relationships between definable texts as a *synchronic* approach.[16] The diachronic approach means that texts are viewed in relationship with each other in temporal sequence. The synchronic approach means that two texts are viewed in a mutual relationship with each other beyond their temporal sequence. The purely diachronic approach is distinguished from intertextuality; the synchronic relationship between definable texts is intertextuality.

A comparison of the Masoretic Text of Hos 11:1, "*umimmiṣrayim qārā'ti libni* (out of Egypt I [God] called my [God's] son [singular])," with the Septuagint "*ex Aigyptou metekalesa ta tekna autou* (out of Egypt I [God] called his [Israel's] children [to another place]")," shows that "*Ex Aigyptou ekalesa ton huion mou* (out of Egypt I called my

---

14. Kristeva, *Desire*, 49–50.
15. See J. Culler, *The Pursuit of Signs* (Ithaca: Cornell University Press, 1981), 106.
16. D. Boyarin, *Intertextuality and the Reading of Midrash* (Bloomington: Indiana University Press, 1990), 135 n. 2.

son)" in Matt 2:15 corresponds to the Masoretic Text and not to the Septuagint.[17] This is clearly a diachronic issue. When, however, readers recognize a mutual relationship between a citation or allusion and a precursor that involves a shift in values, this is a synchronic issue of how the precursor and successor play back and forth on one another. Conventionally, Matt 2:15 is understood as a proof text that violates the context of Hos 11:1. But readers who know Hos 11:1 in its context can play Matthew's citation off against it, identify Jesus as God's Son, add the slaughter of the innocents to the already apparent parallels in plot (Matt 2:16–18), and construe Jesus as recapitulating Israel's exodus from Egypt. Significantly, the movement in Matthew immediately after the citation is not *from* Egypt, as Hosea anticipates, but *to* Egypt,[18] a reiteration of Jacob's — that is, Israel's — sojourn in Egypt.

This kind of synchrony entails a diachronic element in that it presupposes a temporal relationship between a source text and a new text. The diachrony may involve, in fact, at least one more step. Matthew may appropriate Scripture indirectly through interpretive traditions. To anticipate, I will suggest that God's promise to Abraham to give his descendants "this land" (Gen 12:7) is mediated to Matthew by interpretive traditions in Judaism.

A silver symbol on the back of my neighbor's car provides another kind of example of intertextuality. Until one gets quite close, it appears to be a simple design of a fish with some lettering in between two arcs that outline the body and tail. Up close, however, one sees that the body has feet, and the lettering inside the twin arcs is DARWIN. This symbol makes reference to another textual system. Many Christians have silver symbols of a fish on the backs of their cars with the lettering IXTHYS (a Greek acronym for "Jesus Christ,

---

17. The appearance of "my son" (singular) in the Greek versions of Aquila, Symmachus, and Theodotion complicate the issue of source. See R. Gundry, *The Use of the Old Testament in St. Matthew's Gospel with Special Reference to the Messianic Hope* (Leiden: Brill, 1967), 93–94.

18. Powery, *Jesus Reads Scripture*, 125; Gundry, *Use*, 93–94, 195. See D. Moody Smith, "The Use of the Old Testament in the New," in *The Use of the Old Testament in the New and Others Essays: Studies in Honor of W. Stinespring* (ed. J. Efrid; Durham, N.C.: Duke University Press, 1972), 47.

God's Son, Savior") or JESUS between the arcs. The shape of the symbol on my neighbor's car contains the textual pattern of the Christian symbol. My neighbor's symbol trumps the Christian symbol. It takes it over and contains it by inference, but only on its own (Darwinian) terms. The value shifts from an identification with faith to a challenge to faith, presumably in the name of science. Nevertheless, the Christian symbol stands in a dialectical interplay with the Darwinian one, and someone with a Christian perspective can take the Christian symbol as the trump.

The mutual relationship between texts under the synchronic approach possesses the quality of a trope. Much of what parades as intertextuality in biblical study misses this troping. The traditional diachronic approach subjects Matthew's appropriation of Scripture to evaluation as to whether the citation or allusion (1) respects the context of the precursor, (2) is lifted out of its context, or (3) contradicts its context.[19] Such an approach envisions the relationship between the source text and the new text as essentially static. But intertextuality accents a dynamic dialectic between the precursor and the successor in which each stands in degrees of both conflict and consonance with the other. The language is therefore tensive, a quality of language that Robert Tannehill underscored in *The Sword of His Mouth*.[20]

Confronted with allusions and citations, readers may constantly shift perspective to see the successor from the point of view of the precursor or the precursor from the successor's viewpoint — does DARWIN trump IXTHYS, or does IXTHYS trump DARWIN? Or for someone who has integrated science and religion, does the attempted trump in either direction become irrelevant? From the perspective of the precursor, the new text may advance perception beyond the limits of the precursor. From the perspective of the new text, the precursor may activate meaning beyond the limits of the new text.

---

19. See R. Mead, "A Dissenting Opinion about Respect for Context in Old Testament Quotations," *NTS* 10 (1963–64): 279–89; J. Fitzmyer, "The Use of Explicit Old Testament Quotations in Qumran Literature and in the New Testament," *NTS* 7 (1960–61): 305–30.

20. Robert C. Tannehill, *The Sword of His Mouth* (Philadelphia: Fortress, 1975), 11–14, 52–55, et passim.

Finally, readers who view the juxtaposition of intertexts holistically may perceive them together as one figuration that extends meaning beyond the mere sum of the two independent texts.[21]

The tensive interplay among texts is figurative as in the case of metaphors, and as in the case of metaphors it enables readers to envision reality in a new way. Harold Bloom has associated the dialectical relationships between precursor and successor texts with standard figures of speech: irony, synecdoche (a part for the whole or whole for part), metonymy (a name used for something with which it is associated), hyperbole, metaphor, and metalepsis (a trope of a trope).[22] Bloom separates these figurations analytically, but they may function simultaneously.

To give a case, the appropriation of Hos 11:1 in Matt 2:15, "Out of Egypt I called my son," is ironic in that two levels of understanding are going on at the same time, one level with respect to Israel in Hos 11:1 and a second level where Jesus recapitulates Israel's exodus. Interpreters who take Matthew's use of Hosea 11:1 as a proof text are duped by the irony, because they understand it on one level only. Further, the calling of God's son out of Egypt is a synecdoche for the entire exodus. To imply that Jesus recapitulates Israel's history is hyperbole: the text rises to a new level of meaning that represents a gain over the precursor alone. The play on "son" in Hosea is metonymic. That is, the name "son" denotes a people with whom the name is associated, the children of Israel. Finally, Matthew's use of the text is metaleptic, because it makes a figuration on a text that already tropes Israel's relationship with God under the figure of a father caring for his infant.

Enthymeme: Rhetoric of Logic

Consideration of enthymemic rhetoric also presses upon us the metaphorical character of biblical citations and allusions. To examine enthymemic rhetoric is to attempt to follow the logic of arguments

---

21. See R. Brawley, *Text to Text Pours Forth Speech: Voices of Scripture in Luke-Acts* (Bloomington: Indiana University Press, 1995), 8–10.

22. Bloom repeats his analysis in a number of works, e.g., *The Anxiety of Influence: A Theory of Poetry* (New York: Oxford University Press, 1973), 14–16.

that replicate aspects of formal syllogisms, though only approximately. This approximation indeed provokes some purists to set formal logic over against rhetoric. Rhetoric allegedly persuades by reasoning that is effective but defective; logic allegedly demonstrates by proof.[23]

Charles Peirce called an inferential step in forming a hypothesis or generating any new concept an "abduction." Though it is related to *experience,* that is, to a worldview, such an inference has no grounding in previous *knowledge* and is therefore a kind of conjecture.[24] An example is the fresh metaphor in Job 38:8: "when the sea burst forth from the womb." The conventional side of the metaphor is the gushing of amniotic waters from a mother's womb at birth. The creative side is the association of erupting seas with amniotic waters.

Peirce valued the element of surprise in motivating the development of thought. The surprise can be either disappointment or anticipation.[25] Disappointment disrupts the ordinary: "All flesh is grass." Anticipation creates expectation beyond it: "If God so clothes the grass, will God not also clothe you?" But the surprise is also a new thought in that it correlates elements that heretofore were never associated, as in the correlation of the seas with amniotic waters in Job 38:8. Though the conceptual elements preexist in a worldview, they have never been related to each other beforehand. Abduction is, therefore, astute original thinking.

Syllogisms involve three assertions, conventionally called major premise, minor premise, and conclusion. Peirce referred to these as

---

23. So Aristotle, *Rhetoric* 1354a; 1355a. See D. Hellholm, "Enthymemic Argumentation in Paul: The Case of Romans 6," in *Paul in His Hellenistic Context* (ed. T. Engberg-Pedersen; Minneapolis: Fortress, 1995), 127–29. Richard Lanigan shifts the discussion from the logic of rhetoric to the rhetoric of logic, that is, the rhetoric of syllogistic-like enthymemes ("From Enthymeme to Abduction: The Classical Law of Logic and the Postmodern Rule of Rhetoric," in *Recovering Pragmatism's Voice: The Classical Tradition, Rorty, and the Philosophy of Communication* [ed. L. Langsdorf and A. Smith; Albany: SUNY Press, 1995], 52).

24. C. Peirce, "The Logic of Abduction," in *Essays in the Philosophy of Science* (New York: Liberal Arts Press, 1957), 236–37. F. Reilly, *Charles Peirce's Theory of Scientific Method* (New York: Fordham University Press, 1970), 30–31, 37; Lanigan, "From Enthymeme to Abduction," 49–52; P. Ochs, *Peirce, Pragmatism and the Logic of Scripture* (Cambridge: Cambridge University Press, 1998), 60, 114–20, 194; K. Fann, *Peirce's Theory of Abduction* (The Hague: Martinus Nijhoff, 1970), 17–18.

25. Reilly, *Charles Peirce's Theory,* 25.

"rule," "case," and "result." Deductive reasoning follows the pattern rule + case = result. Rule: All the beans from this bag are white. Case: These beans are from this bag. Result: These beans are white. Inductive reasoning inverts the minor and major premises following the pattern case + result = rule. Case: These beans are from this bag. Result: These beans are white. Rule: All the beans from this bag are white. (This is effective reasoning if an investigator draws the beans from the bag one at a time or in handfuls, and the beans are always white.) By contrast, abductive reasoning ends with a case that derives from a known rule and result following the pattern rule + result = case. The abduction is an explanation of a surprising event (result) by reasoning that it is a special case of a general rule. Rule: All the beans from this bag are white. Result: These beans are white. Case: These beans are from this bag.[26]

An abduction is an assertion that a phenomenon belongs to a known class with which it has previously not been associated. More elaborately, the result is an assertion that a particular thing possesses similarity to the general class, and hence, belongs to the class. The recognition of similarity between the class (rule) and the particular (result) leads to a discovery (case) that asserts similarity (1) with the rule and similarity (2) with a result that the case anticipates.[27] To illustrate, Sir Isaac Newton drew an abductive relationship between his proverbial apple falling to the ground and the force that determines the movement of heavenly bodies in relation to one another. A falling apple is a case that exhibits a relationship with gravity, which is the rule, and a relationship with predictable motion between bodies, which is the result that the falling apple anticipates.

Rhetorical enthymemes differ from syllogisms in two respects. First, enthymemes typically leave at least one of the three assertions (rule, result, case) unexpressed. Part of the rhetorical effect is to evoke unexpressed assertions from readers. Not all enthymemes

---

26. Fann, *Peirce's Theory*, 20–21.

27. Lanigan, "From Enthymeme to Abduction," 50; Reilly, *Charles Peirce's Theory*, 32–33, 61; Fann, *Peirce's Theory*, 10, 21; G. Bateson and M. Bateson, *Angels Fear: Towards an Epistemology of the Sacred* (New York: Macmillan, 1987), 174–75.

employ abductive reasoning. In fact, they can follow rather conventional deductive or inductive patterns. When some Pharisees ask Jesus about divorce in Matt 19:3, the interlocutors share with Jesus a conventional unstated rule: proper interpretation of Scripture provides the answer. But what is true of enthymemes in general is also true of enthymemes that involve abductive reasoning. Because such enthymemes leave some assertions unexpressed, they will appear not to have the complete form of a syllogism. In this sense abductive enthymemes are "formally defective." A second distinction between syllogisms and enthymemes is that some unstated assertions may be cultural presuppositions that do not qualify as premises in formal syllogisms. Moreover, abduction is a leap of invention that enables readers to grasp a reality that is not yet proved or disproved by inductive or deductive reasoning. In these senses abductive enthymemes are "materially defective."[28]

In the case concerning divorce, Jesus' interlocutors reason deductively following the pattern rule + case = result. Rule: Interpretation of Scripture is determinative for divorce. For the case, Jesus' interlocutors cite the only text in their Scriptures that deals with the process of divorce, Deut 24:1. This is to say, they cite a conventional text: Moses commands giving a wife a certificate of divorce. Result: Divorce is permissible. Jesus, however, associates Genesis 2 abductively with divorce. He makes a nonconventional new association of Genesis 2 with the known class of texts pertaining to divorce. The shock of the new association evokes new ways of looking at divorce according to the pattern rule + result = case. Rule: God made male and female. Result: God joins the two. Case: There should be no separation. Because this is an abduction, it has the nature of a hypothesis that is subject to attempts to verify or disconfirm it.[29] A historical critical analysis, for example, could claim that in its literary and historical

---

28. Aristotle speaks of enthymemes that are not absolute but probable in particular cases (*Rhetoric* 2.1402a). See Lanigan, "From Enthymeme to Abduction," 52–55; Hellholm, "Enthymemic Argumentation," 121, 127–28, 131; G. Kennedy, *New Testament Interpretation through Rhetorical Criticism* (Chapel Hill: University of North Carolina Press, 1984), 7, 16–17, 49–51; Fann, *Peirce's Theory*, 58–59.

29. See Fann, *Peirce's Theory*, 34–35, 44–51; Hellholm, "Enthymemic Argumentation," 132.

contexts, Genesis 2 has to do with an aetiology of marriage rather than with its dissolution.

Jesus' abduction about God's intention in the creation of human beings then becomes a rule for two deductive enthymemes (rule + case = result). Rule: God joins male and female as God's original intention. Moses' allowance for divorce is, therefore, not the rule as the interlocutors presume, but the case. The result is hardness of heart against God's intention in creation. The other enthymeme is grounded in the same rule: God joins male and female as an original intention. The case is divorce and remarriage, and the result is adultery.

The rhetorical enthymeme is the metaphorical twin of the logical syllogism. Isaiah 40:6–8 illustrates the metaphorical nature of rhetorical enthymemes: "All flesh is grass and all human splendor as a blossom on grass. The grass withers and the blossom falls off. But the word of our God endures forever." Behind the assertion lies a syllogistic-like argument: Grass dies, humans die, humans are grass.[30]

Challenging constructs of reality through the imaginative association of elements heretofore unrelated is tropological. Abduction functions like a fresh metaphor, which also associates something novel with something conventional in order to transform conventional perspectives. Thus, abductive argument begins with shock, a challenge, disorientation. The shock breaks the frames of conventional thinking and confronts readers with a new way to construe reality.

"Blessed Are the Meek"

My proposal is that Jesus' third beatitude in Matthew is marked by both allusive intertextuality and abductive reasoning. Allusions are highly dependent upon cultural currency, as Black's coinage of Dr. Strangeuse is dependent upon the cultural currency of "Dr. Strangelove."[31] For the blessedness of the meek who will inherit the earth, I suggest a cultural repertoire that does not readily meet the eye: God's

---

30. See Bateson and Bateson, *Angels Fear*, 26.
31. In fact, when I presented an earlier form of this essay to a seminar with international participants, a number of them acknowledged that they did not recognize the movie title.

promises to Abraham. The beatitude picks up two prominent themes of the Abrahamic covenant: (1) the blessing in him of all the people of the earth (Gen 12:3) and (2) God's gift of the inheritance of land to his descendants ("seed"; Gen 12:7; 13:14–15).[32]

I indicated earlier that interpretive traditions in Judaism mediate the Abrahamic covenant to Matthew. A part of this tradition is Ps 36:11 LXX (ET, 37:11), with which Matt 5:5 shares a high degree of verbatim agreement. Though Matthew's version contains the textual pattern of Ps 36:11 LXX,[33] Matthew does not merely take it over. Psalm 36:11 LXX is a simple sentence: "*hoi de praeis klēronomēsousin gēn* (the meek will inherit land)." Matthew 5:5 is a complex sentence that identifies those who are blessed in the first part and gives the ground for the blessing in a dependent clause. Matthew also uses the definite article before "land": "*Makarioi hoi praeis, hoti autoi klēronomēsousin tēn gēn* (Blessed are the meek, because they will inherit the land)."

As I indicated earlier, cultural presumptions can serve as unexpressed assertions in enthymemic rhetoric. One such presumption is Abrahamic traditions. It is impossible to trace the development of Abrahamic covenant traditions precisely, but some mileposts along the way are clear. For its part, Ps 36:11 LXX represents a development of the Hebrew version of Ps 37:11. Though the verb *yāraš* can connote "inherit," its nuance is preferably "to take possession." The much more common Hebrew terms for inheriting are the verb *naḥal* and its cognate noun *nāḥălāh*.[34] The Hebrew implicates possession of land; *klēronomeō* in Ps 36:9, 11 LXX accents inheritance.[35]

---

32. See W. Grundmann, *Das Evangelium nach Matthäus* (THNT 1; Berlin: Evangelische Verlagsanstalt, 1968), 126. H. Frankemölle associates the promise of the land with the declaration that Jesus' listeners are the salt of the earth (5:13) (*Matthäus Kommentar*, vol. 1 [Düsseldorf: Patmos, 1994], 211).

33. H. Betz takes Matt 5:5 as an "adaptation" of Psalm 36:11 LXX (*The Sermon on the Mount: A Commentary on the Sermon on the Mount, including the Sermon on the Plain (Matthew 5:3–7:27 and Luke 6:20–49)* [Hermeneia; Minneapolis: Fortress, 1995], 125). See R. Guelich, *The Sermon on the Mount: A Foundation for Understanding* (Waco, Tex.: Word Books, 1982), 101; U. Luz, *Matthew 1–7: A Commentary* (Minneapolis: Augsburg, 1989), 236. The relationship with the LXX makes tracing *praus* to Aramaic or Hebrew unlikely (I. Broer, *Die Seligpreisungen der Bergpredigt: Studien zu ihrer Überlieferung* [Bonn: Peter Hanstein, 1986], 80).

34. J. Herrmann, "*klēronomos,*" *TDNT* 3.769–76.

35. W. Foerster, "*klēronomos,*" *TDNT* 3.779. Psalm 36:11 lacks the eschatological perspective of Matthew (J. Dupont, *Les béatitudes*, Tomes 1–3 [Paris: Gabalda, 1969–73], 3.482).

Further developments of Abrahamic covenant traditions are evident in a broad cultural repertoire. Matthew customarily cites or alludes to Scripture rather than literature of the Second Temple period, but references and allusions are likely mediated through Second Temple traditions. Debates about who qualified as a descendant of Abraham are a part of these traditions. At one extreme, ethnic exclusivism disqualified anyone who was not of Abrahamic lineage. At the other, a spiritualized universality admitted all who followed in the footsteps of Abraham (Paul's view in Rom 4:12). *Jubilees* 22:16–18; 4 Macc 6:17–22; *Psalms of Solomon* 9:9–11; and the *Damascus Document* (CD 12.11) express an ethnic priority for Abraham's descendants over the Gentiles. But *1 Enoch* 89:12–90:36 takes Abraham allegorically to be the ancestor of Gentiles as well as of Israel, whereas Jacob is the ancestor of Israel alone. Josephus also suggests that Abraham was a universal ancestor by deriving Jews from Sarah and Gentiles from Hagar and Keturah.[36]

One trajectory of Jewish tradition made a startling development in the identification of the land that God promised to the descendants of Abraham. In Gen 13:14–15 God promises to give Abraham and his offspring all the land that he can see to the north, south, east, and west. What is this land? It so happens that both the Hebrew *'ereṣ* and the Greek *gē* mean (1) ground (where plants grow), (2) land (territory or country), or (3) earth (the entire planet). The Abrahamic covenant is so charged with interpretive potential that one trajectory of Jewish tradition took the promise of Gen 13:14–15 to mean the entire earth. The specific promise of the land of Canaan (17:8) need not conflict with the promise of the entire earth beyond the inheritance of Canaan. So the tradition pushed the promise into an eschatological future and made it universal — the whole earth.[37]

---

36. Josephus, *Jewish Antiquities* 1 §§220–41; 12 §§225–26. In dependence upon Polyhistor and his sources, Eusebius traces the Assyrians, Africans, the people of Carthage, and Moses' wife Zipporah from Keturah (*Praeparatio evangelica* 9.20; 9.29.1–3). 1 Maccabees 12:21 claims that the Spartans are descended from Abraham.

37. The understanding of the Abrahamic promise as the whole earth appears in Sir 44:19–21; Jubilees 17:3; 19:21; 22:14; 32:18–19; Rom 4:13; 1 Cor 6:2; Heb 2:5. According to Sifre on Deut 34:1–4, when Moses looked into the promised land on Mt. Nebo, God showed him the whole earth. See Philo, *De Vita Mosis* 1.155; *Mekilta Exodus* 14:31. See Dupont, *Béatitudes,*

Matthew's third beatitude is more than likely heir to Abrahamic covenant traditions as mediated through Jewish tradition. It asserts the blessedness of the Abrahamic promise, though the term it uses for "blessed (*makarios*)" is not the characteristic vocabulary that the LXX employs in relation to the Abrahamic covenant (*eulogeō*). On the other hand, Ps 32:12 LXX uses *makarios* in connection with "*klēronomia* (inheritance)," and Paul uses it, under the influence of Ps 31:1–2 LXX (ET, 32:1–2), precisely in relation to the Abrahamic blessing in Rom 4:6–9. An additional reason to infer an intertextual allusion is a widely recognized relationship with Isa 61:1–2 in the immediately preceding beatitude of consolation to those who mourn (Matt 5:4).[38] Matthew's third beatitude, therefore, makes reference to a textual system regarding Abrahamic traditions that it does not contain and with which it is in intertextual interplay.

Hans Dieter Betz raises the question of whether the predicates in the Beatitudes that describe those who are blessed, such as "poor in spirit," are literal or metaphorical and decides for the metaphorical. The poor in spirit are those who understand the human condition as poverty in contrast to arrogance. He takes "the meek" to be a variation on "the poor in spirit" (Matt 5:3). The same reasoning supports taking the second half of the Beatitudes as variations on kingdom of heaven.[39] But beyond mere equivalence, the variations on the poor in spirit and the kingdom of heaven progress toward additional insight, and the parallel repetitions with variation bestow a

---

3.475–86. By missing the allusion to the Abrahamic covenant, Betz takes *hē gē* to mean the whole earth as the place of mission, as in Matt 28:18–20 (*Sermon*, 128).

38. H. Frankemölle, "Die Makarismen (Mt 5,1–12; Lk 6,20–23): Motive und Umfang der redaktionellen Komposition," *BZ* 15 (1971): 59; R. Bultmann, "*penthos, pentheō*," *TDNT* 6:43. W. Davies and D. Allison suggest that Matt 5:4 alludes to Isaiah 61, including the inheritance of the land in 61:7, though their emphasis is on the influence of Isaiah in Q (*A Critical and Exegetical Commentary on the Gospel according to Saint Matthew*, vol. 1 [Edinburgh: T & T Clark, 1988], 436–39, 451). See Guelich, *Sermon*, 80–83, 100.

39. Betz, *Sermon*, 111–16, 125–26, 129, 132. Dupont derives the first and third beatitudes from one alleged Aramaic original (*Béatitudes*, 1:251–52; 3.474, 544). For him, "meek" designates primarily an attitude toward others rather than a social state (3.486–545). See Guelich, *Sermon*, 74–75, 81–82; Davies and Allison, *Matthew*, 1:449; Luz, *Matthew*, 232, 235–36; G. Strecker makes the inheritance of the land simply equivalent to the kingdom of heaven ("Die Makarismen der Bergpredigt," *NTS* 17 [1970–71]: 264). On the starting point of Jesus' proclamation of the kingdom as the extermination of evil and the restoration of God's power, see H. Stegemann, "Der lehrende Jesus," *NZSTh* 24 (1982): 12, 14.

metaphorical flavor on all of the categories of blessedness. They are what Tannehill called "focal-instances" that evoke considerations far beyond their immediate meaning.[40] Further, the tension born from associating blessedness with the absence of accoutrements focuses the blessedness on being rather than having.[41] More to the point, intertextuality endows Matt 5:5 with a metaphorical quality not only in terms of the predicate "meek" but in terms of the figurative interplay of the entire beatitude with Psalm 36 LXX and with Abrahamic covenant traditions.

This metaphorical quality should not be confused, however, with "spiritualizing" the social and political realities of what it means to belong to the meek. The mediation of Abrahamic covenant traditions to Matthew through Psalm 36 LXX underlines the point. Not only is Psalm 36 LXX (ET, 37) suffused with Abrahamic tradition motifs (inheritance of the land occurs at least six times, vv. 9, 11, 18, 22, 29, 34). The wicked also stand over against those to whom the land is promised in two ways. First, because the opponents prosper by unjust behavior, one could be tempted to adopt their behavior in order to prosper like them (vv. 1, 7, 38). Second, the wicked oppress those who are identified as meek in v. 11 by violence. They watch closely for an opportunity, apparently to take advantage of those who live by fair play (v. 12). They are adept at economic abuse by borrowing and failing to repay (v. 21). They use weapons to oppress violently and even to kill the poor and needy (v. 14, 32).

Moreover, the psalm's repeated promise to the poor that they will inherit land indicates that the wicked deprive them of ownership and access to land — the perennial problem of the poor and oppressed,[42] as it is today in Latin America, Zimbabwe, and South Africa. The meek in Matt 5:5 (*praeis*) are identified by their economic, social, and political position as much as they are by their relationship to Jesus,

---

40. Tannehill, *Sword*, 53, 67–77, et passim. See Kennedy, *New Testament Interpretation*, 51.

41. H.-R. Reuter, "Die Bergpredigt als Orientierung unseres Menschseins heute," *ZEE* 23 (1979): 88–90.

42. See W. Carter, *Matthew and the Margins: A Sociopolitical and Religious Reading* (Maryknoll, N.Y.: Orbis, 2000), 132–33.

who also demonstrates what it is to be meek (11:29; 21:5). Further, Walter Wink has shown that such economic, social, and political issues are reflected elsewhere in the context, especially in Jesus' advice about turning the other cheek, giving up one's cloak to a litigant as well as one's coat, and going the second mile (5:39–42).[43]

It is Abrahamic covenant traditions, however, that are mediated to Matthew through Psalm 36 LXX. I attempt to identify some of the intertextual interplay with the caveat that these identifications do not exhaust the interplay. Indeed, the reciprocal play back and forth of intertextual figuration cannot be exhausted. (1) The intertextual relationship is ironic in that there are two levels of understanding. One is the inheritance of the land of Canaan as a fulfillment of the Abrahamic promise. This is the level of understanding in Ps 36:11 LXX. The meek are contrasted with the sinner (*ho hamartōlos,* v. 10), and the psalm constantly reiterates the two ways, contrasting the wicked with those who depend upon God. It thus affirms the continuing inheritance through the distribution of the land of Canaan after the conquest in keeping with the Abrahamic covenant.[44] But Matthew suppresses the possession of Canaan and pushes the inheritance of the earth to a second level far beyond the inheritance of Canaan. (2) This second level of understanding is also hyperbole: when the successor text revisits the inheritance of the land, it rises, like an eye watching a revolving barber's pole, to a higher level. (3) The successor text also participates in metonymy, because as heirs of the earth, the meek are associated with the offspring of Abraham. (4) The intertextual interplay is simultaneously metaleptic. When Jewish tradition pushed the inheritance of the land beyond Canaan, it created a trope on the conquest. The beatitude, therefore, is a figuration on what is already figurative — metalepsis.

Moreover, the beatitude involves abductive reasoning.[45] Psalm 36:11 LXX is a straightforward assertion: "The meek shall inherit

---

43. W. Wink, *Engaging the Powers: Discernment and Resistance in a World of Domination* (vol. 3 of *The Powers;* Minneapolis: Fortress, 1992), 185–93.

44. A. Weiser, *The Psalms: A Commentary* (OTL; Philadelphia: Westminster, 1962), 316–23.

45. Kennedy correctly identifies the syllogistic-like character of the Beatitudes but erroneously categorizes them as deductive (*New Testament Interpretation,* 16, 49–51).

land." In contrast, the basis for the blessedness of the meek in the second clause of Matthew's beatitude gives it a syllogistic-like form. As is usually the case with abductive reasoning, some of the assertions are unexpressed, and readers must supply them. Further, though the assertions of abductive rhetoric may be cultural assumptions that do not qualify as the premises in a formal syllogism, they are valid for persuading everyone who shares the assumptions. In its intertextual interplay, Matt 5:5 makes assertions following the abductive pattern rule + result = case. Rule: The descendants of Abraham will inherit the earth. Result: The meek will inherit the earth. Case: The meek are descendants of Abraham. The beatitude expresses an abductive association between the case and the rule. Thus, the meek belong to the class of the descendants of Abraham. The case also expresses an association with the result that it anticipates: They will inherit the earth. Betz characterizes the "logic" of blessedness as God's justice.[46] The intertextual interplay, however, makes it also a matter of identifying the meek as children of Abraham who are heirs of God's promise.

David Hellholm describes two basic potential functions for the Beatitudes in the Sermon on the Mount: (1) declarations of consolation with a promise of reversal, in which case conditions such as meekness already exist; or (2) ethical exhortations with the promise of reward conditional on fulfilling requirements that do not exist prior to the exhortation. The first is open to hearers to accept the blessing; the second establishes a requirement for the hearers to accept in order to receive the blessing.[47] Mark Allen Powell astutely suggests that the first four beatitudes promise divine reversal for the oppressed, and that the last four demand ethical action on behalf of

---

46. Betz, *Sermon,* 119, 124.

47. D. Hellholm, "Beatitudes and Their Illocutionary Functions," in *Ancient and Modern Perspectives on the Bible and Culture: Essays in Honor of Hans Dieter Betz* (ed. A. Collins; Atlanta: Scholars, 1998), 296–304, 311–12. See Guelich, *Sermon,* 65, 111; Luz, *Matthew,* 229, 238, 243. But announcing a blessing is performative language that confers the blessing. See D. Patte, *The Gospel according to Matthew: A Structural Commentary on Matthew's Faith* (Philadelphia: Fortress, 1987), 67; E. Schweizer, *The Good News according to Matthew* (Atlanta: John Knox, 1975), 81. D. Patte also establishes four distinct legitimate readings that he largely attributes to preunderstanding (*Discipleship according to the Sermon on the Mount: Four Legitimate Readings, Four Plausible Views of Discipleship, and Their Relative Values* [Valley Forge, Pa.: Trinity Press International, 1996).

the oppressed in the first four. According to Hellholm's categories, the first four essentially mean "Blessed are you when you are oppressed." The second four exhort disciples to act on behalf of the oppressed. Powell describes the oppressed in direct universal terms apart from any identification with Israel or with Jesus' disciples.[48] I suggest first, however, that the specifications of Jesus' hearers in 4:23–5:1 presupposes an address to Israelites (see 10:5; 15:24).[49] Universality nevertheless comes indirectly through God's promise that in Abraham all the peoples of the earth would be blessed. In moving to the universal level, the beatitude associates the meek through an abduction with the heirs of Abraham and thus identifies them figuratively with Israel.[50]

Betz takes the third beatitude as a development on "poor in spirit" (5:3) and argues that the context in 5:17–48; 6:25–34; and 7:24–27 compels hearers to understand it as prescribing an ethical stance of becoming aware of the human conditions of poverty or remaining aware of the same with the promise of an eschatological reward.[51] Betz, however, interprets the Sermon on the Mount on the level of a tradition that predates its incorporation into Matthew so that the third beatitude's context is the Sermon on the Mount itself and not the larger context of Matthew.

---

48. M. Powell, "Matthew's Beatitudes: Reversals and Rewards of the Kingdom," *CBQ* 58 (1996): 460–79. Davies and Allison emphasize the performative blessing over a secondary ethical quality (*Matthew*, 1:439–40, 466). For H. Falcke, the Beatitudes address humans in their fundamental situation of need and in their capacity as agents of action ("Die Seligpreisungen der Bergpredigt und das gesellschaftliche Zeugnis der Kirche," *ZEE* 28 [1984]: 380). See Guelich, *Sermon*, 89; D. Allison, *The Sermon on the Mount: Inspiring the Moral Imagination* (New York: Crossroad, 1999), 31, 41–44. Matthew's formulation in the third person implies universality more than the address in the second person in Luke (Strecker, "Makarismen," 256–57). Strecker argues, however, for understanding the first four beatitudes also as ethical prescriptions (262–66, 271). Kennedy takes all of the Beatitudes as ethical, as deliberative rhetoric (*New Testament Interpretation*, 51). *Didache* 3.7 is imperative and clearly prescriptive: *isthi de praus*.

49. See G. Lohfink, *Wem gilt die Bergpredigt? Beiträge zu einer christlichen Ethik* (Freiburg: Herder, 1988), 18–24, 26–35, 107–9, 199–209; Grundmann, *Evangelium nach Matthäus*, 111–15; Frankemölle, *Matthäus Kommentar*, 200–204, 214. Against restricting Jesus' ministry to Israel, see W. D. Davies, *The Setting of the Sermon on the Mount* (Cambridge: Cambridge University Press, 1966), 326–33.

50. Allison overlooks the Abrahamic promise and suggests echoes of Adam and Eve and Moses (*Sermon*, 47–49). See Lohfink, *Wem gilt?* 38.

51. Betz, *Sermon*, 109–10, 118, 130–31, 137–38, 141; Hellholm, "Beatitudes," 324.

By contrast, I wish to place the third beatitude in its Matthean context. First, it appears within an *inclusio* for the entire book that identifies Jesus as "God is with us" (1:23; 28:20). The Sermon on the Mount is thus the proclamation of the one in whom God is present.[52] Second, Matt 4:17 is programmatic: "From then on Jesus began to preach and to say, 'Repent. The kingdom of heaven is at hand.'" As Jack Kingsbury has shown, this narrator's proleptic summary influences the narrative until 16:20.[53] Further, a summary of Jesus' proclamation of the kingdom and his beneficent acts in synagogues introduces the Sermon on the Mount (4:23–25).[54] The Beatitudes, therefore, describe the way things are, as Powell aptly paraphrases, when "heaven rules them."[55] By discarding all literary contexts, Hellholm argues for understanding the Beatitudes on the level of the historical Jesus as present over against an eschatological future.[56] But according to 4:17–25, Jesus' preaching initiates God's rule that is breaking in at the edge where God's future is becoming the present. Jesus' announcement is performative and confers blessing in the present even if the reversal that is the basis for blessedness lies still in the future. "In connection with the proclamation of Jesus the things about which he spoke came to pass."[57]

---

52. Davies affirms Jesus' messianic consciousness (*Setting*, 430–35). See also G. Stanton, "What Is the Law of Christ?" *Ex Auditu* 17 (2001): 52. Reciprocally, the Beatitudes characterize who Jesus is (Davies and Allison, *Matthew*, 1:466). See Allison, *Sermon*, 9, 15.

53. J. Kingsbury, *Matthew as Story* (Philadelphia: Fortress, 1986), 4, 13, 57–77. See Allison, *Sermon*, xi, 9; Luz, *Matthew*, 215, 235; Guelich, *Sermon*, 56. Luz takes 4:17 as an indication that the kingdom is still in the future. Patte supports a kingdom with both present and future dimensions (*Gospel*, 66).

54. Davies, *Setting*, 100, 433.

55. Powell, "Matthew's Beatitudes," 465. "The Beatitudes are . . . the joyful message that one can believe that God the Father . . . is capable of a reversal of all earthly values" (P. Lapide, *Die Bergpredigt — Utopie oder Programm?* [Mainz: Matthias-Grünewald, 1982], 33). Kennedy takes Matt 5:3–13 as a poem that introduces the heart of theme of the Sermon on the Mount, Jesus as fulfillment of the law in 5:17–20 (*New Testament Interpretation*, 43, 48–49, 53–54). For me, 4:17 indicates that the kingdom is thematic.

56. Hellholm, "Beatitudes," 334–40. Betz states that the eschatological concept that God's kingdom is to come in the future does not preclude its reality in the present (*Sermon*, 119). See Luz, *Matthew*, 231; Schweizer, *Good News*, 81, 90.

57. Stegemann, "Der Lehrende Jesus," 17. "The [kingdom] is so near that already its effects are felt" (Dupont, *Béatitudes*, 1:111). See H. Weder, "Beobachtungen zum Verständnis der Bergpredigt Jesu," *EvT* 45 (1985): 56–57; Guelich, *Sermon*, 78, 81, 85, 88, 99, 111. On the future nuance of the dependent clauses formulated in the future, see Strecker, "Makarismen," 261, 263, 271. But there is also for him a present claim of blessedness (274). So also Davies

In the case of Matt 5:5, Jesus asserts that the meek belong to the class "children of Abraham" who are the recipients of the promise that they will inherit the earth. The class "children of Abraham" and the promise are already known. What is new is that the meek belong to the children of Abraham. This intertextual abduction may prod readers to a new construct of reality. First, it disorients by an element of disappointment: the meek are blessed. But then it disorients by anticipation: they will inherit the earth. The new construct is grounded in something ancient, the Abrahamic covenant tradition. But this ancient Abrahamic covenant tradition is revisioned in terms of the kingdom of God and its proclaimer.

---

and Allison, *Matthew*, 1:389–92, 446. See Stanton, "What Is the Law?" 52. The Sermon on the Mount "looks backwards, from the consummation to the present" (Allison, *Sermon*, 12).

8

Of Weeds and Wheat

A Literary Critical Study of Matthew 13:36–43

Carolyn Thomas, SCN

When Jesus told the parables about the kingdom of God, he chose as symbols simple things from agriculture that were known to all his listeners. In the parable of the Weeds among the Wheat (Matt 13:24–30),[1] Jesus uses familiar symbols from nature — weeds are a particularly annoying and common problem, while wheat is positive and life-giving, the basis for the most familiar staple of life. Nevertheless, later the disciples, seeking wisdom, ask for an explanation.

My study of Matt 13:36–43 seeks first to demonstrate that wisdom is the "web"[2] that permeates and holds together the theology of the Gospel and finds the summation of its success and failure in Jesus' explanation of the Weeds among the Wheat. Second, I will show that Jesus, the Son of Man, fulfills his role as the Wisdom of God in the present stage of the kingdom, where both those who reject God's Wisdom and those who accept God's Wisdom dwell together. The first stage of the kingdom ends with the separation of the good from the evil ones: the good will be rewarded with entrance into the kingdom of the Father, whereas the evil ones will be cast into the "furnace of fire" (13:42).

---

1. Scripture and apocryphal citations are from the NRSV; all quotations of the Pseud-epigrapha are from *OTP*.
2. Though I applied the notion of "web" differently, I borrowed it from J. Capel Anderson, *Matthew's Narrative Web: Over, and Over, and Over Again* (Sheffield: JSOT Press, 1994).

In the study of the pericope, I will use the discipline of literary criticism.[3] In so doing, I will treat the passage as a part of the finished form of the Gospel, a unity that cannot be disregarded in the interpretation of any part of the whole. Matthew 13:36–43 is unique to Matthew, and it demonstrates the fate of those who reject Jesus and those who accept him and his words of wisdom.

The Genre and Structure of the Gospel of Matthew

Since Matthew's Gospel is the story of Jesus and has a storyteller or narrator, it is a narrative, albeit a narrative of sacred character. Simply stated, as story, it has a narrator (Matthew), a plot (the story of salvation), a climax (the separation of those inside from those outside), and a principal character (Jesus, God's Wisdom among us).[4]

The structure of the Gospel is of significant importance in the interpretation of Matt 13:36–43, because the structure serves to illustrate the centrality and role of the pericope. In order to convey and emphasize important theological ideas[5] in his narration of Jesus' story, Matthew has used various techniques (e.g., alternation between narrative and sermon, repetition, concentric structure, and so on). More than four decades ago, Charles H. Lohr, SJ, detected symmetry in the structure of Matthew's Gospel, which I find plausible. Instead of Lohr's designated content for the sections, I propose a different content that reflects Jesus as the Wisdom of God, which I believe is more representative of the Gospel. This proposal groups and labels chapters as follows:

---

3. Mark Allan Powell, *What Is Narrative Criticism?* (Minneapolis: Fortress, 1990), 2–4. Other helpful resources are Michael Goldberg, *Theology and Narrative: A Critical Introduction* (Nashville: Abingdon, 1982; Philadelphia: Trinity Press International, 1991). A concise explanation of narrative criticism is that by Anderson, *Matthew's Narrative Web*, 11–45. Robert Alter's *The Art of Biblical Narrative* (New York: Basic Books, 1981) is an insightful literary study of the Bible.

4. See W. A. Beardslee, *Literary Criticism of the New Testament* (Philadelphia: Fortress, 1970), 21. See also R. Scholes and R. Kellogg, *The Nature of Narrative* (London: Oxford University Press, 1966), 4.

5. For my purposes here, it will not be necessary to delve further into the intricacies of narrative, but H. J. Bernard Combrink, "The Structure of the Gospel of Matthew as Narrative," *TynBul* 34 (1983): 69–70, presents further details that one may find helpful.

1–4   Narrative: Birth of Wisdom Incarnate, rejection, and beginnings of ministry

5–7   *Sermon:* Wisdom offers a new interpretation of the Law; all are invited to live in the kingdom

8–9   Narrative: Wisdom heals and invites laborers to the vineyard

10   *Sermon:* Wisdom teaches and sends disciples on mission

11–12 Narrative: Wisdom teaches and heals in spite of rejection

13   *Sermon:* Parables outside for the crowds; explanation inside for disciples

14–17 Narrative: Wisdom rejected by religious leaders, acknowledged by disciples who come to him

18   *Sermon:* Wisdom instructs the church community in love

19–22 Narrative: Wisdom teaches, heals, and invites disciples

23–25 *Sermon:* Woes for those who rejected the kingdom; suffering followed by joy for those who accept it

26–28 Narrative: Final rejection of Wisdom; the resurrection[6]

The literary structure thus highlights the pivotal location of Matt 13:36–42 in the Gospel; at the same time, it illustrates the careful

---

6. Charles H. Lohr, "Oral Techniques in the Gospel of Matthew," *CBQ* 23 (1961): 403–35, especially 427. For variations of the symmetrical chiastic structure of Matthew, see Combrink, "Structure," 61–90; J. C. Fenton, "Inclusio and Chiasmus in 'Matthew,' " *SE* 1 (1959): 174–79. Donald A. Hagner, *Matthew 1–13* (WBC 33A; Dallas, Tex.: Word Books, 1993), offers no structural outline but maintains, along with Jack Dean Kingsbury, *The Parables in Matthew 13* (London: S.P.C.K., 1969), 364, that the two major parts of Matthew's parable chapter are 13:3–35 and 13:36–52. It would be hard not to accept this position, given the obvious break in the narrative by the change of scene from the crowds outside to the disciples inside. The proposed five-book structure of the Gospel purported by many scholars — such as B. W. Bacon in *Studies in Matthew* (New York: Henry Holt, 1930) and more recently John P. Meier, *Matthew* (Wilmington, Del.: Michael Glazier, 1980) — has some plausibility since it seems to reflect the church community's struggle for identity. The five books (chaps 5–7; 8:1–11:1; 11:2–13:52; 13:54–19:1; 19:2–25:46) have an introduction (chaps 1–2) and an epilogue (26:1–28:20). Each book is divided into narrative and discourse. Each book ends with a transition formula that alerts the reader to the beginning of a new "book": "When he/Jesus had finished (saying [all] these things/instructing his twelve disciples/these parables)...." The problem with that structure is that some of the books are not that clearly defined; for example, some of Jesus' teaching runs over into the narrative sections. David R. Bauer, *The Structure of Matthew's Gospel* (Sheffield: Almond, 1988), maintains that the structure rests on "compositional relationships: repetition of comparison; repetition of contrast; repetition of particularization and climax" (137). Regardless of what structure one may espouse, I maintain that Wisdom is the basis of the unity of the Gospel.

alternation between sermon and narrative, in which Wisdom Incarnate reveals the will of the Father in word and action.

Wisdom Christology

To show that Jesus (Emmanuel) is God's Wisdom as manifested in the Son of Man who is among both good and evil people (Matt 13:36–42), there is need to demonstrate the reality of a pervasive wisdom Christology in Matthew's Gospel.

Most frequently, titles attributed to Jesus are the criteria used by scholars to determine major Christologies reflected in New Testament writings. Nevertheless, a pervasive theology of Jesus' identity is also a valid criterion. For example, most scholars agree that wisdom theology is the basis of Jesus' self-revelation in the Gospel of John. Though wisdom theology is not as suffused in Pauline writings,[7] scholars note that Wisdom does appear as a title for Jesus in some of Paul's letters. For example, Christ is referred to as "the wisdom of God" (*theou sophia*) in 1 Cor 1:24 (see also Eph 3:10; Col 2:2–3).[8] So pervasive is wisdom Christology in the Gospel of Matthew[9] that I dare propose that it is the christological web, the underpinning that holds together the role and identity of Jesus and holds Matthew's story together.

In this Gospel, wisdom Christology is more evident in what Jesus says and does than in titles for him. Jesus is never addressed directly as "Wisdom" in the Gospel of Matthew, though more importantly, he makes indirect reference to himself as "Wisdom" in Matt 11:19,

---

7. See Raymond E. Brown, *An Introduction to New Testament Christology* (Mahwah, N.J.: Paulist, 1994), 205–10.

8. Wisdom generally flowed out of a sage's life experiences. As sage, Jesus' experience flowed out of his relationship with the Father. See also Marcus J. Borg, *Conflict, Holiness and Politics in the Teachings of Jesus* (Studies in the Bible and Early Christianity 5; New York: Mellen, 1984), 238. I disagree with Borg, however, who while relating Torah with wisdom speaks of Jesus intensifying "the Torah primarily by applying it to internal dimensions of the human psyche" (238). It seems to me that the driving force for Jesus' interpretation of the Torah was the will of the Father and not, as Borg maintains, his "dispositions, emotions, thoughts and desires" (238) unless we say that these are based in the Father's will.

9. John Kampen, "Aspects of Wisdom in the Gospel of Matthew in Light of the New Qumran Evidence," in *Studies on the Texts of the Desert of Judah* (ed. F. García Martínez and A. S. van der Wande; vol. 35; Leiden: Brill, 2000), relates Matthew's wisdom Christology to Matthew's Jewish community's pastoral needs, which he identifies as understanding their relationship to Jews who were not Christians (238–39).

and he embodies the characteristics of a wisdom teacher (e.g., his teachings that deal with the welfare of human beings and how they might live good lives; his use of imagery in parables, similes, and metaphors;[10] his use of macarisms; his manner of responding to the Pharisees when they try to ensnare him; and so on). Moreover, there are references to wisdom that pertain to, and describe, Jesus (e.g., 11:19), references that appear to highlight the significance of Jesus as Wisdom. This fact is not surprising given that Wisdom literature was popular from the Second Temple period[11] and on into the first century. Scholars using source criticism have demonstrated that Q is concerned with answering certain questions about wisdom: "Is Wisdom to be identified with the Law (Sirach 24[:23–34]), heavenly mysteries (*1 Enoch* 42:1–3), or Christ (Col 1:15–20; John 1:1–18)? Is she to be found in the Jerusalem temple (Sir 24:8–12), everywhere in the cosmos (Wis 7:24–26), in heaven (*1 Enoch* 42:1–3), or in the church (Col 1:18)?"[12] In a period when Wisdom literature was popular and Philo's philosophy, in which wisdom plays a prominent role, was well-known,[13] a first-century author such as Matthew might assume that his readers would recognize the implications and underlying Wisdom literature that guided his story of Jesus as he answered the questions for his church concerning where wisdom was to be found.

Wisdom incarnate demonstrates a great enthusiasm for the kingdom of God similar to Old Testament Wisdom, as Jesus looks for people to heed his voice. Matthew asserts that early in Jesus' ministry, he walked by the Sea of Galilee, called fisherman to be fishers of people (Matt 4:18–22) and to follow him (4:19; 9:9; 10:1–4).

---

10. R. B. Y. Scott, *The Way of Wisdom in the Old Testament* (New York: Macmillan, 1971), 73.

11. The Second Temple period follows the return of the Jewish people from exile in Babylon from 538 B.C.E., when they began to rebuild their temple. The first temple had been destroyed in 587 B.C.E.

12. Richard J. Clifford, *The Wisdom Literature* (Interpreting Biblical Texts Series; Nashville: Abingdon, 1998), 168.

13. Krister Stendahl, *The School of St. Matthew* (Lund: CWK Gleerup, 1954), believes that Wisdom literature was studied in relation to Jesus by Matthew's church community (142). While I agree with Stendahl, I maintain that Matthew's use of Wisdom literature was not unusual for any Jew of the first century.

He went about searching for people to repent and to enter his kingdom: "Now when Jesus had finished instructing his twelve disciples, he went on from there to teach and proclaim his message in their cities" (11:1). Jesus forgave people their sins, and he was criticized for befriending tax collectors and sinners (11:19a). Similarly, Wisdom in the Old Testament is shown to be generous with her gifts to those who come to her, but she is not content to wait for them to approach her. She walks the streets in search of people and calls to them: "Wisdom cries out in the street; in the squares she raises her voice" (Prov 1:20). "Does not Wisdom call?... Beside the gates in front of the town,... she cries out: 'To you, O people, I call' " (Prov 8:1–4; also see Wis 6:16). Likewise, Matthew graphically describes the rejection of both John the Baptist and Jesus, whose mission was to call Israel to repentance, as "the means by which God's wisdom is finally vindicated."[14] Jesus, God's incarnate Wisdom, points to God's plan of salvation: "Yet wisdom is vindicated by her deeds" (Matt 11:19b). In other words, "wisdom does what is right and will finally be vindicated by her deeds."[15]

"Incarnate Wisdom" invites the crowds: "Come to me, all you that are weary and are carrying heavy burdens, and I will give you rest. Take my yoke upon you, and learn from me.... For my yoke is easy, and my burden is light" (Matt 11:28–30). Jesus is referring to instruction on the law as he has interpreted it.[16] The "yoke" that Jesus invites his hearers to take up is that of wisdom, which is identified as the law. The Pharisees regarded the law as the revelation of God's will. Jesus, the personification of the law, which was identified with wisdom in the Old Testament, was himself the revelation of God's will: "Come to me... and learn from me" is an invitation to become his disciples, similar to that of Sir 24:19, "Come to me, [all] you who desire me, and eat your fill of my fruits." As a background for Jesus'

---

14. John P. Meier, *A Marginal Jew* (3 vols.; New York: Doubleday, 1991–2001), 2; (1994): 152–53.

15. Hagner, *Matthew 1–13*, 393.

16. Francis Wright Beare, *The Gospel According to Matthew* (San Francisco: Harper & Row, 1981), 267. Beare is also correct in pointing out that Ben-Sirach understood his study and devotion to the law as the source of joy and rest (267).

invitation in Matt 11:28–30, F. W. Beare rightly points to Proverbs 8, in which Wisdom invites her audience to acquire wisdom through study of the law: "I have good advice and sound wisdom. . . . Hear instruction and be wise, and do not neglect it" (Prov 8:14, 33). Similarly, Sirach also advises: "Acquire wisdom for yourselves without money. Put your neck under her yoke, and let your souls receive instruction" (51:25–27).

In Matt 5:3–11, Jesus, God's Wisdom, proclaims those to be blessed who live by his wisdom. These Beatitudes reflect Wisdom literature in both form and content,[17] as shown in Wis 3:14: "Blessed also is the eunuch whose hands have done no lawless deed, and who has not devised wicked things against the Lord."[18] The last of Matthew's Beatitudes (in chap. 5), "Blessed are you when people revile you and persecute you and utter all kinds of evil against you falsely on my account. Rejoice and be glad, for your reward is great in heaven" (Matt 5:11–12), reflects a future-oriented wisdom similar to *2 Baruch:*[19] "Blessed is he who was not born, or he who was born and died" (10:6). "The anointed one will begin to be revealed" (29:3). Jesus states: "Therefore I send you prophets, sages [*sophous*], and scribes, some of whom you will kill and crucify, and some you will flog in your synagogues and pursue from town to town" (Matt 23:34). Jesus goes on to warn that upon them would come "all the righteous blood shed on earth, from the blood of righteous Abel to the blood of Zechariah son of Barachiah, whom you murdered between the sanctuary and the altar" (23:35). In a similar vein, Baruch attributes the destruction of people to the lack of wisdom: "The giants were born there [in Israel]. . . . God did not choose them, or give them the way to knowledge; so they perished because they had no wisdom, they perished through their folly" (Bar 3:26–28).

---

17. Thus Robert A. Guelich, *The Sermon on the Mount* (Waco, Tex.: Word Books, 1982), 64. Meier alleges that this genre of beatitude was also known in the wisdom literature of ancient Egypt, Greece, and Israel: "On the face of it, a beatitude is a cry of admiration, congratulation, and felicitation" (*Marginal Jew,* 2:323).

18. For similar macarisms, see Sir 14:1–2, 20; 25:8–9; 26:1; 28:19; 31:8; 34:15 (ET, 34:17); 48:11; Tob 13:15–16 (ET, 13:14–15); Bar 4:4; *Psalms of Solomon* 4:23; 5:16; 6:1; 10:1; 17:44; 18:6.

19. Guelich, *Sermon,* 64.

Wisdom and the Torah in Matthew's Gospel

To interpret Jesus' explanation of the Weeds among the Wheat, it is necessary to establish Jesus' role as Wisdom and his association with Torah in the first Gospel. Luke Timothy Johnson rightly suggests that Jesus is the personification of Torah. In the first-century Pharisaic tradition, one who studied Torah was in some way identified with Wisdom. "Haggadic speculation" concluded that Torah was eternal and that those who studied Torah and "took its yoke upon them took on the yoke of the kingdom, which . . . mediated God's presence by means of the *Shekinah.*"[20]

Just as Torah was the revelation of God's will, so also was Jesus to those to whom he chose to reveal his Father (Matt 11:27). When two or three gathered to study Torah, the Shekinah dwelt in their midst. In the Gospel of Matthew, Jesus assured his church that "where two or three are gathered in my name, I am there among them" (18:20). In this Gospel, "Jesus is teacher of Torah, fulfillment of Torah, and the very personification of Torah."[21]

To emphasize Jesus' relation to the law, Matthew portrays Jesus on a mountain as he gives the people a new interpretation of the law (Matt 5–7), a setting that calls to mind God's giving the law to Moses on Sinai: "[Jesus] went up on the mountain; and after he sat down [*kathisantos autou*],[22] his disciples came to him [*proselthan*].[23] Then he began to speak [*anoixas to stoma autou*],[24] and taught them" (5:1–2). Jesus is the eschatological Messiah, who, as Wisdom Incarnate,[25]

20. Luke Timothy Johnson, *The Writings of the New Testament* (Philadelphia: Fortress, 1986), 189.

21. Ibid., 190.

22. The phrase "sat down" indicates Jesus' authority to teach and is frequently used in rabbinic literature to indicate the same.

23. As Hagner, *Matthew 1–13*, correctly notes, "[Jesus' Sermon on the Mount] was to be a special time of teaching for his disciples, who 'came to him.' *Proselthon*, a favorite verb of Matthew in this connection, has cultic connotations and itself points to the messianic character of Jesus" (86).

24. Ibid., 86. Hagner indicates that this phrase is a Semitic idiom used to open a public address.

25. Contrary to the opinion of Frances Taylor Gench, *Wisdom in the Christology of Matthew* (New York: University Press of America, 1997), 209, who concludes that the Gospel of Matthew does not have a wisdom Christology, but rather that it contains only "elements of wisdom tradition, many of which have been assimilated into his very Jewish Gospel." To

renews the law for his people.[26] His new interpretation of the law is put on the level of divine communication. Throughout the Sermon on the Mount, Jesus clarifies his relation to the Mosaic law as the Son of Man who fulfills the law:[27] "Do not think that I have come to abolish the law or the prophets; I have come not to abolish but to fulfill" (5:17).

The close connection between esteem for the law and Wisdom is illustrated in many Old Testament texts. For example, speaking of Wisdom, Baruch asserts: "She is the book of the commandments of God, the law that endures forever. All who hold her fast will live, and those who forsake her will die" (Bar 4:1). In the same book, Zion laments: "Let no one rejoice over me, a widow and bereaved of many; I was left desolate because of the sins of my children, because they turned away from the law of God" (Bar 4:12). Sirach maintains that God commanded Wisdom to find a resting place in Jacob (Sir 24:8–12). Nevertheless, in Matthew's Gospel, Jesus does not find evidence of wisdom in the lives of the scribes and Pharisees, whom he excoriates for killing the prophets as did their ancestors (Matt 23:29–33).

In the Old Testament, "the role of Wisdom among human beings is to teach them the heavenly things that otherwise are too high to be known (Job 11:6–7; Wis 9:16–18), to utter truth (Prov 8:7; Wis 6:22), to give instruction as to what pleases God and the divine will (Wis 8:4; 9:9–10), and thus to lead people to life (Prov 4:13; 8:32–35; Sir 4:12; Bar 4:1) and immortality (Wis 6:18–19)."[28]

Jesus, Wisdom and teacher of Wisdom, represents a new and "definitive interpretation of God's will,"[29] as is demonstrated in the six antitheses in Matt 5:21–48, "You have heard that it was said. . . . But

---

arrive at his conclusion, Gench relies primarily on three texts, Matt 11:2–19; 11:25–30; and 23:29–30.

26. T. L. Donaldson, *Jesus on the Mountain: A Study of Matthean Theology* (JSNTSup 8; Sheffield: JSOT Press, 1985), 111–18.

27. John P. Meier, *The Vision of Matthew* (New York: Paulist, 1979), 62–66.

28. Raymond E. Brown makes this observation regarding the Gospel of John, but it is also applicable to the Gospel of Matthew (*An Introduction to New Testament Christology* [Mahwah, N.J.: Paulist, 1994], 209).

29. Warren Carter, *Matthew* (Peabody, Mass.: Hendrickson, 1996), 86.

I say to you [*egō de legō hymin*]" (5:21–22, 27–28, 31–32, 38–39, 43–44). Jesus assures those who keep the law, as he has interpreted it, that they "will be like a wise man who built his house on rock" (7:24). Those who do not hear and heed his words of wisdom "will be like a foolish man who built his house on sand" (7:26).

Jesus in Matthew's Gospel shows his respect and esteem for the law, while at the same time, as God's Wisdom, he reinterprets it for the Matthew's church. Hence, those who accept and obey the law as elucidated by Incarnate Wisdom become those who inherit the kingdom of the Father in Matt 13:36–40, and those who scorn Jesus' interpretation will be subject to the fires of punishment (13:40–42).

Wisdom in the House

In Matt 13:36, Jesus goes "into the house" (*eis tēn oikian*) and his disciples go with him. This phrase is significant in the Gospel of Matthew; it separates believers from unbelievers. Jesus is a teacher of Wisdom, so that those who are committed, or willing to be committed, go "into the house," where they seek wisdom from Jesus, whose mission was to be a light to the nations (cf. 4:13–16). People are to learn wisdom from Jesus so as to be a light as well: "No one after lighting a lamp puts it under the bushel basket, but on the lampstand, and it gives light to all in the house" (*en tē oikian*; 5:15).

The theme of wisdom is cryptically introduced in the infancy narrative in Matt 1:23 in the application of the prophecy of Isa 7:14 to Jesus: " 'They shall name him Emmanuel,' which means, 'God is with us,' " a name that stresses Jesus' divinity and alludes to Jesus as God's Wisdom. In the Wisdom of Solomon, wisdom as divine is "a breath of the power of God, and a pure emanation of the glory of the Almighty. . . . For she is a reflection of eternal light, . . . an image of his goodness" (Wis 7:25–26). The introduction of the humanity of Wisdom Incarnate and of Jesus as King in Matthew's infancy narrative also has a wisdom basis: "When I was born, I began to breathe the common air. . . . I was nursed with care in swaddling cloths. For no king has had a different beginning of existence" (Wis 7:3–5).

In both the Wisdom of Solomon and Matthew's infancy narrative, those who seek Wisdom find her (Wis 6:12–18; 8:2). The Magi (*magoi*) seek wisdom by questioning the authorities. When the Magi learn the location of his birth and reach Bethlehem, they go into the house (*eis tēn oikian*), the place where wisdom is sought in Jesus, to worship the newborn King (Matt 2:11).[30] Having encountered Wisdom Incarnate, they do not return to the wicked Herod but return home by a different route.

The Magi in the First Gospel are a preview of disciples, who seek Wisdom by questioning Jesus. For example, when the disciples were "in the house," they came to Jesus, saying, "Explain to us the parable of the weeds of the field" (Matt 13:36). Jesus was recognized for his wisdom, and Matthew notes that the people in the synagogue in Jesus' "own country" were astonished at his wisdom: "Where did this man get this wisdom [*Pothen toutō hē sophia hautē*] and these deeds of power? [*kai hai dynameis*]" (13:54).

As God's envoy of wisdom, Jesus fills the role of God's Wisdom personified in his wise words, which brought healing to the sick and outcast. Proverbs, so popular in the first century, attributes healing to wisdom:

> Rash words are like sword thrusts,
> but the tongue of the wise brings healing. (Prov 12:18)

> A bad messenger brings trouble,
> but a faithful envoy, healing. (Prov 13:17)

Esteem for wisdom was universal, but the major obstacle for recognition of Jesus' wisdom lay in the opposition to him and the accusations that he did not keep the law. The narrator comments that the religious leaders "took offense at [Jesus]" (Matt 13:57). These men were unable to perceive in Jesus the wisdom of God, and yet

---

30. In a recent article, Mark Allan Powell, "The Magi as Wise Men: Re-examining a Basic Supposition," *NTS* 46 (2000): 1–20, argues that the implied readers were not expected to envision the magi as learned men, but rather as foolish men. I am not arguing that point here; instead, my concern is that the magi, whether learned or unlearned, are to be understood as seeking wisdom in Jesus.

Solomon's wisdom was appreciated even by the Gentile "queen of the South, . . . because she came from the ends of the earth to listen to the wisdom of Solomon, and see, something greater than Solomon is here!" (12:42).

Jesus offers all the people the opportunity to follow him "into the house" and hence choose wisdom; some do so, and some do not. In speaking to the scribes and Pharisees, Jesus recounts his efforts to bring the crowds to accept Wisdom: "Therefore I send you prophets, sages [*sophous*], and scribes, some of whom you will kill and crucify, and some you will flog in your synagogues and pursue from town to town" (Matt 23:34).

Matthew 13: The Narrative Structure

The concentric structure of the Gospel of Matthew clearly verifies that Matt 13 holds a central place in the Gospel, as an analysis of the narrative structure of this chapter demonstrates:

1. Matthew 13:1–9: These verses identify the location of Jesus as outside ("Jesus went out of the house": *exelthōn ho Iēsous tēs oikias*); the audience is defined as "great crowds" (*ochloi polloi*); and Jesus relates the parable of the Sower and the Seeds that fall on four types of soil. Jesus ends with an appeal for the hearers to take heed of the message of the parable.

2. Matthew 13:10–17: Jesus responds to the disciples' question regarding his speaking to the people in parables. He points to the mystery of positive response to Wisdom Incarnate by some and negative response by others.

3. Matthew 13:18–23: Jesus gives an allegorical explanation of the Parable of the Sower, although no one asked for an explanation.

4. Matthew 13:24–35: Jesus tells the parable of the Kingdom in symbols of wheat and weeds and what will happen to both at the end time.

5. Matthew 13:36–42: Jesus "went into the house. And his disciples approached him" (*ēlthen eis tēn oikian. kai proselthon autō hoi mathētai autou*). In the house, the disciples ask Jesus for an explanation of the parable of the Weeds among the Wheat, and Jesus responds. Those who heed Wisdom Incarnate while the Son of Man is governor of "his kingdom" (*tēs basileias autou*) will be rewarded in the kingdom of the Father. Those who reject Wisdom Incarnate will be handed over to the Son of Man's angels, to be cast into the "furnace of fire." In the meantime, in the first stage of the kingdom, both the good and the bad dwell together. The parable ends with Jesus' exhortation to hear.

6. Matthew 13:44–50: Jesus tells those "in the house" the "secrets of the kingdom" through three short parables. The first two demonstrate the good fortune of those who seek God's Wisdom, while the third reiterates the separation of the good from the evil at the "end of the age."

7. Matthew 13:51–52: The concluding concern for understanding of evangelization on the part of disciples focuses on the aspects of "the continuity and discontinuity of old and new"[31] in the preceding seven parables.

Certainly, there is an intimate connection with Wisdom tradition in the first Gospel, which helps to throw light on the purpose of Matthew 13. Incarnate Wisdom teaches in parables to the crowds (13:1–2), but he reveals the secrets of the kingdom only to disciples (13:11), those who come to him to be filled with the fruits he has to offer. Wisdom, who is justified by her deeds[32] (11:19), prays: "I thank you, Father, Lord of heaven and earth, because you have hidden these things from the wise and the intelligent and have revealed them to infants" (11:25).

---

31. Hagner, *Matthew 1–13*, 401.
32. The parallel phrase in Luke 7:35 has *teknon* ("children"), but in Matthew, Wisdom's *ergon* ("works") corresponds to the "works" of the Messiah in 11:2, which Jesus spells out in terms of his healing of the blind, the lame, and so on.

From Matt 13:36, in which Jesus is said to go inside, Incarnate Wisdom focuses his instructions on the disciples.[33] From Matt 13:15 forward, the disciples are shown to be those who understand.[34] If they don't understand, they ask Jesus to explain the meaning to them: "Then he left the crowds and went into the house. And his disciples approached him, saying, 'Explain to us the parable of the weeds of the field'" (13:36). Seeking for understanding is steeped in Wisdom tradition: "Therefore set your desire on my words; long for them, and you will be instructed" (Wis 6:11; see also Prov 8:17; Sir 6:27; et al.).[35]

Jesus, the teacher of Wisdom, clarifies the need for seeking Wisdom as a gift that will be granted in answer to the seeking: "Ask, and it will be given you; search, and you will find; knock, and the door will be opened for you. For everyone who asks receives, and everyone who searches finds, and for everyone who knocks, the door will be opened" (Matt 7:7–8). The disciples are seekers of Wisdom, and they are rewarded for their asking, seeking, and knocking. They believe that wisdom is to be found in Jesus and his interpretation of the law. "Something greater than the temple is here" (12:6), Jesus assures them. The disciples go "into the house," for they are still learners of wisdom, as Peter demonstrates with his "little faith" (*oligopiste*) in 14:31, followed by all the disciples in 16:8 (cf. 6:30; 8:26; 17:20). Jesus' passion and death reveal further their need to seek and learn more from Incarnate Wisdom.[36]

At this point in the Gospel, those who reject Jesus, God's Wisdom, become hardened in their opposition. Some scholars (Kingsbury and Edwards) see Matthew 13 as the turning point of Matthew's Gospel.[37]

---

33. Leon Morris agrees with this observation but denies the validity of attempts to designate the passage as the center of his Gospel since Matthew does not emphasize these words (*The Gospel According to Matthew* [Grand Rapids: Eerdmans, 1992], 356).

34. David Orton, *The Understanding Scribe* (Sheffield: JSOT Press, 1989), 144.

35. Stephen J. Patterson treats a similar saying in a reconstruction of Q sayings and the Gospel of Thomas (94). For more details, see Patterson's essay, "Wisdom in Q and Thomas," in *In Search of Wisdom* (Louisville: Westminster John Knox, 1993), 188–97.

36. Ben Witherington III, *Jesus the Sage: The Pilgrimage of Wisdom* (Minneapolis: Fortress, 1994), 362.

37. J. D. Kingsbury, *The Parables of Jesus in Matthew 13* (London: S.P.C.K., 1969), 130; Richard A. Edwards, *Matthew's Story of Jesus* (Philadelphia: Fortress, 1985), 47–51.

I see it not only as the turning point but also the summary of the Gospel, as I will explain below. Jesus laments the lack of response from Israel: "How often have I desired to gather your children together as a hen gathers her brood under her wings" (23:37). As Suggs indicates, the connection of this saying with wisdom lies in the connection of wings with the Shekinah (God's presence).[38]

Contrary to the opinion of some scholars,[39] the statement in Matt 13:36 is an indication of a major break in the Gospel. Up to this point in the Gospel, the verb *proserchomai* ("approach") is used eleven times by people who have faith in Jesus (4:11; 5:1; 8:2, 5; 8:19, 25; 9:14, 18, 20, 28; 13:10), and once by the devil, who recognizes Jesus' identity (4:3). Its use in 13:36 signals that the disciples, as the result of their faith, are now being introduced into the mysteries of the kingdom of heaven. Jesus is about to reveal to them the secrets of the end time in 13:36–43. He will explain the mystery of the unrighteous in the kingdom, and that they are to remain among the righteous ones until the judgment, when "the Son of Man will send his angels, and they will collect out of his kingdom all causes of sin and all evildoers, and they will throw them into the furnace of fire, where there will be weeping and gnashing of teeth" (13:41–42).

Matthew 13:36–43:
The Son of Man and Wisdom

The pericope Matthew 13:36–43 sums up the reaction of people to Wisdom Incarnate in the preceding chapters of the Gospel, and it also functions as a preface to the rest of Matthew's Gospel. There is a clear division henceforth between those who respond to Wisdom and those who do not.

Looking at the structure of Matt 13:36–42 is helpful for analyzing the passage:

---

38. M. Jack Suggs, *Wisdom, Christology, and Law in Matthew's Gospel* (Cambridge: Harvard University Press, 1970), 66–67.

39. Morris, *Matthew*, 356.

I. Location of Incarnate Wisdom's interaction with the disciples:

   A. "In the house" (*eis tēn oikian*): The disciples question the teacher of wisdom about the meaning of the parable of the Weeds in the field (v. 36).

II. Wisdom explains the parable

   A. First stage of the kingdom (vv. 37–42)

      1. Both good seed and bad are sown.

      2. The sower of the good seed is the Son of Man (v. 37).

         a. The field is the world (v. 38a).

         b. The good seed means the children of the kingdom (v. 38b).

         c. The weeds are the children of the evil one (v. 38c).

      3. The enemy who sowed them is the devil (v. 39a).

         a. The harvest occurs at the end of the age (v. 39b).

         b. The reapers are angels (v. 39c).

      4. The fate of those who reject Wisdom: Just as the weeds are collected and burned, so will it be at the end of the age (v. 40).

         a. The Son of Man will send his angels (v. 41a),

         b. and they will collect out of his kingdom (v. 41b)

            (1) all causes of sin (v. 41c)

            (2) and all evildoers (v. 41d),

         c. and they will throw them into the furnace of fire, where there will be weeping and gnashing of teeth (v. 42).

   B. Second stage of the kingdom: The reward of the righteous who acknowledge Wisdom (v. 43a)

      1. Then the righteous will shine like the sun in the kingdom of their Father (v. 43a).

III. Exhortation: Let anyone with ears listen (v. 43b)!

In Matt 13:36–43, the structure highlights a break between two stages of God's kingdom — the kingdom governed by the Son of Man (vv. 37–42) and the kingdom of the Father (v. 43). Incarnate Wisdom is the Son of Man, whose kingdom is the first stage in which both those who seek wisdom and those who reject wisdom coexist until the final judgment. Jesus says that the enemy who sowed "the weeds" (*zizania*)[40] is the devil. Nevertheless, Jesus affirms that the weeds are to be left among the wheat so as not to uproot the wheat, which was sown by the Son of Man. The second stage of the kingdom is that of the kingdom of the Father, in which only those who have sought wisdom and entered "into the house" with him have a place.[41]

The disciples recognize and accept Wisdom Incarnate. They have heard his words and witnessed his deeds. They are the "infants" to whom Jesus reveals the mysteries of the kingdom: "I thank you, Father, Lord of heaven and earth, because you have hidden these things from the wise and the intelligent and have revealed them to infants" (Matt 11:25). The disciples choose to gather with Jesus rather than to scatter (12:30). They recognize his wisdom and ask for interpretation of the Weeds among the Wheat, of which Jesus spoke in parable in 13:24–30. From this point on in the Gospel of Matthew, the disciples continue to seek him favorably and become a separate group from the crowd. Hence, 13:36–43 is the climax of Matthew's story of Jesus, God's Wisdom among us.

The Son of Man is he who makes the kingdom possible by sowing the seed (Matt 13:3–8), which becomes the children of the kingdom (13:37). The first stage of the kingdom belongs to him, and yet he claims no advantage over others who suffer in this first stage of the kingdom: "Foxes have holes, and birds of the air have nests; but the Son of Man has nowhere to lay his head" (8:20). He endures criticism because of his concern and love for the suffering and the outcasts in his kingdom (11:19). He is accused of collaborating with Beelzebul, the prince of demons, and performing his works by the

---

40. *Zizania*, sometimes translated "darnel," is a weed that resembles wheat while still in its growth.

41. I did not attempt to distinguish among possible sources, because the literary study of a work is not concerned with such, but rather with the text as it has come to us. Moreover, whatever the traditions Matthew drew upon, he chose to use them and gave them his interpretation through location and redaction. Furthermore, a source study has already been done (e.g., M. Jack Suggs, *Wisdom, Christology, and Law in Matthew's Gospel* [Cambridge: Harvard University Press, 1970]).

power of Satan (12:22–30). Ultimately, the Son of Man is the one who, through obedience to the Father, brought about our salvation.[42]

The Son of Man, who has power over the first stage of the kingdom, is more than human, however, a theme introduced in the infancy narrative. During his ministry, he has power over Satan and evil spirits (Matt 12:22 et al.), and he prays to God as his Father (11:25–30). The Son of Man is also Lord of the Sabbath (12:8), and he has authority to forgive sins (9:6). In this first stage of the kingdom (13:36–42), the weeds (those who reject Jesus) have a chance to repent, to accept Jesus and his teachings, and to be influenced by "the salt of the earth" (those who live his commands; 5:13). The weeds, therefore, are permitted to remain along with the wheat in this first stage of the kingdom, so that the wheat will not be damaged or torn out along with the weeds. The Son of Man is also the eschatological judge who will discern between the weeds and the wheat at the "end of the age" (13:39, 41).

In the explanation of the parable, the Son of Man is the apocalyptic figure who reveals to the disciples the secrets of "his kingdom" (Matt 11:41). John P. Meier signals the importance of the Wisdom of Solomon (2:10–3:12; 4:20–5:23) for understanding Matt 13:38 and the apocalyptic connection with wisdom. The "desire for wisdom leads to a kingdom.... Honor wisdom, so that you may reign [as kings] forever" (Wis 6:20–21). "Living according to divine wisdom assures one of sharing after death in the kingdom of heaven."[43] Thus those who seek to understand are those who are spoken of in the passage as the "children [sons] of the kingdom" (*hoi huioi tēs basileias*).

Jesus, the Son of Man, speaks of the first stage of the kingdom as "his kingdom" (*tēs basileias autou*; Matt 13:41). "All things," Jesus stated earlier in the Gospel, "have been handed over to me by my Father" (11:27a). This stage spans the time of Jesus until the "end of the age." Until that time, the Son of Man still has charge of his

---

42. Gerard Loughlin makes the point that we cannot present an authentic picture of Jesus without the story of his death and resurrection (*Telling God's Story* [Cambridge: Cambridge University Press, 1996], 207).

43. Meier, *Marginal Jew*, 2:249–50.

kingdom and exercises the same loving mercy as shown up to this point in the Gospel. The enemy, the devil, continues to sow seed that is not good. Sinners, nevertheless, still have a chance to repent during this stage of Jesus' governance, and as merciful Son of Man, he is there to forgive them. He has angels at his command (13:41; 16:27) who will carry out the judgment. They are the reapers who gather the weeds and burn them in a furnace of fire.[44] The phrase "the end of the age" (*synteleia tou aiōnos*), appearing in 13:39, 40, 49; 24:3; and 28:20, marks the end of the kingdom ruled by the Son of Man.

The second stage of the kingdom of God is the kingdom of the Father. Those who heed Wisdom in the first stage are to "shine like the sun in the kingdom of their Father" (Matt 13:43).

Conclusions

I have demonstrated that Jesus' explanation of the parable of the Weeds among the Wheat (Matt 13:36–43) is the summary and climax of Matthew's Gospel. Jesus as God's Wisdom Incarnate is the christological web that holds together Matthew's story of Jesus. In Jesus' explanation of the parable, those who heed God's wisdom in Jesus, expressed in his words and actions, are the wheat, and those who reject wisdom are the weeds. Both wheat and weeds coexist in the kingdom of the Son of Man. Jesus, as God's Wisdom among humans, remains in the midst of the church, ready to forgive and heal until the end of the age. At the time of judgment, the Son of Man will send his angels to gather "all causes of evil and all evildoers" from his kingdom, to receive their punishment (13:41–43). The righteous, however, "will shine like the sun in the kingdom of their Father" (13:43).

---

44. Christopher Tuckett, *Christology and the New Testament: Jesus and His Earliest Followers* (Louisville: Westminster John Knox, 2001), 126.

9

The Meaning of "Doubt" in Matthew 28:17

A Narrative-Critical Reading

Fred W. Burnett

Matthew 28:16–20 has long been recognized to be a summary of the main themes of Matthew's narrative,[1] yet "doubt" (*distazō*), which occurs in verse 17, is not a main theme of Matthew. The concept of "little faith" is a theme of Matthean discipleship,[2] but not "doubt," actually having two opposing opinions, or wavering between two opinions.[3] In order to solve the issue of what "doubt" means in 28:17, therefore, commentators have almost unanimously turned to 14:31 as the interpretive key, since 14:31 is the only other occurrence of *distazō* in Matthew and in the New Testament. The consensus of commentators is that in 14:31 "doubt" is synonymous with a faith that is weak and fearful in the face of danger (a "little faith") even though the Lord is present (*kyrie*, 14:30).[4]

---

1. E.g., Günther Bornkamm, "The Risen Lord and the Earthly Jesus: Matthew 28.16–20," in *Essays in Honour of Rudolf Bultmann: The Future of Our Religious Past* (ed. James M. Robinson; New York: Harper & Row, 1971), 205.

2. Gerhard Barth, "Matthew's Understanding of the Law," in *Tradition and Interpretation in Matthew* (ed. Günther Bornkamm, Gerhard Barth, and H. J. Held; London: SCM, 1963), 58–104.

3. On themes of Matthean discipleship, see Jack Dean Kingsbury, *Matthew as Story* (2d ed.; Philadelphia: Fortress, 1988), 129–46; Michael H. Crosby, *House of Disciples: Church, Economics and Justice in Matthew* (Maryknoll, N.Y.: Orbis, 1988); Warren Carter, *Households and Discipleship: A Study of Matthew 19–20* (JSNTSup 103; Sheffield: JSOT Press, 1994); and Richard A. Edwards, *Matthew's Narrative Portrait of Disciples: How the Text-Connoted Reader Is Informed* (Harrisburg, Pa.: Trinity Press International, 1997).

4. Most commentators have followed Günther Bornkamm's argument in "The Stilling of the Storm in Matthew," in *Tradition and Interpretation in Matthew* (ed. G. Bornkamm et al.), 56.

What "doubt" means in Matthew, however, is also linked with the issue of *who* doubts. In 14:31, Jesus' question "Why did you [sing.] doubt?" is clearly addressed to Peter, and perhaps by implication to "the ones (*hoi de*) in the boat," to "the disciples (*hoi de mathētai*)" (14:26). In 14:31, "doubt" primarily refers to Peter's wavering between the opinions about whether or not the Lord will (or can) rescue him from sinking (14:30), but perhaps secondarily to Peter's hesitation about the identity of the figure who is walking on the water. The disciples at first think that Jesus is a "ghost (*phantasma*)" (14:26), and Peter asks the figure for its identity as the *"Lord."* Even though Jesus has just identified himself to the whole group with a direct statement ("It is I," 14:27), Peter still harbors some doubt or hesitation about the figure's identity (*Kyrie, ei sy ei*, 14:27). Peter seems to have the identity issue settled when he boldly requests, "Lord, save me!" (v. 30). In narrative-critical terms, the disciples, including Peter, have already learned that the Lord can control the winds and sea (8:27) and will respond to their petition to be rescued (8:25–26).[5]

In the context of 8:26 the disciples' weak faith is not linked with *distazō* but with *deilos* (timidity). *Deilos* in 8:26 is not necessarily synonymous with *distazō* in 14:31. In the progression of Matthew's narrative the disciples have overcome their "timidity (*deilos*)" that characterized their "little faith" in 8:26, but not their "doubt" (*distazō*). To overcome the doubt that characterizes their "little faith," it takes Jesus' dramatic rescue of Peter in 14:31. Matthew's narrative progression in terms of their "little faith" is, therefore, from "timidity/little faith" to "marveling" (*thaumazō*) at Jesus' power (8:26–27), to "doubt/little faith" (14:31), and finally to "worshiping

---

5. It only seems to confuse things when, e.g., K. Grayston contends that "what Peter feared was the Lord would not save him, but he did" ("The Translation of Matthew 28.17," *JSNT* 21 [1984]: 108). Peter's fear, not his doubt, is specifically related to the fact that he is beginning to sink. In narrative terms, Peter knows from the episode in 8:25–27 that Jesus can save him from sinking, if the figure to whom Peter cries out is, indeed, Jesus. That said, it is probably wise not to split hairs here. As a summary question, Jesus' query in 14:31 ("Why did you doubt?") could refer to Peter's doubt about both Jesus' identity and salvific power. The crucial point is that how "doubt" is understood in 14:31 should not be carried over too quickly to 28:17, if only because of all the intervening narrative between chapters 14 and 28.

(*proskyneō*) him" (28:17),[6] or at least "venerating" him because of his status and function as God's Son (cf. 14:33).[7]

The Meaning of "Doubt" in Matthew 28:17

There are similarities between the scenes in 28:17 and 14:31, and commentators have been instinctively right to compare the two. However, there are also many important narrative differences that affect the meaning of doubt in 28:17, as explicated below. First, I will briefly make clear my own position on the vexing question of the identity of the doubters in 28:17, and then suggest what doubt might mean within that context.

As commonly known, the question of who doubts in 28:17 is usually answered by settling two issues: (1) who is present in this scene, and (2) how *hoi de* should be translated. In terms of narrative criticism it is clear that only "the eleven disciples" and Jesus are present.[8] There is no one else present, even by implication (e.g., disciples other than the Eleven).

The second issue for determining who doubts is more difficult: how to translate *hoi de* in 28:17. Three main possibilities have emerged. They are summarized by P. W. van der Horst:

---

6. In 14:33 "him" seems to refer to Jesus, and *proskyneō* could have the softer meaning of they "venerated" Jesus. Earlier in the narrative Jesus has made it clear — at least to the readers and to the character of Satan — that God alone is to be worshiped and served (4:10; cf. 8:2; 9:18; 15:25; 18:26; and 20:20, where *proskyneō* simply means veneration connected with falling prostrate before Jesus). Admittedly, however, the line between God and Jesus could be a little blurred in 14:33, particularly for Gentile and certain types of Hellenistic Jewish readers. We shall encounter the same ambiguity in 28:17: is God present as a character during this scene and as the exclusive object of the disciples' worship (*proskyneō*)?

7. If "*legontes* (saying)" has instrumental as well as causal overtones in 14:33, then the sense would be that "they (*hoi de*) venerated him [Jesus] by saying, 'Truly, you are God's son.'"

8. Perhaps God has an implied narrative presence, since in my view God as a character is present throughout Matthew's narrative. If God is present as a character in 28:17, it is clear that God does not directly speak or intervene. The object of *proskyneō* is unclear; if it is Jesus, it should be *autō*-, as some copyists have it. It is certainly possible, even likely, to understand "God" as the implied object of *proskyneō* rather than the preceding *auton*, unless the distinction between Jesus and God has almost been lost by the end of Matthew's narrative. If God is the implied object of *proskyneō* in 28:17, then the sense would then be the following: "When they saw Jesus (*auton*), they worshiped [God]."

1. "When they saw him, they worshipped him, but some doubted"; in this translation (the most usual one) *hoi de* refers to some of the disciples.
2. "When they saw him, they worshipped him, but they doubted"; in this translation *hoi de* refers to all of the disciples.
3. "When they saw him, they worshipped him, but others doubted"; in this translation *hoi de* refers to persons other than the disciples.[9]

First, it is often pointed out that normally in Hellenistic Greek *hoi de* should be preceded by *hoi men* if a change of subject is to be understood by the reader.[10] If there is a change of subject, then one translation of 28:17 could be: "They [all of the Eleven] worshipped, but some [of the Eleven? of another group?] doubted." One of the problems with this translation, however, is that there is no preceding *hoi men* to indicate a change of subject from "the eleven disciples" to persons other than the Eleven or to a part of the Eleven ("some of them doubted").[11]

In addition to what is normally the case for *hoi de,* commentators who argue that *hoi de* signals a change of subject in 28:17 base their decision more on a logical assumption than they do on linguistic grounds. The logical assumption is then passed off as a linguistic argument, a procedure that has been far too prevalent in biblical studies.[12] The assumption is an instance of binary thinking that "worship" and "doubt" constitute semantic opposites so that the commentator is forced to make an either/or choice between them. K. L. McKay is an example of this kind of thinking:

---

9. P. W. van der Horst, "Once More: The Translation of *hoi de* in Matthew 28.17," *JSNT* 27 (1986): 27.

10. For a good summary of the basic issues in the debate about the translation of *hoi de* in Matt 28:17 see van der Horst, "Once More"; Grayston, "Translation of Matthew 28.17," 105–9; and, K. L. McKay, "The Use of *hoi de* in Matthew 28.17: A Response to K. Grayston," *JSNT* 24 (1985): 71–72.

11. The issue of whether or not "God" is the implied object of *proskyneō* becomes important once more. If one holds strictly that *hoi de* indicates a change of subject, then the sense would be: "They [*all* of the Eleven] worshiped [God], but some [of the Eleven? others?] doubted that the figure whom they saw was Jesus." Cf. n. 8, above.

12. See, e.g., James Barr, *The Semantics of Biblical Language* (London: SCM, 1983); and Arthur Gibson, *Biblical Semantic Logic: A Preliminary Analysis* (New York: St. Martin's Press, 1981).

It is quite possible in either case [that *hoi de* refers to some other than the Eleven or to a minority of the Eleven] that all worshipped while some both worshipped and doubted; but the proposition that all both worshipped and doubted is untenable without real evidence that *hoi de* was ever used without indicating some change of subject.[13]

Either/or thinking is particularly powerful if it is assumed that "doubt" in Matthew means "unbelief," and that "worship" implies some kind of cognitive certainty. In that case, the logical either/or drives the linguistic explanation so that the pressing question then becomes, "If they worshiped, how could they doubt?"[14]

In light of the fluidity and stylistic diversity of Hellenistic Greek, the use of *hoi de* in Matthew's narrative should be the determining factor for translating the phrase, rather than examples from elsewhere. An analysis of Matthew's use of *hoi de* points clearly to the conclusion that it is all of the Eleven who doubt. As Keith H. Reeves rightly concludes: "Matthew always uses the *hoi de* + verbal construction to refer to a previously mentioned group of people, never in the sense of 'others.' "[15] The translation would then be, "When they saw him, they worshiped, and they doubted."

---

13. McKay, "Use of *hoi de*: A Response," 71–72.

14. Grayston, "Translation of Matthew 28.17," 106. Grayston translates: "When they saw him, they threw themselves down in submission, though they doubted its effect" (108). His view pushes him toward the conclusion that the "doubt" was "a problem of the later church" (cf. also Bornkamm, "Risen Lord and Earthly Jesus," 205). He then refers to the logical problem in which doubt was defined as "unbelief" so that it could not logically accompany a worshipful encounter with the resurrected Jesus. It should be added in passing that arguments that the shorter ending of Matthew might have been the earliest ending are not only unpersuasive but really have little bearing on the issue of *hoi de* in 28:17, particularly since *hoi de* is not in question in textual-critical terms (see George Howard, "A Note on the Short Ending of Matthew," *HTR* 81 [1988]: 117–20).

15. Keith H. Reeves, "They Worshipped Him, and They Doubted: Matthew 28.17," *BT* 49 (1998): 348. Examples of *hoi de* in Matthew show it being consistently used to refer to the previously mentioned group: there is no change of subject (2:5, 9; 4:20, 22; 8:32; 9:31; 14:17; 15:34; 16:7 [some MSS have *tote*], 14; 20:5, 31; 21:25; 22:5; 22:19; 26:15, 66, 67; 27:4, 21, 23, 66; 28:15, 17). Reeves states: "The point of view of the individual or of the sub-group is never set against the point of view of the body as a whole. Consequently, we conclude that *hoi de edistasan* (but they doubted) refers to the eleven disciples as a group" (ibid., 348). Reeves does not address the fact that Matthew does use *hoi de* in 28:16 to change the subject from "the soldiers" in 28:15 (cf. 28:12) to "the Eleven," but this does not argue for a change of subject in 28:17. In 28:17 the *hoi de* continues the narrative subject of 28:16, just as *hoi de* functions this way, for example, in 14:21.

Matthew's use of *hoi de* to refer to the same subject (all of the Eleven) pushes the reading of 28:17 toward a legitimate, though often ignored, meaning of *distazō* in this context: "hesitation."[16] The differences between 28:17 and the narrative situations in Matt 8 and 14 are relevant here, and in light of them I suggest what doubt as "hesitation" might mean in 28:17.

Matthew 28:17 places the Eleven as characters in an entirely new narrative situation. I cannot be exhaustive, but there are major narrative differences between 28:17 and the scene in 14:24–33, which is used to interpret it. First, 28:17 makes no distinction between the disciples as a group and Peter. Peter is not singled out as he is in 14:27–33 as the disciples' spokesperson or as the chief actor. What happens in 28:17 happens to the disciples as a character-group. There is no narrative indication, other than perhaps the contested *hoi de* itself, that doubt only happened to one of them (Peter) or only to some of them. In narrative terms, it is a collective doubt.

Second, in 28:17 the risen Jesus does not rebuke or question their doubt as he does in 8:26 and 14:31. In fact, in 28:17 there is no direct statement either from Jesus or from the disciples; their doubt is the narrator's comment, and their doubt is left standing without an evaluative comment from any of the characters or from the narrator. The lack of comment by both Jesus and the narrator suggests that in Matthew's narrative doubt is left standing as *necessary* to their ongoing worship or veneration of Jesus as they fulfill his new commission.[17]

A Postmodern Suggestion about "Doubt" in Matthew

But what might it mean to say that doubt as "hesitation" is necessary to worship/veneration in Matthew? To suggest an answer to this question, I will first look beyond the surface-narrative differences between Matt 8:23–27; 14:24–33; and 28:17 — important though

---

16. Cf. I. P. Ellis, "But Some Doubted," *NTS* 14 (1967–68): 574–80.

17. In 28:17 there is also no "fear" connected with their doubt, from which Jesus has to rescue them (cf. 8:25–26; 14:26, 30).

they are — to what has transpired at a deeper level in Matthew's narrative from chapter 14 to 28:17. Second, I will explicate "doubt" as "hesitation" in 28:17, using the postmodern notion of "alterity."

The new narrative situation in 28:17 means that the Eleven's doubt can only be partially understood by interpreting it in light of the situation in 14:24–33. In addition to the narrative differences that have already been mentioned, there are at least two structural differences. First, the *place* of spirituality and worship has shifted from "where two or three are gathered" (18:20) in and around Israel to "all nations (*panta ta ethnē*)" (28:19; cf. *oikoumenē*, 24:14).[18] In Matthew's narrative, it is a shift from the idea that the disciples' mission, which up to this point has been conducted in and around Israel (10:5–7) and to each other (Matt 18), is now extended to the whole world. In this regard the "doubt/hesitation" of the Eleven is partly related to that new scheme — a new commission to a new sphere. Most importantly, however, their doubt/hesitation relates to a new form of existence and mode of being for Jesus himself.

The great narrative reversal in 28:17 that makes the disciples' doubt so different than in 14:31 is that Jesus has been raised from the dead: the Eleven are encountering the "Other" in the fullest sense of the word. Part of their doubt/hesitation is between what they are (and what Jesus himself was) as human beings and what Jesus has become. They are experiencing alterity between two forms of existence by encountering Jesus as the resurrected "Other," or the difference between what he was and now appears to be. In their existence the disciples are still what Jesus had been, but now Jesus is what they are *not* and cannot (yet) become.[19] I am not saying that the Evangelist was/is a postmodern writer. However, I am saying that even though the Evangelist surely is not thinking alterity, his narrative expresses it in 28:17

---

18. Cf. Stephen C. Barton, *Discipleship and Family Ties in Mark and Matthew* (SNTSMS 80; New York: Cambridge University Press, 1994), 135.

19. Interestingly, there is no narrative goal in Matthew for the disciples to undergo the same kind of metamorphosis that Jesus himself has experienced (cf. 1 Cor 15:51–55; 2 Cor 3:18), although a transformed existence for the disciples is certainly implied in 19:28 and 26:29; cf. 13:43, 5:12. As a summary of the main themes of Matthew, 28:16–20 would certainly be the place to have the risen Jesus issue a promise of metamorphosis to the Eleven, particularly if he wanted to assuage their doubt.

through the doubt of the Eleven. Alterity is experiencing both the stable ("they worshiped him") and the disruptive movement of an event ("they doubted/hesitated/oscillated"), and this notion catches up the disciples' experience in 28:17.[20]

The lack of direct statements or questions in this scene by both Jesus and the Eleven indicates that worship/doubt is less about a "certainty" that can be articulated in representational language or by empirical demonstration than it is about their experience of alterity. This experience is not "ordinary" consciousness. Their experience is less about thinking together representationally (in doctrines and dogmas), which only posits a knowledge of certainty and presence, than it is about experiencing Jesus' Otherness — his new form of existence with its implied absence and promised presence ("I will be with you always," 28:20).[21]

The new narrative situation in 28:17 has disrupted, perhaps even subverted, the disciples' habitual way of encountering and responding to Jesus. The scene in 28:17 does not simply reinforce their preconceptions as it does in 14:31. The *egō* ("I") who promises to be with them will now be experienced not only as a transformed "I" but also in his empirically demonstrable *absence*.[22] The disciples have

---

20. See Gilles Deleuze and Félix Guattari, *What Is Philosophy?* (trans. Robert Hurley, Mark Seem, and Helen R. Lane; New York: Columbia University Press, 1994), 16, 21, 36, for whom the entire project of philosophy is to think/experience "difference" and "alterity," or the incoherence that allows an experience of "pure" event.

21. For Heidegger, intense doubt (*Destruktion*), i.e., experiencing a dismantling of the whole ontological tradition, is necessary for Being (*Dasein*) to be concretely experienced (Martin Heidegger, *Being and Time* [trans. John Macquarrie and Edward Robinson; New York: Harper & Row, 1962], 49). Derrida carries through Heidegger's notion of *Destruktion* when he reflects on the "de-" in "de-construction." He says that the "de- of *de* construction signifies not the demolition of what is constructing itself, but rather what remains to be thought beyond the constructivist or destructionist scheme" (Jacques Derrida, *Limited, Inc.* (trans. Samuel Welsen; Evanston, Ill.: Northwestern University Press, 1988], 147). The idea of *Destruktion* and deconstruction are similar to the notions of Deleuze and Guattari (see n. 20, above) in their emphasis upon the nonreflective and experiential, and to the notion of *"le différend"* (the experience of alterity) that is expounded by Jean-François Lyotard in *The Differend: Phrases in Dispute* (trans. George van den Abbeele; Theory and History of Literature 46; Minneapolis: University of Minnesota Press, 1988), 13.

22. Fred W. Burnett, "The Undecidability of the Proper Name 'Jesus' in Matthew," *Semeia* 54 (1991): 132–34. Edwards's reader-response analysis of 28:17–18 comes to a similar conclusion: "The implication is that future followers of Jesus will receive the same commands, but will apparently resemble the current disciples as people of little faith, having doubt and fear, but people who nonetheless 'worship' the risen Jesus as the son of the Father" (*Matthew's Narrative Portrait*, 134).

to unlearn what they have previously known. Until now they have worshiped or venerated Jesus while he was present with them. Now, however, with the narrative reversal of the new mode of Jesus' existence, they will experience him through his empirical absence. The presence/absence hierarchy for the disciples has now oscillated to absence/presence. In other words, from now on worship of Jesus cannot (or should not) lead to representational knowledge and the certainty of absolute presence.[23]

The Eleven's "doubt/hesitation" is an instance of otherness in Matthew's text that in its alterity indicates that the disciples experience Jesus in the "not," or the *space between* the binary hierarchy (or opposition) of worship/doubt.[24] The disciples' experience of doubt is not just the inability to choose between two opinions or ideas. It is, rather, the disruption of alterity, in which Jesus as Other is experienced in the space between his new existence/former existence, his presence/absence, and the corresponding space between the worship/doubt of the Eleven. Their experience of alterity means that "they worshipped and doubted."

As with all logocentric narratives such as Matthew, the alteric opening is closed with a direct statement of representational thinking by Jesus himself: he promises that he will continually be with them even though "he" will be empirically absent. With Jesus' promise the absence/presence or worship/doubt of 28:17 regains its ordinary representational position of PRESENCE/absence, though Jesus' absence, like a parasitic ghost (cf. 14:26), will always haunt (and subvert) the certainty of his presence for his disciples.

---

23. The concept of discipleship in Matthew might be coherent, but it is certainly a temporal experience and one of ongoing alterity and flux rather than a once-and-for-all attainment. For a social analysis of discipleship as liminality in Matthew, see Carter, *Households and Discipleship*, 27, 204–18.

24. Cf. Mark C. Taylor, *Altarity* (Chicago: University of Chicago Press, 1987), 230–38.

10

Markan Narrative Christology and the Kingdom of God

*Elizabeth Struthers Malbon**

I have often had occasion to return to Tannehill's article "The Gospel of Mark as Narrative Christology"[1] as an indispensable presupposition of my current larger project, an examination of the characterization of Jesus in the Gospel of Mark, understood as narrative Christology.

Narrative Christology: Following Tannehill's Lead

The opening statement of Tannehill's essay is so clear and compelling that it bears repeating twenty-five years later:

> Jesus is the central figure in the Gospel of Mark, and the author is centrally concerned to present (or re-present) Jesus to his readers so that his significance for their lives becomes clear. He does this in the form of a story. Since this is the case, we need to take seriously the narrative form of Mark in discussing this Gospel's

---

*While I have never been an official student of Dr. Tannehill or an official colleague, I have been one of his national colleagues — like many contributors to this volume, a member with him of the Literary Aspects of the Gospels and Acts Group of the Society of Biblical Literature (1982–99). From before the beginning of this group, Robert Tannehill was an "established" scholar who was wonderfully supportive of the many "promising young scholars" for whom this dynamic group was an important location for scholarly and professional development. My own early work was also juxtaposed with Tannehill's in an almost accidental way: my first scholarly article appeared in *Semeia* 16 (1979), following his pioneering article "The Gospel of Mark as Narrative Christology."

1. Robert C. Tannehill, "The Gospel of Mark as Narrative Christology," *Semeia* 16 (1979): 57–95.

presentation of Jesus Christ. In other words, we need ways of understanding and appreciating Mark as narrative Christology.[2]

The dominant way of investigating Christology — even now, as well as when Tannehill first wrote these words — is by examining christological titles. Tannehill's pioneering move was to focus not on titles abstracted from the narrative but on actions embedded in the plot, although, as he notes, "an understanding of the narrative composition of Mark may allow us to make some observations about the function of particular titles in relation to the developing narrative."[3] Tannehill realizes that Markan characterization is tied to Markan plotting:

> In the Gospel of Mark there is little description of the inner states of the story characters. Instead, characterization takes place through the narration of action. We learn who Jesus is through what he says and does in the context of the action of others. Therefore, the study of character (not in the sense of inner qualities but in the sense of defining characteristics as presented in the story) can only be approached through the study of plot.[4]

Yet Tannehill also brings out the strong connection between the art of characterization and the act of communication. In connecting his essay on Markan narrative Christology to his book *The Sword of His Mouth: Forceful and Imaginative Language in Synoptic Sayings*,[5] Tannehill reiterates:

> Literary composition provides clues to the nature of the act of communication which the words are to make possible. It may provide clues to the speaker's purpose, the conception of the hearers and their needs, and the anticipations of response held

---

2. Ibid., 57.
3. Ibid., 58.
4. Ibid.
5. Robert C. Tannehill, *The Sword of His Mouth: Forceful and Imaginative Language in Synoptic Sayings* (Philadelphia: Fortress; Missoula, Mont.: Scholars, 1975).

by the speaker. It provides clues to the type of influence which the speaker wishes to exercise with regard to the hearer.[6]

In this sense Tannehill regards his essay on Markan narrative Christology as an "extension" of his essay on the disciples in Mark,[7] "which sought to show the author's careful control of emphasis and evaluation, guiding the readers' judgments about the disciples, with possible repercussions for the readers' judgments about themselves."[8] While Tannehill's goal is to "give us a clearer view of the interaction between the author and his first readers," he is quite aware (and even hopeful) that such a view "can also deepen our understanding of what it would mean for a modern reader to read this Gospel well, with full appreciation of its power to challenge."[9]

As Tannehill moves from an overview of what elements are involved in narrative Christology to an analysis of the Markan text itself, the term "commission" becomes central to his explication. Of chief importance is "the commission which Jesus received from God and . . . what Jesus has done (and will do) to fulfill his commission."[10] Behind Jesus' commission stands the "purpose and mission" of God.[11] Moving out from Jesus' commissioning by God is Jesus' commissioning of the disciples. An "ongoing task" in Mark's narrative is that of various groups conspiring to destroy Jesus (3:6).[12] The interaction of the sequences involved in fulfilling these commissions and this task forms the plot of Mark's Gospel.

"In fulfilling his commission, Jesus assumes certain roles in relation to other persons in the narrative," Tannehill continues, "and our understanding of Mark's narrative Christology will be advanced by considering the role relationships."[13] Tannehill finds five role relationships of the Markan Jesus foremost: Jesus' relation to (1) God, (2) his

---

6. Tannehill, "Narrative Christology," 59.
7. Robert C. Tannehill, "The Disciples in Mark: The Function of a Narrative Role," *JR* 57 (1977): 386–405.
8. Tannehill, "Narrative Christology," 59.
9. Ibid., 60.
10. Ibid., 61.
11. Ibid., 62–63.
12. Ibid., 62.
13. Ibid., 63.

disciples, (3) the scribes, Pharisees, and Jerusalem leaders, (4) the supplicants who ask for healing, and (5) the demons. In sketching out a narrative Christology focused on plot, role relations among characters, the communication of the "author" and the "reader," and rhetoric (reiteration, delayed disclosure, irony, and paradox are among a number of rhetorical strategies discussed), Tannehill's essay has led the way for others to develop related ideas.

In 1982, the narrative-critical approach to Mark's Gospel was introduced to a broader audience by the publication of *Mark as Story: An Introduction to the Narrative of a Gospel,* by David Rhoads and Donald Michie.[14] In a way similar to Tannehill's discussion of the plot in terms of "commissions" and "tasks," Rhoads and Michie discuss the plot under these headings:

The Background and Origin of the Conflicts: God's Rule

Jesus versus the Demonic Forces and Nature

Jesus versus the Authorities

Jesus and the Disciples

In the second endnote in the chapter on characters (other chapters are on rhetoric, settings, and plot), Rhoads and Michie cite "the stimulating analysis of Markan characters by Robert Tannehill, 'The Gospel of Mark as Narrative Christology.' "[15]

Naturally enough, Tannehill's essays on Mark as narrative Christology and on the narrative role of the disciples in Mark are cited by Jack Dean Kingsbury in *The Christology of Mark's Gospel* in 1983.[16] Kingsbury's goal is not narrative Christology per se but "a balancing act": "While keeping the reader in touch with the plot of Mark by tracing the development of the motif of the secret of Jesus' identity, I have also attended to what I perceive to be the more stubborn problem of ascertaining the meaning and function of the major titles

---

14. David Rhoads and Donald Michie, *Mark as Story: An Introduction to the Narrative of a Gospel* (Philadelphia: Fortress, 1982). My references here are to this original edition, although a second edition has now appeared: David Rhoads, Joanna Dewey, and Donald Michie, *Mark as Story: An Introduction to the Narrative of a Gospel* (2d ed.; Minneapolis: Fortress, 1999).

15. Rhoads and Michie, *Mark as Story,* 154 n. 2.

16. Jack Dean Kingsbury, *The Christology of Mark's Gospel* (Philadelphia: Fortress, 1983).

of majesty."[17] This is a difficult balancing act, and in my judgment, Kingsbury's attention to christological titles outweighs his attention to narrative functions and roles. In Kingsbury's more popular treatment of Markan Christology, *Conflict in Mark*,[18] we hear an echo of Tannehill's "commissions" and "task" in the division of the material into three stories:

The Story of Jesus

The Story of the Authorities

The Story of the Disciples

Other echoes of Tannehill's approach to Markan narrative Christology could, of course, be sounded. The narrative-critical approach to Christology is categorized as one of three approaches by Jacob Chacko Naluparayil in a review article on "Jesus of the Gospel of Mark":[19]

Main approaches to the christological titles can be divided into three categories: (1) seeking the meaning to the christological titles outside the text; (2) finding the key in the theological interests of the author, often in conjunction with redaction criticism; and (3) in conjunction with narrative criticism, looking for the meaning of the titles within the narrative as they are defined by the act of narration.[20]

Not surprisingly, the first work reviewed in the third category is Tannehill's "The Gospel of Mark as Narrative Christology."[21] Other

---

17. Ibid., ix.

18. Jack Dean Kingsbury, *Conflict in Mark: Jesus, Authorities, Disciples* (Minneapolis: Fortress, 1989).

19. Jacob Chacko Naluparayil, "Jesus of the Gospel of Mark: Present State of Research," *CurBS* 8 (2000): 191–226.

20. Ibid., 192.

21. Ibid., 214. The year of Tannehill's publication is erroneously given as 1980 rather than 1979. After a brief discussion of Tannehill's essay, Naluparayil concludes, "In effect, his Christology turns out to be a Son of God Christology" (214). I believe this misses Tannehill's point and oversimplifies his reading. Naluparayil's comment on Tannehill may well reveal more about Naluparayil's way of reading than about Tannehill's; see below. Pheme Perkins, in summarizing Tannehill's article, concludes more appropriately: "This narrative perspective wants us to see

scholars whose works are discussed under the category of narrative-critical approaches include Rhoads and Michie, Edwin Broadhead,[22] Ole Davidsen,[23] and Peter Müller.[24] In the introduction to his review article, Naluparayil states, "The third approach — the narrative function of the titles — is best illustrated by the work of Kingsbury."[25] Yet, interestingly enough, Naluparayil discusses Kingsbury's work under the subheading "Son of God as the Royal Messiah" rather than under the subheading "Narrative Method and Integrative Christology."[26] Perhaps conventional modesty prevents Naluparayil from doing any more than listing in the bibliography his own large book in this field.[27] In my judgment, Naluparayil, like Kingsbury, allows a christological title (for him, "Son of Man"; for Kingsbury, "Son of God") and concern for abstract (essentialist) christological categories like "identity" to outweigh narratological concerns such as plot and characterization.[28]

Thus, although abstracted christological titles still contend with Markan narrative Christology, the situation has certainly changed since the publication of Tannehill's essay on narrative Christology in 1979. The final paragraph of that essay begins, "The study of Mark

---

that Markan Christology is not limited to one theme or title. It depends on the unfolding impact of the story. None of the titles can express the paradoxes imaged in that story" ("Mark as Narrative Christology," in *Who Is This Christ? Gospel Christology and Contemporary Faith* [ed. Reginald H. Fuller and Pheme Perkins; Philadelphia: Fortress, 1983], 76).

22. Naluparayil ("Jesus," 215) discusses E. K. Broadhead, *Prophet, Son, Messiah: Narrative Form and Function in Mark 14–16* (JSNTSup 97; Sheffield: Sheffield Academic, 1994), but also lists two additional works by Broadhead: *Teaching with Authority: Miracles and Christology in the Gospel of Mark* (JSNTSup 74; Sheffield: Sheffield Academic, 1992); and "Jesus the Nazarene: Narrative Strategy and Christological Imagery in the Gospel of Mark," *JSNT* 52 (1993): 3–19. A more recent book may now be added to this already impressive list: Edwin K. Broadhead, *Naming Jesus: Titular Christology in the Gospel of Mark* (Sheffield: Sheffield Academic, 1999).

23. Ole Davidsen, *The Narrative Jesus: A Semiotic Reading of Mark's Gospel* (Aarhus: Aarhus University Press, 1993).

24. Peter Müller, *"Wer ist dieser?" Jesus in Markusevangelium: Markus als Erzähler* (Biblisch-theologische Studien 27; Neukirchen Vluyn: Neukirchener, 1995).

25. Naluparayil, "Jesus," 192.

26. Ibid., 204.

27. Jacob Chacko Naluparayil, *The Identity of Jesus in Mark: An Essay on Narrative Christology* (Studium Biblicum Franciscanum Analecta 49; Jerusalem: Franciscan Printing, 2000).

28. See my review of Naluparayil, *The Identity of Jesus in Mark,* in *Bib* 4 (2001): 569–73. I thank my colleague Ananda Abeysekara for his helpful comments on the question of "identity" and essentialism.

as a narrative reveals more unity and art in this Gospel than is commonly recognized."[29] It is, in no small part, through the uncommonly forceful and imaginative work of Robert Tannehill — in print and in person — that recognition of "unity and art" in Mark's Gospel is not so uncommon today.

The Markan Jesus on the "Kingdom of God"

Like Tannehill, I began my exploration of Markan characterization with a look at the disciples. Having studied various other Markan characters along the way, however,[30] it took me longer to focus on Jesus than it did Tannehill, who was "seeking to do greater justice to the fact that Jesus is the central character in the Gospel, through whom the Gospel's influence is most fully felt."[31] Now I am concerned to examine the many ways Mark's narrative employs to disclose its central character, Jesus. I am only willing to apply the term "Christology" to Mark's Gospel in the sense of "narrative Christology" as first outlined by Tannehill. What follows is part of a larger project of such narrative Christology, focusing not only on what Jesus does — the actions he initiates (what I call "enacted Christology") — and what the narrator and other characters say about him ("projected Christology"), but also on what Jesus says (and does) in response to what these others say about him ("deflected Christology"), what Jesus says about himself and God ("refracted Christology"), and *how* what other characters do is related to what Jesus says and does ("reflected Christology"[32]).

My focus here is an aspect of Markan "refracted Christology." Not only does the Markan Jesus attempt to deflect attention and

---

29. Tannehill, "Narrative Christology," 88.

30. Seven articles or chapters on Markan characterization are republished in Elizabeth Struthers Malbon, *In the Company of Jesus: Characters in Mark's Gospel* (Louisville: Westminster John Knox, 2000).

31. Tannehill, "Narrative Christology," 59–60.

32. Elizabeth Struthers Malbon, " 'Reflected Christology': An Aspect of Narrative 'Christology' in the Gospel of Mark," *PRSt* 26 (1999; Festschrift for Edgar V. McKnight): 127–45.

honor away from himself and toward God (the focus of my comments elsewhere on "deflected Christology"[33]), but the Markan Jesus
also refracts — or bends — the "Christologies" of other characters
and the narrator. The image comes from the way a prism refracts
"white" light and thus shows its spectral colors. When a thing is
bent and looked at from another angle, something different appears.
The most obvious way in which the Markan Jesus bends the "Christologies" of others is by his statements about the "Son of Man,"
especially in juxtaposition with "christological titles" offered by other
characters. However, the Markan Jesus' statements about the "kingdom of God" may also be seen as refracting the "Christologies" of
other characters and the narrator. No other character or the narrator speaks of the "Son of Man"; no other character speaks of the
"kingdom of God," and the narrator does so but once, just after
Jesus' death (15:43). "Son of Man" and "kingdom of God" depict
the Markan Jesus' distinctive point of view.[34]

In *The Christology of Mark's Gospel,* Kingsbury refers frequently
to what God "thinks" about Jesus, but Mark only narrates two sen-
tences that God says to or about Jesus (1:11; 9:7). Kingsbury says
little about what Jesus says about God, about which Mark narrates considerably more. In terms of systematic theology, one would
distinguish, perhaps dramatically, between "theology" and "Christology." Such abstract distinctions seem less relevant when the task
is understanding the narrative Christology of the Markan Gospel.[35] If
Christology has to do with Jesus, the main character of the narrative,

---

33. Elizabeth Struthers Malbon, "The Christology of Mark's Gospel: Narrative Christology
and the Markan Jesus," in *Who Do You Say That I Am? Essays on Christology* (Festschrift
for Jack Dean Kingsbury; ed. Mark Allan Powell and David R. Bauer; Louisville: Westminster
John Knox, 1999), 33–48; cf. 37 with the previous paragraph of the present essay.

34. Cf. this paragraph with Malbon, "Christology of Mark's Gospel," 44. On the Markan
"Son of Man" sayings, see my essay, "Narrative Christology and the Son of Man: What the
Markan Jesus Says Instead," *BibInt* 11, no 3/4 (2003): 373–85. John R. Donahue, SJ, briefly
discusses "the picture of Jesus as proclaimer of the kingdom and as Son of Man" as "two of the
major metaphors by which Jesus is presented in the Gospel of Mark" ("Jesus as the Parable of
God in the Gospel of Mark," in *Interpreting the Gospels* [ed. James Luther Mays; Philadelphia:
Fortress, 1981], 148–67, quotation from 156; first published in *Int* 32 [1978]: 369–86).

35. Cf. M. Eugene Boring: "For Mark, to tell the story of *Jesus* is to talk about *God,* the
one God. Thus to dispute whether the Markan narrative is theocentric or christocentric is a
misplaced question" ("Markan Christology: God-Language for Jesus?" *NTS* 45 [1999]: 451–
71, quotation from 471).

and if what the main character says is important for understanding him, then a thorough investigation of Markan narrative Christology must consider everything Jesus says.

To make a beginning, I am focusing on two specific topics of Jesus' speech: the "Son of Man," considered elsewhere, and the "kingdom of God," considered here. My investigation of Christology deflected and refracted in Mark suggests that the Markan Jesus is more eager to speak of God than of himself.[36] This narrative fact tells us as much (or more!) about Jesus as it does about God. What the character Jesus says about the "kingdom of God" is thus an important element of Markan narrative Christology.

There are fourteen Markan references to "kingdom of God,"[37] the same number as "Son of Man" references. I do not mention this to suggest some fantastical numerical symbolism (although that would be easy enough to do: fourteen is twice seven; seven is the number of completeness; fourteen represents double completeness; and so on — let the reader smile!). I mention the numbers to note that, at least by frequency, "Son of Man" and "kingdom of God" have a similar

---

36. For an insightful discussion of *theos* (God) as "A Neglected Factor in the Theology of Mark" see John R. Donahue's article by that name in *JBL* 101 (1982): 563–94. Donahue's "overview and general impression" provides an appropriate background for my look at the Markan Jesus' "kingdom of God" statements: "As one would expect, most references to God are on the lips of Jesus. Jesus speaks of God as the creator of the world and the human family (13:19; 10:6), who will bring human history to a close (13:20) and who prepares a place for the elect (13:20, 27; cf. 10:40). God has power to do what is beyond human conception (10:27); is alone good (10:18); issues commands and has a will which is to be followed (3:35; 7:8); is to be addressed as father in prayer (11:25; 14:36); and is the living God of Abraham, Isaac and Jacob (12:27). The observation that there is nothing distinctly new or Christian in this picture of God in respect to the OT or Jewish thought of the time may be true. What is significant, however, is that in Mark, Jesus speaks of God without attributes or ascriptions. With the exception of 11:25 (*ho en tois ouranois*), derivatively in 12:27 (*theos zonton*), and 9:37 (*ton aposteilanta me*), *theos* stands without attributes or ascription, a fact which makes Mark almost singular in the NT."

"Such reserved speech about God is strong especially in contrast to the anthropomorphism of Matthew and the interventionist or salvation history perspective of Luke" (566–67). The Markan Jesus who deflects attention from himself to God honors God with reserved speech.

37. Donahue presents the following data on the Markan use of *theos* (God): "The text of Mark contains the term *theos* forty-eight times. There are fourteen 'kingdom of God' sayings, of which thirteen are on the lips of Jesus, and five appellations of the phrase 'Son of God,' of which three are on the lips of demons, one is the superscription, and one is the final reference by the centurion. Apart from the kingdom sayings Jesus speaks of God directly seventeen times, and *theos* is explicitly used in seven OT citations on the lips of Jesus while in two citations God is the presumed speaker without being explicitly mentioned (7:6 = Isa 29:13; 11:17 = Isa 56:7). There are five other usages of *theos*, two by the narrator (1:14; 2:12) and three by others in the gospel" ("Neglected Factor," 565).

weight in the Markan narrative. All fourteen "Son of Man" statements are on the lips of Jesus; all but one (15:43) of the fourteen
"kingdom of God" statements are his as well. As "Son of Man" is
the Markan Jesus' unique perspective, so "kingdom of God" is his
unique proclamation.[38]

The term "kingdom" comes from the secular world — where David
(11:10) and Herod (6:23) can have kingdoms, along with other nations (13:8). Herod offers to give Herodias's dancing daughter up to
half of his kingdom (6:23). The crowd welcoming Jesus into Jerusalem anticipates "the coming kingdom of our ancestor David!"
(11:10; NRSV here and throughout). Jesus warns four of his disciples
(13:3; but see 13:37) in his eschatological discourse that "nation will
rise against nation, and kingdom against kingdom" (13:8a). "Kingdom" can also be applied metaphorically[39] to the reign of Satan. The
Markan Jesus argues with the scribes who come down from Jerusalem, who accuse him of casting out demons "by the ruler of the
demons" (3:22), that "if a kingdom is divided against itself, that
kingdom cannot stand.... And if Satan has risen up against himself
and is divided, he cannot stand, but his end has come" (3:24, 26).
This is a profound image for Mark's Gospel, for, as one might note
in relation to enacted Christology, the actions of the Markan Jesus as
powerful exorcist of demons and healer, and as authoritative preacher
and teacher as well, serve as evidence that the kingdom of Satan *has*
come to an end because the kingdom of God has begun.

In Mark's Gospel, *basileia,* kingdom, is dominantly used to refer
to the *basileia tou theou,* the "kingdom (rule/reign) of God." Jesus
is often said to preach or to teach, and he is often called "teacher"
in Mark. These narrative facts have clear significance for the enacted

---

38. Donahue asserts: "In taking over the proclamation of the kingdom of God, Mark is
doubtless close to the historical Jesus. However, he does not simply record this tradition but
makes kingdom into a major theological motif which spans the whole Gospel" ("Parable of
God," 156).

39. Obviously there is a metaphorical dimension to the Markan reference to "the coming
kingdom of our ancestor David" (11:10) as well, since David is long dead, but his "kingdom"
is still "coming."

Christology of Mark's Gospel, whereby Jesus' deeds reveal more than others' words. The dominant theme of Jesus' preaching and teaching is the inbreaking of the "kingdom of God."[40] The Gospel's first "kingdom" reference — during the first narrated activity of Jesus' ministry after his baptism and testing have established his commission from God — presents the archetype of Jesus' preaching: "Jesus came to Galilee, proclaiming the good news of God, and saying, 'The time [*kairos*] is fulfilled, and the kingdom of God has come near; repent, and believe in the good news' " (1:14–15). This proclamation, of course, raises more questions than it answers: What is the significance of *kairos?* How is it fulfilled? If the kingdom of God has come near, is it already here, or not yet here? How is Jesus' demand for repentance related to John's (cf. 1:4–5)? What does it mean to *believe* in the good news? Yet, as Tannehill notes, "This scene relates the whole mission of Jesus to the coming of God's kingdom."[41]

The second "kingdom of God" reference is equally significant — and equally cryptic. Whereas the first reference establishes Jesus as the kingdom's proclaimer, the second establishes his followers as its participants. The Markan Jesus, "when he was alone," said to "those who were around him along with the twelve" (4:10): "To you has been given the mystery [*mystērion;* NRSV, secret] of the kingdom of God, but for those outside, everything comes in parables (4:11). As it turns out, being given the *mystērion* is not unlike being given a parable; it is more like being enabled to experience the right questions than knowing the right answer. In fact, receiving the *mystērion* of the "kingdom of God" makes life no easier for Jesus' followers than being the proclaimer of its arrival does for Jesus himself. While the news of God's nearness is good, it is also shocking and demanding. For this reason parables are especially appropriate for communicating news of the "kingdom of God."

---

40. According to Donahue, "By making the kingdom proclamation and sayings such a dominant motif and integrative factor in the Gospel, Mark gives a radically new referent to kingdom" ("Parable of God," 157).

41. Tannehill, "Narrative Christology," 64.

"The kingdom of God is as if . . . " (4:26) and "With what can we compare the kingdom of God?" (4:30) serve as introductory formulas for the Markan Jesus' parabolic speaking in chapter 4. Much has been written about the parables of Jesus, the parables in Mark, and even Jesus as the parable of God in Mark.[42] The present essay is not the place to review or attempt to extend those discussions, although I acknowledge my dependence on what I have learned from them. My question is, rather, how does what the Markan Jesus says about the "kingdom of God" influence the narrative Christology of Mark's Gospel? Do Jesus' images of the "kingdom of God" refract any other conceptions of it? Certainly anyone expecting "kingdom" images of power and glory (conquering armies of celestial beings and cosmic battles) will have been disappointed with the Markan Jesus' talk of planting seeds. Adding to the surprise are the observations that not all the seeds flourish, that we do "not know how" (4:27) those that manage to grow do so, and that a tiny seed grows not into the mighty tree one might expect of a storyteller but into a common shrub, or even a good-sized weed! The images of Jesus' parables in chapter 4 grow out of his proclamation that "the kingdom of God has come near" (1:15); God is a real presence in the world, but God's rule is not (or not yet) overwhelming the world. In terms of narrative Christology, Jesus is one who experiences God's nearness in this surprising way and tries to enable others to experience it as well. One has to have ears to hear, says the parabolic speaker of chapter 4.[43]

In chapter 10, Jesus' metaphoric speaking — and acting — also relies on "kingdom of God" language. The Markan Jesus blesses the little children whom the disciples had apparently tried to turn away (10:13–16) and affirms that "the kingdom of God belongs" "to such as these" (10:14) — powerless children, expected to do as others require — and that "whoever does not receive the kingdom of God as a

---

42. For bibliography, see John R. Donahue, SJ, *The Gospel in Parable* (Philadelphia: Fortress, 1988).

43. As Donahue puts it: "The kingdom of God is not simply as Perrin notes a 'tensive symbol' for God's sovereignty, but is now a metaphor of that power manifest in the life and teaching of Jesus. Jesus is the proclaimer of the kingdom, but in Mark's presentation the kingdom also proclaims Jesus" ("Parable of God," 157).

little child will never enter it" (10:15). Children, low in social status, are the models for those who would enter the kingdom of God. Similarly, and equally surprisingly, the rich, high in social status, present an image of those for whom such entry is somewhere between difficult and impossible. "How hard it will be for those who have wealth to enter the kingdom of God!" (10:23), Jesus tells his disciples after the man who "had many possessions" "was shocked and went away grieving" (10:22) at Jesus' request to give his possessions away to the poor and come, follow him (10:21). The disciples too are perplexed at such words (10:24). But Jesus refracts their status-quo thinking with a colorful image: "It is easier for a camel to go through the eye of a needle than for someone who is rich to enter the kingdom of God" (10:25). If the "kingdom of God" challenges the status quo to this extent, it is no wonder that the established leaders challenge its proclaimer.

It may not be just the rich who have difficulty entering the "kingdom of God." Sandwiched between Jesus' two sayings about this difficulty of the rich is a saying that could have more general import: "Children, how hard it is to enter the kingdom of God!" (10:24). Although there are textual variants that blunt the general impact by adding "for those who trust in riches," the dialogue of Jesus and his disciples in the following verses (10:26–27) suggests the broader application. Disciples: "Then who can be saved?" (10:26). Jesus: "For mortals it is impossible, but not for God; for God all things are possible" (10:27). But however difficult the entry, sacrificing one's power, one's wealth, even — with the Jewish storyteller's usual hyperbole — one's eye is worthwhile, for "it is better for you to enter the kingdom of God with one eye than to have two eyes and to be thrown into hell" (9:47). If the "kingdom of God" is this demanding, it is no wonder that its proclaimer infuriates his foes and challenges his followers.

Since the kingdom of Satan is being overthrown (see 3:23–27), choices must be made. Those who hear Jesus' proclamation, like the Jesus who proclaims it, live at a decisive moment in time — a *kairos*. Just after the baptism and testing scenes in the wilderness, the Markan

Jesus announces that the *kairos* is fulfilled (1:15). Just before the transfiguration scene on the high mountain, Jesus announces that "there are some standing here who will not taste death until they see that the kingdom of God has come with power" (9:1). At the close of the Last Supper scene, Jesus announces, "I will never again drink of the fruit of the vine until that day when I drink it new in the kingdom of God" (14:25). The kingdom of God has come, and yet the kingdom of God is still to come. It is not a mere matter of chronology, in which already and not yet are mutually exclusive, but a *kairos*.[44]

The kingdom of God has come near, but one must be given its *mystērion;* one must have eyes to see and ears to hear. Some do. The Markan Jesus says to a scribe (surprisingly enough) with whom he has been discussing the greatest commandment, "You are not far from the kingdom of God" (12:34). Not only has the kingdom of God come near you, but you have come near the kingdom of God! One must receive the *mystērion* that one is given. And after Jesus can say no more about the kingdom, having "breathed his last" (15:39), the *narrator* picks up the phrase for the first — and only — time, in describing Joseph of Arimathea, "a respected member of the council" (very possibly the council that condemned Jesus to death[45]), as one "who was also himself waiting expectantly [or "looking"; *prosdechomenos*] for the kingdom of God" (15:43). The kingdom has come and is coming. The narrator, picking up Jesus' "kingdom" language, invites the implied audience to share the position of Joseph of Arimathea.

The kingdom has come (1:15); the kingdom is coming (9:1; 12:34; 14:25; cf. 15:43) — that is what the Markan Jesus says. And what the Markan Jesus says is a significant clue to the Markan Gospel's

---

44. Cf. M. Eugene Boring on the tensive nature of history and eschatology in Mark: "The eschatological battle with Satan has already been won and demons flee before the triumphant Christ, for the eschaton has arrived and the world is different. But also the world still goes on as before. To speak of this situation as '*zwischen den Zeiten*' is to make it more chronological than Mark in fact wants to make it.... Diachronic language cannot do justice to the synchronic reality which struggles to be expressed." ("The Christology of Mark: Hermeneutical Issues for Systematic Theology," *Semeia* 30 [1984]: 125–53, quotation from 140).

45. Contra Kingsbury, *Conflict,* 123–24 n. 46, 125 n. 87.

"Christology." Although the Markan narrator proclaims Jesus as the "Christ, the Son of God," the Markan Jesus proclaims the inbreaking of the "kingdom of God." The deflected, refracted (and enacted) Christology of the Markan Jesus is "theology."[46] The one anointed by God (Messiah, Christ), chosen by God (Son of God; see Ps 2), and obedient to God (a son of God in Jewish usage) is the one who senses that God is near, even if others do not, and faithfully proclaims God's presence as good news.

Narrative Christology, Kingdom, and Parable: In Lieu of a Conclusion

As proclaimer of the surprising "kingdom of God" (and speaker of the puzzling "Son of Man" statements), the Markan Jesus is, as John Donahue has artfully shown, presented as the parable of God in the Gospel of Mark.[47] Following C. H. Dodd's influential definition of a parable, Donahue illustrates how each element applies to an aspect of Mark's portrayal of Jesus. I also suggest that Dodd's definition of a parable parallels the aspects of Markan narrative Christology I have labeled Christology deflected and refracted (and enacted and reflected). In *The Parables of the Kingdom* Dodd wrote: "At its simplest the parable is a metaphor or simile drawn from nature or common life, arresting the hearer by its vividness or strangeness, and leaving the mind in sufficient doubt about its precise application to tease it into active thought."[48] The story of Jesus of Nazareth has metaphoric

---

46. In the sense of *narrative* "theology," not systematic theology. Cf. Michael L. Cook, SJ: "In an ultimate sense the most important character in Mark's story world is God. . . . Jesus' view of God, inseparable from God's view of Jesus, is expressed throughout the gospel" (*Christology as a Narrative Quest* [Collegeville, Minn.: Liturgical Press, 1997], 96). Cf. also Boring: "In the Markan narrative, to encounter Jesus is to deal with God" ("Christology of Mark," 139).

47. See the full citation in note 35, above. "Since parable has now become not simply a description of a select group of sayings of Jesus, but an independent hermeneutical and theological category," Donahue argues, "we will propose that Mark's Gospel can be presented as a narrative parable of the meaning of the life and death of Jesus." "Such a [parabolic] reading means that the Gospel's presentation of Jesus is always 'open-ended' and always calls for revisioning and restatement" ("Parable of God," 149, 155).

48. C. H. Dodd, *The Parables of the Kingdom* (Glasgow: Collins, 1961), 16.

significance but is "drawn from...common life."[49] Enacted Christology stresses how much is revealed about Jesus in his actions, rather than in what others say about him. Reflected Christology illustrates within the narrative the metaphoric power of Jesus' life that extends beyond the narrative. But Jesus' actions and his words — especially about the "Son of Man" and the "kingdom of God" — are so vivid and strange, even in relation to the narrator, that they arrest the audience, leave doubt, and tease the audience into active thought.

In the terms of Tannehill, who initiated the discussion of Markan narrative Christology:

> To a surprising degree Jesus' action, rather than replacing the action of others, calls forth the action of others. Jesus becomes the ameliorator of others in that he incites them to become ameliorators for themselves and others. In other words, Jesus functions frequently as an influencer, one who moves others to action.[50]

The key issue involving Jesus is not "identity" but influence. Markan narrative Christology focuses not on essence (What is Jesus' nature?) but on process (What are the dynamics of the relationships Jesus establishes and encourages?). The parables of the kingdom of God demand response, and so does their Markan "parabler." The narrative christological question for Mark's Gospel is not "Who is Jesus?" but "What will his hearers do?"

In the terms I have applied to Markan narrative Christology here, the deflected and refracted Christology of the Markan narrative challenges the implied audience to deal with the tension between an assertive narrator who proclaims "Jesus Christ, the Son of God" and a reticent Jesus who deflects attention and honor, challenges traditional views, and insistently proclaims not himself but God. By

---

49. Cf. Donahue: "In Mark, Jesus is truly the parable of God, but the way to God is not through any docetic circumvention of the human Jesus. In the case of Jesus himself, no less than in the parables he utters, the scandal of the human is the starting point for the unfolding of the mystery of God" ("Parable of God," 160).

50. Tannehill, "Narrative Christology," 63.

creating this tension between narrator and protagonist, the Markan implied author is able to present Jesus the parabler as a parable, as one who teases others into active thought. The implied author of Mark sets up this tension to draw in the implied audience — not to resolve the tension but to receive it as the *mystērion* that is given, to receive it, as Tannehill also hopes, "with full appreciation of its power to challenge."[51]

---

51. Ibid., 60.

11

Creating the Kingdom

The Performance of Mark as Revelatory Event

Whitney Shiner

Nearly twenty-five years ago Robert Tannehill published *The Sword of His Mouth*, a pioneering work in the rhetoric of the Gospels. In this work he drew attention to the importance of literary and rhetorical style in the creation of meaning in the Synoptic Gospels. He took interpreters to task for reducing the meaning of the biblical text to clear assertions about historical facts or theological propositions. "There are other types of language," he insisted, "which have their own values, of which interpretation must take account." Deep or expressive language presents meaning through its manner of expression, so that meaning cannot be abstracted from the language in which it is imbedded.[1] One of the important functions of expressive language is to lead readers to new visions of themselves and their worlds. Following Ray Hart, Tannehill argued that imagination is the medium of revelatory knowledge. "Revelation, as God's call to man to be man, is mediated through the imagination, which, as the will's mental mode, makes possible the modification of the will, the principle of order at the center of man's being."[2] Revelation takes the route of art and rhetoric to enter into the soul. In particular, Tannehill was interested in imaginative and forceful language as the medium of revelation.

---

1. Robert C. Tannehill, *The Sword of His Mouth: Forceful and Imaginative Language in Synoptic Sayings* (Seimeia Supplements 1; Philadelphia: Fortress; Missoula, Mont.: Scholars, 1975), 11–13; quotation from p. 11.
2. Ibid., 21–22; quotation from p. 22.

This article follows Tannehill's insight that the Gospels are not only records of revelation but are intended to serve as a vehicles of revelation. While Tannehill concerned himself with the way that the style of the Gospel language worked upon our imaginations to bring about revelation, I am here concerned with the way the performance of the Gospel functions as a revelatory event.

In the years since the publication of *The Sword of His Mouth*, scholars have become much more aware of the importance of oral expression in the culture of the first century. At that time oral speech still remained primary. Except for bureaucratic functions, writing was largely understood as a record of oral speech, either speech delivered at a previous time or speech to be delivered in the future or at a distance. The letters remained dead on the page until brought to life by a human voice. The ancients understood deeply the point made by Tannehill in *The Sword of His Mouth*. Communication is much more than propositions. It is emotion. It is the authority of a personal presence. It is the forcefulness of a passionate delivery.

How would the Gospel have been delivered in such a culture? Based on available analogies, the following seem most likely: the Gospel would have been presented orally. The text would have been presented from memory, the performer having memorized the narrative either word for word or more likely in its general structure and flow. The presentation style would have been dramatic, with a full range of voice inflection and gesturing. The style would be considered extremely bombastic by most twenty-first century American standards. Dialogue would have been presented in character. There would be an emphasis on creating an emotional impact. The performer would make use of dialogue to address his audience directly. And the listeners would be extremely involved in the performance through their own reactions to the narrative, applauding the triumphs of Jesus and the performer and reviling Jesus' opponents.[3]

---

3. For a more detailed analysis of the oral nature of first-century culture and of the manner in which one would expect the Gospels to be presented within that culture, see Whitney Shiner, *Proclaiming the Gospel: First-Century Performance of Mark* (Harrisburg, Pa.: Trinity Press International, 2003). Some of the material in this chapter appears in that work as well.

The two points most important for this essay are the emotional nature of an expected performance and the phenomenon of dialogue being experienced as direct address by the audience.

This line of investigation assumes that with an oral performance the proper subject for interpretation is the performance event rather than the text. The text of Mark provides clues to the nature of the performance event, but I am intending here to exegete the reconstructed event rather than the text itself. Actual performance events would vary widely. Even within a particular performance, different members of the audience would have quite different experiences. Thus the claim I am making for my exegesis is rather limited: the text as we have it seems to correlate well with the type of experience I am suggesting.

Liminality and Revelation

It is my belief that the performance of the Gospel served to induce a particular social and psychological state in the audience that facilitated an experience of revelation. This revelation may have come through something experienced after the completion of the performance. Specifically, if the Gospel narrative was performed in conjunction with baptism, the revelation may have occurred in the experience of baptism as mediated through the liminal state induced by the performance.[4] The revelation may also have come through the experience of the performance itself. The Gospel performance leads the audience to strongly identify with the death of Jesus. The early church seems to have considered such an experience of identification to be transformative and revelatory.

---

4. The performance of Mark as part of a baptism ritual has been suggested by a number of scholars, including Robin Scroggs and Kent I. Groff, "Baptism in Mark: Dying and Rising with Christ," *JBL* 92 (1973): 531–48; Benoit Standaert, *L'Évangile selon Marc: Composition et genre littéraire* (Nijmegen: Stichting Studentenpers, 1978); Augustine Stock, *The Method and Message of Mark* (Wilmington, Del.: Michael Glazier, 1989); and Mark McVann, "Baptism, Miracles, and Boundary Jumping in Mark," *BTB* 21 (1991): 151–57. For a critique of the idea, see Ernest Best, *Mark: The Gospel as Story* (Edinburgh: T & T Clark, 1983), 95–98.

This social and psychological state conducive of revelation has been designated liminality by the anthropologist Victor Turner.[5] Turner used the term to describe a transitional state that occurs in many rites of passage.[6] Arnold van Gennep had earlier argued that all rituals associated with passage from one state to another are marked by three phases: separation from the earlier state; margin or limen (threshold), in which the ritual subject possesses the attributes of neither state; and aggregation, in which the subject is reintegrated into society in his or her new state.[7]

The liminal state, Turner argues, is one outside of structure. Liminality may be likened to death, to being in the womb, to darkness, to the wilderness, and to an eclipse of the sun or moon. Liminal persons may be described as possessing nothing. They have no status, property, or anything indicating their normal status or role or distinguishing them from other neophytes. Their behavior is normally passive or humble and obedient to their instructor. Often they are expected to accept arbitrary punishment. Among themselves, neophytes develop an intense comradeship and egalitarianism, which Turner

---

5. Mark McVann has applied the concept to the Gospel of Mark in "The Passion in Mark: Transformation Ritual," *BTB* 18 (1988): 96–101; and "Baptism," 151–57. See also Carol Schersten LaHurd, "Biblical Exorcism and Reader Response to Ritual in Narrative," in *The Daemonic Imagination: Biblical Text and Secular Story* (ed. Robert Detweiler and William G. Doty; American Academy of Religion Studies in Religion 60; Atlanta: Scholars, 1990), 53–63; idem, "Reader Response to Ritual Elements in Mark 5:1–20," *BTB* 20 (1990): 154–60; Mark McVann, ed., "Transformations, Passages, and Processes: Ritual Approaches to Biblical Texts," *Semeia* 67 (1994); esp. Mark McVann, "Reading Mark Ritually: Honor-Shame and the Ritual of Baptism," *Semeia* 67 (1994): 179–98; and reply by Carol Schersten LaHurd, "Exactly What's Ritual about the Experience of Reading/Hearing Mark's Gospel?" *Semeia* 67 (1994): 199–208; A. Kirk, "Crossing the Boundary: Liminality and Transformative Wisdom in Q," *NTS* 45 (1999): 1–18.

Wayne A. Meeks has applied the concept to early Christian baptism in *The First Urban Christians: The Social World of the Apostle Paul* (New Haven: Yale University Press, 1983), 88–89. J. Randall Nichols has applied the concept of liminality to contemporary Christian worship in "Worship as Anti-Structure: The Contribution of Victor Turner," *ThTo* 41 (1985): 401–9. See also Mark Kline Taylor, "In Praise of Shaky Ground: The Liminal Christ and Cultural Pluralism," *ThTo* 43 (1986): 36–51.

6. Victor Turner, "Betwixt and Between: The Liminal Period in *Rites de Passage*," *Proceedings of the American Ethnological Society* (Seattle: University of Washington Press, 1964); reprinted in idem, ed., *The Forest of Symbols: Aspects of Ndembu Ritual* (Ithaca: Cornell University Press, 1967), 93–111; idem, *The Ritual Process: Structure and Anti-Structure* (Ithaca: Cornell University Press, 1969).

7. Arnold van Gennep, *The Rites of Passage* (London: Routledge & Kegan Paul, 1909).

designated as communitas. The liminal state is characterized by low-liness, homogeneity, equality, comradeship, anonymity, unselfishness, sacredness, sacred instruction, silence, suspension of kinship rights and obligations, and acceptance of pain and suffering.[8]

It will be helpful if we distinguish between various aspects of liminality. On the one hand, there is a socially defined state of being outside of the normal structures of society. This is an objective state that can be recognized by those outside of the ritual as well as those undergoing the ritual. This I will call *social liminality*. On the other hand, there is the interior state of those undergoing the ritual, which I will call *liminal consciousness*. The liminal consciousness may be further distinguished into a *disintegrative* aspect, the disorientation caused by loss of structure and the physical and psychological stresses which the initiate experiences; and an *integrative* aspect, the feeling of communitas and oneness that may be part of the liminal experience.

While the concept of liminality was developed to describe a short-term state that takes place within a ritual, there are cases where the liminal state continues on a long-term basis. Turner notes the connection between liminality and millenarian movements. In millenarian movements, society as a whole is understood as going through a transformation. The old structures have passed. The new ones have not yet arrived. The liminal state continues until God acts to end it.[9]

Turner also notes that in Christianity, as in other major religions, many of the qualities of liminality are regarded as enduring religious virtues. The religious person is expected to live in a state of continual liminality.[10] The Gospel of Mark presents an ideology of living liminally. The last shall be first; the first shall be last. The Son of Man came not to be served but to serve. Whoever wishes to save her life will lose it. Sell all you have and follow me. Those who do the will of God are my mother and brothers and sisters. There are also frequent scenes of liminal action: John the Baptist in the wilderness, the baptism and temptation of Jesus, the disciples abandoning their

8. Turner, *Ritual Process*, 106–7.
9. Ibid., 111–12; 153–54.
10. Ibid., 107–8.

homes and jobs and families in obedience to Jesus, the wandering life of Jesus and his disciples, esoteric teaching, Jesus' acceptance of death.[11] All this is put in a context of cosmic liminality. The world itself is undergoing a transformation from its earlier state into the coming kingdom of God.

Liminality is related to revelation in three different ways. First, the integrative experience of liminal consciousness is itself a revelation of the divine. Most societies recognize those undergoing rites of passage as sacred in recognition of the fact that the liminal experience of the primordial oneness of humanity apart from the specific structures of particular societies is closer to the divine than is ordinary structured social life. The liminal experience of oneness is intended to carry over into ordinary life as a restraint on the selfishness that is a part of everyday social activity. As Turner states,

> In preindustrial and early industrial societies with multiplex social relations, spontaneous communitas appears to be very frequently associated with mystical power and to be regarded as a charism or grace sent by the deities or ancestors. Nevertheless, by impetrative ritual means, attempts are made, mostly in the phases of liminal seclusion, to cause the deities or ancestors to bring this charism of communitas among men.[12]

While it is hoped that the deities will respond to entreaty, it is much more likely that they will if other aspects of liminal consciousness are created through ritual means. The ritual itself is a form of entreaty for the gift of communitas.

Second, the liminal state makes one more receptive to the sacred, often esoteric, instruction that one receives in the course of the rite of passage. The original source of such instruction is often understood

---

11. McVann has noted that several of these narrative events fit the ritual pattern of separation, liminality, reintegration. McVann argues that the trial and death of Jesus should be understood as a ritual of status elevation. While there are certainly strong parallels, not all experiences of liminality are ritual. Ritual implies both intention on the part of a ritual official and recognition of the ritual efficacy on the part of some community. See McVann, "Passion in Mark," 96–101; "Baptism," 151–57; "Reading Mark Ritually," 179–98.

12. Turner, *Ritual Process*, 137–38.

to be divine, and the liminal state allows those being instructed to recover aspects of the original revelatory experience. As Turner states,

> The arcane knowledge or *"gnosis"* obtained in the liminal period is felt to change the inmost nature of the neophyte, impressing him, as a seal impresses wax, with the characteristics of his new state. It is not a mere acquisition of knowledge, but a change in being.[13]

Third, in some cases the liminal state is expected to facilitate a personal revelation from the divine or the spiritual world. The vision quest practiced by some North American peoples is one example. Another is found in the West African groups in which initiation into the priesthood of a divinity includes possession by the divinity. The early Christian parallel would be reception of the Holy Spirit during baptism.

Gospel Performance as Liminal Event

I have already suggested that the Gospel of Mark presents an ideology of liminality and numerous accounts of liminal events. The same could be said of the other canonical Gospels, but Mark goes beyond the narrative of liminality to create a liminal consciousness in the listeners. Many of the well-known features of the Gospel contribute to this effect. In my experience, the effect of these features is often much more pronounced in oral performance.

The Ending

Let us begin with the end. The ending is the most important point in any narrative in determining the lasting effect that is impressed upon the audience. The ending of the Gospel of Mark may be one of the most bizarre in the history of literature. A typical narrative plot is in its basic structure similar to a rite of passage. There is a more or less stable initial state. The initial state is disrupted through conflict and

---

13. Turner, *Forest of Symbols,* 102.

tension. The conflict or tension is resolved into a new more or less stable state. Aristotle's definition of tragedy as the catharsis of pity and fear recognizes this pattern.[14] We begin watching a tragedy in our ordinary state as members of a structured society. The experience of pity and fear temporarily moves us outside of our ordinary selves to some more primal level. Catharsis and closure allow us to return to our ordinary lives, though somewhat transformed by the experience. Mark does not allow us to experience this return to a stable state.

This is one of the points at which my experience as a performer of Mark is very different from my experience as a silent reader. As a silent reader I have never been bothered by the ending of Mark. It is curious, but in the twentieth century we became used to curious endings and lack of closure. As a silent reader my reaction is one of approbation. That is so Markan. Even at the end he does not let up. He never allows us to domesticate Jesus. As a performer, however, I find the ending extremely disconcerting. As a performer, I feel an obligation to bring the performance to a close. There is something quite impolite about not providing closure, and I have found no way to make Mark appear closed. The audience expects the empty tomb to provide closure and a structure with which we can return to our ordinary reality. Women running away in fear is obviously not the end. The audience is staring with expectation: *Provide us with an ending!* On occasion I have felt impelled to add, "The End," just to get myself off the hook. Almost always someone asks incredulously, "Is *that* how it ends?" The lack of closure leaves us in liminality. We are brought out of our ordinary reality by the preceding narrative, and we are given no map for how to return.

There are other associations between the ending and liminality. The resurrection of Jesus is an immense disruption of the normal structures of life and death. The women are prevented from fulfilling their social obligations. They are given new obligations, which they fail to fulfill. The purposeful breach of social or religious obligation is a common way of inducing liminality in rites of passage.[15] Early

---

14. Aristotle, *Poetica* 6.2; 1449b.
15. Turner, *Ritual Process*, 160–62.

Christians may have become used to breaking certain social and religious conventions in their lives as Christians. Hence, the failure of the women to fulfill their new obligations presented within the text, to go and tell the disciples and Peter, must have been much more effective in the production of this liminality that disrupts burial obligations. Finally, the sense of fear and awe that pervades the ending is frequently part of liminal consciousness.

The Crucifixion

Of course, the ending cannot leave us in liminality unless the preceding portions of the Gospel have already brought us there. The passion scene immediately preceding the nonending creates a particularly strong need for catharsis and closure; the passion scene is absolutely brilliant as a provocation to the liminal state. This is another place where performance of the Gospel has radically transformed my understanding. The crucifixion scene ranks next to the ending as the most disconcerting part of the Gospel to perform.

Mark's approach to the crucifixion is curious. It is not triumphalistic or heroic, like the passion in John or Luke. Nor does it describe in excruciating detail the physical torments of his death, as do the martyrdom scenes in the books of Maccabees. Instead, the suffering of Jesus is expressed through the mockery and the cry of dereliction.

The reason I find the crucifixion scene hard to perform is that it does not allow me to do what I feel I ought to be doing. What I want to do is to express sympathy for the pain of Jesus and my own sorrow at his death. The discussions of pathos in the rhetorical handbooks lead me to expect that a first-century performer would adopt the same approach.[16] When I first performed the Gospel, that is what I did. I would choke up a little and get misty-eyed and present the scene as if watching it from the outside, from afar. The rhetorical handbooks, however, say that in the presentation of narrative one should try to

---

16. [Aristotle], *Rhetorica ad Alexandrum* 34, 1439b–1440a; 36, 1444b–1445a; Quintilian, *Institutio oratoria* 6.1.53.

present a scene as realistically as possible, and speech should be done in character.[17] If I follow those rules, the scene changes radically.

The cry of dereliction I enjoy. I have one line to express the suffering of Jesus. I muster up every ounce of pain I have felt in my life and cry in a loud voice, *"Eloi! Eloi! Lema sabachthani?"* Then I get to repeat it in English (15:34). This cry is quite cathartic for me, though it appears to be disconcerting for the audience.

It is the mockery that is disconcerting to perform. I want to be presenting sympathy for Jesus. Instead, I am standing in front of everyone, yelling insults at Jesus while he is dying in pain: *Hey, **Messiah**! King of **Israel**! Come on down from the cross so that we might see and believe!*[18] *Nyah, nyah, nyah, nyah, nyah.* When I read that silently, I think of the cleverness of Mark's irony. When I perform it, it just seems nasty. Almost the entire scene consists of mockery. About halfway through the scene, it begins to feel quite bizarre. This is the foundational narrative of Christianity. This is the climactic scene around which the whole narrative is built. I am standing here yelling blasphemous things at Jesus. The audience is sitting there listening to me insult Jesus. What a strange way to celebrate the Son of God! If I wanted to hear someone revile Jesus, I could go out on the street and find one of Vespasian's soldiers, or I could go down to the synagogue and debate with the Pharisees. The assembly of God's people should be the one place where I do not have to put up with that.

Mark's passion story is absolutely brilliant for two reasons. First, he re-creates the one part of Jesus' suffering that I can experience in the audience. If the performer describes the physical agony of crucifixion, it is something external to me. It is something I sympathize with. If the performer describes the mental anguish of Jesus, it is still

---

17. Aristotle, *Rhetorica* 3.11; 1411b; anon., *Rhetorica ad Herennium* 4.47.60; 4.48.61; 4.49.62; Cicero, *De oratore* 3.40.160; Quintilian, *Inst.* 3.8.51; 4.1.47; 4.5.22; 6.2.29–36; 10.2.26; Longinus, *Ars Rhetorica* (Walz 9.567 = Spengel-Hammer 1.2.194); Seneca the Elder, *Controversiae* 2.4.8.

18. From this point on, I am abandoning the normal conventions for quotations from Scripture. Text from Mark will be italicized rather than placed within quotation marks, and no chapter and verse citations will be given. This is done to minimize distracting visual elements and create a more oral-friendly typography. Italicized elements should be read with full emotional inflection.

external to me. My reaction is still one of sympathy. If the performer yells insults at Jesus, I experience that directly. That SOB is insulting Jesus, and since Jesus is *my* Lord and *my* Savior, that SOB is insulting me. This is one of the places where dialogue in the narrative becomes direct address to the audience. Mark puts the audience directly in the place of Jesus.

Ritualized abuse is a common feature of rites of passage. Commenting on the arbitrary punishment that is part of many such rituals, Turner remarks, "It is as though they [the initiates] are being reduced or ground down to a uniform condition to be fashioned anew."[19] The initiate has to accept the abuse with humility. Mark's audience cannot fight back against this abuse. The performer has been granted authority to tell the story. It is ritual. I have to distance myself from my ego and accept it.

The state of liminality involves not only a loss of the socially structured sense of self but also the suppression of the ego self, which is so closely bound up with it. Abuse produces liminality only when I do not engage in my normal emotional reaction to it. This is the second brilliant thing about the crucifixion scene in terms of the production of liminality. My natural emotional reaction is totally subverted. I want to feel sympathy for Jesus. Instead, I experience someone heaping abuse on him. The cry of dereliction looks like a place where I ought to be able to indulge in a little sympathy. This is just raw pain. It ought to be easy to sympathize with this pain, but Mark does not grant me a pause for me to experience that. Instead, I meet some fool in the narrative thinking he is calling for Elijah. The rapid switching among strong unprocessed emotions is disorienting and further serves to induce a liminal consciousness.

Another feature of the passion narrative that facilitates liminality is the enacted destruction of the primary social institution for mediation between God and humanity. *And the curtain of the temple was ripped in two, from top to bottom.* Any gesture indicating the ripping of the curtain is necessarily violent. The performer is expected to make

---

19. Turner, *Ritual Process*, 95.

the destruction of the curtain present for the listeners. If Mark is performed after the destruction of the temple, such an enactment would certainly bring to mind that recent event. Since Mark does not recount the gory details of the crucifixion itself, this in performance is the most violent part of the scene. Thus the enacted violence in the scene is the cosmic violence of the destruction of the temple, which must in some way have been experienced personally, in much the same way that many Americans experienced the destruction of the World Trade Towers as an attack on themselves. Ritualized violence is frequently used to induce the liminal state. Mark has produced the same effect here through the conjunction of violent gestures with the reminder of a violent event that has affected the audience deeply.

Liminality-Inducing Features throughout the Gospel

I do not have time to describe in detail the liminality-inducing features found throughout the Gospel, but a listing of some of those features suggests there is a great enough density of them that one could expect the performance of the Gospel to invoke a liminal consciousness in its audience.

First, the Gospel frequently enacts ritualized abuse, which is often part of rites of passage. Every time I perform the Gospel I am amazed at how frequently Jesus appears to be angry, irritated, or frustrated: *Do you not understand? How then will you understand all the parables? Cowards! Have you still no faith? Isaiah prophesied well about you hypocrites! Do you not yet understand? Why does this generation seek a sign? Why are you talking about not having bread?* In oral narration, where dialogue is also experienced as direct address, the audience experiences all these scoldings as addressed to themselves. One can distance oneself to some extent from the scolding, depending on how much one identifies with the various characters, but one at least experiences the performer addressing a great deal of frustration at oneself. The narrative Jesus, embodied in the performer, stands in the position of the ritual leader heaping abuse on the initiate. The audience cannot object, both because of the position given to Jesus and because of the ritualization of the abuse as narrative.

In addition to the scoldings of Jesus, the audience is subjected to various attacks and insinuations launched by the opponents of Jesus: *Why is he eating with tax collectors and sinners? Why don't your followers fast? Why are they doing unlawful things on the Sabbath? He has Beelzebul, and by the ruler of demons he casts out demons! Is this not the carpenter?* At least in these cases, one is allowed to feel vindicated by Jesus, but such narrated attacks underline the audience's separation from the larger society.

The unmasking of Peter in the denial scene is another place in the narrative where the audience is under attack: *You also were with Jesus the Nazarene! This person is one of them! Surely you are one of them, for you also are a Galilean!* If denunciation could lead to social ostracism or even death, enacted denunciation must have been seriously disturbing.

Second, the Gospel makes authoritative demands on the audience to leave the comfortable structures of society: *Come! Follow me! They left their father Zebedee in the boat with the hired hands and followed him. Take nothing on the road except a staff! Sell all you have and give it to the poor!* When Anthony heard those passages, he experienced them as a personal call to the liminal life. We do not know enough about the communities where Mark was performed to know if the listeners had already taken such steps themselves. If so, the passages would reinforce their liminal position outside the structures of society. If not, they are faced with extraordinary demands to abandon those structures.

Third, the Gospel undermines and relativizes many of the structures of society: *Who are my mother and my brothers? The last shall be first and the first shall be last. Give to Caesar the things that are Caesar's, and give to God the things that are God's.* All the religious authorities are discredited, and the temple, the central institution of Judaism, is subjected to attack. Money is denigrated as an impediment to receiving the kingdom of God.

The much-discussed failures of the disciples similarly undercut the structures of the church. The highest authorities of the church, the ones on whom we rely for all our knowledge of Jesus, are torn down and insulted before our very eyes. They are afraid and confused, called cowards and the embodiment of Satan. They do not understand the teaching of Jesus. Their quest for power and glory is ridiculed. They abandon Jesus to death.

Mark acknowledges the hierarchy of the church. The twelve are commissioned by Jesus. Peter, James, and John hold a privileged position. But within the performance of the Gospel the church structure is not allowed to function as a substitute for the structures of society. We float without structure, faced only with the authority of Jesus.

Fourth, the Gospel relativizes the audience's normal state of perception. The messianic secret, the use of parables as masks of meaning, the ambiguity of miracles as pointers to meaning, the misunderstanding of the disciples — all these suggest the need to step outside the ordinary structures of thought in order to grasp true meaning.

Fifth, the Gospel invokes a state of awe and fear associated with the divine: *What is this? They were amazed. We have never seen anything like this. They were pleading with him to leave their region. They thought they saw a ghost and cried out, for they all saw him and were terrified. He did not know what to say, for they were terrified.*

Sixth, the Gospel enacts the casting out of demons of the audience and subjects the audience to the abuse of demons: *What have you to do with us, Jesus of Nazareth? Have you come to destroy us? Be silent! Come out of him! What have you to do with me, Jesus, Son of the Most High God? I adjure you by God, do not torment me! Come out of the man, you unclean spirit! Get behind me, Satan!* Since exorcism produces a transition from one state to another, it necessarily requires a transition through liminality and symbolizes the liminal state. We have later evidence that the expulsion of evil spirits was included in the ritual of baptism, presumably because such cleansing moved the initiate out of his or her former unclean state to the liminal, unstructured state in preparation for baptism.[20]

---

20. Arabic *Canons of Hippolytus* 19, 29; Cyril, *Procatechesis* 14 (PG 33.355); Augustine, *Epistulae* 194.46 (PL 33.890); *Contra Julian* 3.8 (PL 34.705).

Seventh, the Gospel makes frequent allusions to death and the danger that the audience faced: *The Son of Man will suffer many things and be rejected by the elders and the high priests and the scribes and be killed. Pick up your cross and follow me! Are you able to drink the cup that I drink? Brother will hand over brother to death and a father his child.*

Eighth, the Gospel repeatedly invalidates or suppresses the expected emotional reaction of the audience. I noted this in the discussion of the crucifixion scene. We find it in many other places as well. In part, the fast pace of the Gospel does not allow for the processing of emotion, but there are frequent places where there is a deliberate reversal of emotion: *You are my Son, the Beloved; with you I am well pleased.* The audience feels good: *And immediately the Spirit drove him out into the wilderness, and he was in the wilderness forty days, tempted by Satan.* We did not get to celebrate that very long: *To you has been given the mystery of the rule of God.* It does not get much better than that. *Do you not know this parable? How then will you recognize all of the parables?* Mark has a similar approach to more negative emotions. John the Baptist is senselessly killed; his disciples collect his body and head for burial. We expect the audience to feel some sorrow, but the narrative immediately continues with an emotionally incongruous scene of the disciples returning from their mission, telling all they did and taught.

Many of the features of the messianic secret serve the function of cutting off expected emotional reactions. Given the degree to which audiences in the first century seem to have reacted with applause or catcalls, such constant undermining of emotional reaction must have involved a considerable degree of ego suppression. *You are the Messiah!* We ought to applaud. *And he rebuked them, so that they might not tell anyone about him.* Very quickly we descend to *Get behind me, Satan!* The transfiguration scene is similar: *This is my Son, the Beloved. Listen to him!* Get ready to applaud. *He ordered them to tell no one about what they had seen.* Maybe next time. The commands to silence after healings function the same way. If a healing ends with an acclamation, *We have never seen anything like this,* we are able to applaud and express our emotion. When it ends with a command to silence, we cannot. This explains why we hear commands to silence even in improbable situations, such as the raising of Jairus's daughter. It is impossible for the girl's parents not to tell people that their child has been healed. The command to silence is instead directed at the performer's audience, in order to suppress their reaction. The silencing of the demons functions in a similar way. If someone confesses Jesus to be the Holy One of God or the Son of God, we would expect the audience to react favorably and applaud. The silencing of the demons cuts off that reaction.

Ninth, through the commands to silence as well as other means, the Gospel creates an aura of secrecy. The transmission of secret knowledge is a frequent part of the rites of passage associated with liminality. Liminality and secrecy reinforce each other. The secrets separate us from others in society. Liminal consciousness imparts to knowledge a sense of esoteric profundity.

Tenth, the Gospel enacts a state of communitas among the listeners: *Here are my mother and my brothers! To you has been given the mystery of the rule of God.* The performer as Jesus calls his audience *Children.* He promises them a hundredfold brothers and sisters, mothers and children. He imparts secrets.

Eleventh, the Gospel makes authoritative claims on the audience to live in a state of liminality and communitas: *Whoever wants to be first must be last of all and servant of all. Whoever wishes to be first among you must be a slave of all.*

Together, I would argue, all these features serve to create in those experiencing the Gospel performance a liminal consciousness that can serve as a vehicle of revelation.

The Revelation Mediated by the Gospel

What is the content of the revelation that is mediated by the liminal consciousness induced by the Gospel performance? Let me suggest two possible answers.

A number of scholars have suggested that the Gospel of Mark was performed as part of an extended baptism ritual.[21] I can think of no more powerful setting for the performance of the Gospel than immediately before baptism. In the ritual of baptism, the initiate goes through a liminal stage, and the psychological power of the ritual is greatly increased by the creation of a more profound level of liminal consciousness. The ritual of baptism and ensuing welcome into the community of the church would provide the missing closure to the Gospel and the catharsis of the unresolved emotions that the performance has produced. Since some of the most powerful of those emotions concern the death of Jesus and confusion in the face of the resurrection, it is easy to imagine how those unresolved emotions might lead to a profound identification between one's own symbolic death in baptism and the death of Jesus.

The constant concern of the Gospel with understanding the true meanings hidden behind the facade of story and action would prepare the initiate to make such a connection. The liminal state would make the initiate open to other revelatory experiences as well. It is possible that the one performing the baptism may have been able to induce an ecstatic experience of the Holy Spirit though the laying on of hands, as in Acts 8:17.[22] In that case, the postbaptismal reception of the Spirit and the resurrection of Jesus would tend to merge as well.

If the Gospel was performed as preparation for the Lord's Supper, it would similarly facilitate a relationship between the death of Jesus and the bread and wine, deepening the connection between those elements and the sacrificial body and blood of Jesus.

Such a revelatory experience would depend on the performance of the Gospel in a particular ritual situation. Given the apparent parallel in the mystery religions, it is certainly possible that the Gospel might have been used in such a setting. Apuleius's description of the experience of initiation into the mysteries of Isis suggests that the initiate

---

21. See note 4.
22. I have seen a similar induction of an ecstatic state in Afro-Caribbean worship. In that situation, the officiating priestess or priest causes the initiate to enter a trance, one of the deities takes control of the initiate's body, and the initiate performs the characteristic dance of the deity.

experienced some revelation of the goddess.[23] Lucian tells us that all the mystery initiations included pantomime, and it seems likely that such performances were intended to facilitate the intended experience.[24] Dio Chrysostom also reports the use of dance in the mystery initiations. In a rite called enthronement, the initiates are seated and the priests dance around them.[25] Thus Gentiles in the Greco-Roman world would have been used to performance as a means of facilitating revelatory experiences. Turner includes ancient mysteries in the evidence for a cross-cultural pattern of ritual that includes a stage of liminality.[26]

In one of the more emotional passages in his letter to the Galatians, Paul takes his audience to task as foolish Galatians, before whose eyes Jesus Christ was publicly exhibited as crucified (Gal 3:1). Hans Dieter Betz has recognized that the public exhibition to which the passage refers was most likely an emotional retelling of the passion narrative. According to the rhetorical handbooks, the goal of narrative is to make the audience feel present at the actual event. Good narrative is a dramatic reenactment.[27] The reminder of this portrayal serves as a link between baptismal language about being crucified with Christ and rhetorical questions that couple the reception of the Spirit with hearing and faith. This line of argument suggests that Paul associated the passion narrative in some way with baptism and the reception of the Spirit. He implies that the passion narrative should have had a profound impact on his audience, which should give them a proper understanding of the relationship between the cross of Christ and salvation. The experience of the passion narrative and the associated reception of the Spirit should be enough to lead one to believe that the covenant recorded in Scripture has now been superseded.

If the Gospel was not performed in conjunction with such a ritual, however, it might still serve to facilitate a revelatory experience.

---

23. Apuleius, *Metamorphoses* 11.23–24.
24. Lucian, *De saltatione* 15–17.
25. Dio Chrysostom, *De dei cognitione* = Or. 12.33.
26. Turner, *Forest of Symbols*, 102–3, 108.
27. Hans Dieter Betz, *Galatians: A Commentary on Paul's Letters to the Churches in Galatia* (Hermeneia; Philadelphia: Fortress, 1979), 131.

Knowledge received by an individual in a liminal state can affect a person much more profoundly than knowledge received in an ordinary state of consciousness, because of the experience of sacredness associated with it. If the Gospel is not preparatory to another experience, then the experience of the Gospel itself becomes the mediated knowledge. The concluding death and resurrection scene would be imbued with a supraordinary reality and clothed with an aura of the sacred.

12

Wielding the Sword

The Sayings of Jesus
in Recent Markan Scholarship

Sharyn Dowd

Robert Tannehill is responsible for some of the most important work that has been done on the sayings of Jesus. This essay discusses the development of the classification and study of Jesus' sayings with particular attention to scholarship on the Gospel of Mark.[1]

Classification of Sayings:
From Dibelius to Tannehill

The study of the sayings of Jesus was central in the work of the form critics, who focused on the small units of the Jesus tradition. Martin Dibelius used the term "paradigm" for sayings units.[2] Rudolf Bultmann divided the sayings material into apophthegms and dominical sayings. He defined the apophthegms as "sayings of Jesus set in a brief context," and further subdivided them into the controversy,

---

1. The title of Robert Tannehill's influential monograph, *The Sword of His Mouth* (Semeia Supplements 1; Philadelphia: Fortress, Missoula, Mont.: Scholars, 1975) is one source for the title of this essay. I appreciate the helpful critique of an earlier version of this work by the Mark Task Force of the Catholic Biblical Association (Aug. 4, 2002), and in particular the insightful response by Hugh M. Humphrey (see n. 63, below).

2. Martin Dibelius, *From Tradition to Gospel* (German original, 1919; trans. B. L. Wolf; 2d ed.; New York: Charles Scribner's Sons, 1935), 26, 37–69. For a discussion of the beginnings of the form-critical study of the sayings, see V. K. Robbins, "Chreia and Pronouncement Story in Synoptic Studies," in *Patterns of Persuasion in the Gospels* (ed. B. L. Mack and V. K. Robbins; Sonoma, Calif.: Polebridge, 1989), 2–11 and V. K. Robbins, "Form Criticism: New Testament," *ABD* 2:841–44.

the school dialogue, and the biographical apophthegm.[3] Vincent Taylor introduced the term that came to dominate the study of sayings material among English-speaking scholars; he classified Dibelius's "paradigm" and Bultmann's "apophthegm" as the "pronouncement story."[4]

Dibelius's initial interest had been in the early Christian sermon, but much form-critical work focused on historical issues in an attempt to recover the exact words of Jesus himself by peeling away the interpretive material added by the early Christians as they used the sayings in teaching and preaching. Redaction criticism paid more attention to the function of the sayings in their Gospel contexts, but tended to focus on the editorial changes made to the purportedly earliest form of each unit. Then in 1975 Robert Tannehill led the way into a literary and rhetorical study of the pronouncement stories with his book *The Sword of His Mouth.*

In this monograph, Tannehill foreshadowed the reader-oriented approaches to the Gospels that became so influential in biblical studies during the last decade of the twentieth century. He did this by calling for careful attention to the "forceful and imaginative language" of the synoptic sayings units.[5] Tannehill argued for a combination of literary and rhetorical approaches, because, in the words of P. J. Corbett, the sayings of Jesus "have designs on an audience."[6] His careful analysis of seventeen passages demonstrated the fruitfulness of this approach.

The analysis begun in *The Sword of His Mouth* was followed up by the SBL Pronouncement Story Group of 1975–1981, which published its findings in *Semeia* 20: *Pronouncement Stories,* edited by

---

3. Rudolf Bultmann, *The History of the Synoptic Tradition* (German original, 1931; trans. J. Marsh; rev. ed.; New York: Harper & Row, 1968), 11–69. See Robbins, "Form Criticism," 842.

4. Vincent Taylor, *Formation of the Gospel Tradition* (London: Macmillan, 1953), 29–30, 63–87. See R. C. Tannehill, "Introduction: The Pronouncement Story and Its Types," *Semeia* 20 (1981): 1.

5. Tannehill, *The Sword of His Mouth,* 1.

6. Ibid., 18–19.

Tannehill.[7] The purpose of the group's research was to develop a classification system for pronouncement stories and to attempt to apply it to such stories, not only in the Gospels, but also in Hellenistic and Jewish literature of approximately the same historical period as the Gospels.

In the introduction to this volume, Tannehill defined the pronouncement story as "a brief narrative in which the climactic (and often final) element is a pronouncement, which is presented as a particular person's response to something said or observed on a particular occasion of the past."[8] In keeping with the direction set by *The Sword of His Mouth* and by Tannehill's "Attitudinal Shift in Synoptic Pronouncement Stories,"[9] the work of the Pronouncement Story Group eschewed historical questions and created a typology that would "provide clues to the rhetorical function of the story, the way in which the storyteller is seeking to influence the reader."[10] Most of the articles, however, gave much more attention to classification than to rhetorical analysis.

It was clear that the pronouncement story was an important feature of pagan Hellenistic biographical and didactic narratives in the first two centuries of the common era, though it was found to be rare in the Hellenistic Jewish and early noncanonical Christian works surveyed. Although Bultmann had argued that the synoptic "controversy" and "scholastic" dialogues were comparable to, and derived from, rabbinic models,[11] Gary Porton argued forcefully that this was not the case, and that in fact the Tannaitic stratum of rabbinic

---

7. For this volume *Pronouncement Stories*, R. C. Tannehill wrote the "Introduction" and "Varieties of Synoptic Pronouncement Stories," *Semeia* 20 (1981): 1–13, 101–19.

8. Tannehill, "Introduction," 1. See also R. C. Tannehill, "Types and Functions of Apophthegms in the Synoptic Gospels," *ANRW* II.25.2 (1984): 1792–1829. The focus on particularity distinguishes pronouncement stories from more generalized proverbial material.

9. R. C. Tannehill, "Attitudinal Shift in Synoptic Pronouncement Stories," in *Orientation by Disorientation: Studies in Literary Criticism and Biblical Literary Criticism in Honor of William A. Beardslee* (ed. R. A. Spencer; Pittsburgh: Pickwick, 1980), 183–97.

10. Tannehill, "Introduction," 5–6. Tannehill's approach to rhetorical theory was apparently influenced by Heinrich Lausberg, *Handbuch der literarischen Rhetorik* (2 Aufl.; 2 vols.; Munich: Max Hueber, 1973), which is cited both in *Sword* and in *Semeia* 20.

11. Bultmann, *History*, 42.

literature contains few pronouncement stories.[12] This research led naturally to the question as to whether various types of sayings material had been classified and discussed by Hellenistic authors. As early as 1944, R. O. P. Taylor had called for more attention to the Hellenistic handbooks of preliminary rhetorical exercises (*progymnasmata*) as a basis for Gospel form criticism. In the second phase of the SBL Pronouncement Story Group Taylor's suggestion was taken up.

Pronouncement Stories and *Chreiai*

This second phase (1981–87) was led by Vernon Robbins, who was collaborating with the scholars working on the Claremont Chreia Project during the same period.[13] Thus, by the time a second collection of SBL Pronouncement Story Group papers was published,[14] the ancient rhetorical category of the *chreia* was being used as a tool in the analysis of what Taylor and Tannehill had called the "pronouncement story."[15]

The word Greek *chreia* (Latin: *chria*) literally means "need." According to the earliest definition, that of Theon of Alexandria, the chreia is so called "because of its excellence, for more than the

---

12. Gary G. Porton, "The Pronouncement Story in Tannaitic Literature: A Review of Bultmann's Theory," *Semeia* 20 (1981): 81–99. In an interesting reversal of Bultmann's thesis, A. J. Avery-Peck argued that the stories identified as pronouncement stories by Porton "use the types of argument discussed by Hermogenes and common within Hellenistic rhetoric" ("Rhetorical Argumentation in Early Rabbinic Pronouncement Stories," *Semeia* 64 [1994]: 49). Avery-Peck, however, attributed this not to the influence of Greek rhetors on the Tannaim, but to the claim that "within broad historical and geographical limits, rhetorical art remains the same from literature to literature" (49). Using a different classification, Marion Moeser found similarities between what she called the "anecdotes" in the Mishnah and in the Gospel of Mark, but she did not attempt to support Bultmann's claim that the Gospel units were derived from Palestinian rabbinic practice ("The Anecdote in the Cultural Worlds of the First Gospel: A Study of Brief Stories in the *Demonax*, the Mishnah, and Mark 8:27–10:15" [Ph.D. diss., University of Notre Dame, 1998]).

13. The director of the Claremont project was Edward N. O'Neil of the University of Southern California; the New Testament scholars involved in the project included Ronald Hock, Burton Mack, and James Butts.

14. Vernon K. Robbins, ed., *The Rhetoric of Pronouncement*, in *Semeia* 64 (issued 1993; copyright 1994).

15. V. K. Robbins, "Introduction: Using Rhetorical Discussions of the Chreia to Interpret Pronouncement Stories," *Semeia* 64 (1994): vii–xvii. Based on a comparison of the definitions, it appears that Tannehill's pronouncement story is a subcategory of the chreia, perhaps a "response-chreia." See Tannehill, "Introduction," 1, and Robbins, "Introduction," xv.

other exercises it is useful (*chreiōdēs*) in many ways for life" (*Progymnasmata* 3.19–20).[16] Theon defines the chreia as "a concise statement or action which [sic] is attributed with aptness to some specified character or to something analogous to a character" (3.2–3). Thus, the chreia was always associated with a person, usually an exemplary one.

Many Hellenistic people made collections of chreiai, and a few collections were published.[17] The memorization of such sayings was encouraged for personal edification. Plutarch wrote to the daughter of a friend: "I would have you read what Timoxena wrote to Aristylla about the love of ornament, and try to memorize it.... Familiarize yourself... with the sayings of good and wise people" (Plutarch, *Conjugalia praecepta* 145E). Such a practice would, Plutarch believed, contribute to the character of his former pupil Eurydice and enhance her conversational skills.[18] In addition to their usefulness for character formation, the chreiai were used by orators when preparing speeches, and by writers such as Plutarch, Aulus Gellius, Lucian of Samosata, Diogenes Laertius, Aelian, Philostratus, and Stobaeus.[19]

The writing and manipulation of chreiai was one of the preliminary exercises (*progymnasmata*) in the curriculum of Greek and Roman education. This curriculum is described differently by different writers, but it appears to have had three levels. First, of course, students had to learn to read and write, being required to copy previously written texts. At the second level, students were drilled in preliminary exercises in which they wrote and developed small units of text such as the fable, the description, the speech-in-character, the comparison, and so on. In the preliminary exercises of Theon, the chreia

---

16. A text of Theon with translation may be found in James R. Butts, "The *Progymnasmata* of Theon: A New Text with Translation and Commentary" (Ph.D. diss., The Claremont Graduate School, 1986).

17. R. F. Hock, "General Introduction to Volume 1," in *The Progymnasmata* (ed. R. F. Hock and E. N. O'Neil; vol. 1 of *The Chreia in Ancient Rhetoric*; Atlanta: Scholars, 1986), 8.

18. Translation corrected from that of Donald Russell in *Plutarch's "Advice to the Bride and Groom" and "A Consolation to His Wife"* (ed. Sarah B. Pomeroy; New York: Oxford University Press, 1999). Timoxena was Plutarch's wife, but the treatise she wrote is not extant (Sarah B. Pomeroy, "Reflections on Plutarch, *Advice to the Bride and Groom*," in *Plutarch's "Advice*," 55). See also Moeser, "Anecdote," 96.

19. Hock, "Introduction," 5.

is the first exercise to be taught to students. After they had learned to compose these shorter units, students went on to the third level of education to prepare for public life by writing entire practice speeches under the tutelage of a rhetor. Only after they had mastered this stage would they be ready to speak in actual situations such as the law court, the civic assembly, the funeral service, or on occasions of public celebration.[20] Theon, in his chapter on pedagogy, writes:

> So then, these subjects I have set forth not because I think that they are all suitable to every beginner, but in order that we might see that practice in the exercises is absolutely necessary, not only for those who intend to be orators, but also if someone wants to be a poet or prose writer, or if he wants to acquire facility with some other form of writing. For these exercises are, so to speak, the foundation stones for every form of writing. (*Prog.* 2.138–43)

The *progymnasmata* were not the most basic level of education, but the mastery of these skills would have been necessary for anyone who could have put together a coherent and persuasive narrative like the Gospel of Mark.

Theon and other writers of preliminary exercises[21] organize their discussions of the chreia in a common pattern: (1) definition and sometimes discussions differentiating the chreia from other forms;

---

20. Butts, "Theon," 23; Moeser, "Anecdote," 62–67. The standard work on this topic in the relevant period is Stanley F. Bonner, *Education in Ancient Rome: From the Elder Cato to the Younger Pliny* (Berkeley: University of California Press, 1977). Although Theon wrote sometime between the mid-first and the early-second centuries C.E., there is strong evidence for the use of such exercises at least as early as the first century B.C.E. (Hock, "Introduction," 10).

21. The extant examples in chronological order: Theon of Alexandria (mid to late first century C.E. to early second century C.E.); Hermogenes of Tarsus (161 to not later than 230–238, translated into Latin by Priscian [mid-fifth-early-sixth centuries]); Aphthonius of Antioch (late-fourth-early-fifth centuries); Nicolaus of Myra (ca. 430–late-fifth/early-sixth centuries); an anonymous fragment in Codex Vaticanus 5216, copied fifteenth-sixteenth century). The texts and translations of the chreia discussions are collected in Hock and O'Neil, eds., *Progymnasmata*. The chreia discussion is, however, only one section of the *Progymnasmata*. For an English translation of Theon, Hermogenes, Aphthonius, Nicolaus, and selected excerpts and fragments of other works, see George A. Kennedy, *Progymnasmata: Greek Textbooks of Prose Composition Introductory to the Study of Rhetoric* (Atlanta: SBL, 2003; Writings from the Greco-Roman World 10; Leiden and Boston: Brill, 2003).

(2) descriptions and labels for the various types of chreiai; and (3) exercises to be performed on the chreiai. This essay will skip over the sometimes-complicated typologies in order to examine three of the exercises that students were taught. Of the exercises discussed by Theon, the most relevant to Gospel study are the recitation in the same or different words, and the expansion and condensation exercises.

The first and most basic exercise discussed by Theon is "recitation": "We try to the best of our ability to express the assigned chreia very clearly in the same words or in others as well" (*Prog* 3.143–45). It is not important that the student reproduce the exact wording of the original, but that the sense be clear.

The exercises that Theon calls "expansion" and "condensation" are so important that his examples are quoted in full:

> For example, a concise chreia: Epaminondas, as he was dying childless, said to his friends: "I have left two daughters — the victory at Leuctra and the one at Mantinea." Let us expand like this: Epaminondas, the Theban general, was of course a good man in time of peace, and when war against the Lacedaemonians came to his country, he displayed many outstanding deeds of great courage. As a Boeotarch at Leuctra, he triumphed over the enemy, and while campaigning and fighting for his country, he died at Mantinea. While he was dying of his wounds and his friends were lamenting, among other things, that he was dying childless, he smiled and said: "Stop weeping, friends, for I have left you two immortal daughters: two victories of our country over the Lacedaemonians, the one at Leuctra, who is the older, and the younger, who is just now being born at Mantinea." (*Prog.* 3.227–40)

The example stops there, but it is obvious that since Theon says a chreia may be either expanded or condensed, students would have been expected to shorten the second version to the first by editing out all the extraneous material, that is, all the material not necessary for one to understand the saying.

Hermogenes of Tarsus (second–third century C.E.) discusses all the exercises to be performed on the chreia under the rubric of "elaboration" (*ergasia*). Unlike Theon's advice about "expanding" (form of *epekteinomai*) the chreia, Hermogenes' "elaboration" produces a complete argument. His example is the following chreia: "Isocrates said that education's root is bitter, [but] its fruit is sweet." The elaboration has the following elements:

1. Praise: "Isocrates was wise," and you amplify the subject moderately.

2. Then the chreia: "He said thus and so," and you are not to express it simply, but rather by amplifying the presentation.

3. Then the rationale: "For the most important affairs generally succeed because of toil, and once they have succeeded, they bring pleasure."

4. Then the statement from the opposite: "For ordinary affairs do not need toil, and they have an outcome that is entirely without pleasure; but serious affairs have the opposite outcome."

5. Then the statement from analogy: "For just as it is the lot of farmers to reap their fruits after working with the land, so also is it for those working with words."

6. Then the statement from example: "Demosthenes, after locking himself in a room and toiling long, later reaped his fruits: wreaths and public acclamations."

7. It is also possible to argue from the statement by an authority: For example, Hesiod said, "In front of virtue gods have ordained sweat." And another poet says, "At the price of toil do the gods sell every good to us."

8. At the end you are to add an exhortation to the effect that it is necessary to heed the one who has spoken or acted.[22]

Burton Mack and Edward O'Neil point out that although Hermogenes is writing in the second century, his pattern of elaboration is

---

22. Hock and O'Neil, *Progymnasmata*, 7–8.

quite similar to the steps outlined in the *Rhetorica ad Herennium* for the elaboration of a maxim (*gnōmē*), which differs from a chreia only in that the maxim is unattributed. Since the *Rhetorica ad Herennium* dates from the first century B.C.E, it is reasonable to assume that Hermogenes follows an earlier tradition that Theon revises.[23] The differences between the expansion of Theon, which merely makes the chreia longer and more detailed, and the elaboration of Hermogenes, which develops the chreia into an argument, are important; the two exercises should not be confused.

Since this attention to the chreia exercises in the *progymnasmata* by New Testament scholars had been motivated by an interest in Gospel sayings material, and since both Vernon Robbins and Burton Mack were working on the Gospel of Mark in the 1980s, several analyses of chreiai have either focused on Mark or on materials in the triple tradition.[24] The 1998 Notre Dame dissertation "The Anecdote in the Cultural Worlds of the First Gospel: A Study of Brief Stories in the *Demonax,* the Mishnah, and Mark 8:27–10:45," by Marion C. Moeser, examines the chreiai in the central section of Mark and responds to previous chreia studies.[25]

Examples of Applications to the Gospel of Mark

Applications of information in the *progymnasmata* discussions of chreiai have focused on identifying chreia expansions and elaborations in the Gospel. The expansion is a simple exercise in which details are added, but a full argument is not developed. Moeser reads Mark 8:31–33 as an expansion of a mixed chreia, which would have

---

23. B. L. Mack and E. N. O'Neil, "The Chreia Discussion of Hermogenes of Tarsus: Introduction," in Hock and O'Neil, *Progymnasmata,* 161.

24. E.g., B. Mack, *A Myth of Innocence: Mark and Christian Origins* (Philadelphia: Fortress, 1988); Mack and Robbins, *Patterns of Persuasion;* Miriam Dean-Otting and Vernon K. Robbins, "Biblical Sources for Pronouncement Stories in the Gospels," *Semeia* 64 (1994): 95–115; Rod Parrott, "Conflict and Rhetoric in Mark 2:23–28," *Semeia* 64 (1994): 117–37.

25. Moeser's dissertation, "Anecdote," was directed by Adela Yarbro Collins and Mary Rose D'Angelo. Ben Witherington III (*The Gospel of Mark: A Socio-Rhetorical Commentary* [Grand Rapids: Eerdmans, 2001], 10 n. 31) refers to two other unpublished dissertations that I have not yet been able to consult: D. M. Young, "Whoever Has Ears to Hear" (Ph.D. diss., Vanderbilt University, 1994); and J. E. Phelan, "Rhetoric and Meaning in Mark 6.30–8:10" (Ph.D. diss., Northwestern University, 1985).

been something like this: "When Peter rebuked Jesus for predicting his suffering and death, Jesus turned to the disciples and said, 'Get behind me, Satan, for you are setting your mind not on divine things but on human things!' "[26] This is a mixed chreia because it includes both a saying and an action (turning) (Hermogenes, *Progymnasmata* 6.10).[27] Everything else in 8:31–33 supplements this (theoretical) basic chreia. The expansion does not change the meaning of the basic chreia; it adds details.[28] The details may be part of the situation that provokes the saying as well as part of the saying itself, as in the expansion of the chreia concerning Epaminondas's last words.[29]

Elaboration, it will be recalled, is the construction of an argument from a chreia. Elaboration may be illustrated by two different analyses of Mark 2:23–28. Vernon Robbins analyzed the passage as follows:

Introduction
One sabbath he was going alongside through the grainfields; and his disciples began to make a path, plucking the heads of grain.

Statement of the case
And the Pharisees were saying to him, "Look, why are they doing on the sabbath what is not lawful?"

Refutation (example as precedent)
And he said to them, "Have you never read what David did when he and his companions were in need and hungry? How he entered the house of God when Abiathar was high priest, and

---

26. Moeser, "Anecdote, 259.

27. Hock and O'Neil, *Progymnasmata*, 174–75; Moeser, "Anecdote," 259.

28. The assessment of Donahue and Harrington regarding the passion predictions is typical: Though "it is likely that Jesus recognized that his teachings and actions...might well get him into trouble,...it is hard to escape the impression that the language of these texts has been influenced to some extent by the events described in Mark 14–16" (J. R. Donahue and D. J. Harrington, *The Gospel of Mark* [SP 2; Collegeville, Minn.: Liturgical Press, 2002], 266). Similarly, though she does not comment on historical plausibility, Moeser, "Anecdote," 258–60 assumes that a reference to the passion prediction was part of the original chreia, so that Mark is not responsible for the idea, only for the choice of words.

29. See above.

ate the bread of the Presence, which it is not lawful to eat except for the priests, and even gave it to those with him?

Conclusion (chreia as enthymemic rationale)
And he said to them, "The sabbath was made for the sake of man, not man for the sabbath. Therefore the Son of Man is lord even of the sabbath."[30]

Since the enthymeme is an incomplete syllogism, Robbins proposes that the full syllogism might run something like this:

General premise: The sabbath was made by God for man.

Presupposed concrete premise: The Son of Man came with God's authority to serve man with that which God created for man.

Conclusion: Therefore, the Son of Man is lord even of the sabbath [so that he has the authority to use it to serve the needs of man].

In this case, the middle premise is supported in the Markan narrative by 2:10 and 10:45.[31] This analysis does not fit the pattern of a chreia elaboration in the *progymnasmata* because "when judicial rhetoric occurs in a pronouncement story instead of a speech, the introduction and the statement regularly emerge in narrative clauses and speech that establish the setting, and the proof and conclusion occur in response to the setting."[32]

Rod Parrott took issue with Robbins's analysis because the thesis of the argument (often a chreia) was not explicit; it was merely implicit in the setting and statement of the facts (the thesis in this argument would be that what the disciples did was not "unlawful").[33] Parrott argued instead that the original statement of the chreia was 2:27, but

---

30. Robbins, "Plucking Grain on the Sabbath," in *Patterns of Persuasion* (ed. Mack and Robbins), 110, 123–35.
31. Ibid., 126.
32. Ibid., 109.
33. Parrott, "Conflict and Rhetoric," 122–23.

the chreia now functions as part of the argument, while the thesis comes at the end (2:28).[34] This yields the following analysis:

Citation of authority	"Have you never read . . . "
Example	"How David . . . "
Rationale	"The Sabbath was made for man,
Converse	not man for the Sabbath."
Thesis	"So the Son of man is lord even of the Sabbath."[35]

Parrott is still left with the problem of explaining why the thesis should be at the end rather than near the beginning, as in the handbooks. His answer is that according to *Rhetorica ad Herennium* 1.6.9–7.11 and Quintilian's *Institutio oratoria* 4.1.42–45, a hostile audience (the Pharisees) makes it necessary to change the order of argumentation from deductive (thesis first) to inductive (thesis last, as conclusion).[36]

Reception of Chreia Studies in Markan Scholarship

If the results of chreia analysis are taken seriously, there are important implications for our understanding of the transmission and redaction of the Jesus traditions. Since students were taught not only to lengthen chreiai and to elaborate them into arguments but also to shorten them, the traditional form-critical belief that the expanded version must be the later one is mistaken. Further, Bultmann's assumption that the saying is always primary and its setting and action secondary is also disproved by what we have learned from the *progymnasmata*.[37] Nevertheless, chreia analysis has been perceived by some to be a challenge to the historical accuracy (and therefore, presumably, the authority) of the sayings of Jesus in Mark.

---

34. Ibid., 125.
35. Ibid., 124.
36. Ibid., 126–28.
37. Robbins, "Chreia and Pronouncement Story," 18. Tannehill had already argued that "a pronouncement story is a story with narrative tension and movement, not just a saying with a narrative setting which can be ignored" ("Varieties," 117).

Both Robert H. Gundry[38] and Ben Witherington III[39] attempt to deny the presence of chreia expansion or elaboration in the Gospel of Mark. In commenting on Mark's version of the temple incident (11:15–17), Gundry takes issue with Hock's observation that Mark's version seems to be an expansion of the basic chreia found in Luke 19:45–46.[40] Gundry comments: "If Luke uses Mark's version (as is commonly thought), the shorter version of the temple-cleansing in Luke 19:45–46 does not show Mark's version to be an expanded *chreia*."[41] Gundry's objection assumes two things that are not assumed by Hock's observation: (1) Mark would only have recorded traditions exactly as he found them and, according to the two-source theory, (2) the version in Mark is the earlier one, which Luke has condensed.[42]

But one of the interesting questions raised by chreia studies is whether taking the *progymnasmata* seriously might reduce the importance of synoptic source theory. What Hock seems to be suggesting is that the temple incident was remembered as a basic chreia, which Luke "recites," but Mark "expands." It is important to remember that students were taught both to expand and to condense chreiai. Even if Mark is a source for Luke, it is still possible (though not demonstrable) that Mark's source was a basic chreia that Mark expanded and Luke subsequently condensed.[43]

---

38. Robert H. Gundry, *Mark: A Commentary on His Apology for the Cross* (Grand Rapids: Eerdmans, 1993).

39. Witherington, *Mark*.

40. Hock, "Introduction," 41.

41. Gundry, *Mark*, 647.

42. For some reason, neither Gundry (*Mark*) nor Witherington (*Mark*) seems to regard condensing a chreia to be a distortion of the tradition, but they seem to think it necessary to deny that Mark expanded or elaborated a chreia. The only possible rationale for this is that condensation is not seen as a problem because it does not introduce the possibility of adding nonhistorical details, whereas to admit expansion or elaboration would mean that there might be a word, phrase, or even a paragraph in the account that did not actually come from the lips of Jesus of Nazareth.

43. It is also possible, of course, that Mark's initial contact with the chreia was in the expanded form that he reproduces. See also Gundry, *Mark*, 516, where he objects at length to Robbins's admittedly theoretical reconstruction of a basic chreia that Robbins thinks is expanded in Mark 9:33–37. Gundry's final argument is "the absence of pre-Marcan [sic] literary remains." But this fact says nothing about whether or not the author of Mark is employing rhetorical techniques.

Witherington's 2001 commentary has as its subtitle "A Socio-Rhetorical Commentary," so it is worth considering how he uses chreia analysis. He begins his discussion by presenting chreiai as "the end product of [a writer's] boiling down of larger and more cumbersome accounts."[44] Since this claim is not documented, it must rely on the argument that occurs on the next page:

> Aphtonius [*sic*] the Sophist reminds his listeners that a *chreia* is a *concise* statement of *apomnēmoneumata*, which may be translated memoirs, recollections, or memoranda. The recollection is sometimes told at considerable length on its own merits because of its subject matter, but the *chreia* must be brief and pointed, referring to a particular person. The word *apomnemonēumata* is important, for it is precisely the word Justin Martyr uses for the Gospel material (*Apol.* 1.67). They are based on the apostle's memoirs or recollections, so to speak. Like the term *diēgēsis*, or narrative, which Luke uses (Luke 1:1–4), "recollections" can be seen as longer, less precisely formed pieces of tradition which could serve as the basis for the creation of a *chreia*.

This paragraph makes the assumption that both Justin (second century) and Aphthonius (fourth–fifth century) are using the term *apomnēmoneumata* in the same way: to designate a long written work implied by the English translation "memoir." The context of Justin's remark is public reading from the *apomnēmoneumata* of the apostles, so he is referring either to some form of narrative or at least to a written collection of "reminiscences." Aphthonius, a teacher of rhetoric, begins his discussion of the chreia in the manner that had become standard by the fourth century, with a definition: "A chreia is a concise reminiscence (*apomnēmoneuma syntomon*) aptly attributed to some character" (*Progymnasmata* 3, 20).[45] All Aphthonius says is that the chreia is something remembered, that it is concise, and that it is attributed, by contrast with a maxim (*gnōmē*) that is unattributed

---

44. Witherington, *Mark*, 9.
45. Hock and O'Neil, *Progymnasmata*, 224–25.

because it is thought to be general wisdom, not the saying of a particular wise person. Aphthonius does not say, here or elsewhere, that an *apomnēmoneuma* is anything like a "large cumbersome account," from which a chreia must be "boiled down."

In fact, Theon, author of the earliest *Progymnasmata*, has this to say: "The chreia is concise, while the reminiscence is sometimes expanded (*epekteinetai*)" (3.15–16). This suggests, not that the chreia is created by condensing a reminiscence, but rather that a reminiscence might be an expansion or extension of a chreia.[46] Writers of the *progymnasmata* do not say anything at all about how chreia are created, only about how they are recited and manipulated. They treat chreiai as givens—raw materials with which the student works.

Witherington confuses the exercise "expansion" with the exercise "elaboration." At one point he concedes (not about Mark, but about "ancient biographers"), "Of course there was expansion, arrangement, rephrasing, but source material was indeed used."[47] On the next page, however, he writes, "Do we also have examples of expansions of *chreiae*, called *ergasiae* (elaborations), in Mark? This is the contention of Mack in particular, and it requires close scrutiny."[48] Here he is using the terms "expansion" and "elaboration" as synonyms,[49] and the argument that follows here and throughout the commentary is concerned to show that Mark neither adds anything to the traditions he received, nor develops arguments from them.

Witherington regards the Papias testimony as an exact account of how the traditions about Jesus were transmitted from Peter to John

---

46. This appears to be the understanding of R. M. Grant, *The Earliest Lives of Jesus* (New York: Harper & Brothers, 1961), 15.

47. Witherington, *Mark*, 12.

48. Ibid., 13.

49. Witherington goes on to object to Mack's analysis of Mark 14:3–9 (Mack and Robbins, *Patterns of Persuasion*, 92–93) on the grounds that it does not follow the instructions in the *progymnasmata* (Witherington, *Mark*, 13–14). This is, in fact, a problem with identifying elaborations in any Gospel narrative, because the handbook examples show how to use a chreia as the thesis of an argument. That is, the voice of the person doing the elaborating is always different from the voice of the person to whom the chreia is attributed. Some of the analyses of Mack and Robbins have Jesus elaborating his own chreia, a strategy the *progymnasmata* do not discuss. Therefore, Mack and Robbins sometimes introduce strategies from the rhetorical handbooks in addition to the preliminary exercises.

Mark, but there is some confusion in Witherington's discussion. Here is his translation:

> And this is what the Elder said, "Mark, who became Peter's *hermēneutēs*, accurately wrote, though not in order (*taxei*), as many of the things said and done by the Lord as he had noted (*emnēmoneusen*). For he neither heard the Lord nor followed him, but afterwards, as I said, followed Peter, who composed his teachings according to the *chreiae* and not as a rhetorical arrangement (*syntaxin*) of the Lord's sayings. So Mark made no mistake in writing some things just as he recollected (*apemnēmoneusen*) them. For he was careful of this one thing, to leave nothing he heard out and to say nothing falsely."[50]

Witherington summarizes: "The claim, then, is quite straightforward here. While Peter shaped his teaching in the form of chreiae, Mark followed his lead and took the larger recollections and accurately summarized the tradition. He made a narrative out of the individual chreiae."[51] This correctly identifies Peter as the one whom "the Elder" says transmitted the tradition in the form of chreiai. Earlier, however, Witherington had claimed that it was Mark who "formed his source material into *chreiai*."[52] Witherington seems to be saying that when a tradition from Peter was not short enough to be a chreia, Mark shortened it and then made a story out of Peter's chreiai and the ones that he (Mark) had composed. But the places where Mark has a longer version than another Synoptic Gospel belie this explanation.

Witherington further uses the Papias statement to prove that there can be no rhetorical arguments in the Gospel:

> Recall that in our discussion of the *progymnasta*, [*sic*] what is supposed to follow the *chreia*, if it is used as a thesis statement, is the *taxis*, the arguments in order in an elaboration. In short,

---

50. Witherington, *Mark*, 22.
51. Ibid., 23.
52. Ibid., 14.

what we are being told is that Mark would *not* compose his Gospel according to prescribed rhetorical form if he were to follow the dictates of the *progymnasta* [*sic*]. . . . In other words, Papias is saying that we *don't* have what Mack and Robbins believe they have found in Mark's Gospel (and the other Synoptics).[53]

The difficulty here is that even if Eusebius's version of the Elder's version of what Peter and Mark did is historically accurate (which it may be), it cannot be used to exclude analyses of the text of Mark itself. The Elder may have been mistaken, or may have had a reason for denying that the Gospel was rhetorically organized, even if *taxei* has the technical meaning here that Witherington asserts (but does not demonstrate) that it does.

Witherington's final argument based on the testimony is that, since "Theon says the two greatest faults *chreiae* can have are either leaving out essential information or telling what is false," the last sentence of the testimony exonerates "Mark of these charges."[54] This statement about Theon is simply false. Nowhere does Theon say anything like "the two greatest faults *chreiae* can have are either leaving out essential information or telling what is false."[55] And since Theon insists

---

53. Ibid., 23.
54. Ibid.
55. Witherington, *Mark*, cites R. P. Martin, *Mark: Evangelist and Theologian* (Grand Rapids: Zondervan, 1972), 82. Martin writes: "In fact, Mark is exonerated in Papias' 'final' sentence of the twin charges which Theon brings against a *chreia*, viz., it leaves out material and it tells what is false." Martin cites Theon in L. Spengel, *Rhetores Graeci*, vol. 2 (Leipzig: Teubner, 1854), 104 (lines 15–18); and Grant, *Earliest Lives*, 14–18. Martin does not say that Theon regards falsity and incompleteness as the two greatest faults a *chreia* can manifest. Martin (*Mark*, 82) does, however, distort Grant's statement: "Now according to the rules laid down by the rhetoricians, a *chreia* can be criticized on the grounds (among others) that it leaves things out or that what it tells is false" (Grant, *Earliest Lives*, 18). Grant is apparently the only one of the three who has actually read Theon. In the section describing the various ways in which chreiae can be used in argumentation, Theon explains that chreiae can be refuted for any of nine faults: obscurity, excess, incompleteness, impossibility, implausibility, falsity, disadvantageousness, uselessness, and shamefulness (*Prog* 3.241–44). Seven of these criticisms have to do with the content of the chreia, not with its transmission. Only "implausibility" criticizes the transmission of the chreia; it is applied when it is unlikely that the person to whom the chreia is attributed actually said it (3.261–63). To assert that one of the chreia found in Mark is "false" or "incomplete" would be to criticize the speaker, meaning Jesus, not Mark. Further, Theon does not rank these faults; he does not say that falsity and incompleteness are "the two greatest faults" of chreiae. To sum up, Theon's discussion of "falsity" and "incompleteness" have nothing to do with historicity and cannot be used in arguments about historicity, as Witherington and Martin would have known had they actually read the text.

that any writer must know how to perform a number of alterations and expansions of chreiai, then it follows that Mark would still be "exonerated" of errors of omission or commission even if he manipulated the chreiai from the Jesus tradition as prescribed in the handbooks. In fact, the Papias testimony claims that Mark was careful "to leave out nothing he heard and to say nothing falsely." No claim is made that Mark did not expand the chreiai or use them in a rhetorical argument, as long as the tradition was not essentially falsified. And again, the Papias testimony cannot be used as evidence against the text of Mark itself.

There are a few chreia studies of which Witherington approves, at least in part, but when any claim is made that the author of Mark has arranged the material into a rhetorical argument, Witherington objects.[56] When the case is made so strongly that he can find no fault with it, he demurs in an attempt to take the onus of rhetoric off the author and transfer it to the audience: "G. Salyer has made an impressive case that we have in this section two *chreiae* (7:6–7 and 14–15), and that Mark has edited the rest of this section so that *it would appear to his Gentile audience to be elaborations of these chreiae.*"[57]

The resistance in Gundry and Witherington to the idea of flexibility in the use of the sayings traditions seems to be an extension to rhetorical analysis the traditional evangelical suspicion of form criticism. E. V. McKnight writes, "The emphasis on the creativity of the early church has been seen by some as a denigration of the role of Jesus as a teacher and the place of eyewitnesses."[58] This is reflected in Witherington's remark that the ancients did not regard the chreia

---

56. See, e.g., the discussion of Theon, *Prog.* 3:20–35, in Witherington, *Mark,* 153–60.

57. Witherington, *Mark,* 224 (emphasis added). Reference is to G. Salyer, "Rhetoric, Purity, and Play: Aspects of Mark 7.1–23," *Semeia* 64 (1994): 139–69.

58. E. V. McKnight, "Form and Redaction Criticism" in *The New Testament and Its Modern Interpreters* (ed. E. J. Epp and G. W. MacRae; Atlanta: Scholars, 1989), 152. Donahue and Harrington (*Mark,* 7) point out that many Catholic scholars have also been skeptical of form-criticism's assumption that much of the sayings tradition was created by the early church. Of course, the reception of the work of Robbins and Mack (*Patterns of Persuasion*) was probably not helped by their early association with the Jesus Seminar or by Mack's book, *Myth of Innocence,* which blamed the author of Mark for all subsequent Christian anti-Semitism as well as for the Reagan-era "Star Wars" defense program (355–56, 368–76).

as "created out of thin air."[59] In this, Witherington is quite correct, but observing that Mark expanded or elaborated traditional chreiai is not a claim that he invented them out of thin air, or that anyone did. Nevertheless, classical scholars have warned that since the same saying is attributed to several different teachers, and some "stock" questions seem allegedly to be asked of every philosopher, it is a mistake to base historical arguments on chreiai,[60] and there is no reason for New Testament scholars to ignore this caveat.

But historical questions aside, chreia studies have so far made little impact on commentary exegesis on the Gospel of Mark. The principal effect has been on the introductory sections of commentaries, especially on the way scholars interpret the Papias testimony, in which the word chreia appears.[61] In their introductory discussion of form criticism, Donahue and Harrington devote a paragraph to the chreia and its importance and ubiquity in the early education of children in the period during which Mark was written,[62] but they do not discuss the chreiai in the commentary exegesis.

This failure of chreia studies to make an impact on Markan scholarship outside the circles of rhetorical criticism is not, for the most part, due to concerns about historicity. There are at least five other possible reasons, perhaps the foremost being biblical scholars' unfamiliarity with the Hellenistic rhetorical tradition and with its extensive technical terminology.[63] In addition, its origin in form criticism may cause chreia studies to be perceived as useful primarily for

---

59. Witherington, *Mark*, 12.

60. Hock, "Introduction," 42–46.

61. The phrase says that Peter *pros tas chreias epoieito tas didaskalias*. Joel Marcus retains the traditional translation, "used to give teaching as necessity demanded" (*Mark 1–8: A New Translation with Introduction and Commentary* [AB 27; New York: Doubleday, 2000], 22). Gundry (*Mark*, 1037) translates, "teaching in accord with the anecdotes," while Witherington (*Mark*, 22) leaves *chreiai* untranslated (see above), as does Christopher Bryan (*A Preface to Mark: Notes on the Gospel in Its Literary and Cultural Settings* [New York: Oxford University Press, 1993], 127): "used to give teaching formulated into *chreiai*." See also Bryan's discussion in *Preface*, 126–28.

62. Donahue and Harrington, *Mark*, 7.

63. "The work has not reached significant status yet," according to Hugh M. Humphrey, "On Chreia Studies in the Gospel of Mark: A Response" (unpublished paper, Catholic Biblical Association Task Force on Mark, Aug. 4, 2002), 5. The jargon barrier was at least one reason for the early demise of structuralism as a method in biblical studies.

investigating pre-Markan traditions in a period in which many interpreters are more interested in the literary aspects of the final form of
the text.[64]

In the third place, there is still a tendency in Markan scholarship
to prefer to read the Gospel exclusively in the light of the Hebrew
Bible and its interpretation at the time of Jesus. Hellenism is still
understood by some as a corrupting overlay on the earthy simplicity
of the Galilean peasant and his humble followers. Even though Mark
writes in Greek for a Hellenistic audience, Mark is seen as living
within the same basic worldview as that of Jesus, about whom he
writes. In addition, there is Mark's reputation as an unsophisticated
writer, as Joel Marcus reminds us:

> As opposed to scholars who regard him and other New Tes-
> tament writers as sophisticated practitioners of the Hellenistic
> rhetorical arts (e.g., Standaert, *Marc;* Robbins, *Teacher;* Mack
> and Robbins, *Patterns*), we should never forget the dismay felt
> by the rhetorically trained Augustine when he first turned to the
> biblical writings after years of studying the classics: "To me they
> seemed quite unworthy of comparison with the stately prose of
> Cicero (*Confessions* [3.5.9])."[65]

But to say that Mark's writing is not worthy of comparison with
Cicero's is the equivalent of saying that the short story of a high
school graduate is not worthy of comparison with the work of Twain
or O'Henry. Such an evaluation does not mean that the high school
student and the accomplished writer were not using the same basic
conventions of the genre; it merely asserts that one result is much
better than the other.

But there may be yet another explanation for the lack of enthusiasm among Mark scholars for chreia analysis; some of the exegetical

---

64. For an attempt to use some of the results of chreia analysis in the service of a literary
reading of Mark, see my *Reading Mark: A Literary and Theological Commentary on the Second
Gospel* (Macon, Ga.: Smyth & Helwys, 2000).

65. Marcus, *Mark 1–8,* 60.

results so far can seem modest in light of the effort expended.[66] For example, after Parrott's closely argued analysis of the story of plucking grain on the Sabbath, he concludes that the purpose of the rhetorical development "in the life of the early community [was] to provide self-definition and support."[67] In fact, even Moeser's finding that Jesus is portrayed as a persuasive teacher in 8:27–10:45 could also have been discerned from the fact that "five times in this section of Mark Jesus is addressed as 'Teacher,' and eleven anecdotes present teachings of Jesus,"[68] along with the observation that throughout the Gospel of Mark Jesus wins every argument with his opponents, finally silencing them altogether (12:34b).

Moeser has compared the use of anecdotes in Mark and in Lucian's *Demonax* while keeping one eye on the *progymnasmata*. This approach, expanded to other Hellenistic biographies and to the whole narrative of Mark, would likely yield richer results than have so far been achieved.[69] In addition, the question needs to be reconsidered. Instead of asking what level of rhetoric can plausibly be attributed to a particular Gospel writer, it would be more interesting to ask how the text would have been heard in the Greek-speaking Roman world of the first century.[70]

A study of what the *progymnasmata* and other rhetorical handbooks have to say about effective language needs to be combined with an examination of the rhetoric actually found in the Hellenistic

---

66. In 1989 Burton Mack wrote, "There is no guarantee that learning to read these stories as chreiai will put us in touch with things we have not known in some way or another all along, much less help us solve the pack of problems with which the synoptic tradition confronts us" ("Elaboration of the Chreia in the Hellenistic School," in *Patterns of Persuasion*, 66).

67. Parrott, "Conflict and Rhetoric," 132.

68. Moeser, "Anecdote," 313.

69. Richard A. Burridge has begun this work in his contributions to *Handbook of Classical Rhetoric in the Hellenistic Period: 330 B.C.–A.D. 400* (ed. Stanley E. Porter; Boston/Leiden: Brill, 2001): "Biography," 371–91, and "The Gospels and Acts," 507–32. Burridge ("Biography," 371–91) points out that both the *bioi* and the Gospels are dissimilar in significant ways to oratory, which was the main concern of the rhetorical handbooks. Mikeal Parsons has found evidence of rhetorical techniques in the Gospel of Luke: "Luke and the Progymnasmata: A Preliminary Investigation into the Preliminary Exercises," in Mikeal Parsons, *Luke: Storyteller, Interpreter, and Evangelist* (Peabody, Mass.: Hendrickson, forthcoming).

70. This is the shift made by Witherington, *Mark*, 224, in commenting on Salyer's analysis in "Rhetoric, Purity, and Play."

biographies. Such a study should help us to discover how the "forceful and imaginative language" in the Gospels, so ably set forth by Robert Tannehill, would have been heard by a Hellenistic audience accustomed to its culture's modes of persuasion.

13

The Church and the Resurrection

Another Look at the Ending of Mark

Sharon H. Ringe

The abrupt ending of Mark — the absence of appearance narratives, the puzzling ending with the conjunction *gar* (for), the women's frightened silence — used to prompt scholars to flights of imagination. Commentators working in earlier periods often speculated about lost endings or tragic interruptions of the evangelist's work. In recent years the question they have posed is "why?" or "so what?" instead of whether the author really intended such an ending. Now we puzzle over the meaning of the text as we have it in the best manuscripts, and the implications of the Gospel's ending for Markan theology and redaction.[1]

Several factors have prompted that shift of emphasis. First, critics have recognized that there is no way to know "authorial intent" beyond what is actually written in a text or stated elsewhere by an author him- or herself. Second, various forms of literary criticism have directed our attention to the text itself instead of to the world behind the text,[2] whether on the plane of events in the life of the historical Jesus or of the author's community, which held the focus of most earlier work. Robert Tannehill, in whose honor this essay is offered, has been a pioneer in several aspects of that study. In particular, he has

---

1. For a summary of such explanations, see Bruce M. Metzger, *The Text of the New Testament: Its Transmission, Corruption, and Restoration* (3d ed.; New York: Oxford University Press, 1992), 228. For a discussion of the various endings proposed for this Gospel found in the manuscripts, see Michael W. Holmes, "To Be Continued . . . The Many Endings of the Gospel of Mark," *BRev* 17 (Aug. 2001): 12–23, 48–50.

2. For a summary of some of those findings, see Joel F. Williams, "Literary Approaches to the End of Mark's Gospel," *JETS* 42 (1999): 21–35.

done significant work in the subdiscipline of narrative criticism on both Mark and Luke,[3] which has set the background and standard for my own study. Finally, again prompted by the model of Professor Tannehill's work, interpreters are looking at the effect of biblical writings on their audience. In particular, we have learned to ask about the theological questions and concerns embedded in the text, in contrast to the earlier agenda of fitting the early biblical material into subsequent systematic theological agenda of the church.

All of these developments have informed this study. It was prompted specifically, however, by the discussion of Mark in Norman Perrin's final work, *The Resurrection according to Matthew, Mark, and Luke*,[4] the proofreading of which was completed only a few days before his death in November of 1976. Perrin suggests three reasons why the ending is appropriate to, and consistent with, the Markan theological agenda: (1) the interpretation of the passion and resurrection in the central section of the Gospel (8:22–10:52); (2) Galilee as the symbol for the Gentile mission; and (3) the motif of failed discipleship before and after the resurrection as an indication that Mark's own church must live in the interim between crucifixion and Parousia, when Jesus' past suffering serves as a model for the disciples' present suffering. I want to suggest that the ongoing daily life of the church, and not an assumed concern with its eschatological locus, provides us with a pastoral-theological context and interpretation for the ending of the Gospel at 16:8. That concern is related also to earlier references to the resurrection or to the resurrected Lord in the Gospel (not just in the central section) and to the meaning of "Galilee," in keeping with Perrin's literary-critical observations. The literary and theological function of the ending of the Gospel, in turn, provides a clue to the narrative and theological integrity of Mark's Gospel.

―――――――――――――――

3. Robert C. Tannehill, *A Mirror for Disciples: A Study of the Gospel of Mark* (Nashville: Discipleship Resources, 1977); idem, "The Gospel of Mark as Narrative Christology," *Semeia* 16 (1979): 57–95; idem, *The Narrative Unity of Luke-Acts: A Literary Interpretation* (2 vols.; Philadelphia: Fortress, 1986–90).

4. Norman Perrin, *The Resurrection according to Matthew, Mark, and Luke* (Philadelphia: Fortress, 1977).

Earlier References to the Resurrection
and to the Resurrected Lord

Perrin's examination of the central section of Mark calls attention to the passion predictions and the narrative of the Transfiguration (9:2–8) as central to our understanding of Mark's view of the resurrection.[5] The three formal passion predictions (8:31; 9:31; 10:33–34) tell us little about Mark's understanding of the resurrection. According to Perrin, they tell us more about Mark's view of the centrality of the passion in understanding both Mark's Christology and his view of the parallel fate of John the Baptist, Jesus, and the Christian martyrs. The summaries of the passion are richly textured, and they are shaped by declarations of betrayal (*paradidōmi*) and suffering. In contrast to the variety in the summaries of the passion, concerning the resurrection Mark says only that "after three days" he will "rise." The verb used in each case is *anistēmi,* twice in the future tense and once as an aorist infinitive completing the verb *dei* (8:31). If one accepts the likelihood that these "predictions" are in fact post-Easter summaries either by Mark himself or by the pre-Markan church, these formulas appear to reflect either an early stage in the church's life, when the resurrection was simply proclaimed and when appearance narratives had not yet been developed,[6] or else a creedal formula indicating the centrality of fact and not form or manner of resurrection in the church's confession.

The empty-tomb narrative (16:1–8) confirms Mark's focus on proclamation and not narrative as vehicle for presenting the resurrection.[7] The words of the young man (16:6–7) affirm simply that he has been raised (aor. pass. of *egeirō*), is absent from the tomb, and is going before them to Galilee. The special mention of a report to "his disciples and Peter" may situate the story at the level

---

5. Ibid., 19–25.

6. Reginald H. Fuller, *The Formation of the Resurrection Narratives* (New York: Macmillan, 1971), 66–67.

7. Raymond Fisher ("The Empty Tomb Story in Mark: Its Origin and Significance," *Neot* 33 [1991]: 559–77), on the other hand, interprets Mark's formulation of the empty-tomb story to express the resurrection as reflective of the transition from oral tradition to written text, and of the need to bring primitive oral traditions concerning the resurrection into conformity with Pauline theology.

of church elaboration reflected in the lists of recipients of appearances without narration of details or circumstances, such as the one in 1 Cor 15:3–8. Just as that list is significant primarily as a warrant of Paul's apostolic mission, so we might also anticipate such a referent in Mark's truncated list as well, as the discussion below of the significance of Galilee in this Gospel indeed bears out.

Mark's apparently minimal interest in details surrounding the resurrection is corroborated, according to Perrin, by the transfiguration narrative. That narrative, Perrin says, represents "the state of Jesus after his resurrection." The crucial point is not any continuing manner of presence on earth as the resurrected one, but rather that "he is in heaven with Moses and Elijah awaiting the moment of his return to earth as Son of Man." From this, Perrin concludes that Mark's real concern is about the Parousia, focal point of hope and longing during the difficult meantime of the church.[8] Other scholars similarly conclude that for Mark the resurrection itself is not all that important, but rather it is a provisional stage anticipating the Parousia. They base their conclusion on details of the empty-tomb narrative itself. Many who draw this conclusion point to the future tense of *horaō*, used in Parousia predictions in Mark 13:26 (*opsontai*) and 14:62 (*opsesthe*).[9]

Because that usage to refer to the Parousia is not exclusive, and the same verb can refer to resurrection traditions too (albeit in other biblical books, as in Matt 28:7, 10; John 20:18, 25, 29; 1 Cor 9:1), John Dominic Crossan points to the possibility of an anti-Jerusalem motif in Mark. Opposition to, or at least rivalry with, the Jerusalem church would, according to this argument, lead Mark to want to discredit reports of appearances to Peter (such as that in 1 Cor 15:3–5a) in favor of a new center in the Markan community. He posits that place as at once the location of Jesus' past ministry, the place of current mission (in particular, mission to the errant Jerusalem-centered

---

8. Perrin, *Resurrection*, 24–25.
9. Ernst Lohmeyer (*Das Evangelium des Markus* [Göttingen: Vandenhoeck & Ruprecht, 1954], 354–55) represents this line of argument.

church), and especially the locus of Christ's anticipated eschatological return.[10] In a similar vein, Theodore Weeden pursues the theme of Mark's opposition to the disciples, seeing in the postresurrection failure of the women portrayed in the empty-tomb narrative the final straw leading to Mark's view of Jesus as "absent not just from the grave. He has completely left the human scene and will not return until the Parousia."[11]

Both of these scholars have bolstered their argument with prior conclusions about Mark's agenda. Furthermore, several details in 16:1–8 do not seem to support a Parousia interpretation. For example, there is the present tense of *proagei* in 16:7 and, except for the young man in the shining robe (*stolē leukē*) mentioned in 16:5, the absence of the vocabulary of glory associated with the Parousia. These findings compel both Pheme Perkins and Ernest Best (as well as others) to conclude against a Parousia reference,[12] and require us to push on as well.

It may indeed be true, as Perrin suggests, that the transfiguration narrative commends itself to our attention as Mark's view of the resurrected Christ read back into the account of Jesus' earthly ministry. Nevertheless, two additional pericopes found earlier in the Gospel include details hinting that they too should be seen in light of the resurrection. They are the two narratives of the storms on the "Sea" of Galilee (4:35–41 and 6:45–52).[13] These two narratives have many details in common, from their setting on the "Sea" of Galilee at evening (and on into the night), to the daunting winds and the fearful disciples.

---

10. John Dominic Crossan, "Empty Tomb and Absent Lord," in *The Passion in Mark: Studies in Mark 14–16* (ed. Werner H. Kelber; Philadelphia: Fortress, 1976), 146.

11. Theodore J. Weeden, *Mark — Traditions in Conflict* (Philadelphia: Fortress, 1971), 110.

12. Pheme Perkins, *Resurrection: New Testament Witness and Contemporary Reflection* (Garden City, N.Y.: Doubleday, 1984), 120; Ernest Best, *Following Jesus: Discipleship in Mark* (JSNTSup 4; Sheffield: Sheffield University Press, 1981), 240–41.

13. Not all scholars agree that these are stories of the resurrected Christ. Eduard Schweizer, for example, represents the majority position that considers them stories depicting Jesus' divine or wonder-working power during his earthly life (*The Good News According to Mark* [trans. D. H. Madvig; Atlanta: John Knox, 1970], 108–10, 141–42). The discussion below, however, identifies dimensions of these narratives warranting my conclusion that they are appearance stories.

The first of the stories (4:35–41) has several aspects that give it a certain verisimilitude. Winds blowing from the Mediterranean Sea on the west, eastward through Pigeon Pass do give rise to sudden storms on the lake that can catch even experienced sailors far from port. There may have been an occasion during Jesus' ministry with the disciples when they were caught in such a storm, with an exhausted Jesus sleeping in the stern of the boat. When he was finally awakened by the nervous disciples, he reassured them, and as suddenly as it had started, the storm stopped. Whatever may have happened, if any actual event did underlie the account, it was nevertheless remembered, shaped, and narrated as having a causal relationship between Jesus' alert presence and the meteorological calm.

Several details suggest that the narrative has been further shaped as a story of the risen Lord. First, the disciples and only the disciples are present, as they are in the appearance stories in the other Gospels. The community is gathered, and in a place apart. They are in a boat, early a symbol for the Christian church. Jesus has been sleeping (a common metaphor for death) and awakens. Life and death are at stake in the storm, and Jesus is the one who holds the key to both. At issue are faith and fear. Six times in Mark the disciples are said to be gripped by the fear that is a blend of awe and terror (*phobos,* or the verb *phobeomai*). Two of them are in these stormy sea journeys (4:41; 6:50). Two others accompany passion predictions (9:32; 10:32). The others are at the transfiguration (9:6) and at the empty tomb (16:8). Despite the fact that Jesus' "rebuking" (*epitimaō*) of the storm is language appropriate to an exorcism (as in 1:25, 34; 3:12) or to Jesus' confrontation of Peter/Satan (8:33), the reaction of fear marks what has transpired as an epiphany.[14]

In short, here we seem to be glimpsing questions faced by Mark's church in the midst of the storms they encountered — questions of faith, fear, life, and death, in which the crucified and risen Lord is recognized as present with them continually in their need — still in the nighttime of the life of the church, and not only on the "day"

---

14. Edwin K. Broadhead, *Mark* (Sheffield: Sheffield Academic, 2001), 49.

of the Parousia, and when the journey still continues to the "other side."[15] In that painful meantime of the church, the cosmic authority of the exalted Lord is already affirmed as fact. It is the same authority that opened the way for Israel's liberation from Egypt through the Red Sea.[16] Furthermore, as God delivered humankind from the chaos symbolized by the sea (Pss 65:7; 68:22; 89:9; 95:5; 104:7; 106:9; 107:23–29; Jonah 1:4–5, 10), so now does the risen Christ.[17] The significance of Mark's innovative designation of Galilee as a *thalassa* is now clear. This one whom even the wind and the sea obey is the risen Christ who acts with full divine power and authority.

The same themes of epiphany and divine authority in the now risen Christ are intensified in the second storm narrative (6:45–52).[18] Jesus has forced (*anankazō*, Mark 6:45) them to set out alone. "If the first journey was made under the 'protection' of the present Jesus, in the second the disciples are compelled to make the crossing on their own."[19] As is the case in the resurrection appearance stories in the other Gospels, when Jesus does appear, he is not recognized (see Matt 28:17; Luke 24:13–35, 37, 41; John 20:14–16; 21:4–7). Instead, the disciples think they have seen a ghost (*phantasma*). They are afraid, this time because of Jesus' presence as the "I AM" (the emphatic form, *egō eimi*; cf. Exod 3:14) who quells the storm, and not by the ferocity of the storm itself. Yet they ought to have understood because of "the loaves" (Mark 6:52).

The account in 6:47–52 follows the account of the feeding of the five thousand (6:30–44). The implication of 6:52 is that their confusion and fear when Jesus appears reflects their failure to understand the feeding they have just witnessed. In 8:14–21 a similar picture

---

15. Best, *Following Jesus*, 232.

16. The word *thalassa* compels that connection. It occurs fifteen times in Exod 14 (LXX), where the story of that sea crossing is narrated. See the discussion of the links between these two narratives in William Richard Stegner, "Jesus' Walking on the Water: Mark 6.45–52," in *The Gospels and the Scriptures of Israel* (ed. Craig A. Evans and W. Richard Stegner; JSNTSup 104; Sheffield: Sheffield Academic, 1994), 217–21.

17. Ched Myers, *Binding the Strong Man: A Political Reading of Mark's Story of Jesus* (Maryknoll, N.Y.: Orbis Books, 1988), 196.

18. Broadhead (*Mark*, 66–67) recognizes a particularly close connection between this narrative and that in John 21:4–7.

19. Ibid., 196.

linking distress on a sea journey "to the other side" with failure to understand the feeding underlines the theological weight of the story. The word seems to me to be clearly from and to Mark's church, rowing into the winds of struggling mission, of political reality (the war either at hand or just past), and of opposition outside the boat and faltering faith within. Yet if they can come to know the Risen One present with them in the "boat" and in the eucharistic memory of the loaves as well as in remembering how the hungry have been fed, they can endure.[20]

Mark has indeed moved beyond mere proclamation of the resurrection and in narrative form affirms its power. By incorporating resurrection narratives such as the sea journeys in the body of the Gospel, Mark presents the resurrection not as providing glimpses of the Risen One in those first few days after Easter — glimpses which can only be remembered in the long meantime — but rather as being the basis for the ongoing presence of Christ in the church. He is indeed going before us to "Galilee."

The Meaning of Galilee in Mark

Clearly the young man's reference to Jesus' going before them to Galilee (16:7) echoes Jesus' promise in 14:28. Galilee is the only place mentioned in this Gospel in connection with post-Easter hopes. At issue still is what "Galilee" meant to Mark. Was it merely a geographical designation, perhaps indicating the place where Mark's church was centered? Was it purely symbolic? Or was it some blend of the two? Perrin follows much of British scholarship in concluding that for Mark, Galilee is symbolic of the Gentile mission.[21] Recognizing that

---

20. Charles Homer Giblin argues that Mark links the loaves and Jesus' presence with the disciples in their boat in an apocalyptic correlation of the theological symbols of Eucharist and Parousia ("The Beginning of the Ongoing Gospel: Mk 1,2–16,8," in *The Four Gospels, 1992: Festschrift Frans Neirynck* [ed. Frans van Segbroeck et al.; 3 vols.; BETL 100; Leuven: Leuven University Press/Peeters, 1992], 2:979). His positing of the Parousia as the time of presence of Christ in the church is predicated on his assumption of an apocalyptic framework for the entire Gospel.

21. Perrin, *Resurrection*, 26–27.

Galilee is not Gentile territory, Fuller tempers that assertion by see-ing it as the place *"from which the mission goes out to the Gentiles"* (emphasis his) through the apostolic mission of the church.[22]

It is tempting to posit Galilee as the literal location of Mark's church and thus as symbolic of the early church in general, or even to see the blossoming of a Jerusalem-Galilee dispute over the legitimacy of the Gentile mission (with Galilee representing the more inclusive side of the argument).[23] Yet the text of the Gospel suggests a simpler solution. If one accepts, as I do, that Mark's was the first Gospel, then when Mark's church reached the end of what we now call 16:8, *kai oudeni ouden eipan: ephobounto gar,* they would have been sent back immediately to the beginning of the Gospel, *archē tou euan-geliou Iēsou Christou* (1:1). That beginning does not take us to the Jerusalem suburbs as the place where the Risen One is met (as in Luke 24; John 20). Rather, after an introduction that links Jesus to John the Baptist and to Jesus' baptism by John and his testing in the wilderness by Satan (1:2–13), we are taken to the beginning of Jesus' ministry in Galilee (1:14–15), where we encounter not only the Nazarene of historical memory, but also the Christ known in the post-Easter community.[24] Through their own proclamation of Jesus and through their acceptance of Jesus' call to discipleship, the hearers or readers of the Gospel are in a position to complete "the gospel of Jesus Christ, the Son of God" that Mark has begun.[25]

What is at stake is not simply the rereading of the written work, but rather its completion through the lived experience of the church, in

---

22. Fuller, *Formation*, 62, 67; see also Perkins, *Resurrection*, 120.

23. Crossan, "Empty Tomb," 149; Werner H. Kelber, *The Kingdom in Mark: A New Place and a New Time* (Philadelphia: Fortress, 1974), 130–40. See also the discussion in Edwin K. Broadhead, *Prophet, Son, Messiah: Narrative Form and Function in Mark 14–16* (Sheffield: Sheffield Academic, 1994), 242–43.

24. Edwin K. Broadhead builds his interpretation of Mark's Christology and of the Gospel as a whole on the links between the ending of Mark and the Galilee as the locus of Jesus' ministry. See his discussions in *Prophet, Son, Messiah*, 241–46; *Mark*, 147–49; "In Search of the Gospel: Research Trends in Mark 14–16," *ABR* 43 (1995): 47–49.

25. John Paul Heil, "The Progressive Narrative Pattern of Mark 14,53–16,8," *Bib* 73 (1992): 357. A similar point is argued by J. David Hester, who concludes that the "inconclusive" ending "requires actual readers, disappointed by the role they are expected to play (implied reader) to enter the story and act upon it" ("Dramatic Inconclusion: Irony and the Narrative Rhetoric of the Ending of Mark," *JSNT* 57 [1995]: 84).

which the Risen One accompanies them, and indeed goes on ahead of them, as Jesus has done from the beginning.[26] The Gospel of Mark thus works like a continuous-play compact disk: as soon as it appears to end, the story begins again, with teachings, healings, the calls of disciples, incidents at table. In the church's retelling of the story, which is also the proclamation of their own lived experience of the Risen One in their midst, Jesus is present again — a *mnēmosynon* (reminder) that re-presents the moments of salvation.[27]

Galilee is thus both symbol and place, insofar as it is that place (everyplace) where Jesus is known and met, where disciples are called, taught, led, comforted, astounded, afraid, and in awe again in the church.[28] There the Jesus who called the disciples once continues to call those who hear the story, and that same Jesus is present now as the Risen and therefore Living One — the same one whose life was authenticated by God in the drama of Easter, and who will return again in glory at the last day. The "beginning" ("This is the *beginning* of the gospel of Jesus Christ . . . ") is thus Jesus' life as it was remembered to have happened and to have been important, for the story goes on precisely in the life and proclamation of the church that continues to tell the story. The present and even the future (*opsesthe*) points of reference are the same as the past: Galilee.

The Irony of Mark's Ending

The words of the young man at the tomb are words of hope and promise. Just as both Peter (in his denials) and the disciples (in their flight) represent a double collapse of the community, they are specifically to be recipients of the proclamation of fact ("He has been raised;

---

26. Giblin, "Beginning of the Ongoing Gospel," 2:978.

27. Although they reach the conclusion by other routes, other scholars also posit Galilee as the locus of Christ's presence in the proclamation of the church. See, for example, Willi Marxsen, *Mark the Evangelist: Studies on the Redaction History of the Gospel* (trans. J. Boyce et al.; Nashville: Abingdon, 1969), 86, 91; Tannehill, *Mirror for Disciples*, 116–17; Myers, *Binding the Strong Man*, 398–99; David Rhoads, Joanna Dewey, and Donald Michie, *Mark as Story: An Introduction to the Narrative of a Gospel* (2d ed.; Minneapolis: Fortress, 1999), 72.

28. Robert Tannehill points to Mark 13 as indicative of the postresurrection situation of the Markan church, when the anticipated shift from the disciples' apparent failure to their possible faithfulness is actually realized ("Narrative Christology," 83).

he is not here") and promise ("you will see him"). Like the disciples in the appearance stories of the other Gospels, here the women at the empty tomb receive an apostolic commission that aims at reversing the command of secrecy that has pervaded the Gospel until the end.[29] The secret is no longer necessary, because in the fact of crucifixion the true identity of the Human One (*ho huios tou anthrōpou*) has been revealed, and in the commission all are sent back to the places where the earlier deed/words of God's reign have been proclaimed.

But despite the words of the young man, the women's response is said to be silence and fear. Does Mark intend to say that they have now failed as had Peter and the others earlier? It sounds that way, and it sounds further as though their failure to bring the message to "his disciples and Peter" would take away the possibility that the others' failures might be overcome. The report of the women's response would lend credence to those who conclude that for Mark there is no resurrected Christ, and that the report "He is not here" refers to his permanent absence until the Parousia.[30] We might even say, with Frank Kermode, that Mark's ending with the enclitic *gar* was as weak as James Joyce's ending of *Finnegans Wake* with the word "the," whose strength comes only from its being the first word in the book as well as the last. No such redemption, according to Kermode, awaits Mark's *gar:* "Mark's book began with a trumpet call: 'This is the beginning of the gospel of Jesus Christ, the Son of God.' It ends with this faint whisper of timid women."[31]

As I see it, that allegedly "weak" ending of Mark finds its strength not in a grammatical finesse, but in literary irony, for Mark includes the report of the women's fearful silence. His "omniscient narrator" received the word somehow — perhaps in the lived experience of Mark's community. Perhaps awareness of the presence of the Risen One happened for Mark's community without the high drama that might find its way into appearance stories. Instead, in what Henri

---

29. Thomas Boomershine, "Mark 16:8 and the Apostolic Commission," *JBL* 100 (1981): 225.

30. Weeden, *Mark*, 114–15.

31. Frank Kermode, *The Genesis of Secrecy: On the Interpretation of Narrative* (Cambridge: Harvard University Press, 1979), 67–68.

Nouwen calls the intimacy of absence,[32] there came a discovery among Jesus' closest followers that it was as if the one who had cared for them and challenged them before Jesus' death continued to do so; it was as if Jesus were still (or again) with them.

The woman's anointing of Jesus as the Christ (14:3–9) replaced the customary anointing by the women at the grave because in the truth of Mark's community, which was the point of his proclamation of the Gospel, Jesus was absent from the tomb and, as the risen Christ, was present with them, continuing to comfort and transform them in the retelling of the stories and the remembering of the church. For Mark, the message is clear: Christ is risen indeed!

---

32. Henri J. M. Nouwen, *In Memoriam* (Notre Dame, Ind.: Ave Maria, 1980), 37.

14

The Sensory-Aesthetic Texture of the Compassionate Samaritan Parable in Luke 10

Vernon K. Robbins

It is a special honor and pleasure to write an essay that gives tribute to Robert C. Tannehill's contribution to New Testament interpretation. I first saw and heard him when he read a paper at a meeting of the Society of Biblical Literature in the early 1970s on the rhetorical force of the repetitive patterns in "The Birds and the Lilies" passage in Matt 6:25–33//Luke 12:22–31.[1] This paper persuaded me that it was important to incorporate aesthetic literary and rhetorical interpretation into mainline biblical commentary. Since then, the question has been how to formulate a richer, fuller understanding of the emergence and effect of Christianity in the world by incorporating these dynamics in biblical commentary.

In the same mode, this essay interprets the parable traditionally called the Good Samaritan in its Lukan context.[2] The inclusion of all of the Lukan narration calls attention to the interplay between Jesus' description of the Samaritan as compassionate (*esplanchnisthē,*

---

1. Robert C. Tannehill, "The Birds and the Lilies," later published in R. C. Tannehill, *The Sword of His Mouth* (Semeia Supplements 1; Philadelphia: Fortress; Missoula, Mont.: Scholars, 1975), 60–67.
2. I am grateful to Robert von Thaden for his skillful bibliographical assistance for this essay. For an alternative title for the parable as "From Jerusalem to Jericho," see Bernard Brandon Scott, *Hear Then the Parable: A Commentary on the Parables of Jesus* (Minneapolis: Fortress, 1989), 189.

10:33) and the lawyer's description of him as merciful (*eleos,* 10:37).[3] Careful attention to Lukan discourse reveals that no adjective for "good" (*agathos* or *kalos*) occurs either in the parable or in the interchange between Jesus and the lawyer. Instead, the focus is on the response of all of one's body to the needs of others, no matter what the circumstances or who the people might be.

Tannehill started to bring his views on this Lukan passage into print already in 1974 when he responded to essays by Daniel Patte and John Dominic Crossan on the genre and narrative structure of the parable.[4] He complimented Patte for "tak[ing] account of the clear three-fold structure of the Good Samaritan (three potential helpers approach the injured man) and . . . relat[ing] this to the fact that the parable begins as the story of the injured man."[5] In turn, he complimented Crossan for "catch[ing] the proper emphasis when he says that Luke 10:30 is the 'initial situation' which establishes the traveler as wounded and so prepares for what follows. It provides the occasion for a story rather than being the basic story sequence."[6] In the context of these comments, Tannehill emphasized "the importance of rhetorical highlighting effects"[7] in *particular* stories as a key for interpretation of them. Calling attention to the presence of the three-fold pattern that is "so common in popular storytelling," he asserted, "Our attention is focused on the third traveler before he arrives, and this heightens the shock when we discover that he neither fits the pattern of cultural expectation nor the pattern of expectation created by the series priest, Levite."[8]

With these emphases, Tannehill was introducing an intricate and complex literary, rhetorical, and cultural mode of analysis and

---

3. German interpreters regularly capture this dimension of the parable with the adjective *barmherzig*; e.g., Gerhard Sellin, "Lukas als Gleichniserzähler: Die Erzählung vom barmherzigen Samariter (Lk 10:25–37)," *ZNW* 65 (1974): 166–89; 66 (1975): 2–59.

4. Robert C. Tannehill, "Comments on the Articles of Daniel Patte and John Dominic Crossan," *Semeia* 2 (1974): 113–16.

5. Ibid., 114.

6. Ibid.

7. Ibid., 115.

8. Ibid. Later he explained that the logical sequence would be priest, Levite, lay Israelite: Robert C. Tannehill, *Luke* (ANTC; Nashville: Abingdon, 1996), 183.

interpretation.[9] Moreover, the mode of interpretation is implicitly social in its orientation.[10] These strategies were coming into the field of New Testament interpretation during the 1970s especially through the influence of Amos N. Wilder and William A. Beardslee.[11] In the present essay, my purpose is to build on the insights Tannehill has contributed in broad ways to our field of study and in special ways to the Gospel of Luke. The essay emphasizes the sensory-aesthetic texture[12] of the story of the Good Samaritan in its Lukan context to present a "full-bodied interpretation." In particular, I present analysis and interpretation of "body zones"[13] to enrich and expand the literary, rhetorical, social, and cultural mode of interpretation Tannehill has been nurturing for more than thirty years.

The Topos of Love in Lukan Narration

In his commentary on the Gospel of Luke, Tannehill observes that Luke 10:25–37 focuses on "love of neighbor."[14] A sociorhetorical approach to this story focuses on "love" as a topos.[15] This portion of text reconfigures the topos of love for God in Jewish culture into the topos of enacting mercy for a wounded person. In Carolyn Miller's terms:

---

9. See his first full literary analysis of Luke: Robert C. Tannehill, *The Gospel According to Luke* (vol. 1 of *The Narrative Unity of Luke-Acts: A Literary Interpretation;* Philadelphia: Fortress, 1986).

10. See the emphasis on social dimensions in Tannehill, *Luke,* 28–29.

11. Cf. Amos N. Wilder, "Scholars, Theologians, and Ancient Rhetoric," *JBL* 75 (1956): 1–11; idem, *Early Christian Rhetoric: The Language of the Gospel* (New York: Harper & Row, 1964); William A. Beardslee, *Literary Criticism of the New Testament* (Philadelphia: Fortress, 1970); Richard A. Spencer, ed., *Orientation by Disorientation: Studies in Literary Criticism and Biblical Literary Criticism: Presented in Honor of William A. Beardslee* (Pittsburgh: Pickwick, 1980).

12. Vernon K. Robbins, *Exploring the Texture of Texts: A Guide to Socio-Rhetorical Interpretation* (Harrisburg, Pa.: Trinity Press International, 1996), 29–36; idem, *The Tapestry of Early Christian Discourse: Rhetoric, Society and Ideology* (London and New York: Routledge, 1996), 64–65, 89–91.

13. Bruce C. Malina, *The New Testament World: Insights from Cultural Anthropology* (rev. ed.; Louisville: Westminster John Knox, 1993), 73–81; Robbins, *Exploring,* 30–36.

14. Tannehill, *Luke,* 181–85.

15. For basic insights into a sociorhetorical approach to topoi (plural of topos), see Vernon K. Robbins, "The Intertexture of Apocalyptic Discourse in the Gospel of Mark," in *The Intertexture of Apocalyptic Discourse in the New Testament* (ed. Duane F. Watson; SBLSymS 14; Atlanta: SBL, 2002), 11–15.

The *topos* is a conceptual space without fully specified or speci-
fiable contents; it is a region of productive uncertainty. It is
a "problem space," but rather than circumscribing or delim-
iting the problem, rather than being a closed space or container
within which one searches, it is a space, or a located perspective,
from which one searches. I am thinking here of the linguistic notion of "semantic space." . . . Such semantic networks may
be conditioned both by the peculiarities of community history
and by apparently logical relationships (like opposition and
inclusion).[16]

Opening-middle-closing texture[17] is prominent in Luke 10:25–37,
and the opening texture establishes the sociocultural topos of love
through dialogue between Jesus and a lawyer who stands up to test
Jesus (10:25). When the lawyer introduces the topos of "inheriting eternal life" (10:25), Jesus responds with the topos of "written
Torah" (10:26), to which the lawyer responds with the topos of
"love for God and for neighbor" (10:27). Once the topos of love
(*agapān/agapē*) emerges, it does not occur again in the overall interchange between Jesus and the lawyer. Instead, the topos of love
functions as a semantic space into which the discourse weaves multiple meanings. When the response of the lawyer moves to the topos of
neighbor, the dialogue, through the strategy of a story within a story,
reconfigures the topos of love into the topos of "mercy (*eleos*)" in
the remark of the lawyer in the closing scene (10:37). Since the topos
of mercy had widespread Mediterranean valence during the first century,[18] the persuasive force of its social rhetoric had a potential to
reach beyond the confines of Jewish and eastern Mediterranean culture into the widest horizons of Mediterranean culture, and even into
almost any culture in the world.

---

16. Carolyn R. Miller, "The Aristotelean *Topos*: Hunting for Novelty," in *Rereading Aristotle's Rhetoric* (ed. Alan G. Gross and Arthur E. Walzer; Carbondale and Edwardsville: Southern
Illinois University Press, 2000), 141.

17. Robbins, *Tapestry*, 50–53, 70–72; idem, *Exploring*, 19–21.

18. Rudolf Bultmann, "eleos, eleeo, eleemon, eleemosune, aneleos, aneleemon," *TDNT*
2:477–87.

The semantic space for reconfiguring love of God into mercy for a wounded man emerges from written Torah, which Jewish people by the first century of the common era presupposed to be a conventional resource for inheriting eternal life (cf. Lev 18:5). The intertexture of the lawyer's recitation creates the semantic space. The lawyer does not introduce the topos of love "from the air." Rather, when Jesus asks the lawyer what is written in the Torah, the lawyer exhibits the characteristics of a Jew who has learned not only the first verse of the Shema but also essential related passages. These passages include Deut 6:6–7 (NRSV): "Keep these words that I am commanding you today in your heart. Recite them to your children and talk about them when you are at home and when you are away, when you lie down and when you rise." This lawyer has kept the words of the Shema in his heart. When Jesus asks him to recite words "written in the Torah," he is able not only to recite the portion of the Shema in Deut 6:5, which Jews were to recite twice daily (sunrise, sunset: Deut 6:7),[19] but also to recite Lev 19:18 about loving one's neighbor, which is linked to the Shema through the introductory command, "love" (LXX: *agapēseis*). The ability of the lawyer to link another Torah passage containing the word *love* to the Shema shows that this lawyer not only holds the Shema in his heart, but also readily knows other portions of the Torah.

Once the dialogue between Jesus and the lawyer has brought the topos of love of God into speech and linked it with the topos of neighbor, Jesus could have continued to the end of the scene with a monologue that elaborated these topoi. When there is such an approach in Lukan discourse, there is no closing scene that reintroduces the initial interlocutor with Jesus (cf. 11:1–13;[20]

---

19. Cf. m. Berakhoth 1:1–4; cf. Joseph A. Fitzmyer, *The Gospel According to Luke: Introduction, Translation, and Notes* (AB 28–28A; 2 vols.; Garden City, N.Y.: Doubleday, 1981–85), 2:878.

20. See Vernon K. Robbins, "From Enthymeme to Theology in Luke 11:1–13," in *Literary Studies in Luke-Acts: A Collection of Essays in Honor of Joseph B. Tyson* (ed. R. P. Thompson and T. E. Phillips; Macon, Ga.: Mercer University Press, 1998), 191–214. Online: http://www.emory.edu/COLLEGE/RELIGION/faculty/robbins/Theology/theology191.html.

11:14–36;[21] 15:1–32). Luke 10:25–37, in contrast, presents an overall story with opening-middle-closing texture. The opening scene
contains dialogue between Jesus and a lawyer that introduces the
topos "love of neighbor" (10:25–28). In the middle scene (10:29–
35), Jesus continues the dialogue with a story that contains its
own opening-middle-closing texture (10:30, 31–34, 35). The closing
scene reaches its conclusion in dialogue that reconfigures the topos
of love of neighbor into the topos of mercy (10:36–37). The result is a story within a story: a story about a Samaritan helping a
wounded man within a story about an encounter between Jesus and
a lawyer.[22]

A special feature of the narrational texture[23] of Luke 10:25–37 is
the presence of questions in each portion of the overall story. In the
opening scene, the lawyer asks Jesus a question (10:25) and Jesus
responds with two questions (10:26). The middle scene opens with a
second question by the lawyer (10:29), and the closing scene opens
with a question by Jesus. All of these questions truly seek information.
In rhetorical terminology, they are inquiries, rather than simple questions that can be answered "yes" or "no," or questions calling for an
explanation.[24] None of the questions is simply rhetorical, and no response is simply a retort. All of the dialogue earnestly seeks answers
to difficult issues. Indeed, a remarkable feature of the overall story
is the absence of explicitly rhetorical constituents of argumentative
discourse, such as rationales, contraries or opposites, analogies, conditional constructions, pronouncements of authoritative testimony,
and conclusions (cf. Luke 11:1–13, 14–36; 15:1–32).

---

21. See Vernon K. Robbins, "Beelzebul Controversy in Mark and Luke: Rhetorical and Social
Analysis," *Forum* 7.3–4 (1991): 261–77; cf. idem, "Rhetorical Composition and the Beelzebul
Controversy," in *Patterns of Persuasion in the Gospels* (ed. B. L. Mack and V. K. Robbins;
Sonoma, Calif.: Polebridge, 1989), 185–91.

22. Cf. the perceptive rhetorical interpretation of the unit as *exordium* (10:25–28), *definitio*
or redefinition of the issue (10:29–35), *peroratio* including the final imperative (10:36–37):
J. Ian H. McDonald, "Rhetorical Issue and Rhetorical Strategy in Luke 10.25–37 and Acts
10.1–11.18," in *Rhetoric and the New Testament: Essays from the 1992 Heidelberg Conference*
(ed. S. E. Porter and T. H. Olbricht; JSNTSup 90; Sheffield: Sheffield Academic, 1993), 66–67.

23. Robbins, *Exploring*, 15–19; idem, *Tapestry*, 53–58, 72–77.

24. See Ronald F. Hock and Edward N. O'Neil, eds., *The Progymnasmata* (vol. 1 of *The
Chreia in Ancient Rhetoric*; Atlanta: Scholars, 1986), 84–87.

Rhetography and Body Zones in the Overall Story

At this point it will be helpful to introduce two new words for interpretation. In rhetorical terms, argumentative discourse containing rationales, contraries or opposites, analogies, conditional constructions, authoritative written testimony, and conclusions can appropriately be called rhetology, expressible (*rhētos*)[25] reasoning (*logos*). In contrast, pictorial narration can appropriately be called rhetography, expressible graphic images.[26] Often, Lukan pictorial narration (rhetography) contains explicit rhetological features. For example, even though Luke 15:1–32 is highly pictorial, featuring three rhetographical parables in a sequence, it contains explicitly argumentative constituents in the form of rhetorical questions (15:4, 8), rationales (15:6, 9, 24, 27, 32), analogies (15:7, 10), contraries (15:28–30), and a conclusion (15:32). In contrast, Luke 10:25–37 contains only two implicit conclusions in the form of commands: (1) "You have answered aright; [therefore] do this and you will live" (10:28); (2) [The Samaritan showed mercy, which makes him a true neighbor. Therefore] "go and do likewise" (Luke 10:37). In Luke 10:25–37, the vehicle of persuasion is dominantly pictorial narration (rhetography) rather than argumentative reasoning (rhetology).[27]

The focus on bodily enactment ("go and do")[28] of statements in written Torah (10:27) and in actions in a story (10:33–35) calls for interpretive strategies guided by a taxonomy of body zones in Mediterranean antiquity. In 1979, Bruce J. Malina introduced a three-zone model for interpreting texts featuring dyadic personalities in Mediterranean antiquity,[29] and it has yielded important information

---

25. See the *"rhēt-"* words in Polybius, *Histories* 32.6.7 (to give a stated [*rhēten*] answer); Plato, *Theatetus* 205d, 205e (syllables are expressible [*rhētai*]); *Epistulai* 341c (subject matter that admits of verbal expression [*rhēton*]), 341d (things which can be stated [*rhēta*]).

26. Cf. the term "theography" in Jack Miles, *God: A Biography* (New York: Vintage Books, 1996), 12.

27. Cf. McDonald, "Rhetorical Issue," 67: "Jesus' own rhetoric appears to have allowed him to develop parabolic presentation to the point at which telling became showing and his hearers encountered the reality which his discourse conveyed."

28. See the reference to "body-reality": L. W. Mazamisa, *Beatific Comradeship: An Exegetical-Hermeneutical Study on Lk. 10:25–37* (Kampen: J. H. Kok, 1987), 102.

29. Bruce J. Malina, "The Individual and the Community — Personality in the Social World of Early Christianity," *BTB* 9 (1979): 126–38; idem, *New Testament World*, 73–82.

when interpreters have applied it. John J. Pilch has summarized the approach as follows:[30]

Human beings consist of three mutually interpenetrating yet distinguishable symbolic zones for interacting with various environments: (1) the zone of emotion-fused thought (heart-eyes); (2) the zone of self-expressive speech (mouth-ears); and (3) the zone of purposeful action (hands-feet).

	Bodily parts	Functions
Zone 1:	heart/eyes	emotion-fused thought
Zone 2:	mouth/ears	self-expressive speech
Zone 3:	hands/feet	purposeful action

Malina has listed an extensive number of nouns, verbs, and adjectives to guide interpreters in commentary on body zones.[31] In the context of this taxonomy, the effect of the recitation of the Shema in Luke 10:27 appears to refer to the entire human body in its intersubjective relation to God and to other people. The verse lists heart and mind (*dianoia*), which are agents of emotion-fused thought.[32] Malina does not list "strength," but this would appear to apply especially to people's hands and feet, the agents of purposeful action. When the verse refers to soul (*psychē*), it appears to refer to the entire person in relation to God and to others. The words of Joseph Fitzmyer seem highly appropriate when he writes, with reference to the body parts mentioned in Luke 10:27: "As a group, they sum up the totality of personal life."[33]

In the opening and closing of the overall story, then, the lawyer has articulated guidelines from the Torah concerning the response of a person's entire body both to God and to the neighbor. But even more than this is present in the pictorial depiction of the dialogue between Jesus and the lawyer. The lawyer opens the episode by using

---

30. John J. Pilch, "Sickness and Healing in Luke-Acts," in *The Social World of Luke-Acts: Models for Interpretation* (ed. J. H. Neyrey; Peabody, Mass.: Hendrickson, 1991), 204.
31. Malina, *New Testament World*, 74–75.
32. Ibid., 74.
33. Fitzmyer, *Luke*, 2:880.

his feet to stand up (*anestē*, 10:25) and his mouth to speak. Thus, he begins by enacting both the body zone of purposeful action and the body zone of self-expressive speech. Jesus responds with his own self-expressive speech by asking the lawyer (*nomikos*), whom he perceives to be a scribe,[34] to activate his emotion-fused thought. Since the eyes take information into the heart, the primary location for emotion-fused thought, Jesus asks the lawyer to activate the mode of remembering what his eyes have brought into his heart from written Torah. The effect of Jesus' response is to turn the lawyer's testing of Jesus' emotion-fused thought (10:25) into Jesus' testing of the lawyer's emotion-fused thought (10:26). The lawyer fulfills the test very well. He is able to produce the emotion-fused thought of the Shema plus Lev 19:18 in a manner that receives Jesus' approval.

But then Jesus issues one more test for the lawyer. The lawyer must bring into purposive action the emotion-fused thought he has presented so well in self-expressive speech. He must do what he has said. Since Jesus' statement is so close to statements in the Torah, such as "You shall keep my statutes and my ordinances; by doing so one shall live: I am the LORD" (Lev 18:5 NRSV), the lawyer should have no difficulty understanding Jesus' reasoning. Thus, a hearer might reasonably expect the dialogue between Jesus and the lawyer to end at this point. The lawyer certainly would not ask Jesus why he should do these things, because the presence of the statements in the Torah provides a comprehensive rationale. One does what is in the Torah, because the Torah is God's self-expressive speech concerning God's emotion-fused thought and purposive action. Humans receive benefits from God by understanding this "three body zone" revelation from God and doing what the revelation asks them to do.

The dialogue between Jesus and the lawyer does not end at this point: the lawyer continues the interaction by means of his self-expressive speech.[35] The meaning of the narrational comment that the

---

34. Cf. ibid., 1:676: "The term *nomikos* is probably only a synonym for *grammateus*, 'scribe.' "

35. Perhaps one should understand the lawyer as a teacher of the law whose profession gives prominence to his self-expressive speech. See the reference to "teachers of the law" (*nomodidaskaloi*) in Luke 5:17: cf. Fitzmyer, *Luke*, 1:581.

lawyer wanted "*dikaiōsai* (to justify)"[36] himself (10:29) is not clear. Perhaps it means that Jesus has won the respect of the lawyer, and the lawyer now wants guidelines about the meaning of "my neighbor," so he can adopt practices that will keep him from being guilty of wrong action in the future.[37] Thus, it could mean he is "wanting to keep himself innocent from wrongdoing." Perhaps it simply introduces a "combative ethos."[38] Most interpreters assign negative motives to the lawyer, suggesting that he is trying to save face.[39] Tannehill perceives the wording to mean either that the lawyer has a "false concern with his own position"[40] or that he "is suspicious and unreceptive."[41] Whatever the case, Jesus "took up"[42] the question and continued the dialogue by telling a story (10:30–35).

When the story is over, Jesus asks the lawyer to activate his emotion-fused thoughts once again, but this time in relation to the story rather than in relation to the Torah. The key is in the question "Which of these three...seems to you?" (*tis toutōn tōn triōn...dokei soi?* 10:36), rather than "What is written?" (*ti gegraptai?* 10:26). Jesus has presented a case to the lawyer and now asks him to function as a judge and announce a decision about the three men who saw the wounded man by the road. With this rhetorical move, Jesus is asking the lawyer to shift from his usual practice of making official decisions about different verses in the Torah, to a decision about different people in a realistic situation in the lives of people.

The decisive rhetorical effect of the dialogue is to change the focus from "Who is my neighbor?" (10:29) to "How does a person become

---

36. Variant *dikaioun* (present active infinitive).

37. Kenneth E. Bailey, *Through Peasant Eyes: More Lukan Parables, Their Culture and Style* (Grand Rapids: Eerdmans, 1980 [combined ed.: *Poet and Peasant;* and, *Through Peasant Eyes: A Literary-Cultural Approach to the Parables in Luke,* 1983]), 39; cf. Luke 23:47; 7:29.

38. McDonald, "Rhetorical Issue," 66.

39. The strongest case against a more positive reading is Luke 16:15; cf. 18:9, 14, 21. Cf. Fitzmyer, *Luke,* 2:886: " 'desiring to vindicate himself,' to show he was right in posing the question that he had originally proposed to Jesus, even though it found such a simple answer." For a range of possible meanings, see Darrell L. Bock, *Luke,* vol. 2: *9:51–24:53* (BECNT; Grand Rapids: Baker Books, 1996), 1027–28.

40. Tannehill, *Narrative Unity,* 1:179.

41. Tannehill, *Luke,* 181.

42. Cf. LXX: Job 2:4; 32:6; 40:1; Dan 3:28; Fitzmyer, *Luke,* 2:886.

a neighbor?" (10:36). Thus, Jesus' question is, "Which of these three, do you think, became (*gegonenai*)[43] a neighbor to the man who fell among the robbers?" The lawyer readily responds with perceptive judgment: "The one who did mercy with him" (10:37). With this response, the lawyer shows that he has the ability to make judgments about haggadah (narrative) as well as halakah (legal scripture). When he moves to haggadah, he also moves beyond whatever limitations to the topos "neighbor" he may find in the Torah to "mercy," which is an important topos in prophetic literature and Mediterranean culture at large.

There was debate among Jews concerning the precise meaning of the "neighbor" toward which one must show love "as yourself." The Greek word for neighbor, *plēsion,* means "one who is near."[44] It was conventional to consider the mandate to "love your neighbor" to re-fer first and foremost to fellow Israelites, with an extension to loving the sojourner in the land as yourself (Lev 19:34; cf. Deut 10:19).[45] Some Jews understood the Torah to require a person to show love to "all people."[46] No matter exactly who one might understand the neighbor to be, people are being asked to love God and neighbor with their entire body. Hence, the Torah could be understood to require that if a Samaritan sojourning in Judea were attacked, robbed, and beaten, Israelites should enact love for the Samaritan as they would for themselves. In the story, of course, the reverse is the case. The sojourner in the land enacts love for the wounded Judean.

Wesley H. Wachob's interpretation of "mercy" (*eleos*) in James 2:13 is highly pertinent to Luke 10:37, since James 2:8–13 also reconfigures the topos of "loving your neighbor as yourself" into

---

43. John Nolland, *Luke 9:21–18:34* (WBC 35B; Dallas, Tex.: Word Books, 1993), 596.
44. Tannehill, *Luke*, 182.
45. Fitzmyer, *Luke*, 880–81.
46. *Letter of Aristeas* 228: "[The king's] question was, 'To whom must one show favor?' The answer was, 'To his parents, always, for God's very commandment concerns the honor due to parents. Next (and closely connected) he reckons the honor due to friends, calling the friend an equal of one's own self. You do well if you bring all men into friendship with yourself'" (*OTP* 2:28); cf. *Testament of Zebulon* 5:1: "Now, my children, I tell you to keep the Lord's commands; show mercy to your neighbor, have compassion on all, not only human beings but to dumb animals" (*OTP* 1:806); Nolland, *Luke 9:21–18:34*, 584.

"doing mercy."[47] Wachob explains that "Aristotle defined the 'emotion' *eleos* as 'a kind of pain [*lupē*] excited by the sight of evil [*kakō*], deadly or painful, which befalls one who does not deserve it'" (*Rhetorica* 2.8.2).[48] In Jewish and Christian literature, mercy becomes "an attribute of God. . . . Specifically, it is an attribute of action, something that God does."[49] In addition, "in the LXX *eleos* [or *eleēmosynē*] is demanded by God of those to whom God shows love" (LXX: Mic 6:8; Zech 7:9–10; Jer 9:23; Hos 12:7; cf. Dan 4:27; Sir 3:30; 40:17; and Tob 4:9–11).[50] As a result of the rhetography (graphic narration) of the story of the wounded man in Luke 10:30–35, the lawyer's emotion-fused thought moves to the conclusion that even a despised person who "does mercy" toward someone in dire need has become "a neighbor," and this provides a link for understanding the meaning of neighbor in Lev 19:18.

Thus, the lawyer is making a halakhic judgment that the one who "becomes a neighbor to someone in need" is fulfilling the Torah injunction to "love your neighbor as yourself." When the lawyer makes this judgment, Jesus simply reconfigures the standard Torah injunction "Do this and you will live" (Lev 18:5) to "Go and do likewise" (Luke 10:37). The special question we must now ask is, "What sociorhetorical features in Jesus' story made it possible to imagine that an expert in Jewish halakah might be moved to such a perception of 'loving your neighbor as yourself' by this story?" This requires that we turn to the inner story about the Samaritan's helping of the wounded man alongside the road.

Rhetography and Body Zones
in the Story within the Story

The presence of the story about the Samaritan within the story about the lawyer establishes two interacting rhetographies in this portion

---

47. Wesley H. Wachob, *The Voice of Jesus in the Social Rhetoric of James* (SNTSMS 106; Cambridge: Cambridge University Press, 2000), 104–13, 132–34, 179–80.
48. Ibid., 179.
49. Ibid., 133.
50. Ibid., 134.

of Luke. The picture of the lawyer's performance in relation to Jesus interacts with the picture of the Samaritan's performance in relation to the priest and Levite. In the previous section, we have seen the effect of the story within the story on the lawyer. In this section, the goal is to discern how the story within the story could be perceived to have the particular effect the discourse assigns to it.

Repetitive texture[51] in the story within the story emphasizes a sequence of "seeing" and "passing by on the other side" (*idōn antiparēlthen*, 10:31, 32). Jesus' story about the wounded man presupposes that if Lev 19:18 were present in the hearts of the priest and Levite in a mode of "remembrance of the Torah," their hearts would move them toward merciful purposive action when their eyes brought the information to their hearts that a man was lying half-dead alongside the road. The narration in Luke 10:31–32, however, presents no movement within the emotion-fused thought of the priest and Levite, like hate, fear, disdain, disgust, or anger.[52] They fulfill the description of people in Isa 6:9 who "seeing do not see" (cf. Luke 8:10).

The verb describing the purposive action is intensified with the prefix *anti-*, indicating that each man did not simply pass "alongside" the man but alongside "on the opposite side" (*antiparēlthen*). The narration certainly does not imply that they passed by on the other side so they would not step on him and harm him more. It can mean, however, that they passed by at a distance that kept the information about the wounded man from becoming more fully present and vivid to their hearts through their eyes. Their feet purposefully took their eyes further away from the wounded man and his injuries.

After Jesus' narration uses twenty Greek words to describe the event that leaves the man lying alongside the road (10:30), it describes the action of the priest in twelve (or fourteen) Greek words (10:31), and the action of the Levite in eleven (or twelve) Greek words (10:32). This means that the narrational length of the description of the setting

---

51. Robbins, *Exploring*, 8–9; idem, *Tapestry*, 46–50, 66–69.

52. E.g., there is no remark that the priest feared that he may become impure by touching a corpse, even if this is a possibility. See Scott, *Hear*, 195–97; cf. Richard Bauckham, "The Scrupulous Priest and the Good Samaritan: Jesus' Parabolic Interpretation of the Law of Moses," *NTS* 44 (1998): 475–89.

and the description of the two men who pass by is almost equivalent (20 to 23 [or 26]).[53] In contrast, the narration uses sixty Greek words to describe the actions of the Samaritan. This means that the detailed description of the actions of the Samaritan is three times longer than either the description of the initial setting or the actions of the priest and Levite.

Jesus' description of the response of the Samaritan to the wounded man is so lengthy because it presents a detailed progression of concrete compassionate moments[54] that show the response of the Samaritan "with his entire body."[55] The story starts by describing the Samaritan as "journeying" (*hodeuōn*), which suggests that he is engaged in purposive action toward a specific destination. Displaying progressive texture,[56] however, it asserts that "journeying he came to him and seeing him he was moved with compassion" (*idōn esplanchnisthē*, 10:33), rather than "seeing him he passed by on the other side" (*idōn antiparēlthen*, 10:31, 32).[57] In contrast to Isa 6:9, which the priest and Levite enact, the Samaritan "seeing does see and, moved with compassion, he understands what must be done." Just as moving along the road naturally brought him to the half-dead man, so seeing the man naturally produced a movement of compassion within his "innermost parts" (*esplanchnisthē*). M. J. J. Menken has discovered that "Luke puts *splanchnizesthai* and *splanchna* — whether it comes from his source or from his own pen — in various ways in the numerical centre of a passage, to give it the emphasis it apparently deserves from his point of view."[58] In the story of the Compassionate Samaritan, it marks the movement within the emotion-fused thought of the Samaritan that begins a sequence in which he shows love to the wounded man "with all his heart" (cf. 10:27).

53. Cf. the word count in Bock, *Luke*, 2:1032.
54. Bock, *Luke*, 2:1032, uses the phrase "concrete compassionate units" to describe the Samaritan's actions.
55. Cf. Tannehill, *Luke*, 184.
56. Robbins, *Exploring*, 9–14; idem, *Tapestry*, 46–50, 69–70.
57. Cf. Scott, *Hear*, 193.
58. M. J. J. Menken, "The Position of *Splanchnizesthai* and *Splanchna* in the Gospel of Luke," *NovT* 30 (1988): 114.

As we have seen in the previous section, when this story within the story is over, the lawyer describes the Samaritan as "the one who did mercy" (*ho poiēsas to eleos*, 10:37).[59] Careful analysis shows that he performed eight progressive acts of compassion.[60] The first act of the Samaritan was "seeing, he made his eyes to see." When his eyes really saw, they took the pitiful sight into his heart, which moved him with compassion (10:33). The second act of the Samaritan was to turn toward a new form of purposive action with his feet. He turns away from his "journeying" to "go toward" the wounded man (*proselthōn*, 10:34). The third and fourth acts of compassion occur when the Samaritan puts his hands, the other agency of purposive action, to work. Pouring on oil and wine, he binds up the wounds of the man (10:34). The fifth act of compassion occurs when he lifts the man onto his own beast of burden, not only using his hands with skill but also with "all their strength" (cf. 10:27).

Once the wounded man is on the beast of burden, the Samaritan enacts the sixth act of compassion by turning his feet toward an inn, taking the man there, and caring for him (10:34). With these actions, he continues to use his feet and hands "with all their functions" for the sake of the wounded man. The seventh act of compassion occurs when the Samaritan takes out two denarii on the next day and gives them to the innkeeper (10:35). With this action, he is not only loving the wounded man with his hands but also with his soul (*psychē*, 10:27), his very being and livelihood (cf. 21:4). The eighth act of compassion occurs when the Samaritan uses his self-expressive speech, telling the innkeeper to take care of the wounded man, and promising that he will return to pay whatever additional expense is owed (10:35). At this point, the Samaritan uses the third body zone associated with the mouth and ears to make a promise out of his heart and mind (cf. 10:27) that he will use his feet to return to the

---

59. See the analysis of *poieō* in the opening and closing scenes: John O. York, *The Last Shall Be First: The Rhetoric of Reversal in Luke* (JSNTSup 46; Sheffield: Sheffield Academic, 1991), 131.

60. Bock, *Luke*, 2:1032–33, without the aid of a taxonomy of body zones, details six concrete compassionate units: (1) he comes up to him; (2) binds his wounds; (3) anoints the cuts with oil and wine; (4) loads the man on his mule; (5) takes him to an inn; (6) provides care and comfort to the man.

inn and use his hands to pay the innkeeper an additional amount. In an eightfold progression, then, the narration describes the Samaritan loving his neighbor with "his whole heart, his whole soul, his whole strength, and his whole mind" (10:27). And surely the overall context implies that these actions exhibit the Samaritan's complete love for God and all that God has created.

As is well-known, the deep shock of the parable comes from the presence of the Samaritan as the "folkloric third person" who comes along in the story within the story.[61] As Tannehill has indicated, the logical progression would have been priest, Levite, and lay Israelite.[62] The result, in the words of John O. York, is a "bipolar reversal": "The shameful Samaritan is shown to be honorable by his actions; the honored Jews are shameful because of their inaction."[63] The history of Judean disdain for Samaritans as a despised outgroup has been detailed well recently by Philip F. Esler.[64] It is possible, however, that 2 Chr 28:5–15 functioned as a precedent for Samaritans helping wounded Judeans.[65] Of particular interest is the detailed description of the actions of the Samaritans:

> [Certain chiefs] took the captives, and with the booty they clothed all that were naked among them; they clothed them, gave them sandals, provided them with food and drink, and anointed them; and carrying all the feeble among them on donkeys, they brought them to their kindred at Jericho, the city of palm trees. Then they returned to Samaria. (2 Chr 28:15 NRSV)

---

61. For Samaritans, see Scott, *Hear*, 192; and Philip F. Esler, "Jesus and the Reduction of Intergroup Conflict: The Parable of the Good Samaritan in Light of Social Identity Theory," *BibInt* 8 (2000): 329–32.

62. Tannehill, *Luke*, 183; cf. Scott, *Hear*, 197–99; Michel Gourgues, "The Priest, the Levite, and the Samaritan Revisited: A Critical Note on Luke 10:31–35," *JBL* 117 (1998): 712.

63. York, *Last Shall Be First*, 132.

64. Esler, "Jesus and the Reduction of Intergroup Conflict," 329–32.

65. F. Scott Spencer, "2 Chronicles 28:5–15 and the Parable of the Good Samaritan," *WTJ* 46 (1984): 317–49. A major problem with this essay is a single focus on what Jesus may have known and thought, rather than on the possible role of the passage in Lukan discourse; cf. Vernon K. Robbins, "The Socio-Rhetorical Role of Old Testament Scripture in Luke 4–19," in *Z Nového Zákona/From the New Testament: Sborník k narozeninám Prof. ThDr. Zdenka Sázavy* (ed. Hana Tonzarová and Petr Melmuk; Prague: Vydala Církev československá husitská, 2001), 81–93.

The function of these Samaritans as "ministers of healing"[66] suggests that earlier in biblical discourse these people had shown that they knew what obedience to Lev 19:18 means.[67] If this passage does have an intertextual relation to the Lukan story, it is yet another example of the manner in which stories in Lukan discourse are powerful vehicles for configuring and reconfiguring Torah, Prophets, and Psalms in a continuation of the story of Israel through the story of Jesus of Nazareth (Luke 24:44).

Conclusion

For many years Robert C. Tannehill has shown a keen interest in "forceful and imaginative language" and in "pattern and tension" in Gospel stories.[68] The story of the Compassionate Samaritan within the story of the lawyer seeking eternal life exhibits both qualities. Throughout, the story features pattern and tension of various kinds. First, there is the pattern and tension with the dialogue between Jesus and the lawyer as the lawyer moves through a series of steps to an identification of the Samaritan as "the one who did mercy." Second, there is pattern and tension in the story of the wounded man as "seeing" finally progresses to "compassion," which unfolds in an eightfold progression of actions in which the Samaritan activates his emotion-fused thought, purposeful action, and self-expressive speech. Third, there is pattern in tension between the Samaritan, who "did mercy" with his "whole heart, soul, strength, and mind," and the lawyer, who earnestly uses emotion-fused thought and self-expressive speech to find out how to inherit eternal life, but has yet to fulfill what he has thought and said by "going and doing likewise."

In the language of Tannehill, the shock of the embodiment of compassion in the Samaritan stretches love of neighbor "until it becomes love of enemy (as in 6:27–36), except that it is more unsettling."[69] The forceful and imaginative discourse presents the

---

66. F. S. Spencer, "2 Chronicles 28:5–15," 327–33.
67. Ibid., 334–37.
68. Tannehill, *Sword*, 11–58.
69. Tannehill, *Luke*, 184.

Samaritan not only as "bearer of God's eternal mercy" but as "the Irruptive Other."[70] Therefore, this story within a story functions beyond metaphor and analogy by becoming a tensive pictorial narration of "the substance of a new reality."[71] In the language of Brendan Byrne:

> This is the way to inherit eternal life. The God whom one is attempting to love with all one's heart is the God who reaches out to the world in compassion in the same way as the good Samaritan did. In the ministry of Jesus, which the Church has to continue, God offers extravagant, life-giving hospitality to wounded and half-dead humanity. The way to eternal life is to allow oneself to become an active instrument and channel of that same boundary-breaking hospitality.[72]

---

70. Mazamisa, *Beatific Comradeship*, 164–65.
71. McDonald, "Rhetorical Issue," 67.
72. Brendan Byrne, *The Hospitality of God: A Reading of Luke's Gospel* (Collegeville, Minn.: Liturgical Press, 2000), 101–2.

15

The Forgotten Famine

Personal Responsibility
in Luke's Parable of "the Prodigal Son"

Mark Allan Powell

In my teaching, I sometimes employ a close-reading exercise that I learned from David Rhoads. Here is how Rhoads describes the exercise in an appendix to his book *Mark as Story:*

> (1) Pair off and both read/study the episode silently; (2) Both close books, then the first person recounts to the other what he or she read, as faithfully as possible; (3) Both now look at the episode and see what details were accurately remembered and what was omitted, added, or changed in telling.[1]

In my classes, at least, this exercise sometimes allows students to note the sort of "redactional changes" that they inevitably make in their own reception of a text. It is especially intriguing when patterns of recollection emerge and when these seem to align with certain factors of social location (race, gender, age, and so forth).

The Famine in Popular Memory

We employed this exercise one day with the story of "the Prodigal Son" in Luke 15:11–32. On that day, twelve seminary students read the text carefully, then recounted it from memory to twelve partners. Not one of them mentioned the famine to which Jesus

---

1. David Rhoads with Joanna Dewey and Donald Michie, *Mark as Story: An Introduction to the Narrative of a Gospel* (2d ed.; Minneapolis: Fortress, 1999), 154.

refers in 15:14, an omission that I took as striking for its unanimity. Thus, I organized a more controlled study involving ultimately a hundred diverse respondents, only six of whom mentioned the famine in their oral recounting of Luke's tale. The famine-forgetters, furthermore, comprised persons of diverse gender, race, age, economic status, and religious affiliation. No factor of social location seemed to have any statistically relevant impact on the likelihood that a reader would or would not remember the famine reference when recounting Luke's tale.

All hundred respondents were Americans. The next logical step, then, was to survey non-American readers, and I had the opportunity to do this when I spent a portion of 2001 on sabbatical in Eastern Europe. There, I polled diverse respondents in the city of St. Petersburg, Russia. I was only able to access a sample one-half the size of that in America (50 total respondents as opposed to 100), but a shocking forty-two of these specifically mentioned the famine when they retold the story that they had just been asked to read. Again, the likelihood of such recall could not be linked statistically to any specific factor(s) of social location within the St. Petersburg sample. The only factor that emerged as relevant in this survey was the geographical one.

One probably does not need to look too far for a social or psychological explanation for this data. In 1941, the German army laid siege to the city of St. Petersburg (then Leningrad) and subjected its inhabitants to what was in effect a 900–day famine. During that time, 670,000 people died of starvation. Some of the current inhabitants of the city are survivors of that horror; more are descendants of survivors. Other residents represent a new generation of immigrants, but even for these, a collective memory remains strong in the cultural milieu. In modern St. Petersburg, typical social issues (abortion, care of the elderly, imprisonment of lawbreakers, socialized medicine, and so on) are often considered through the lens of an important question: *but what if there is not enough food?* And no one thinks it odd for university students to write papers on "The Ethics of Cannibalism." It is, I think, not surprising that in *this* social location, more than four-fifths of the people who read Luke's story of "the Prodigal

Son" and then repeat it from memory do not forget that there was a famine.

What difference does it make? One might argue that the mention of a famine in Luke's account is not only a minor detail but a superfluous one. The elements of the plot in this portion of the story seem to be (a) the young man acquires his inheritance prematurely; (b) he squanders his fortune in a faraway land; (c) a famine comes; and (d) the young man is left in dire straits. The rhetorical function of the third movement (the arrival of the famine) seems to be simply to intensify the young man's plight. It is not causative and thus appears to be expendable. The narrative progression would make perfect sense without the "c" element at all. To test this, try reading the text of Luke 15:13–14, omitting the italicized words below:

> A few days later the younger son gathered all he had and traveled to a distant country, and there he squandered his property in dissolute living. When he had spent everything, *a severe famine took place throughout that country, and* he began to be in need. (NRSV throughout except as noted)

This, in effect, is how most American readers *do* receive the text. The famine is an unnecessary plot element and so is subconsciously dropped from the story. The Russians, we might surmise, are prone to notice the unnecessary element for understandable existential reasons, but that element remains superfluous nonetheless. My survey, then, could be of human interest even if it reveals little of relevance for exegetical interpretation.

But consider this: the *b* element in the scene summary above could also be viewed as unnecessary, so long as the *c* element were retained. The narrative progression would also make sense without the *b* element, and if that element were eliminated no one would ever suspect anything was missing. Again, read the text omitting the italicized words:

> A few days later the younger son gathered all he had and traveled to a distant country, and *there he squandered his property in*

dissolute living. When he had spent everything, a severe famine took place throughout that country, and he began to be in need.

How intriguing, then, that a goodly number of Russian readers, when recounting the story from memory, made no mention of the boy squandering his property. In fact, only seventeen of the fifty respondents made mention of this point, which had been remembered by all the Americans. Here are the percentages of what was recalled

| *Americans* | squandering, 100% | famine, 6% |
| *Russians* | squandering, 34% | famine, 84% |

Many of the Russian readers, in other words, assigned causative value to the plot element of the famine and regarded Luke's mention of the boy squandering his fortune as a superfluous (and hence forgettable) point. For them, perhaps, the reverse of the logic presented above would apply: a severe famine *alone* is sufficient to explain why a young man would end up hungry and in need; the fact that this man had previously squandered his property merely intensifies the situation.

Luke's text identifies two factors as contributing to the situation of a young man being in need: he squandered his property, and a severe famine came upon the land. Logically, either factor could have accounted for the situation, but both are stated. I do not see any *exegetical* reason for privileging one factor over the other or for regarding either as superfluous. Yet readers, who inevitably bring interpretative biases to texts, have done this, and the choices that they have made in so doing appear to reflect their social locations.

The Famine Detail in Scholarship

So far, however, we are only describing the unstudied responses of nonprofessional readers. Critical exegetical method strives to transcend cultural prejudices and to enable scholarly readers to see what others would miss. Thus, I turned next to the library to discover what role Luke's mention of a famine (15:14) has played in scholarly exegesis of this parable. What follows is a comprehensive account of everything that fifty-five scholars have to say on the famine:

Arndt, William F.[2]	[not mentioned]
Blomberg, Craig[3]	[not mentioned]
Bock, Darrell[4]	Some of the boy's hard time is not his own doing. . . . Now comes another blow — famine. Nature makes his bad situation worse.
Borsch, Frederick[5]	[not mentioned]
Boucher, Madeleine[6]	[mentioned without comment]
Caird, G. B.[7]	[not mentioned]
Craddock, Fred[8]	[not mentioned]
Creed, John[9]	[not mentioned]
Culpepper, R. Alan[10]	The famine only hastened his impoverishment.
Danker, Frederick[11]	[not mentioned]
Dillersberger, J.[12]	[not mentioned]
Dodd, C. H.[13]	[not mentioned]
Donahue, John R.[14]	[mentioned without comment]
Ellis, E. Earle[15]	[not mentioned]
Evans, Craig A.[16]	[not mentioned]
Evans, C. F.[17]	[not mentioned]

2. William F. Arndt, *The Gospel According to St. Luke* (St. Louis: Concordia, 1956).
3. Craig Blomberg, *Interpreting the Parables* (Downers Grove, Ill.: InterVarsity, 1990).
4. Darrell L. Bock, *Luke* (BECNT; 2 vols.; Grand Rapids: Baker Books, 1996), 2.1311.
5. Frederick Houk Borsch, *Many Things in Parables: Extravagant Stories of New Community* (Philadelphia: Fortress, 1988).
6. Madeleine I. Boucher, *The Parables* (New Testament Message; rev. ed.; Wilmington, Del.: Michael Glazier, 1983), 106.
7. G. B. Caird, *Saint Luke* (PNTC; Middlesex, U.K.: Penguin Books, 1963).
8. Fred B. Craddock, *Luke* (IBC; Louisville: John Knox, 1990).
9. John Martin Creed, *The Gospel According to St. Luke* (London: Macmillan, 1953).
10. R. Alan Culpepper, "Luke," in *Luke, John* (vol. 9 of *NIB*; Nashville: Abingdon, 1995), 301.
11. Frederick Danker, *Jesus and the New Age: A Commentary on St. Luke's Gospel* (Philadelphia: Fortress, 1988).
12. Joseph Dillersberger, *The Gospel of Saint Luke* (Westminster: Newman, 1958).
13. C. H. Dodd, *The Parables of the Kingdom* (rev. ed.; London: Collins, 1961).
14. John R. Donahue, *The Gospel in Parable* (Philadelphia: Fortress, 1988), 153.
15. E. Earle Ellis, *The Gospel of Luke* (NCB; Grand Rapids: Eerdmans, 1966).
16. Craig A. Evans, *Luke* (NIBCNT; Peabody, Mass.: Hendrickson, 1990).
17. C. F. Evans, *Saint Luke* (TPINTC; Philadelphia: Trinity Press International, 1990).

Fitzmyer, Joseph[18]	[not mentioned]
Ford, D. W. C.[19]	[not mentioned]
Ford, Richard Q.[20]	[not mentioned]
Geldenhuys, Norval[21]	[mentioned without comment]
Glen, J. Stanley[22]	[not mentioned]
Gooding, David[23]	[not mentioned]
Goulder, Michael[24]	[Luke's parable] has a younger son like Joseph who goes to a far country.... There was a great famine in that country that ultimately brings the family together once more.
Green, Joel[25]	The deteriorating situation of the younger son is compounded by the onset of a famine.... The general effects of a depressed economy in the midst of famine might be reason enough for Jesus' observation that "no one gave him anything."
Hannam, Wilfrid[26]	[not mentioned]
Hendrickx, Herman[27]	"A (great) famine arose" is a biblical expression. In a country which suffered ten famines in about 200 years (from 169 B.C. to A.D. 70), famine was a powerful image.
Hendriksen, William[28]	Things went from bad to worse. His money is gone; the famine arrives. Moreover, this new disaster has struck not only the *place* where he has happened to be living at that time, but the entire *country!* He himself had nothing left and he could not expect help from anyone else.

---

18. Joseph Fitzmyer, *The Gospel According to Luke* (2 vols.; AB 28–28A; Garden City, N.Y.: Doubleday, 1981–85).

19. D. W. Cleverley Ford, *A Reading of Saint Luke's Gospel* (London: Hodder & Stoughton, 1967).

20. Richard Q. Ford, *The Parables of Jesus: Recovering the Art of Listening* (Minneapolis: Fortress, 1997).

21. Norval Geldenhuys, *Commentary on the Gospel of Luke* (NICNT; Grand Rapids: Eerdmans, 1979), 407.

22. J. Stanley Glen, *The Parables of Conflict in Luke* (Philadelphia: Westminster, 1962).

23. David Gooding, *According to Luke: A New Exposition of the Third Gospel* (Grand Rapids: Eerdmans, 1987).

24. Michael D. Goulder, *Luke: A New Paradigm* (JSNTSup 20; 2 vols.; Sheffield: Sheffield Academic, 1989), 2:611.

25. Joel Green, *The Gospel of Luke* (NICNT; Grand Rapids, Eerdmans, 1997), 580–81.

26. Wilfrid L. Hannam, *Luke the Evangelist: A Study of His Purpose* (New York: Abingdon, 1935).

27. Herman Hendrickx, *The Parables of Jesus* (San Francisco: Harper & Row, 1983), 152.

28. William Hendriksen, *New Testament Commentary: Exposition of the Gospel According to Luke* (Grand Rapids: Baker Books, 1978), 753.

Hobbs, Herschel[29]	[mentioned without comment]
Hultgren, Arland[30]	All goes downhill, including factors beyond his control or fault. A severe famine strikes, which he could not have anticipated when he left home.
Hunter, Archibald[31]	[not mentioned]
Jeremias, Joachim[32]	[not mentioned]
Johnson, Luke T.[33]	Biblical literature suggests that this was a frequent occurrence in an area in which agriculture was always a hazardous enterprise.
Kilgallen, John[34]	[not mentioned]
Lambrecht, Jan[35]	[not mentioned]
LaVerdiere, Eugene[36]	[not mentioned]
Leaney, A. R. C.[37]	[not mentioned]
Lenski, R. C. H.[38]	It is then that the famine sets in, one that the entire country cannot remove because it is so strong.
Marshall, I. H.[39]	[not mentioned]
Miller, Donald[40]	[not mentioned]
Morgan, G. C.[41]	[not mentioned]

---

29. Herschel H. Hobbs, *An Exposition of the Gospel of Luke* (Grand Rapids: Baker Books, 1966).

30. Arland J. Hultgren, *The Parables of Jesus: A Commentary* (Grand Rapids: Eerdmans, 2000), 75.

31. Archibald M. Hunter, *Interpreting the Parables* (Philadelphia: Westminster, 1960); idem, *The Parables Then and Now* (Philadelphia: Westminster, 1971). Hunter does not mention the famine in either of these two works, both of which discuss the parable.

32. Joachim Jeremias, *The Parables of Jesus* (2d ed.; New York: Charles Scribner's Sons, 1954).

33. Luke Timothy Johnson, *The Gospel of Luke* (SP; Collegeville, Minn.: Liturgical Press, 1991), 237.

34. John J. Kilgallen, *A Brief Commentary on the Gospel of Luke* (New York: Paulist, 1988).

35. Jan Lambrecht, *Once More Astonished: The Parables of Jesus* (New York: Crossroad, 1981).

36. Eugene LaVerdiere, *Luke* (New Testament Message; Collegeville, Minn.: Liturgical Press, 1980).

37. A. R. C. Leaney, *The Gospel According to St. Luke* (HNTC; New York: Harper and Brothers, 1958).

38. R. C. H. Lenski, *Interpretation of St. Luke's Gospel* (Columbus, Ohio: Wartburg, 1946), 810.

39. I. H. Marshall, *The Gospel of Luke* (NIGTC; Grand Rapids: Eerdmans, 1978).

40. Donald G. Miller, *The Gospel According to Luke* (LBC; Richmond: John Knox, 1959).

41. G. Campbell Morgan, *The Gospel According to Luke* (New York: Fleming H. Revell, 1931).

Morris, Leon[42]	Two disasters struck him simultaneously. . . . The famine was not his fault but it increased his difficulties. People who might have helped him would find their own circumstances more straitened.
Nolland, John[43]	Luke has a "severe famine" also in 4:25 and Acts 11:28. . . . At the point when his money is gone and he is vulnerable, "nature" intervenes against this dissolute young man.
Perkins, Pheme[44]	He is subject to famine and destitution. He does not rescue the country and his family from it as Joseph does. This boy is almost a parody of the Joseph/Jacob type.
Plummer, Alfred[45]	The working of Providence is manifested in coincidences. Just when he had spent everything, a famine, and a severe one, arose in precisely the land to which he had gone to enjoy himself.
Ragg, Lonsdale[46]	[probable allusion to famine] It was Providence, by circumstances outside his own control and responsibility, that brought home to him the folly of his recklessness.
Ringe, Sharon[47]	[mentioned without comment]
Scott, Bernard[48]	A famine, a feared scourge of the ancient world, draws the audience's sympathy toward the son, for though he is responsible for his fate, he is not responsible for this downward turn.
Schweizer, Eduard[49]	[probable allusion to famine] Neither is his situation entirely his own fault.
Stein, Robert[50]	[mentioned without comment]
Stöger, Alois[51]	In times of famine, even a wealthy person finds it hard to make ends meet. But what about a person who has no means whatsoever?

---

42. Leon Morris, *Luke* (TNTC; Grand Rapids: Eerdmans, 1974), 264.

43. John Nolland, *Luke* (WBC; 3 vols.; Waco, Tex.: Word Books, 1989–93), 2:783.

44. Pheme Perkins, *Hearing the Parables of Jesus* (New York: Paulist, 1981), 54.

45. Alfred Plummer, *The Gospel according to St. Luke* (ICC; 4th ed.; New York: Charles Scribner's Sons, 1901), 373.

46. Lonsdale Ragg, *St. Luke* (London: Methuen, 1922), 211.

47. Sharon Ringe, *Luke* (Westminster Bible Companion; Louisville: Westminster John Knox, 1995), 207.

48. Bernard Brandon Scott, *Hear Then the Parable: A Commentary on the Parables of Jesus* (Minneapolis: Fortress, 1989), 114.

49. Eduard Schweizer, *The Good News according to Luke* (Atlanta: John Knox, 1984), 248.

50. Robert H. Stein, *An Introduction to the Parables of Jesus* (Philadelphia: Westminster, 1981), 120.

51. Alois Stöger, *The Gospel According to St. Luke* (New Testament for Spiritual Reading; New York: Crossroad, 1981), 43.

Summers, Ray[52]	[not mentioned]
Talbert, Charles[53]	[not mentioned]
Tannehill, Robert[54]	[not mentioned]
Thompson, G. H. P.[55]	[not mentioned]
Tiede, David[56]	He did not cause the famine, but he did not save his money to meet such problems either.

The most obvious lesson I draw from this survey is that scholars who are conducting line-by-line close readings of the text have often attributed no more significance to the mention of the famine than American readers who forget that such mention is even made. For thirty-seven of the fifty-five scholars surveyed, the famine has no impact whatsoever on their interpretation of the text; it either is not mentioned at all, or is just barely mentioned, without comment. Among the eighteen who do take the reference into account, most seem to regard the narrative role of the famine as being to intensify a situation that in any case would have been dire. Thus, Western commentaries, like American readers, tend to regard the famine as an almost superfluous detail or, more than half the time, as a *completely* superfluous detail.

We might at least be suspicious that our inattention to the famine in Luke's account is a factor of our social location and, thus, a product of interpretative bias. Indeed, those in the biblical guild who are primarily interested in discerning how texts might have been received by their *original* audiences might want to consider the implications of the remarks by Hendrickx and Johnson (above). If, in fact, the world in which Jesus' stories were told and/or that in which Luke's Gospel was written endured frequent severe famines, then it seems likely that the original audience for this parable might have heard it more in the manner of the Russian readers I surveyed than in the manner

---

52. Ray Summers, *Commentary on Luke* (Waco, Tex.: Word Books, 1972).
53. Charles H. Talbert, *Reading Luke: A Literary and Theological Commentary on the Third Gospel* (New York: Crossroad, 1986).
54. Robert C. Tannehill, *Luke* (ANTC; Nashville: Abingdon, 1996).
55. G. H. P. Thompson, *The Gospel according to Luke* (New Clarendon Bible; Oxford: Oxford University Press, 1972).
56. David L. Tiede, *Luke* (ACNT; Minneapolis: Augsburg, 1988), 278.

of American readers or Western scholars. In any case, I would like
to put the interpretative question this way: if we assume an implied
audience that is familiar with famine and its effects, how might that
assumption affect interpretation of the text?

The Role of Personal Responsibility
in the Lukan Parable

The mention of the famine serves at least to encourage a note of sympathy for the younger son (cf. Scott, above). Whatever *else* might be
said about this young man (cf. 15:30), the famine was not his fault
(cf. also Bock, Hultgren, Morris, Ragg, Schweizer, Tiede). Accordingly, when Western scholarship treats the famine as a parenthetical
element in the parable (or ignores it altogether), the young man's cul-
pability comes to the fore and threatens to take center stage. At a
popular level, the first act of this parable (15:11–24) is typically read
and preached as a quintessential tale of repentance (though the word
repentance does not actually occur). It is a story of an irresponsible
and immoral boy who comes to realize the error of his ways and returns, confessing his sin, to a father who welcomes his penitent child.
I would not want to argue that this element of personal responsibility
(or irresponsibility) is absent from the story, but there are considerations that might lead us to question whether it should be regarded as
central to it.

The Parable Offers a Poor Paradigm for Moral Reform

The narrator of the story (Jesus) never says that the young man's
dire straits are the result of immoral or unseemly behavior. The
older brother, of course, is quick to make that allegation in verse 30
("this son of yours, . . . who has devoured your property with prostitutes"), but the implied audience is hardly expected to regard this
brother's point of view as reliable.[57] Furthermore, the younger son

---

57. Caird is more cautious than some about normalizing the elder brother's perspective: "His
brother, not trying to be just, let alone charitable, chose to believe that he had added profligacy
to extravagance, but he had no more evidence for the harlots than his imagination and bad

does not confess to any specific instances of wickedness. In his proposed (15:18) and actual (15:21) confessions, he acknowledges only that he has sinned against heaven and before his father, without indicating just what that sin might have entailed. At least, we might surmise that the details of his sin are irrelevant to the story. At most, we could propose that the boy repents of one thing only: his decision to request his share of the inheritance and to leave his father's house. This, after all, is the only matter that he attempts to undo. Not surprisingly, Eastern interpretations of the story have typically differed from Western ones on this point. Western audiences tend to link the unnamed sin with the squandering of property; Easterners generally assume it to be the act of separation from family.[58]

All the narrator says is that the boy squandered (*diaskorpizō*, 15:13; cf. 16:1) his property by living in ways that may be described as *asōtōs* — and the history of translation for that hapax legomenon is interesting. The word *asōtōs* appears to be a negation of *sōtōs,* a nonrecurring adjective related to *sōtēria* (salvation). Literally, then, the text simply states that the boy spent his money in a manner that may be regarded as the opposite of *saving* it; by extension, the text might (but need not) imply that he spent this money in ways that were not *salutary.* Western translations of the Bible have favored the latter sense:

KJV	1611	wasted his substance with riotous living
NAB	1941	squandered his inheritance on a life of dissipation
RSV	1946	squandered his property in loose living
NEB	1961	squandered it in reckless living
NASB	1963	squandered his estate with loose living
JB	1985	squandered his money on a life of debauchery
TEV	1966	wasted his money in reckless living

---

temper could supply" (*Saint Luke,* 183). Arndt, however, has no problem adopting the older brother's point of view: "The far country was not so distant that no news of his conduct could reach his father and brother, as is evident from v. 30" (*St. Luke,* 350). So, too, Bock (*Luke,* 2:1311).

58. Hultgren, *Parables of Jesus,* 77.

NIV	1973	squandered his wealth in wild living
NJB	1985	squandered his money on a life of debauchery
REB	1989	squandered it in dissolute living
NRSV	1991	squandered his property in dissolute living
CEV	1995	wasted all his money in wild living

In the East, however, translations have consistently rendered the word in its more literal sense. Kenneth Bailey notes, "With the one exception of the Old Syriac, our Syriac and Arabic versions for 1800 years have consistently translated 'expensive' or 'luxurious' or 'spendthrift living' with no hint of immorality."[59]

Some justification might be found for either Eastern or Western translations. In an article on the term, Werner Foerster notes a primal sense of "incurable" in some literature (to be *asōtōs* is to be "hopelessly sick") and suggests that the term came to be associated with dissipation and thus with various vices, especially gluttony. Nevertheless, Foerster maintains that the occurrence of *asōtōs* in Luke 15:13 depicts the life of "the prodigal" as "simply carefree and spendthrift," without further specification.[60]

Western commentators, however, often pick up the possible implication of immorality and run with it:[61]

Bock	The son throws away his wealth through an undisciplined, wild life.[62]
Culpepper	He quickly squanders his inheritance, living fast and loose (cf. Prov. 29:3).[63]
Glen	Like an irresponsible youth who for the first time is out from under the discipline of his father and who

---

59. Kenneth E. Bailey, *Finding the Lost: Cultural Keys to Luke 15* (St. Louis: Concordia Publishing House, 1992), 123.

60. Werner Foerster, "*asōtōs, asōtia*," in *TDNT* 1:506–7. Foerster does allow that the related term *asotia*, used three times in the New Testament (Eph 5:18; Titus 1:6; 1 Pet 4:4), signifies "wild and disorderly living."

61. Schweizer is an exception: "No immorality is mentioned. He merely squanders his money 'stupidly' " (*Luke*, 248).

62. Bock, *Luke*, 2:1311, makes the source of his observation explicit by adding, "Luke 15:30 speaks of the son's time with prostitutes" (2.1311 n. 13).

63. Culpepper, "Luke," 301.

> thinks of his new freedom only as an opportunity for indulgence, he apparently yielded to his every desire.[64]

Goulder   He goes abroad and lives a sinful life.[65]

Hobbs   The headstrong youth wasted his substance in riotous living. This means he went the whole route in sinful indulgence.[66]

Perkins   The prodigal wastes his inheritance on sexual misconduct.[67]

Stein   We do not read that he lost his money by means of poor investments or even by theft. On the contrary, the text suggests that the "prodigal son" wasted his money on "wine, women, and song."[68]

Again, we discover that commentators in the East have offered different interpretations. Bailey reports on some of these:[69]

Author 1   [The boy] wasted his possessions living luxuriously.

Author 2   [He was enamored of] a love of luxury and splendor.

Author 3   [He pursued] a life full of entertainment and amusement.

Author 4   [He was] troublefree.

In all of these instances, the boy's level of irresponsibility is somewhat muted, or at least construed quite differently than in the Western readings.[70] The main point of Eastern interpretations is simply that the boy *spent* his money instead of *saving* it.

Reader-response critics might recognize that both types of readings go beyond what the text has to offer and yet both may be defended

---

64. Glen, *Parables of Conflict*, 27.
65. Goulder, *Luke*, 2:610.
66. Hobbs, *Exposition of Luke*, 235.
67. Perkins, *Hearing the Parables*, 54.
68. Stein, *Introduction to the Parables*, 119.
69. Cited in Bailey, *Finding the Lost*, 123.
70. Given the Lukan prejudice against the wealthy, one might argue that spending one's wealth on finery is wicked in and of itself (cf. 16:19). But neither the Lukan text nor the Eastern (much less Western) interpretations of it seem to develop this potential trajectory. The boy is not portrayed as inordinately wealthy, nor is he faulted for a failure to help the poor.

as actualizing ambiguities inherent in the text. Since the term *asōtōs* can carry connotations of either foolishness or immorality, readers are free to assign either value to it. The text is inherently polyvalent at this point; still, it is intriguing that the different ways of reading the passage have tended to match the different social locations of readers.

Before going on, I want to note briefly one other reason why the Eastern preference for regarding the boy as foolish might be commended. Even Western scholars have sometimes noted connections between this story and the tale of Joseph in Genesis 37–50: (a) sibling rivalry between a young son and older brother(s); (b) the young son ends up separated from his father in a far country; (c) the young son is regarded as dead by his father, who later rejoices to learn that he is alive; (d) the father gives his young son a ring and a robe, as Pharaoh gives to Joseph in Gen 41:42; (e) the father embraces his son in a noticeable display of affection, as Joseph does his father in Gen 46:29. Incredibly, some of the scholars who list such parallels fail to notice that both stories also include a famine.[71] Most interpreters who find intertextual allusions to Genesis, furthermore, see the young son in Luke's parable as something of an antitype to Joseph: he is not sold into slavery against his will but voluntarily abandons his father's home for another land; in the far country he goes from riches to rags instead of vice versa; at the end of the story he travels home to be welcomed by his father instead of staying put to welcome a father who travels to see him. In this light a few have actually suggested that the boy is Joseph's alter ego with regard to morality. Whereas Joseph establishes himself as a paragon of virtue by resisting the lure of Potiphar's wife, the young son in this parable allegedly yields to the temptations of harlots.[72]

I think this moral comparison is a bit of a stretch, especially in view of a far more likely contrast: Joseph is regarded as the wisest man in

---

71. Scholars who list parallels to the Joseph story include Borsch, *Many Things in Parables*, 40; Goulder, *Luke*, 2:611; Jeremias, *Parables of Jesus*, 130; Perkins, *Hearing the Parables*, 54. Borsch and Jeremias make no mention of the famine. See also John Drury, *The Parables in the Gospels* (New York: Crossroad, 1985), 144.

72. Drury, *Parables*, 144; Perkins, *Hearing the Parables*, 54.

all Egypt because he foresees that a famine is coming and prepares for it; the son in this parable is the opposite of wise (hence, foolish) because he does *not* foresee that a famine could come and does nothing to prepare for it. Joseph's moral virtue did not help him to prepare for a famine. His (divinely granted) wisdom is what allowed him to prepare for famine. Accordingly, if the boy in Luke's parable is to be viewed as some kind of anti-Joseph, his lack of wisdom rather than his lack of moral virtue would be the characteristic that counts.

I don't want to go too far, however, in substituting one overly specific reading of the text for another. I have tried to demonstrate that a reasonable case can be made for the Eastern tradition that regards the younger son as foolish rather than as immoral because the opposite reading is so well-established in Western scholarship. But my transcendent observation is that the emphasis of the parable is not on personal responsibility (or irresponsibility) in either sense. The parable offers a poor paradigm for reformation, in that (a) it does not indicate clearly whether a penchant for sinful behavior or simple folly is responsible for the boy's dereliction, and (b) it does not offer readers much reason to believe that the boy will henceforth be improved in either arena. Neither the boy's lack of wisdom or moral virtue is ultimately essential to the story. What is important is that a famine catches the young man unawares. *Why* it catches him unawares — because he was foolish or because he was immoral — seems irrelevant, or at least it seems irrelevant to *some*. It matters not a whit to the father, though apparently it does matter to the older brother (15:30) and to most modern interpreters.

The Parable Is Offered as Part of a Triad

The parable follows two others in which responsibility for becoming lost is not an issue. The parables of the Lost Sheep (15:3–7) and the Lost Coin (15:8–10) clearly emphasize the joy of recovery without prejudice toward what caused the lost to become lost in the first place. There is no suggestion that the sheep was a bad sheep for running away, much less that it learned its lesson from this adventure and will stay with the flock from now on. There is no indication that the coin was inadequate in some way that made it easy to lose (or easier to lose than, say, brighter, shinier coins). The point is simply that what was lost (for whatever reason) has been found, and that this is a cause for joy. Naturally, the third parable need not be restricted from developing themes not present in the first two, but its placement within the triad suggests that the lost sinner's personal responsibility (for becoming lost and/or found) is a subsidiary element at best. Cleverley Ford notes well the irrelevance of cause "for a man [*sic*] becoming lost" in Luke 15:

> He could be lost by stupidity (like a sheep) or through misfortune (like a coin rolling away) or by wilfulness like the younger son in the story....Nothing mattered except that the lost was an outsider and needed to be made an insider. Inclusiveness is the right attitude, exclusiveness the wrong one.[73]

The third story *is* more developed than the others and it does differ from them in attributing motivation to the lost entity. But even then, the claim that is ultimately advanced is not that the son "has returned" but that he has "been found" (15:24, 32). This may seem odd, since the father has not appeared to do anything to find the boy.[74] But this is the very element that links the parable to its predecessors. All three stories may be about repentance, but they illustrate repentance as a gift of God — as a divine initiative through which God restores the lost — rather than (primarily) as a moral act by which people make life-changing decisions. Neither the sheep nor the coin make such decisions, and the significance of the son's decision is muted by the father's decree that the boy "was lost and has been found." Such language characterizes the young son as a passive object that has been acted upon (like the sheep or coin) rather than as an actor who has determined his own destiny.[75]

---

73. Ford, *Reading*, 367.

74. Though the father claims that his son has "been found," the story never indicates that the father or anyone else sought him, much less found him. Thus Morgan writes: "In the first two (parables), that which is lost is sought. In the last one, that which is lost, seeks....Thus within the sweep of the parable(s), Calvinists and Arminians find their place" (*Luke*, 181).

75. Along these same lines, the emphasis in all three parables seems to be on the one who finds rather than on that which is found. Scholarship on the third parable has consistently

The primary change that occurs in all three stories is a simple change in status: from "lost" to "found." Yet Luke makes bold to identify that change in status as exemplary of what he calls "repentance" (15:7, 10). Western readers, I think, often regard the third story (not using the word *repentance*) as a better illustration of repentance than the first two (using the word), and this may be an indication that we do not grasp what Luke means to communicate about that theme. The third story may offer the best illustration of a character making a life-changing decision, but what if such decisions are not as definitive of repentance for Luke as they are for us? Perhaps we should begin by asking, How exactly does the finding of the sheep or coin exemplify the repentance of a sinner? It doesn't — unless one thinks of repentance more as *recovery* than as *reformation*. Then, we may notice that the father in the third parable does not celebrate because his son has "come to himself" (15:17) or because he has "come back" (the language the older brother uses in 15:30), but because he has "been found." The emphasis remains on recovery in a way consistent with the main theme of the first two stories.

It may seem odd to Western readers to think of *repentance* in this way (with primary emphasis on recovery rather than reformation), but twice in the book of Acts repentance is explicitly described as a gift: repentance and forgiveness of sins is something that the exalted Jesus gives to Israel (Acts 5:31). When Cornelius and his associates are baptized with the Holy Spirit, Peter realizes that "God has given even to the Gentiles the repentance that leads to life" (Acts 11:18).[76] To speak of repentance as a gift in this sense is about as strange as (and therefore consistent with) a shepherd chasing down a lost sheep,

---

recognized that it is primarily about "a man who has two sons" (15:11), that the father is the main character of the third parable, as the shepherd is of the first and the woman of the second. For one thing, the father is the only character featured in the introduction (15:11–12), in the first act concerning the younger son (15:13–23), and in the second act concerning the older son (15:25–32).

76. Commentators are virtually unanimous in taking the expressions in these verses as an idiomatic way of saying, "God has granted *the opportunity for* repentance" to Israel and to Gentiles. Even so, the choice of idiom is significant. We need not argue that idioms or parables should be read literally to recognize their connotative force: the idiom employed in Acts 5:31 and 11:18, like the idioms in Luke 15:24, 32 and the parables in Luke 15:3–10, emphasize the "result" element of recovery in their depiction of repentance.

returning it to the fold, and then maintaining that it has "repented." Or, it is a bit like a father claiming that his lost son has "been found" when the boy appears to have come home of his own accord, confessing his sins and pleading for help. In all cases, the concept of repentance seems to be defined by result (reunion) rather than cause. There is little interest in who initiates the reunion or in why it must be initiated, or in whether and by whom it might be maintained. Repentance can be said to have occurred when the lost have been recovered, and personal responsibility (for being found) or irresponsibility (for being lost) are not prominent themes.

The Parable Is Presented as a Response to Grumbling

The story is told as a response to the grumbling of the Pharisees and scribes over the fact that Jesus "welcomes sinners and eats with them" (15:2; cf. 5:30; 19:7). Jeremias, for instance, identifies Luke 15:11–32 as "primarily an apologetic parable, in which Jesus vindicates his table companionship with sinners." He insists, "Jesus thus claims that in his actions the love of God to the repentant sinner is made effectual."[77] Still, as is often noted, the complaint of the religious leaders is not that Jesus is *reforming* sinners. Luke's Pharisees would presumably have had few problems with Jesus sharing table fellowship with former tax collectors and ex-sinners who had mended their wicked ways. The grumbling is precipitated by a welcome of current sinners. Certainly, there is no reason to assume that Levi's party guests in 5:29 had all abandoned their appalling profession after the example of their host (5:27–28).[78] Yet Jesus eats with them. He also describes the (current) tax collector in Luke 18:9–14 as "justified" in the eyes of the God when the man has merely acknowledged his sin without offering any assurance of abandoning it. Similarly, the woman who anoints Jesus' feet in Luke 7:36–50 is identified as "a

---

77. Jeremias, *Parables of Jesus*, 132.

78. Indeed, there is no assurance that Levi/Matthew himself has abandoned the unsavory profession of tax-collecting altogether, since he is not subsequently listed among Jesus' disciples (Luke 6:14–16; cf. "Matthew" in Matt. 9:9; 10:3). Likewise, Zacchaeus might serve as an example of a reformed tax collector (19:1–10), though he clearly does not abandon the profession completely. From the Pharisees' perspective, his pledge to be honest (cf. 3:12–13) and to give generously to the poor would signal partial reformation at best.

sinner," meaning a current sinner. On *that* point, Jesus, Simon the Pharisee, and Luke's narrator all seem to agree (7:37, 39). She perhaps is a prostitute, and if so, there is no hint that she will not still be a prostitute tomorrow. Jesus says only that her many sins are forgiven and that her faith has saved her; there is no admonition to "go and sin no more."[79] In terms of social situation, of course, there is evidence that most tax collectors and prostitutes were slaves, for whom reformation (at least as defined by career change) was not an option.[80]

The grumbling of the scribes and Pharisees, then, concerns Jesus' announced and enacted policy of proclaiming a kingdom of God that includes unreformed sinners. Accordingly, the parable in Luke 15:11–32 can only serve as an effective response to such grumbling if the son is assumed to return to his father in an essentially unreformed state. What exactly has changed? He has undergone an attitude adjustment in one important regard: he now regrets leaving his father's house, where he would have been protected from famine. He calls his decision to leave that haven a "sin." Still, the story gives no indication that anything *else* has changed. If we take *asōtōs* in the most literal sense and regard the boy as a fool who did not know how to manage his money, we have no reason to believe that he will now be any wiser with regard to such matters. Or, if we allow that the boy may have squandered his fortune fulfilling lusts of the flesh, the story gives us no reason to assume that those appetites will have been squelched or that the boy will have attained sufficient moral fiber to resist them. The only relevant transformation in the young man is that at the beginning of the story he does not want to be in his father's house, and at the end he does. Indeed, at the beginning, he is so desperate *not to be* in his father's house that he eschews convention by requesting an early payment of his inheritance and moves to a far country. At

---

79. When I have invited readers to recount the story from memory in the manner described at the start of this chapter, more than half add the words (probably derived from John 8:11) to what Luke actually quotes Jesus as saying in 7:50. Thus, their subconscious "memory" creates an account of moral reformation out of a story that seems to focus only on inclusion (via forgiveness) of an apparently unreformed sinner.

80. Luise Schottroff and Wolfgang Stegemann, *Jesus and the Hope of the Poor* (Maryknoll, N.Y.: Orbis, 1986), 8, 15.

the end, he is so desperate *to be* in his father's house that he would relinquish his status as a son and accept the role of a hired servant.

Summary

Western interpreters have tended to regard Luke's story of "the Prodigal Son" (even that title is revealing!) as a tale of moral repentance, as a story that depicts sin as personal irresponsibility, illustrates the consequences of such sin, and then locates the key to redemption in an individual decision to reverse one's course through humble confession and capitulation to the authority against which one formerly rebelled. To sustain this reading, such interpreters have had to make a number of assumptions about matters that are not actually stated in the text. They have (1) assumed that squandering possessions should be prioritized over famine as the main cause of the boy's affliction; (2) assumed that the property was squandered in ways that involve wickedness, not just foolishness; (3) assumed that the boy's generic confession of sin includes repentance for the (assumed) vices that he committed in squandering his money; and (4) assumed that once the young man — who is assumed to have repented of these assumed vices — is back in his father's house, he will strive to live as he should have lived previously. As indicated, this chain of assumptions begins with a troublesome decision to all but ignore the mention of a famine in 15:14, a detail that threatens to shift the focus away from the boy's irresponsibility to the vicissitudes of life in a treacherous world. In the interests of sustaining their preferred interpretation, readers have also been willing to disconnect the story from the other two with which it is grouped and to neglect its role as a response to complaints about Jesus welcoming (unreformed) sinners.

What if we do not make these assumptions and follow this line of interpretation? What if, as a start, we notice the famine and treat it as an essential part of the narrative? The story then becomes a tale of recovery, not reformation: it is about the recovery of a boy who might have perished. The point is that the recovery of such a boy should be an occasion for rejoicing, not grumbling. The assumptions listed above become unnecessary, and the story fits well with its context, scoring essentially the same main point as its two companions and offering a threefold response to the grumbling of 15:2. The "prodigal" himself recedes in importance, and the father comes to the fore. This father illustrates the proper response to recovery of what was thought lost. The older son illustrates an inappropriate attitude analogous to that of the scribes and Pharisees.

Some Concluding, (Almost) Postmodern Thoughts

What we have in Luke 15:11–32 is a story about a young man who gets lost, just as the sheep and the coin before him. This time, we recognize a slight element of personal responsibility: the boy made a foolish (and possibly wicked) decision to leave the safety of his father's home and to go out into the world alone. He compounded this error predictably by wasting his money in foolish (and possibly wicked) ways. But then a famine came, and whose fault was that?

A couple of the commentators surveyed above (Plummer, Ragg) suggest that readers are to assume God (ironically termed Providence) sent the famine, effectively starving an entire country in the interest of expediting an important realization on the part of its only significant inhabitant. Alternatively, Bock and Nolland suggest that we attribute the famine to "Nature." But what does Luke's Gospel tell us about Providence and nature (creation)?

In Luke 12, Jesus urges his disciples to trust creation and Providence: "Do not worry about your life, what you will eat, or about your body, what you will wear. For life is more than food, and the body more than clothing. Consider the ravens: they neither sow nor reap, they have neither storehouse nor barn, and yet God feeds them" (Luke 12:22–24). Well, *sometimes* God feeds them — and yet Luke 15:14 seems to undermine this advice. How many ravens starved in that far country when famine came upon the land?

Notably, Jesus preceded his encouragement to trust nature (Providence) with a different parable about a man as foolish as the young lad we have been discussing, though in this case, the foolishness would take a quite different form. In Luke 12, we hear of a man who stores his crops (12:17) and grain (12:18) in barns so that he will have "ample goods laid up for many years" (12:19). This man is a fool because he dies while nature is still on his side, while his land is "producing abundantly" (12:16). But what if he had lived long enough to see the famine that arrives just three chapters later? Who would have been the fool then? The one with barns full of grain, or the one who had squandered his property without worrying about his life, what he would eat, or his body, what he would wear?

If Luke 15:14 seems to deconstruct the teaching of chapter 12, it may be because neither section of this Gospel is intended to provide instruction regarding financial management (12:14). The Lukan Jesus seems to recognize that this world has a certain "damned if you do, and damned if you don't" ambience to it. This is a world where God does feed birds and clothe lilies, but it is also a world where wolves kill lambs (10:3), foxes hunt chickens (Luke 13:31–35), and even those sparrows so treasured by God have a market value below five-for-two-cents (12:6). It is a world where famine may arise without the sort of divine premonition once granted to Joseph. In such a world, advice is not what is needed, for the wise course of action in one instance might prove to be one's undoing in another. In that regard, we should not even take the boy's desertion of his father as an action that would be universally condemned (cf. Luke 9:59–60).

Jesus' parables, least of all the story of the man with two sons, do not offer advice for surviving life's treacheries. Jesus urges his followers to trust creation and Providence, apparently knowing full well that such trust will *ultimately* prove to be misplaced. But, then, in this parable, he offers something more. A main point of the parable, I think, is that there *is* a "father's house," a place of safety unaffected by famine or sloth, where tables can be perpetually filled with food and rooms with music and dancing. There *is* such a place. Sometimes, perhaps, it is here on this earth, when nature is temporarily cooperative. Within the world of Luke's story, this wondrous place (sometimes called "the kingdom of God") seems almost perpetually to be found in a circle around Jesus who, in this Gospel, appears to be "always eating" (to quote Robert Karris[81]) and likening life in his company to an ongoing wedding feast (5:33–34; but then see 5:35). Otherwise, this place (the father's house or God's kingdom) might be found in a community of people who share their possessions with such a spirit that there is "not a needy person among them" (Acts 4:34). Or, ultimately, it may only exist in heaven, where the hungry are filled (Luke 6:21) and the limits of any entity that can "kill the body, and after that do nothing more" (12:4) have been exhausted. This parable promises first and foremost that such a place exists and that whenever and wherever it is found, there should be celebration.

Second, the parable insists that the foolish and/or wicked belong in this place of safety; indeed, of all people, they need to be there the most, since foolishness and/or wickedness are factors that place people at special risk. The world is populated by sinners and fools, but that is not all. The world *itself* needs correction — a point that is lost when Luke's famine is forgotten. Luke's Jesus finds joy in the recovery of those who (for whatever reason) have fallen victim to the world's treachery. And, conversely, he sees tragedy in the tribulation of those who (for whatever reason) are not recovered. Indeed, it is a tragedy worthy of tears when little chicks will not gather under the wings of Mother Jesus for the protection she would offer them (Luke 13:31–35). Whether such chicks are naughty or foolish is quite irrelevant; with foxes like Herod on the loose, their fate seems assured. The Lukan Jesus comes not to seek and to reform but to seek and to save (19:10). He seeks to recover the lost and bring them into the house of their father or gather them under the bosom of their mother, where they will be safe from famines and foxes.

---

81. Robert J. Karris, *Luke: Artist and Theologian* (Theological Inquiries; New York: Paulist, 1985), 47–78.

16

"There the ? Will Gather Together" (Luke 17:37)

Bird-Watching as an Exegetical Activity

Gail R. O'Day

The invitation to contribute to this volume identified its proposed title as "Lilies of the Field and Birds of the Air: Literary Encounters with the Reign of God" and requested that contributors write an essay that reflected Professor Tannehill's two lifelong interests of New Testament interpretation and nature, especially bird-watching. As a backyard bird enthusiast myself, I warmed to the challenge of finding an intellectual and theological connection between two such seemingly disparate activities. While sparrows (Luke 12:6–7) or even ravens (Luke 12:24) might be more appealing birds to "watch," the bird that caught my exegetical and ornithological eye was the bird of Luke 17:37b, "Where the corpse is, there the vultures will gather" (NRSV). This essay will explore how inaccurate bird-watching by modern critical scholarship has distorted the interpretation of this saying of Jesus.

Vultures or Eagles?

The Greek text of Luke 17:37b names the birds in Jesus' saying as *hoi aetoi*. *Aetos* is the Greek word for eagle,[1] which is how its other New Testament occurrences (Rev 4:7; 8:13; 12:14) are translated.

---

1. BDAG, 22; LSJ, s.v.

There is a Greek word for vulture, *gyps*,[2] and the lists of unclean birds in Lev 11:13–19 and Deut 14:12–18 make clear that eagles and vultures are two different bird species: each is included separately in the two lists. Contemporary English translations of Luke 17:37b (and its parallel in Matt 24:28), however, seem to ignore this distinction and consistently translate *oi aetoi* as vultures.[3]

The widespread agreement among contemporary English translations notwithstanding, the translation of *aetos* in verse 37b as vulture rather than eagle is a relatively recent development. The Vulgate of Luke 17:37b reads, "Ubicumque fuerit corpus, illuc congregabuntur et aquilae," with *aetoi* translated as "eagles" (*aquilae*). The earliest English language translations, culminating in the KJV, all consistently identify the birds of Luke 17:37b as "eagles":

West Saxon Gospels ca. 990	Swa hwar swa se lichama bið þyder beoð *earnas* gegaderud.[4]
late Wycliffe ca. 1394	Where euer the bodi schal be, thidur schulen be gaderid togidere also *the eglis*.
Tyndale 1530–34	Whersoever ye body shalbe thyther will *the egles* resoorte.
Miles Coverdale 1535	Where so euer ye deed carcase is there wil *ye Aegles* be gathered together.
KJV 1611	Wheresoever the body is, thither will *the eagles* be gathered together.

In the United States, one of the earliest examples of translating *aetoi* as vultures rather than eagles is Goodspeed's New Testament (1931). The RSV (1952), however, kept with the long-standing tradition of translating *hoi aetoi* as "eagles," but included a text note that reads "or vultures."[5]

---

2. *Gyps* (vulture) does not appear in the New Testament but is used six times in the LXX (Lev 11:14; Deut 14:13; Job 5:7; 15:23; 23:7; 39:27). See also *gryps* (likely the great bearded vulture [LSJ, s.v.]) in LXX (Lev 11:13; Deut 14:12).

3. In addition to the NRSV, see also REB, NJB, NIV, NAB.

4. "Just so where the body is, there will the eagles be gathered." Cf. also the West Saxon Gospel, ca. 1175. I want to thank Derek Olsen, an Emory University Ph.D. student, for helping me locate these translations.

5. This translation pattern holds in other languages as well. In the 1534 Luther Bible (Wittenberg), Luther translates v. 37b as "Wo das Aas ist / da samlen sich auch die Adeler

Bird-Watching

How does one explain the development in modern historical critical research of this translation tradition and attendant interpretation
of Luke 17:37b? The answer seems to be that scholars' assumptions
about birds and bird behavior informed how the verse was interpreted and understood, which in turn seemed to necessitate a shift in
translation. A few representative comments from Lukan interpreters
will suffice to demonstrate ways in which the science of ornithology
has determined the art of biblical exegesis.

Alfred Plummer, in his International Critical Commentary volume
on Luke, observes about verse 37b, "The griffon vulture is probably
meant. ... Eagles neither fly in flocks nor feed on carrion. During the
Crimean War, griffon vultures, which had scarcely been around Se-
bastapol, collected in numbers, 'from the ends of the earth.' "[6] Joseph
Fitzmyer writes, "From earlier times Greek *aetos* (or *aietos*) designated the 'eagle,' the graceful bird of speed. Cf. Rev 4:7; 8:13; 12:14.
Even though ancient natural historians knew the difference between
an 'eagle' and a 'vulture,' ... it was not always easy to distinguish
them in flight."[7] And C. F. Evans writes, "The Greek word *aetos* must
mean 'vulture' (so RSV margin) rather than eagle, since the eagle is
not a carrion-eating bird."[8]

In addition to drawing on their own bird knowledge (note Plummer's comment), Lukan scholars point to two types of written sources
for their confident assertions about eagles and vultures in antiquity:
the natural histories of Aristotle and Pliny and the Old Testament, especially Job 39:27–30.[9] The bird-watching of these ancient

---

[the eagles]." In the 1984 Luther Bible (Deutsche Bibelgesellschaft Stuttgart), v. 37b reads,
"Wo das Aas ist, da sammeln sich auch die Geier [the vultures]."

   6. Alfred Plummer, *The Gospel according to St. Luke* (ICC; New York: Scribner's, 1907),
410.

   7. Joseph Fitzmyer, *The Gospel according to Luke*, vol. 2: *X–XXIV* (AB 28A; Garden City,
N.Y.: Doubleday, 1985), 1173.

   8. C. F. Evans, *Saint Luke* (London: SCM; Philadelphia: Trinity Press International,
1990), 633.

   9. See, for example, the full citations of the commentators cited in notes 6–8 (above).

naturalists, however, is more attentive to species differentiation than is the bird-watching of modern interpreters.[10]

Aristotle's bird classifications in book 8 (9) of *Historia animalium* contain an extended discussion of eagles in 8.32. Aristotle notes "numerous kinds" of eagles and describes six different types. One of these types is described as "resembling a vulture" (*gypi homoios*) in physical appearance, and Aristotle notes that the bird "takes dead animals" (*ta tethneota pherōn*). Aristotle is clear, however, that despite the physical resemblance, the bird in question is nonetheless an eagle (*aetos*). Pliny the Elder (*Naturalis historia* 10.3) follows Aristotle's classification of six kinds of eagles and repeats Aristotle's observation that one type of eagle "resembles a vulture."[11] Most important for the conclusions scholars reach on the basis of Pliny's classifications, Pliny elaborates on Aristotle's vague observation about this eagle's habit of taking dead animals. Pliny writes, "It is the only eagle that carries away the dead bodies of its prey; all the others after killing alight on the spot."[12] Scholars regularly point to this observation to show that Pliny (and by association Aristotle) here has in view a vulture, not an eagle.[13] A careful reading, though, shows that the ornithological contrast here does not distinguish this eagle by the kind of food that it eats but by where and when it eats its food. Pliny does not say that this variety of eagle is a carrion eater, but that it moves the prey it has killed to another spot before eating it. On the basis of Pliny's extended description, it is fair to assume that this is the behavior that Aristotle described as well. Scholars read Aristotle's phrase, "takes dead animals," as if *pherō* means eat or consume, but

---

10. See Warren Carter, "Are There Imperial Texts in This Class? Intertextual Eagles and Matthean Eschatology as 'Lights Out' Time for Imperial Rome," *JBL* 122 (2003): 467–87. Carter's focus is on Matt 24:28 and the importance of reclaiming the interpretation of eagles there as symbols of the Roman Empire. Carter also concludes that the ancient sources do not support equating eagles and vultures.

11. Item quarti generis est percnopeterus, eadem oripelargus, vulturina specie alis minimis, reliqua magnitudine antecellens....

12. Sola aquilarum examinata aufert corpora, ceterae cum occidere considunt.

13. So BDAG, 21, which provides a special definition for *aetos* in Matt 24:28//Luke 17:37: "Eating carrion, in the proverb (cf. Job 39:30) Mt 24:28; Lk 17:37 (where vulture is meant; Arist[otle], *H[ist.] A[n.]* 9, 32, 592b, 1ff and Pliny, *Hist. Nat.* 10, 3 also class the vulture among the eagles.)"

there is no precedent for such a meaning.[14] Aristotle means exactly what Pliny takes him to mean: this eagle "carries away" (*aufert*) its prey before consuming it.

A careful reading of Job 39:26–30 also calls into question the bird-watching skills of interpreters of Luke 17:37b. In this section of the whirlwind speech, the voice of God turns to bird behavior to under-score the difference between God's knowledge and power and Job's:

> Is it by your wisdom that the hawk soars,
>   and spreads its wings toward the south?
> Is it at your command that the eagle mounts up
>   and makes its nest on high?
> It lives on the rock and makes its home
>   in the fastness of the rocky crag.
> From there it spies the prey;
>   its eyes see it from far away.
> Its young ones suck up blood;
>   and where the slain are, there it is. (NRSV)

In the English and the Masoretic Text, there are only two birds in question in this passage — the hawk of verse 26 and the eagle of verses 27–30. Yet the Septuagint (LXX), its translators perhaps more attuned to the subtleties of bird behavior, inserts a third bird into the unit. In the LXX, verses 27–28 read:

> epi de sō prostagmati hypsoutai aetos,
> gyps de epi nossias autou kathestheis aulizetai
> ep' exochē petras kai apokruphō;[15]

Here verses 29–30 refer explicitly to the vulture (*gyps*), belying any notion that the behaviors of eagles and vultures are subsumed into one another. On the basis of the LXX of Job 39:27–30, then, one

---

14. It is also interesting to note that scholars make a similar erroneous assumption about the meaning of *(epi)sunagō* in Luke 17:37//Matt 24:28. Commentators assume that vultures must be in view because only vultures eat carrion, but the verse actually says nothing about eating, only that *hoi aetoi* will gather together. See Carter, "Imperial Text," 471.

15. "Is it at your command that the eagle soars, and that the vulture makes its nest and lives in the protection and hiddenness of the rock?"

cannot say that the Greek word *aetos* can double as the word for vulture.[16]

Does modern ornithology provide any support for the assumptions interpreters bring to Luke 17:37b? The traditional classification of vultures in bird books is alongside hawks and eagles, because all are diurnal raptors, birds of prey who hunt by day. Vultures belong to the family Cathartidae, while hawks and eagles belong to the family Accipitridae. Aristotle's observations on the six kinds of eagles stand up remarkably well next to the observations of modern ornithologists, as both note family similarities and distinct differences. Neither classifies the vulture as an eagle, even as both note the "strong (even if only superficial) resemblance between the groups."[17] Like Aristotle, modern field observation notes that the "Golden Eagle can be mistaken for Turkey Vulture and even some buteos [hawks], but note the much larger size, relatively long wings, steady flight."[18]

Ancient natural historians and modern field observers are quite clear on the distinctions between eagles and vultures. As in antiquity, there is no contemporary evidence that "eagle" functions as a generic word for "bird of prey." To say that one can have difficulty distinguishing between some kinds of eagles and vultures in flight does not lead inevitably, as most modern commentators seem to assume,[19] to the conclusion that therefore one would confuse the nouns one uses to speak of these birds. To paraphrase Gertrude Stein, "An eagle is an eagle is an eagle."[20]

The Wild Bird Chase

The translation of *hoi aetoi* as "vultures" and interpretations based on that translation predetermine the way Luke 17:37 is understood.

---

16. So Carter, "Imperial Text," 469.

17. David Allen Sibley, *The Sibley Guide to Birds* (National Audubon Society; New York: Knopf, 2000), 106.

18. Ibid., 126.

19. Cf. the comment of Fitzmyer, *Luke*, cited above.

20. Gertrude Stein, "Rose is a rose is a rose is a rose," in "Sacred Emily;" first published in *Geography and Plays* (Boston: The Four Seas Co., 1922; repr., New York: Haskell House, 1967).

There is a circular logic to the arguments offered in support of "vultures": Based on the evidence of the natural sciences, *hoi aetoi* must mean "vultures" because of the references to "body (*sōma*)" and "gather together."[21] Yet at the same time, interpreters argue that because *hoi aetoi* must mean vultures, the behavior described in 17:37b must be that associated with vultures as described by ornithologists.

This circular logic and its appeal to the natural sciences has the effect of turning Luke 17:37b into a literal statement about birds and their behavior. Interpreters appropriate Luke's words here almost as if they belong to the genre of natural history found in Aristotle or Pliny. Interpreters seem to assume that the statement about bird behavior is a straightforward description, and that once one recognizes the bird behavior in question, the meaning of the verse is known. This can be seen most readily in the frequent assumption that "where the corpse is, there the vultures will gather" is a common proverb based on an example from nature. Yet multiple attestations of such a "common" proverb do not seem to exist.[22]

Job 39:30 is regularly referred to as the proof of the existence of such a proverb,[23] but the context of this verse in the whirlwind speech, as well as the LXX's addition of *gyps* (noted above), make reliance on Job suspect. The bird behaviors cited in 39:26–30, like the references to nature throughout Job 39–41, are not put forward as examples from which one is to draw a generalized or illustrative truth, as is the case with proverbs (cf. the use of bird behavior in Prov 23:5), but as very specific indicators of the power and providence of God. The nature references throughout Job 39–41 do provide a glimpse into ancient Hebrew understandings of the natural world, but Job 39–41 is not a source for proverbs.

The translation of *hoi aetoi* as "vultures" aids the interpreter in identifying a recognizable natural phenomenon to which the words

---

21. The one significant difference between Luke 17:37 and Matt 24:28 is the word for "body." Matthew 24:28 reads *ptōma*, "corpse," whereas Luke 17:37 has the more ambiguous *sōma*. *Sōma* does not necessarily mean "corpse," but it is used with that meaning elsewhere in Luke (23:55 and 24:3, 23). *Ptōma* does not occur in Luke.

22. See Carter, "Imperial Texts," 469–72, for a review of the primary source data.

23. E.g., BDAG, 21.

point. This identification removes much of the interpretive difficulty of the verse, however. The reader is no longer challenged to discover what the verse "means": what one already knows about vultures provides a meaning and obviates further questions. The interpreter's only remaining task is to figure out what this example of vulture behavior means in its context.

Modern critical commentators invariably point first in their explanatory remarks to what is known about vultures and then work to fit that understanding into Luke 17:37.[24] As a result, two traits of vultures are highlighted: the inevitability of the appearance of a carrion eater at the site of a corpse, or the speed and suddenness with which a carrion eater discovers a corpse.[25] A third alternative is to highlight the visibility in the sky of circling birds of prey, although this alternative is proposed more for the Matthean context of this saying than its Lukan context.[26] With this bird behavior in view, commentators then posit that this saying is intended as an analogy: as it is with vultures and corpses, so it is with the days of the Son of Man. This analogy is posited even though there are no comparative particles or adverbs (e.g., *hōs*, *houtōs*) in the verse.

In assuming that Jesus' words about *hoi aetoi* can function only as an analogy, commentators also have to reread and/or rewrite the question that evokes these words. Luke 13:37a contains the first (and only) words that Jesus' disciples speak in response to Jesus' teaching about the days of the Son of Man that began in verse 22. The disciples ask a very short and simple question, "Where, Lord?" (*Pou, kyrie*; v. 37a). Because verse 37b is interpreted as an analogy from nature (and so would more logically answer the question "How?"), commentators are forced to posit either: (a) that the disciples ask the wrong question; (b) that Jesus does not answer their question directly; or (c) some combination of the two (e.g., Jesus knew that the

---

24. The commentators cited in notes 6–8 illustrate the pattern found in all major commentaries on this verse.

25. For inevitability, see Fitzmyer, *Luke*, 1173; for suddenness, see François Bovon, *L'Evangile selon Saint Luc, 15,1–19,27* (CNT, Deuxième Séries, IIIc; Geneva: Labor et Fides, 2001), 159–60.

26. Heinz O. Guenther, "Where 'Eagles' Draw Together," *Foundation and Facets Forum 5* (1989): 141–47.

disciples meant "How"). The notes in the *New Oxford Annotated Bible* (NRSV) on Luke 17:37 ably demonstrate this perspective:

> Jesus' answer is a significant appeal to faith. The questioners wish to know *where* the Messiah and his people will be located. Instead of answering them directly, Jesus warns: As surely as vultures find the carcass, so surely will divine judgment come; therefore always be ready![27]

A reading of the words of 17:37a and 37b without the presumption of the vulture analogy, however, suggests that Jesus answers the disciples' question very directly: they ask a question of location ("where [*pou*]?") and he provides them with one (*hopou*). The vocabulary of verse 37 suggests a quite careful connection between Jesus' response and the question to which he responds, which is nonetheless ignored by commentators because it does not fit their presuppositions about vultures and the "proverb" that Jesus is speaking. For these interpreters, a sense of the logic and order of the natural world becomes the determining interpretive lens, regardless of whether the ornithological or exegetical data actually support these assumptions. The translation of *hoi aetoi* as "vultures" instead of "eagles" became an assumed and unexamined "fact," and inaccurate exegesis inevitably followed from inaccurate bird-watching.

Three Blackbirds in a Tree

> I was of three minds,
> Like a tree
> In which there are three blackbirds.
> (Wallace Stevens)[28]

The main casualty from reading Luke 17:37b as a literal account of bird behavior is losing the possibility of reading Jesus' words here

---

27. Bruce M. Metzger and Roland E. Murphy, eds., *The New Oxford Annotated Bible*, NRSV (New York: Oxford University Press, 1991), loc. cit.

28. "Thirteen Ways of Looking at a Blackbird," in Wallace Stevens, *The Collected Poems* (New York: Vintage Books, 1990).

as spoken in language as richly figurative and evocative as the preceding teachings in verses 22–36 and the following parable in 18:1–8. Because the translation "vultures" removes any tension intrinsic to Jesus' words in verse 37b, the saying becomes so easy to appropriate that the possibility that Jesus is speaking in any categories other than the most obvious disappears as an interpretive option. As a result, verse 37b becomes the one verse to be taken "literally" in an otherwise figurative context. Interpreters do not assume that Jesus intends verses 31–36 to be taken literally, for example, nor do they assume that the parable of the Widow and the Judge recounts an actual court proceeding (or that coherence between the court proceedings and the parable is essential to its meaning).[29] Yet the interpretation of 37b hinges on establishing a correspondence between Jesus' words and the bird behavior. That this bird saying might be intentionally disjunctive in its context, asking the reader to create a mental image that does not have a literal corollary in the natural world, is excluded from consideration.

As an interpretive exercise, what happens if we return to the centuries-long tradition of translating *hoi aetoi* as "eagles"? Since vultures became the translation of choice in large measure because of the inconsistencies its use eliminated, one may have to shift reading strategies. Instead of reading 17:37 as an almost self-contained proverb and as an observation that must be confirmable from natural history, interpreters may need to read first for the theological and literary function of the eagles saying in this section of Luke.

The interpreters of the early church, who assumed that *hoi aetoi* (or *aquilae*) signified eagles, provide useful conversation partners in exploring a different reading strategy.[30] Unlike the strategy of modern

---

29. Although see J. D. M. Derrett, "Law in the New Testament: The Parable of the Unjust Judge," *NTS* 18 (1971–72): 178–91, who does place this parable in the context of first-century jurisprudence.

30. Another strategy, which I will not pursue in this essay, is to read Luke 17:37//Matt 24:28 in conversation with the apocalyptic literature of the Roman period. "Eagles" were a well-known symbol of the Roman Empire: the image of an eagle was carried by Roman armies. Reading this saying in an apocalyptic context restores the possible political dimension of this symbolism. See Warren Carter, "Imperial Texts," and note 10 (above). This reading strategy seems more appropriate for the saying's appearance in Matthew than in Luke, because Matthew sets Jesus' speech in Jerusalem, but it should still be considered as one of the possible

critical commentators noted above, these early interpreters took as their defining point of reference what they already knew about the revelation of God as contained in all the books of Scripture. The church fathers made use of the resources of their contemporary natural science where appropriate,[31] but their hermeneutical assumption was that the gospel provided the framework in which to understand natural science, not the other way around.

The interpretations of many early church fathers on this saying of Jesus are readily available in Thomas Aquinas's compendium of patristic teaching *Catena aurea*.[32] Aquinas begins the catena with the consensus patristic and medieval understanding of this verse:

> Another sign He adds of His coming, "Wheresoever the body is, thither will the eagles be gathered together." The eagles denote the company of the Angels, Martyrs, and Saints.

There is no attempt made in this interpretation to take "eagles" literally as an example of a particular bird species whose behavior needs to be classified before one can engage the substance of the saying. "Eagles" is clearly taken as purely symbolic and evocative language, so that Jesus' saying is not a proverb from nature, but a proclamation "of His coming." What reading strategy leads to this interpretation? The words that precede the Scripture quotation are key: "another sign He adds of His coming." This consensus interpretation of the early church gives primary importance to this saying being spoken in the context of a collection of sayings about the coming of the Son of Man, who for these readers is Jesus himself. The "body" is understood not as a corpse, but as the body of Christ, the Son of Man. As a result, the birds do not come to the body to

---

meanings that Jesus' saying can generate once the interpreter is freed from the constraints imposed by dependence on a flawed appropriation of natural science. See Fitzmyer, *Luke*, 1173, who acknowledges that there may be an allusion to the Roman Empire here. This reading shares an important trait with the patristic readings discussed below: it assumes that Jesus speaks in symbolic discourse.

31. E.g., Origen's and Augustine's use of Pliny.

32. http://ccel.org/a/aquinas/catena/Matthew/ch.24htm. This catena is of Matt 24:28, but the patristic commentators take Luke 17:37//Matt 24:28 as the same saying. All of the patristic quotations in the following pages come from *Catena aurea*. For the consensus reading, see John Chrysostom, *Homilies on Matthew*, 77.

eat carrion, since there is no carrion to eat. Unlike contemporary interpretations, this means that one does not need to manufacture a definition for *episynago* that includes "eating."[33] There is no sense that Luke 17:37//Matt 24:28 is a self-contained proverb from nature, but rather that its meaning coheres with the sayings that precede it. It is an eschatological announcement about the coming of the Son of Man.

In this reading, Jesus' saying is not a warning or admonition (as in comments on p. 296, above) but a celebration of the coming of the Son of Man. This celebration will be marked by the gathering together of the company of "angels, martyrs, and saints," the heavenly winged creatures.

Modern critical scholarship is quick to dismiss this reading,[34] and it is not my intent to present this patristic interpretation as the "correct" reading of Luke 17:37//Matt 24:28. It seems unlikely that the Lukan Jesus had second- and third-century C.E. conceptions of martyrs and saints in view here. It is my intent, however, to suggest that this patristic interpretation (as well as the others given below) may offer a way of reading a text that is attuned to what the biblical text may say rather than to what it cannot mean, with the result that it presents multiple possibilities and not the single answer.

This patristic interpretation, as odd as it seems to modern sensibilities, does not really substitute flights of theological fancy for close reading of the biblical texts. Rather, it is more closely attuned to the context in which this saying is found in Luke and Matthew than many historical critical interpretations that proceed as if the defining context is ornithology, not eschatology. This consensus reading attends to the setting of the passage in a discourse about the day of the Son of Man and so reads the verse as a distinctive saying of Jesus and not a common proverb.

Jerome, like modern critics, appeals to examples from bird life, but to a quite different end:

---

33. See note 14 (above).

34. Plummer (*Luke*, 410) writes, "The patristic interpretation of the saints gathering round the glorified body of Christ is equally unsuitable to the context."

By an instance from nature, which we daily see, we are instructed in a sacrament of Christ. Eagles and vultures are said to scent dead bodies even beyond sea, and to flock to feed upon them. If then birds, not having the gift of reason, by instinct alone find out where lays a dead body, separated by so great space of country, how much more ought the whole multitude of believers to hasten to Christ, whose lightning goeth forth out of the east, and shines even to the west? We may understand by the carcase here, or corpse, which in the Latin is more expressively "cadaver," an allusion to the passion of Christ's death.

These comments, which Aquinas draws from Jerome's *Commentary on Matthew,* have much more depth and detail than the generic consensus view just discussed. Attending to the specifics of ornithology is not paramount for Jerome, since he generalizes about birds of prey and their behavior. Instead, Jerome argues from nature on the basis of "from the lesser to the greater": if so with birds, how much more so with humans. The key to reading nature is the way in which it provides "a sacrament of Christ." Jerome engages in theological interpretation, not bad science.

As with the consensus perspective, the hermeneutical key for Jerome lies in recognizing this saying as a teaching of Jesus about the coming of the Son of Man. "Body" is not read generically, but with the very specific referent of the body of Christ. Unlike modern interpretations, the activity of the birds is not given an ominous note, but is something for believers to emulate. The saying is read as invitation, not admonition. The image of the gathering eagles presents a vision of the community of believers gathered around the body of Christ.

Jerome's closing comments about the passion of Christ reflect another patristic bent in the interpretation of Luke 17:37//Matt 24:28, illustrated even more clearly in this quote from Hilary:

That we might not be ignorant of the place in which He should come, He adds this, "Wheresoever the carcase, &c." He calls the Saints "eagles," from the spiritual flight of their bodies, and shews that their gathering shall be to the place of His passion, the Angels guiding them thither; and rightly should we look for His coming in glory there, where He wrought for us eternal glory by the suffering of His bodily humiliation.

Because Luke 17:37//Matt 24:28 occurs in a series of sayings about the coming of the Son of Man, "corpse," whether (Luke's) *sōma* or (Matthew's) *ptōma*, is taken to evoke the crucified body of Jesus. This reading intersects with the church fathers' observations of the natural world and the behavior of birds of prey. The natural world is theologically evocative, not exegetically constraining. The context of the saying as an eschatological teaching of Jesus again is determinative. The gathering together of birds of prey at a corpse provides a way of envisioning the gathering of the faithful at the passion. This reading also attends to the immediate setting of the saying in Luke, as it answers the disciples' question of "where." The place of the eschatological event is at the passion.

These patristic interpretations also are attuned to another aspect of context that eludes most modern critical commentators. Jesus' eschatological sayings envision a world in which the constraints and strictures of the natural world will be transformed by the coming of the Son of Man. The imagery of the natural world that provides the context for Luke 17:37//Matt 24:28 challenges everyday assumptions about how the natural world coheres. In Luke, the saying is immediately preceded by the teaching about one being taken and another left (17:35–36), a teaching that completely subverts assumed values about the natural order. In Matthew, it is followed immediately by language about the darkening of the sun and moon and the descent of the stars. Nothing in its context suggests that Jesus' saying intends to conform with the canons of the natural world (as the translation of *hoi aetoi* as vultures assumes). The natural world is not presented as the control on eschatological expectations. Instead, eschatological expectations are the lens through which one's vision of the natural world is refracted.

The remaining three quotes from Aquinas's catena speak to this eschatological transformation. The image of the company of heaven flocking around the passion of Christ comes closer to capturing the symbolic potential of Jesus' saying about eagles than the literalistic reading of verse 37b as a proverb about vultures eating carrion.

> ORIGEN: And observe, He says not vultures or crows, but "eagles," shewing the lordliness and royalty of all who have believed in the Lord's passion.

> JEROME: They are called eagles whose youth is renewed as the eagle's, and who take to themselves wings that they may come to Christ's passion.[35]

> GREGORY: We may understand this, "Wheresoever the carcase is," as meaning, I who incarnate sit on the throne of heaven, as soon as I shall have loosed the souls of the elect from the flesh, will exalt them to heavenly places.

The quotation from Gregory introduces yet another level of meaning. Just as the body of Christ was exalted, so, too, will be the souls of the elect. Gregory plays out fully the eschatological context of this saying, interpreting Luke 17:37//Matt 24:28 as a vision of the final resurrection of the dead.

Rather than restricting what Luke 17:37 may mean, the church fathers' knowledge and observation of birds generates multiple possibilities of meaning. Jerome and others are more concerned with locating their reading of the natural world within what they know about God than the other way around. The patristic and medieval interpreters rightly recognized that *hoi aetoi* is a symbol, not an entry in a bird book, and so read in ways that honor the form and function of Jesus' saying. By contrast, the modern historical critical interpretation of Luke 17:37//Matt 24:28 has relied on unexamined assumptions from ornithology and natural history to provide it with a definitive reading of this verse that shuts out all other interpretive options.

---

35. In these comments, Jerome reads "eagles" through the lens of Ps 102:5 (ET, 103:5) and Isa 40:31, an illustration of the patristic and medieval practice of interpreting Scripture by Scripture.

The goal of this interpretive exercise is not to pit ancient and modern interpretation against one another, or to argue for one of the patristic options as the "correct" interpretation of Luke 17:37. To do so would violate the shift in reading strategy that the exercise was designed to highlight: that the meaning potential of symbolic discourse suffers when it is reduced to one definitive reading. The translation and interpretive history of Luke 17:37 demonstrates what happens when such interpretive reduction occurs, since the circular and uncritical application of ornithology by modern commentators governs even the translation of the verse and so predetermines what can and cannot be said. The patristic readings are illuminating because they show the range of interpretive practices that reenter the picture once Luke 17:37 is freed from the constraints wrongly imposed by translating *hoi aetoi* as vultures.

Like Wallace Stevens's "Thirteen Ways of Looking at a Blackbird," the interpretive exercise in this essay is a reminder of the richness that comes from recognizing that just as there is more than one blackbird in the tree, there is more than one meaning in any given biblical text. The modern interpretive direction is often away from the "three minds" that Stevens's poem celebrates and toward a uniformity of mind and interpretation. Bird-watching and biblical exegesis, however, are both more engaging arts when their practitioners attend to all the blackbirds in the textual tree.[36]

---

36. Over the course of the days when I was writing this paper, I observed the following birds in and around my backyard: northern cardinal, Carolina chickadee, tufted titmouse, white-throated sparrow, American robin, eastern towhee, American goldfinch, house finch, cedar waxwing, northern mockingbird, common grackle, mourning dove, American crow, red-shouldered hawk, red-tailed hawk, red-bellied woodpecker, downy woodpecker, blue jay, pine warbler, yellow-rumped warbler, brown-headed nuthatch, white-breasted nuthatch, Carolina wren, brown thrasher. I also heard a barred owl and a pileated woodpecker. No eagles or vultures, though.

17

"Ministers of Divine Providence"

Diodorus Siculus and Luke the Evangelist on the Rhetorical Significance of the Audience in Narrative "Arrangement"

David P. Moessner

It has been the aspiration of certain of these writers [of universal histories] to draw (*agagein*) all humanity — who, though united to one another by kinship are yet separated by place and time — into one and the same narrative account (*syntaxis*), and so, as it were, have shown themselves to be ministers of Divine Providence (*hypourgoi tēs theias pronoias*). (Diodorus Siculus, *Library of History* 1.1.3)[1]

Thus Diodorus Siculus styles himself and links his forty-volume history of the inhabited world[2] to the well-intentioned attempts of those who have preceded him. Yet Diodorus continues in his opening

---

1. My translation from the LCL Greek text, *Diodorus of Sicily*, vol. 1 (Cambridge: Harvard University Press, 1946).

2. Of the forty volumes composed, only fifteen are extant in their more or less completed form; the rest are in various fragmentary states; see, e.g., C. Rubincam, "How Many Books Did Diodorus Siculus Originally Intend to Write?" *CQ* 48 (1998): 229–33, esp. p. 232. For the relation of Diodorus to previous Hellenistic historians, see esp. Adele C. Scafuro, "Universal History and the Genres of Greek Historiography" (Ph.D. diss., Yale University, 1984), 116–54, 205–62; K. S. Sacks, *Diodorus Siculus and the First Century* (Princeton: Princeton University Press, 1990); G. Wirth, *Diodor und das Ende des Hellenismus: Mutmassungen zu einem fast unbekannten Historiker* (Sitzungsberichte, Österreichische Akademie der Wissenschaften, Philosophisch-historische Klasse, 600; Vienna: Verlag der Österreichische Akademie der Wissenschaften, 1993). For the relation to the Latin historians Justin and Curtius, see, e.g., N. G. L. Hammond, *Three Historians of Alexander the Great: The So-called Vulgate Authors, Diodorus, Justin and Curtius* (Cambridge: Cambridge University Press, 1983).

flourish[3] (1.3.1–8) to detail the deficiencies of those predecessors and even suggest that his is the first authentic universal history in recent memory, since he alone traces the mythic origins of the human family down to his own day (ca. 59 B.C.E.) (1.3.3–6).[4] While other historians have "closed their narratives"[5] with Philip, or Alexander, or even the Diadochi or the Epigoni,

> yet, despite the number and importance of the events following these and extending even to our own lifetime which have been overlooked, no historian has written up an account of them within the scope of a single narrative (*mias syntaxeōs perigraphē pragmateusasthai*), due to the magnitude of the undertaking. (1.3.3)[6]

Diodorus's alleged superiority to other historians echoes a common *topos* of Hellenistic historiographical *prooimia* such that his lofty self-commendation perhaps will not seem so "unseemly."[7] On the other hand, what may appear as striking in this rather eloquent

---

3. The *prooimion* to book 1 also functions as a prologue to the whole work; the style is more eloquent than the rest of the work. See, e.g., A. Burton, *Diodorus Siculus Book I: A Commentary* (Leiden: Brill, 1972), 35: "Diodorus's general introduction to his history... reaches a degree of eloquence unsurpassed by any other author, and far superior to the rest of his work." For a detailed analysis of Diodorus's style, see J. Palm, *Über Sprache und Stil des Diodorus von Sizilien: Ein Beitrag zur Beleuchtung der hellenistischen Prosa* (Lund: C. W. K. Gleerup, 1955), e.g., 194: "DS [Diodorus] beim Stilisieren im wesentlichen selbständig vorgegangen ist und dem aus den Quellen übernommenen Material ein neues, modernes sprachliches Gewand gegeben hat."

4. For discussions of the dating of the last events treated by Diodorus, see Sacks, *Diodorus Siculus and the First Century,* 160–203. Sacks concludes that Diodorus changed his original plan of ending the work with the contemporary events of 46 B.C. (1.5.1) to conclude with 60 B.C.E. (1.4.7): "Outspokenly admiring of the Dictator, yet mildly hostile toward the Empire and especially its new ruler, Diodorus thought it best to eliminate contemporary history from his work. Too many people had a stake in the rendering of their past for an émigré to detail it with candor" (160–61); cf. Rubincam, "How Many Books?" 229: "His [Diodorus's] originally intended terminus was most likely the triple triumph of Julius Caesar.... The decision in favour of an earlier terminus will have been due either to simple fatigue or to disillusionment with the course followed by Caesar's heir after 44 B.C. and anxiety about the dangers of dealing with events of a too recent and controversial past." Ironically, then, Diodorus did not meet his primary criticism of others!

5. Diodorus, *Hist* 1.3.3: *katestrepsan tas syntaxeis*.

6. Unless otherwise indicated, all translations are mine.

7. Cf., e.g., T. Rajak, "Josephus and the 'Archaeology' of the Jews," *JJS* 33 (1982): 465–77; D. P. Moessner, "The Appeal and Power of Poetics (Luke 1:1–4): Luke's Superior Credentials (*parēkolouthēkoti*), Narrative Sequence (*kathexēs*), and Firmness of Understanding (*asphaleia*) for the Reader," in *Jesus and the Heritage of Israel* (ed. D. P. Moessner; vol. 1 of *Luke the Interpreter of Israel*; Harrisburg, Pa.: Trinity Press International, 1999), 84–123, esp. pp. 85–97.

self-appraisal is the extent to which his superior narrative account purports to *benefit the readers*. When composed properly, history narrative motivates humans to aspire to that true morality disclosed through the very workings of Providence:

> In general, then, it is because of that commemoration of good deeds which history accords human beings that some of them have been induced to become the founders of cities ... and that many have aspired to discover new sciences and arts in order to benefit the race of humankind. And since complete happiness can be attained only through the combination of all these activities, the foremost title of praise must be awarded to that which more than any other thing is their cause, that is, to history, ... [that] herald of the divine voice. (1.2.1, 3)[8]

Diodorus goes on to hail *historia* as "guardian of the high achievements," "witness ... to the evil deeds of the wicked," and the "benefactor of the entire human race ... the mother-city (*mētr-o-polis*) of philosophy as a whole" (1.2.2). It is indeed as a mouthpiece for "Fate" and "Providence" and their interweavings of the whole inhabited world "as though the affairs of one city/state" (*polis*) that he, Diodorus, the true universal historian, serves "most sublimely" as "the minister of Providence" "to all humanity who love and seek the truth" (*pasōn euchrēstotatēn syntaxaito tois philanagnōstousin*, 1.3.6).

It is the argument of this short tribute to Professor Tannehill's monumental contribution that Diodorus's emphases on the extent to which his audience will be impacted and even inspired to particular courses of action should not come as a surprise. As is well-known, it is precisely during the cultural transition from the primacy of orality to orality *and* literacy in the late Hellenistic period that rhetoric establishes itself as a discrete discipline, complete with a metalanguage of epistemology, categories for adjudicating "truth" claims of performed speech, and school traditions of instruction and

---

8. Slightly revised from C. H. Oldfather's translation, LCL, vol. 1.

performance, including narrative production.[9] But more than that, positively stated, Diodorus's zeal to reconfigure events of the past in order to instruct his audience in the moral lessons that history provides — purposefully structuring his narrative to be the primary vehicle for conveying these messages — continues a fundamental Hellenistic narrative hermeneutic originating in, and developing out of, the earlier stages of "composed orality."[10] Similar to his contemporaries, Diodorus appeals to his readers/auditors as the ultimate judge of his narrative performance, since the narrative hermeneutic that he engages integrates into its very epistemology the audience's participation and comprehension. The "proof" of the narrative's success is in the "pudding" of audience impact. Rhetoric's pervasive influence and a standard narrative hermeneutics thus work hand in hand.

A century or so later, Luke the Evangelist makes a similar pitch. He informs his audience from the beginning that he is not fully satisfied with the narrative attempts of "the many" to render an account of the "events/affairs that have come to fruition among us" (Luke 1:1–4). My argument also intends to show that Luke's opening justifications for yet another narrative presentation makes perfect sense within this pervasive, conventional narrative (diegetic) hermeneutic. Independently of each other, Diodorus and Luke conceive their compositions from within this standard *diegetic* epistemology and can thus be so construed. Taken together, however, Diodorus's rationale for writing may possibly serve further to illumine Luke's desire to add to the number of "the many." I hope that, in some small way, this comparison may shed some light on the significance of Luke's continuation of fulfilled events through a second volume and thus be a fitting contribution for Robert Tannehill, whose pioneer publications

---

9. Cf. R. L. Enos, *Greek Rhetoric before Aristotle* (Prospect Heights, Ill.: Waveland, 1993), esp. pp. 41–90; and bibliography, 141–54; C. G. Thomas and E. K. Webb, "From Orality to Rhetoric: An Intellectual Transformation," in *Persuasion: Greek Rhetoric in Action* (ed. I. Worthington; London/New York: Routledge, 1994), 3–25, esp. pp. 16–23; M. Gagarin, "Probability and Persuasion: Plato and Early Greek Rhetoric," in *Persuasion* (ed. Worthington), 46–64.

10. For the function of audience participation and persuasion through the heuristic, eristic, and protreptic modes of discourse in the composed orality of Homer and the rhapsodes, see esp. Enos, *Greek Rhetoric before Aristotle*, 1–22.

in the poetic performance of the two-volume Luke-Acts has — for the reader — produced a most sublime benefit![11]

The Tria-lectic Dynamic

As I have delineated elsewhere, the commonly shared epistemology of narrative that informs both Diodorus and Luke is articulated already in the fourth century B.C.E. in Aristotle's *Poetics*.[12] In the course of expounding the distinctive features of poetic *mimesis* in tragedy and epic[13], Aristotle's presentation posits the fundamentals of the standard narrative poetics.

Of the six ingredients of poetic *mimēsis* introduced by Aristotle in *Poetics* 6, the three most constitutive and defined as "objects" of the "poet's" *mimēsis* are "plot" (*mythos/praxeis*), "character" (*ta ēthē*), and "thought" (*dianoia*). These three then comprise the structural rudiments of composed orality, whether of dramatic presentation or narrative performance.

> The most important of these is the arrangement of the incidents (*hē tōn pragmatōn systasis*), ... and the end aimed at is [the representation] not of qualities of character (*ta ēthē*) but of some action. ... [The characters] do not therefore act to represent character traits or qualities (*ta ēthē mimēsontai*), but

---

11. See esp. Robert C. Tannehill's groundbreaking two-volume *The Narrative Unity of Luke-Acts: A Literary Interpretation* (2 vols.; Minneapolis: Fortress, 1986–1990).

12. D. P. Moessner, "Dionysius' Narrative 'Arrangement' (*oikonomia*) as the Hermeneutical Key to Luke's Re-Vision of the 'Many,' " in *Paul, Luke and the Graeco-Roman World: Essays in Honour of Alexander J. M. Wedderburn* (ed. A. Christophersen et al.; JSNTSup. 217; Sheffield: Sheffield Academic, 2002), 149–64, esp. pp. 151–53.

13. Cf. e.g., S. Halliwell, *The Poetics of Aristotle: Translation and Commentary* (London: Duckworth, 1987); L. Cooper, *The Poetics of Aristotle: Its Meaning and Influence* (New York: Longman, Green, 1927), esp. pp. 15–62; S. H. Butcher, *Aristotle's Theory of Poetry and Fine Art* (New York: Dover Publications, 1951), esp. pp. 121–27; Manfred Fuhrmann, trans. and ed., *Aristoteles: Poetik* (Dialog mit der Antike 7; Munich: Heimeran, 1976), esp. pp. 25–31; G. M. A. Grube, *The Greek and Roman Critics* (London: Methuen, 1965), 70–92; D. A. Russell, *Criticism in Antiquity* (Berkeley and Los Angeles: University of California Press, 1981), 99–113; K. Eden, *Poetic and Legal Fiction in the Aristotelian Tradition* (Princeton: Princeton University Press, 1986), 69–75; W. Trimpi, *Muses of One Mind: The Literary Analysis of Experience and Its Continuity* (Princeton: Princeton University Press, 1983), 50–63; M. Heath, *Unity in Greek Poetics* (Oxford: Clarendon, 1989), 38–55; Paul Ricoeur, *Time and Narrative* (3 vols.; Chicago: University of Chicago Press, 1984–88), 1:31–51.

characters are included for the sake of the action (*dia tas prax-eis*).... The plot (*mythos*) then is the first principle and, as it were, the soul of tragedy:[14] character comes second.... Third comes "thought" (*dianoia*). (6.15–40, trans. mine)

According to Aristotle, every good tragedy or epic represents a "single action" with a unique sequence of *beginning, middle,* and *end* in which a main actor undergoes a major turn of events (*metabasis*) from good to bad or the reverse (the latter as in comedy). Every character, event, or action is arranged with all the other characters, actions, or events for the sake of this single action into a unique and dynamic causal nexus of a balanced, beautiful whole, that is to say, "plot," all with the specific purpose of eliciting the emotive reaction or "*katharsis* (catharsis)" of the audience as one of "pity and fear."[15] The extent to which this audience impact (cf. modern reader response) is integral to the very raison d'être of the poet's undertaking cannot be overemphasized. The goal that the poet must keep vividly before his or her mind for every dimension and section of the drama or narrative epic is the *kathartic* response of the audience:

> For the plot (*mythos*) should be so structured (*synestanai*) that, even without seeing it performed, the person who hears the events that occur experiences horror and pity at what comes about.... And since the poet should create the pleasure (*hēdonē*) which comes from pity and fear through *mimēsis*, obviously this should *be built into the events* (*en tois pragmasin empoiēteon*). (*Poetics* 14.1–13, emphasis added)[16]

Here we encounter two fundamental components of what we can term a *tria-lectics* of Hellenistic poetics: (1) the particular form of the actions (*plot*), which (2) is structured by the "poet" toward a specific impact upon the audience. The third component is already implicit:

---

14. Or as Aristotle himself states in *Poetics* 9.25–29, "The poet (*poiētēs*) must be a 'maker' (*poiētēs*) not of verses but of plots/stories (*mythoi*), since he/she is a poet by virtue of [his/her] 'representation' (*mimēsis*), and what he/she represents (*mimeitai*) are actions/events (*praxeis*)" (trans. mine; numeration follows *Aristotle*, LCL, vol. 23 [2d ed., 1995]).

15. Aristotle, *Poetics* 6–8, 13–14, 17.

16. Trans. S. Halliwell, *Aristotle*, LCL, vol. 23 (2d ed.; 1995).

the author's/poet's *intention of the mind* (*dianoia*) to compose a plot that issues in the intended audience result. But to describe this authorial intention more directly, we must turn to Aristotle's more nuanced development of the third object of *mimēsis:* "thought" (*dianoia*).

As is commonly agreed, Aristotle employs *dianoia* in two different senses:[17] (1) On the one hand, *dianoia* "appears wherever in the dialogue they [the characters] put forward an argument (*apodeiknyousi*) or deliver a general view on matters (*katholou ti apophainontai*)" (*Poetics* 6.[1450b] 10–11). Thus *dianoia* in this more focused sense is constitutive of character development, which in turn is determinative of the quality of action. (2) *Dianoia*, however, may also refer to the poet's own point of view or orientation to the whole of the work, which is expressed through the overall form and content of the work itself. *Dianoia* in this wider sense is essentially the rhetoric of the text, because the expression of an author's intent always entails selected language, arranged in specific ways for the purpose of desired effects upon an audience.

Consequently, for any writer to be effective, argues Aristotle in *Poetics* 19, she or he must follow the principles (*idea*) laid down by the master art, whether involving persuasion, emotional effect, or perspectives on the relative importance of anything. Accordingly, it is ultimately the author's/poet's control of the overall ideological "thought" of the composition through control of the intermeshing actions, characters, and characters' points of viewing or understanding (*dianoia*) that produces a coherent *poiēma* with distinct significances for the audience. Aristotle can even appeal to the formal arrangement of the *pragmata* (*mythos*) through the *dianoia* of the poet such that the overall impact will be the same on any observer or reader. Indeed, speeches or dialogue should be included only when the emplotted action *itself* does not create the desired effect upon the audience of pity and fear: "For what would be the point of the speaker, if the required effect were evident even without speech?" (*Poetics* 19.7–8). So tightly interwoven is authorial intention (*dianoia* in the broader

---

17. E.g., S. Halliwell, *Poetics of Aristotle*, esp. on chap. 6 of the *Poetics*.

sense) with the structured plot and its impact upon the audience that Aristotle argues that the poet can commit an "incidental error" — such as an impossible detail in depicting life — as long as the larger action becomes more lifelike or convincing in producing the desired impact of fear and pity. "It [the error] is justifiable if the poet thus achieves the object (*telos*) of *poiesis* . . . and makes that part or some other part of the poem more striking" (25.23–24, trans. mine).

To sum up, the *Poetics* presents a tria-lectic poetics of "composed orality" that consists of authorial intention (cf. *dianoia*), the arrangement of the actions or events (cf. *mythos*), and the impact upon the audience (cf. *katharsis*). All three components are interdynamically related such that no single component can operate without the concurrent enabling engagement of the other two. This tria-lectic dynamic of narrative epistemology constitutes the standard poetics of the Hellenistic period; its tria-lectic interaction rendered the truth claims of the text.

Integration of Linear and Lateral Cause-Effect Nexuses

Diodorus criticizes his predecessors, as we have seen, for not extending the narrative compass to more recent events, which in his estimation are laden with world significance (*Hist.* 1.3.3). But it would be wrong to conclude that scope alone epitomizes his concern to immortalize the good deeds of the past through the divine voice of historical narrative. In recounting why he himself decided to undertake such an overwhelming responsibility, he cites a fundamental flaw in the power of his predecessors' narratives to deliver the desired benefits to the readers. The "working out" or "disposition" of their compositions do not measure up to the task (*ou mēn exeirgasthai pros to sympheron kata to dynaton tas pragmateias autōn*)" (1.3.1). He gives two main types of deficient history narratives: (1) "Independent" or "self-contained" (*autoteleis*) wars of a single people or city as the sole focus (1.3.2); (2) universal sweeps that lack attention to some major nation or city/state, or to proper chronology, or to accounts of the "barbarians," or to the "ancient legends," or that break off before the intended conclusion because of the death of the author (1.3.2).

In both categories — whether insufficient scope or chronology — what is missing are the interconnections among peoples and events both "vertically" through time and "horizontally" through the cause-effect nexuses of the interweavings of Providence. By contrast, his "single narrative" will "begin with the most ancient times and record to the best of his ability the affairs of the entire world down to his own day, so far as they have been handed down to memory, as though they were the affairs of some single city (*hōsper tinos mias poleōs*)" (1.3.6). It is this synoptic intercalating of happenings as *one larger process of a larger force unfolding* that constitutes the "greater" benefit purportedly lacking in the other histories. Both form and content must inhere in order to cohere!

That this integration of both a linear chronological trajectory and a lateral synchronological compass in Diodorus's own estimation distinguishes his conception from the accomplishments of previous historians is evidenced in four passages.[18]

Fusing Synchronic and Diachronic Streams (History 1.3.8)

Diodorus climaxes his own decision to write by summarizing the greater benefit of his narrative configuration:

> The reason for this is that, in the first place, it is not easy for those who propose to go through the writings of so many historians to procure the books which come to be needed and, in the second place, that, because the works vary so widely and are so numerous, the recovery of past events becomes extremely difficult of comprehension and of attainment (*dysephiktos hē tōn pepragmenōn analēpsis*); whereas, on the other hand, the account which keeps within the limits of a single narrative (*he d' en mias syntaxeōs perigraphē pragmateia*) and contains a

---

18. Scafuro, *Universal History*, is one of the few to treat these critical epistemological aspects of the poetics of narrative historiography in any detail; see esp. 205–62.

connected account of events (*to tōn praxeōn eiromenon ec-housa*) facilitates the reading and contains such recovery of the past (*tēn men anagnōsin hetoimēn parechetai*) in a form that is perfectly easy to follow (*tēn d' analēpsin echei pantelōs euparakoloutheton*).

Both the sheer chronological sweep and the wide swath of interconnections are impossible for *the reader to grasp* ("follow," *parakolouthetos*; cf. Luke 1:3–4) unless both dimensions are fused together through the interwoven poetics (plot) of the one narrative. As Diodorus goes on to say, "A history of this nature [Diodorus's narrative] must be held to surpass all others to the same degree as the whole is more useful than the part and continuity [more useful] than discontinuity, and, again, as an event whose date has been accurately determined is more useful than one of which it is not known in what period it happened" (1.3.8). In other words, synchronic and diachronic streams must both flow together as one.

Balancing Narrative Arrangement (History 5.1.1–4)

The synthesis of both chronological and synchronological dimensions is especially manifest in the short *prooimion* to book 5. Now Diodorus draws upon the poetics-rhetorical term "management/arrangement" (*oikonomia*), taken from the world of "household management," to describe the proper balance between linear and lateral connections in historiographical narrative's purview.[19] Without the proper balance or "arrangement" of the "varied material" by a skilled author, the reader is deprived of the fuller experience that history has to teach. Sequence or "order" (*taxis*) is one vector of narrative "arrangement" that is relatively easy to monitor in drawing comparisons among several writers.[20]

---

19. On an *oikonomia* "system" of Hellenistic poetics that was developing already from before the time of Aristotle and on into the imperial period, see esp. R. Meijering, *Literary and Rhetorical Theories in Greek Scholia* (Groningen: E. Forsten, 1987), esp. 171–225; cf. R. S. Reid, " 'Neither Oratory nor Dialogue': Dionysius of Halicarnassus and the Genre of Plato's *Apology*," *Rhetoric Society Quarterly* 27 (1997): 63–90, esp. 67–72.

20. For a more developed system of "arrangement" in the younger contemporary Dionysius of Halicarnassus, which includes "division/partitioning" (*diairesis*), "order/sequence" (*taxis*),

Thus Diodorus, in promoting his own balanced "arrangement," singles out his predecessor Timaeus as performing admirably in narrating detailed and accurate chronology, as well as doing justice to the vicarious quality of historical accounts that pull the reader into sync with its lessons. It would seem that in both diachronic and synchronic concerns, Timaeus has written exemplary narrative. Yet there is a major problem that — again — destroys *for the reader* the balance between the two:

> Some historians indeed, although they are worthy objects of praise in the matter of style (*kata tēn lexin*) and in the breadth of experience derived from the events which they record (*kata tēn polypeirian tōn anagraphomenon praxeon*), have nevertheless fallen short in respect of the way in which they have handled the matter of arrangement (*kata tēn oikonomian*), with the result that, whereas the effort and care which they expended *receive the approbation of their readers* (*apodochēs tynchanein para tois anaginōskousi*), yet the order (*tēn de taxin*) which they gave to the material they have recorded is *the object of just censure.* Timaeus, for example, bestowed, it is true, the greatest attention upon the precision of his chronology and had due regard for the breadth of knowledge gained through experience, but he is criticized with good reason for his untimely and lengthy censures, and because of the excess to which he went in censuring, he has been given by some men [*sic*] the name Epitimaeus or Censurer. (5.1.2, trans. Oldfather, emphasis added)

The reader is deprived, not simply because lengthy censures consume precious narrative space; rather, such passages also break up the "continuity" (cf. *to syneches*, 1.3.8) of the finely meshed linear and lateral connectors and thus break up the reader's ability to follow the narrative lessons the author wishes to convey. Hence, Diodorus considers Timaeus's "arrangement" and thus "management" of the

---

and "method or effectiveness of development" (*exargasia*), see Reid, "'Neither Oratory nor Dialogue,'" 67–83; Moessner, "Dionysius' Narrative 'Arrangement,'" 153–64.

reader in both diachronic and synchronic matters to be defective. Or, more generally, his "order" does not serve his larger purposes (5.1.3). By contrast, Ephorus elicited the well-deserved reputation of a successful writer of "universal history," since both his "style" and his "arrangement" were skillfully conceived and executed, and the reader duly rewarded (*ou monon kata tēn lexin, alla kai kata tēn oikonomian epiteteuche*) (5.1.4).

Diodorus goes on to relate that Ephorus's procedure in "arrangement" was to limit each "book" to only those events which fell under a "single topic" (*kata genos*). Diodorus then claims that he too is adhering to this model and will incorporate in book 5 only material that relates to Sicily (5.1.4). However, as he proceeds to include also accounts of islands on either side of Sicily that were influential in Sicily's growth, it is clear that lateral dimensions as well as the linear developments of Sicily's history are integral to good "arrangement." The point of theoretical contrast between his predecessors should not be underestimated. Unlike Timaeus's account, Diodorus's narrative fabric will deliver the maximum "returns" *for the reader.* His "order" will not disrupt the reader since both chronological and synchronological trajectories will mesh and convey the desired messages. It is, of course, another matter whether Diodorus lived up to his lofty goal. With respect to chronological scope, according to his original plan, he evidently did not complete his narrative down to his own day, to the fate-filled events of the beginning of the Roman Empire. Thus the great irony remains that he could not improve upon the very features for which he chiefly criticized his predecessors.[21] Moreover, Diodorus's synchronic abilities have generally been regarded as at best "second-rate,"[22] though K. S. Sacks has gone a long way in "rehabilitating" Diodorus's contribution, both in the treatment of his

---

21. See note 4 (above).

22. Cf., e.g., P. J. Stylianou, *A Historical Commentary on Diodorus Siculus Book 15* (Oxford: Clarendon, 1998), 1: "For the cardinal fact about Diodorus is that he was a second-rate epitomator who generally used first-rate sources"; A. Burton, *Diodorus Siculus Book I*, 1: "The very title of the work indicates that little more is to be expected than a convenient compilation of earlier historical writings. And in spite of the noble declarations in his introduction, Diodorus seems generally to have achieved little more than this."

sources as well as his own compositional skills.[23] But what is undeniable, however, is the tria-lectic poetics of authorial intent, narrative vehicle of that intent, and realized intent for the reader that Diodorus espouses here.

Treating a Single Topic in Full Scope (History 15.95.4)

Sacks makes a persuasive case that the close of book 15 discloses Diodorus's meaning of good "arrangement" "according to a single topic" (*kata genos*) or to "a full account" (cf. *autoteleis,* 16.1–3). In declaring that he is on task by closing book 15 with the events that led up to King Philip, Diodorus announces that book 16 will begin (*archomai*) with Philip's accession to the throne and include "all the achievements of this king to his death (*teleutē*), including in its compass (*symperilambanontes*) those other events as well which have occurred in the known portions of the world" (15.95.4). Sacks points out that Diodorus refers back to the beginning of book 15, where he outlines his scope as *beginning* with the war of the Persians against Evagoras in Cyprus and *ending* with the year preceding the reign of Philip, son of Amyntas. A single topic appears to consist of the full scope of the nexus of cause and effect of important events surrounding a ruler or actions of a city/state, which in turn are related to other key movements and developments within the larger work.

Completing Accounts for Moral Instruction (History 16.1.1–3)

When Diodorus does begin book 16, he reiterates the principle of "a single topic" or "complete account" but reformulates this procedure through an appeal to the conventional tria-lectic hermeneutic in a way that scholars like Sacks have not appreciated.[24] Diodorus gives

---

23. See esp. Sacks, *Diodorus Siculus and the First Century,* 3–8, "Introduction."

24. Sacks (ibid., 95) speaks only of a "commonplace" *topos* of historical literature as "express[ing] fears that materials that are uninteresting or unhistorical will not attract the reader (1.1; 1.4)." His citation of the proem of book 1 and his severing as two different issues Diodorus's discussion in book 20 of the interruption of the narrative continuity by unneeded speeches (20.1–2) from the narrative problems of presenting simultaneous events (20.43.7) shows further his failure to grasp the organic cluster of audience comprehension, authorial intent, and authorial "management."

as his rationale for composing books "that are complete in them-selves (*autoteleis*)" (16.1) the requirement that the audience be able to "remember" what is presented because the narrative itself is "intel-ligible/comprehensible" to the readers (*tēn historian eumnēmoneuton kai saphē genesthai tois anaginōskousin*; 16.1.1).

> For incomplete accounts of actions (*hēmiteleis praxeis*) in which the culminating events exhibit no continuity with the beginning events (*ouk echousai syneches tais archais to peras*) interrupt the interest even of avid readers (*mesolabousi tēn epithymian tōn philanagnōstountōn*), whereas those accounts that do exhibit the continuity of the narrative (*to tēs diēgēseos syneches*) up to the very conclusion of the events (*mechri tēs teleutēs*) produce a narrative account that is well-roundedly complete (*apērtismenēn tēn tōn praxeōn echousin apangelian*). (16.1.2)

Without the reader fully involved in following the significance of the author's narrative connections, even the most skillful of literati will fail the test. *Autoteleis* accounts lead the reader to the right moral con-clusions that history is teaching; these lessons are "clear" (*saphē*) if the historian as minister of Divine Providence re-presents those moral truths through the mimetic connections of the narrative. *Hēmiteleis* accounts simply do not supply the proper emplotment of significance (*to syneches*) *for the reader.* As in Aristotle's *Poetics,* we note the same conception of a complete and balanced narrative that shows how *beginning* points develop through a *middle* series of connections to the causally effected *end* events. Diodorus goes on to say that in the particular cases where the "events themselves" seem to "cohere naturally" and thus "work together" with "those who are writing his-tory" (*hē physis autē tōn prachthentōn synergē tois syngrapheusi*), it behooves the historian to perceive that pattern as heuristic for the entirety of the narrative: "s/he must not deviate at all from this principle!" (16.1.2).

To sum up, Diodorus regards his predecessors' universal histories to be wanting in either "vertical scope" or "horizontal sweep" or both. In matters of starting and ending points of a diachronological

presentation (through time), as well as synchronological interconnections among contemporary nations/city-states, Diodorus intends
to fulfill his obligation as a "mouthpiece" for Providence by better "management" of his audience's comprehension of the workings
of Providence. Only a new narrative "arrangement" can accomplish
that goal.

Luke's Vertical Chronology and Horizontal Synchrony

Luke also wants to compose a narrative that better illumines his audience vis-à-vis "events come to fruition" through an overarching
"plan of God."[25] The tria-lectic Hellenistic poetics — with audience
comprehension built into the very structure of the composition — is
explicit in Luke 1:3–4 (*edoxe kamoi... kathexēs soi grapsai, kratiste
Theophile, hina epignōs peri hōn katēchēthēs logōn tēn asphaleian*).
The import of *asphaleia* for Luke's readers becomes clear from its
adverbial sense in Acts 2:36: "Let the whole house of Israel know
therefore with *clear certainty* (*asphalōs*) that God established him
as both Lord and Christ, this Jesus whom you crucified." Adjectival
senses of *asphales* in Acts are linked with verbs of "understanding"
and "writing," just as with "most excellent Theophilus" in Luke
1:4 (e.g., Acts 25:26–26:25, "most excellent Festus," who has not
"firmly grasped" anything about the accusations against Paul "in
order to write" his superior [*asphales ti grapsai*, 25:26]. He therefore
needs further illumination from those who are competent to judge
Paul's case; cf. Acts 21:34; 22:30). *Asphaleia* thus combines both
the senses of "clarity" (*saphēneia*) and "security" (*asphalēs*).[26] Luke
is not satisfied that "the many" can provide a "firm grasp" for his

---

25. Luke 7:30; Acts 2:23; 4:28; 5:38–39; 13:36; 20:27; cf. 27:42–43. For an illuminating
treatment of this notion in several Hellenistic writers, including Diodorus, Dionysius of Halicarnassus, Josephus, and Luke, see J. T. Squires, *The Plan of God in Luke-Acts* (SNTSMS 76;
Cambridge: Cambridge University Press, 1993), esp. 15–52. Squires compares the formulations of providence and divine control over history in the various writers but does not treat the
narrative epistemology that shapes the more comprehensive narrative configurations of those
formulations.

26. Cf. the only other instance of *asphaleia* in Luke-Acts, in Acts 5:23, with its literal sense
and referent, "the securely locked" prison gates! Cf. Bauer on *asphalōs* in Acts 2:36: "know
beyond a doubt" (BDAG, s.v.); RSV: "know assuredly."

audience. Like Diodorus, he too must put forward a new narrative arrangement.

That this new narrative configuration will be different from "the many" in both diachronological scope and synchronic emplotment seems evident from a variety of indications. The limited scope of this chapter, however, will confine us to the following two observations.

Luke 24:13–53 and Acts 1:1–14: The "Plan of God" in the "Opening of the Scriptures"

Luke seems to go out of his way to make it clear that his volume 2 is not simply a sequel that is ancillary or even secondary to the first, but rather is part and parcel of one narrative enterprise. By overlapping Luke 24 with Acts 1 chronologically and synchron(olog)ically, the audience learns that one emplotment of one "plan of God" is being enacted:

1. *Chronologically*, Luke 24:50–51 ends with Jesus "being taking up into heaven." Acts 1 begins with a secondary prologue that defers to the primary prologue ("O Theophilus," Acts 1:1→Luke 1:3) and summarizes the chronological scope of volume 1 as beginning with a "beginning" point in which Jesus acts and teaches until the "day in which he was taken up" (*hōn ērxato ho Iēsous...achri hēs hēmeras...anelēmphthē*, Acts 1:1b–2). The end boundary of the first volume is acknowledged, yet verse 3 of Acts 1 launches into an emplotment which recontextualizes Luke 24:13–49 into a distinctive new period. Now the reader learns that Jesus did not appear just twice on the day of resurrection before being taken up (24:13–35, 36–49); instead, there were "many" such "proofs" during a longer period between resurrection and ascension ("through forty days," Acts 1:3). In particular, Jesus' appearance to the gathered group in 24:36–49 must be seen in a new light. This encounter, in fact, may be a "type scene" emblematic of the whole (new!) period between the women's first belief in the resurrected one (Luke 24:1–12) and Jesus' being "taking up" from them (Acts 1:11–14).

2. *Synchronically*, Acts 1:3–8 recasts Luke 24:36–49 into the main plot of volume 2. Jesus' "opening of the Scriptures" and charge

to "the Eleven and those with them" to take to "all the nations" the new comprehension of all these Scriptures (Luke 24:44–47) sets the course of events in Acts and prepares the reader for the radically new apostolic "opening of the Scriptures" in the leading speeches of Acts (2:14–36; 3:12–26; 4:8–12, 23–31; 5:29–32). Now the whole of Israel must understand that all of their Scriptures come to their goal in Jesus as "the Christ" and that all must "have a change of mind/repent" concerning all that "Jesus began to do and to teach" (Acts 1:1) (e.g., 2:36: "Let the whole household of Israel know with clear certainty:... this Jesus whom you crucified."). Even the role and replacement of the betrayer in this "apostolic ministry" was forecast in Scripture (Acts 1:15–26, esp. v. 25). In sum, the true apostolic tradition concerning the "kingdom of God" is defined and reconstituted as apostolic "witness" to the "plan of God" in all the Scriptures (Luke 24:48: "these things of which you are witnesses"→Acts 2:23: "You executed this one [who was] delivered over through the preordained plan and prescience of God"→Acts 2:32: "this Jesus whom God raised, of which we are all witnesses"; and so on).[27]

3. *Jesus as the Proemial Voice:* Luke does something most unusual when he has Jesus, the main actor of the first volume, "interrupt" to speak out of the mouth of the narrator as the latter reintroduces Jesus' prophetic command from Luke 24 to begin the second volume (Acts 1:4a→1:4b). This technique of moving from "indirect" to "direct speech" within a short, secondary *prooimion* delivers a striking message: Jesus the resurrected Christ, the authoritative voice of volume 1 — not the narrator — forecasts to apostolic witness and reader alike the plot of the continuing narrative to be the fulfillment of his own prophecy in the legacy of his witnesses in the "kingdom of God" ("You are witnesses of these things,... but wait... until you are clothed with power from on high"→"to await the promise of my Father which you heard from me"→"but you shall receive power... and

---

27. See also my discussion of the overlap of Luke 24 and Acts 1:1–14, in D. P. Moessner, "The Lukan Prologues in the Light of Ancient Narrative Hermeneutics: *Parēkolouthēkoti* and the Credentialed Author," in *The Unity of Luke-Acts* (ed. J. Verheyden; BETL 142; Leuven: Leuven University Press/Peeters, 1999), 399–418, esp. 402–3.

be my witnesses...to the end of the earth," Luke 24:48–49→Acts 1:4b→Acts 1:8). The intricate web of Acts 1:1–8 with Luke 24:36–49 is indeed telling for the whole "arrangement" of Luke-Acts.

Luke 1:1 and Acts 1:8: "Events Come to Fruition in Our Midst" through "Witnesses into All the Nations"

Jesus' summary of what "stands written in the Scriptures" "concerning himself" as "the Christ" would seem to suggest that "witness" to this Christ "into all the nations" (*eis panta ta ethnē*) also stands at the heart of this scriptural fulfillment (Luke 24:44–49, esp. vv. 47b–48). Is it possible that none of the "many" other narratives with which Luke is familiar incorporates this witness to the nations such that this desideratum constitutes a major motivation for Luke himself to undertake a narrative compilation? Is it possible that, similar to Diodorus, Luke's dissatisfaction with the other accounts includes their failure to extend their diachronological sweeps far enough into more recent events, and because of that gap, fail to show how these later events themselves demonstrate the fuller flowering/fruition (*peplērophorēmenōn,* Luke 1:1) of the earlier fulfillment(s) of "the plan of God"? Do we perhaps have a clue already in Luke 1:1 when the inscribed author hints at "events come to fruition *in our midst*" which he now wishes to configure into the narrative in order to ensure a "firmer grasp" of the whole for the likes of Theophilus?

Our scope cannot cover the enigmatic ending of Acts, whether it is a fitting "conclusion" (*teleutē*) to the whole. But whatever else Luke may be referring to in his plan "to write to you in a distinctive sequence" (*kathexēs soi grapsai,* Luke 1:3), *kathexēs* would appear to denote both diachronological and synchronic "ordering," as we learn from Acts 11:4. There the term *kathexēs* in Peter's "laying out" to those of the circumcision in Jerusalem his experiences with Cornelius connotes, as it does in Luke 1:3, an ordering that brings narratological sense within the larger plot that is unfolding.[28] More precisely, it is

---

28. See, e.g., my treatment of *kathexēs* in D. P. Moessner, "The Meaning of *KATHEXĒS* in the Lukan Prologue as a Key to the Distinctive Contribution of Luke's Narrative Among the 'Many,' " in *The Four Gospels, 1992: Festschrift Frans Neirynck* (ed. Frans van Segbroeck

the content of that exposition and its intertwining with other parts of the Luke-Acts narrative that point to the critical significance of the Cornelius material within the larger emplotment. This content and intertwining may showcase a significant reason why Luke extended, beyond "the many" other attempts, both the linear and lateral scope of the "events come to fruition."

In Acts 11:15 Peter links the falling of the Spirit upon Cornelius's household to the falling of the Spirit upon himself and the Jewish believers "at the beginning" (*en archē*), namely, the "beginning" of Pentecost as depicted in Acts 2. But this seminal event is immediately interpreted as the fulfillment of the proemial voice in Acts 1:4b–8, at the beginning of volume 2! "I remembered the word of the Lord, how he said, 'John baptized with water, but you shall be baptized with the Holy Spirit' " (11:16→1:4b–5). We have just seen that this voice functions as a linchpin, pulling the two volumes together into one plot of the apostolic witness of and to the resurrected, rejected Christ. But this means that Peter is now hearing the voice of the forty-day interim as confirming his sending to the "unclean" Gentile Cornelius. But more than that, when Peter presents his report at the apostolic assembly in Acts 15, he now looks back to that period known as "from the days of the beginning" (*aph' hēmerōn archaiōn*, 15:7) as the time when God chose him to speak the gospel to *the nations* (*ta ethnē*). The echo of Acts 1:8 as well as the voice from heaven "not to call what God has cleansed unclean" (Acts 11:9b) reverberate here as one (Acts 15:7–9). It is no less than the proemial voice of the resurrected, crucified Christ of "all that stands written" (Luke 24:44) who had commanded Peter to fulfill those Scriptures by being a witness to the nations! The message in Luke's different "arrangement" from "the many" is hard to miss. Luke provides the synchronic threading of the Cornelius event with the baptism of the Holy Spirit at the beginning of the church (vol. 2), which in turn is stitched to the

---

et al.; 3 vols.; BETL 100; Leuven: Leuven University Press/Peeters, 1992), 2:1513–28. For ten renderings of the sense and referent of *kathexēs* in Luke 1:3, including Prof. Tannehill's "narrative order" (toward a unified story), see D. P. Moessner, "The Appeal and Power of Poetics," 98 n. 44).

prophecy of John the Baptist who inaugurates Jesus' public ministry: "beginning from John's baptism until the day he [Jesus] was taken up from us" (Luke 3:16→vol. 1→Luke 24:48–49→Acts 1:4b→Acts 1:22→Acts 11:16). Thus Luke "manages" his audience to the "clear certainty" (*asphaleia*) that the messianic witness to the Gentiles is part and parcel of the scriptural "plan of God." By composing a "vertical" chronology and a "horizontal" synchrony distinct from "the many," Luke shows how the divine voice that commissioned Jesus the Christ resounded through the divine voice of the crucified, resurrected one to commission the apostles to the Gentiles (Luke 3:15–22→Luke 24:44–49→Acts 1:4b–8). Through these nexuses of cause and effect, Luke indeed shows himself to be a "minister of Divine Providence" (Diodorus, *Hist.* 1.1.3).

18

Postcolonial Reflections on Reading Luke-Acts from Cabo San Lucas and Other Places

Jeffrey L. Staley

Reading Luke-Acts in My Study, in Bothell, Washington, Looking East

Of all the documents in the New Testament, the two-volume work we call Luke-Acts seems most amenable to postcolonial interpretation.[1] Motifs of travel, numerous geographical references, Diasporic and ethnic concerns, and issues of empire, mimicry, and hybridity — all these are central concerns of many postcolonial critics and are vividly represented in Luke-Acts. Furthermore, these topics have played important roles in Christian Europe's missionizing and colonizing strategies of the past. In contemporary scholarly debates the battle continues to rage over the question of whether Luke-Acts is largely sympathetic to Roman imperial power and elite society or opposed to them.

The thesis of this essay will be that, like many a subaltern living under imperial rule, the two-volume work reflects conflicting perspectives that are introduced in the first four chapters of Luke. Many times the author/narrator and "his" characters positively mimic the behavior of their Roman overlords. But at other times there is a powerful rejection of its imperial ethos. Likewise (Lukewise?), commentaries,

---

1. Some parts of this essay appeared in an earlier form in "Narrative Structure (Self-Stricture) in Luke 4:14–9:62: The United States of Luke's Story World," *Semeia* 72 (1995): 173–213.

even postcolonial ones, can easily end up replicating the totalizing power and authority of the very colonial empires they have dismantled, by being written in a rhetorical mode that silences conversation and dialogue. In light of this latter concern, I have chosen to write this essay from a variety of places and with alternating voices in hope that readers will feel free to insert their voices into the postcolonial dialogue over these texts.

Reading Luke-Acts in Cabo San Lucas, Baja Mexico

I have decided to take Luke-Acts along with me on my family's summer vacation, and I am reading it now, in the fierce desert landscape of Baja California. My family and I have flown nearly two thousand miles south from the rainy, overcast skies of the Pacific Northwest, to bask for a week in the June sun at San José del Cabo. We got suckered into one of those condo deals — "We'll give you a free week in Cabo — all you have to do is pay for your flight down there, and listen to a one-hour sales presentation."

Thanks to airline frequent-flyer miles racked up by attending professional meetings with other biblical scholars, we only have to pay for two full-fare tickets. My youngest child and I fly free. My wife and I are taking advantage of the system, we think. We do not plan on buying a condo or a time-share. We carefully rehearsed our no's all the way down here, and we plan on keeping our noses out of everyone else's business deals.

At home we had been telling people that we were going to Cabo San Lucas. But that is not really true. We are much closer to San José than to San Lucas. And there is an important difference between the two. San José — Saint Joseph in English — is just two miles north of where we are staying. Guidebooks say that it is a colonial Spanish outpost, founded by eighteenth-century Roman Catholic priests. San Lucas — or Saint Luke — is ten miles southwest of us, a neocolonial town. Nothing was there fifty years ago except a quiet harbor for deep-sea fishing boats, and a big rock with a hole in it. But now, with the advent of cheap airline flights and air-conditioning, Cabo has become a destination desert resort for sun-and-surf-starved North Americans like us.

If I could change the language buzzing around my ears and the flora and fauna I see just beyond the edge of the swimming pool where I am lounging, I could be at Eilat, Israel, or somewhere on the edge of the Judean wilderness with Luke's John, "preparing the way of the Lord." But I cannot change the geography, and so I put on my sunglasses, dip my toes in the lukewarm pool, and prepare to read the Third Gospel.

Reading from the Big "Rez" — Mapping the Plot of Luke-Acts

The place where I grew up was not much different from Eilat, Israel, the Judean wilderness, or the arid land around Cabo San Lucas, where I am now lounging, thinking about reading the Third Gospel. My childhood was formed largely by the geography of the southwestern United States, where I was raised in a high-desert region known as the Four Corners. There is, however, no such thing as the Four Corners, even though a U.S. National Monument bears that name. At least with Cabo San Lucas, there was a landmark — that giant of a rock poking its head out of the roiling waters of the Gulf of California a few miles down the beach from where I am now reading. But with the Four Corners there isn't even an observable landmark. It is a place of pure geometry, a place invented by the colonialist dreams of United States presidents, government surveyors, and creative cartographers. It is a typographical construct on a map, not a topographical constant.

The first time I visited the Four Corners — the spot near the San Juan River where the states of Utah, Colorado, Arizona, and New Mexico meet — was much different from this, my first visit to the tip of Baja California. I was young then, and I had to beg my parents to turn off the newly finished highway bisecting the Navajo Reservation and drive up a six-mile, unmarked dirt trail from Teec Nos Pos Trading Post. I was forced to endure my parents' stony "I told you so" looks as I stared at the four-inch square, one-foot high concrete post and asked incredulously, "Is that all there is to it?"

I toured the town of Cabo San Lucas yesterday and repeated the same words I said at the Four Corners forty years ago: "Is that all there is to it?" Like the Four Corners, Cabo San Lucas is also the invention of colonialist dreams — or better put, it is a neocolonialist nightmare — with its Planet Hollywood, outlet stores, and every other hybrid fast food and hotel chain that many North Americans desire when traveling.

A few years ago my children and I visited my childhood home on the Navajo Reservation. On the way to the place where I grew up, we stopped at the Four Corners. I was surprised to find that this time I had to slow down for a tollbooth a short distance from the monument. The Navajo Nation was charging each tourist a tithe of $1.50 to enter the sacred *bilagháana* (white man's) site. As we approached the ceremonial grounds, I saw a large, three-tiered plaza emblazoned with the insignias of the four hallowed states, and above the plaza a scaffold rose like a postcolonial prayer in an azure sky. Faithful pilgrims quietly lined up below that rood loft, waiting their turn to take a sacramental photograph of family members straddling all four states. On the perimeter of the plaza Indians in sticky Denver Bronco T-shirts hawked native foods and crafts. A Navajo woman I met at one of the craft stalls told me the tribe was thinking of building a motel and RV campground at the shrine overlooking the San Juan River. Planet Hollywood can't be far behind.

Like those hot and sweaty pilgrims queued at the Four Corners a few years ago — or like those of us passing quietly through customs at the airport in Baja California a few days ago — I feel that I have lived my life in lines marked on the shifting sands of literary theory and biblical criticism. And I continually am trying to balance on the political borders of these ofttimes contradictory worlds. So it should come as no surprise that as I open Luke-Acts at poolside in Cabo San Lucas and begin to plod through it, I find myself making lines in the margins of the text. I am now dividing the story into nine major narrative states (four for Luke and five for Acts), divisions that inadvertently mimic the colonialist cartography of my childhood on the big Rez.

These nine states, as the Lukan prologue rather obliquely puts it, are directly related to "those events that have been fulfilled among us" (1:1; cf. Acts 3:18; 13:32; 15:13–15); or as Jesus later says (quoting Isa 61:1–2), they are related to the proclamation of "the year of the Lord's favor" (Luke 4:19). The "fulfillment of events" is repeatedly connected to a "salvation" (liberation, rescue, restoration, jubilation — pick your favorite word) that is present in Jesus' words and deeds (Luke 2:30; 24:19, 21; Acts 1:6); a "salvation" that spreads topsy-turvy from Jerusalem to the "ends of the earth" (Acts 1:8). In the first book, Luke 4:14; 10:1; and 20:1 mark major turning points within this general plot movement, as Jesus faces rejection and moves toward his martyrdom in Jerusalem. In the second book, however, Acts 8:4, 15:36; 21:1; and 27:1 mark major shifts in this plot movement, with Jerusalem functioning centripetally against the centrifuge of Paul's ever-expanding Gentile mission.

The four plot sequences in the Gospel of Luke roughly correspond to the geographic movements of Jesus. The introductory sequence centers upon events related to the births of Jesus and John, and these men's initial public appearances in Judea (Luke 1:5–4:13). The second sequence centers upon Jesus' Galilean ministry (Luke 4:14–9:62). After Jesus reaches adulthood and has proven his divine parentage in a test with the devil (Luke 4:1–13), this section focuses upon Jesus' growing reputation and activity as a prophet, and the increasing opposition to him. There is also an important progressive development in Jesus' Galilean ministry — a particular "order" (*kathexēs*, Luke 1:3) that moves from city to countryside, synagogue to house, from Jew to Gentile, and ultimately, from Jerusalem to Rome. I think this order is constructed largely to parallel the author's conception of Paul's missionary activity in Acts, where hybrid characters like the Ethiopian eunuch, Timothy, and Lydia inhabit the borders of transgressed geographic and ethnic boundaries.

The third narrative sequence in the Gospel of Luke is the well-known, highly artificial "travel section" (like my artificial travel vacation in Baja California), where Jesus purposely journeys toward Jerusalem and death (Luke 10:1–19:48; see especially 9:51; 13:33–35; 18:31–33). Finally, the fourth sequence centers on Jesus' Jerusalem ministry, with his subsequent arrest, trial, death, and resurrection (Luke 20:1–24:53). Me? I'm here in Cabo San Lucas, looking for a little rest and resurrection, without all that other negative stuff.

After a brief prologue that echoes Luke 1:1–4, the book of Acts falls into five general plot/geographical sequences. The first sequence focuses on how the apostles and their associates announce God's Christ to and in Israel (Acts 1:6–8:3). The second sequence is clearly transitional, for the bearers of the message of God's imperial reign (*euangelizesthai,* Acts 8:4, 12, 25, 35, 40) travel beyond the boundaries of Israel, going as far west as Pisidian Antioch and coming in contact with a wide range of hybrid characters (Acts 8:4–15:35). In the third sequence, Paul journeys into Macedonia and Achaia, where he has increasing contact with Roman officials and power (15:36–20:38). In the fourth sequence, Paul journeys back to Jerusalem and Judea, defending his message before Jewish and Roman officials (Acts 21:1–26:32). Finally, the fifth geographic sequence of Acts confirms Paul as the primary witness to God's promised universal "salvation" as he travels the dangerous, watery road to the imperial city of Rome, where he defends his message (Acts 27:1–28:31). A lot of traveling for a man without any frequent-flier miles.

Like the Navajo Nation's ironic, postcolonial manipulation of the Four Corners National Monument, or the neocolonial Mexican destination resort of Cabo San Lucas, the plot progression of Luke-Acts can be seen as one of (ironic?) colonial mimicry and triumphalism. In Acts, Paul, the Diaspora Jew, mimics Roman imperial power when he appeals, as a Roman citizen, to its courts of justice. Similarly, Jesus, the apostles, and Paul, having been rejected by their Jewish forebears, turn around and "conquer" the pagan Roman Empire by proclaiming the good news (the verb *euangelizesthai* occurs twenty-five times in Luke-Acts and is drenched in the ideology of empire). In many ways, the Western church has been a living testament to Luke-Acts' double-pronged, colonialist ideology. But the geographical movement from

Jerusalem to Rome, with its strategy of colonialist mimicry, can also be construed differently in this two-volume work — as perhaps part of a larger tragic plot that God (fantastically) uses for some positive end (Acts 28:25–28). I wonder, lazily, whether Cabo San Lucas can be saved from Planet Hollywood. Or if the craft stalls at the Four Corners, overlooking the San Juan River, can overcome the world.

Reading Luke-Acts in My Study, in Bothell, Washington, Looking East — Literary Mimicry and Heteroglossia in Luke 1:1–4

From the commentaries lining my refurbished desk in Bothell, Washington, I have learned that the elevated Greek of the Lukan prologue has fascinated biblical scholars for over a hundred years. In this single complex sentence, the author-narrator seems consciously to emulate the prefaces of ancient Greek historiographers such as Diodorus Siculus and Dionysius of Halicarnassus. But as soon as the preface is done, the narrative style abruptly changes. For the next two chapters the narrator will mimic the Semitic syntax and vocabulary of the Septuagint. The style changes so dramatically that many commentators have argued that the author must have borrowed heavily from a collection of Maccabean hymns in Hebrew, or an Aramaic account of Jesus' birth. However, since the same Septuagint style also dominates the first five chapters of Acts, it is more likely that the author is simply an adept storyteller, one who is able to mimic a variety of narrative styles with ease.

From a postcolonial perspective, the radical juxtapositioning of literary styles reminds one of Mikhail Bakhtin's concept of heteroglossia,[2] where two different dialects create a narrative dialogue and destabilize the narrative's power centers. Here in Luke-Acts, the double-voicing may initially seem to connote a narrator who is seeking to legitimate his account by utilizing the literary codes of the

---

2. Simon Dentith, *Bakhtinian Thought: An Introductory Reader* (New York: Routledge, 1995), 195–224.

colonizer. The elegant style of the prologue, coupled with the evocation of the patron, Theophilus (whether a real person or a fictive character is hotly debated), adds a further note of legitimacy to the subsequent narrative. Regardless of where the narrator's sympathies lie (is he pro-Empire or anti-Empire?), he is able to move about in elite society and mimic the voice and tone of colonial powers. Like Esther, he seems adept at passing:[3] he can so mimic the colonizer that he can pass as the colonized when he wants to, when it suits his fancy.

"Nativism" in Luke 1:5–4:13

According to John Oliver Perry, "nativism" can be defined as a militant, aggressive assertion of one's native cultural heritage. As a literary movement, it aspires to counterbalance the homogenizing cultural effects of colonialism,[4] and thus has a share in the multivocal world of postcolonialism. Under this definition, Luke 1:5–4:13, the first major plot sequence of the Gospel, could be described as nativist since it focuses on the Jerusalem temple with its ancient priestly purity codes, incorporates songs that recall the glory days of Israel's Davidic monarchy (Luke 1:51–55, 68–73), and mimics a Septuagintal narrative style (e.g., "in those days," "righteous before God," "answering, said"). All this in the face of the homogenizing power of Roman imperialism (Luke 2:1; 3:1), and in a text likely written no more than ten to fifteen years after Roman legions had destroyed the Jewish temple and decimated the traditional land of Israel.

But after a general prologue (1:1–4) the story proper begins — and what a proper story it is. The plot sequence is set off from what follows in 4:14ff. in two important ways. First, there is a geographical change between Luke 1:5–4:13 and 4:14ff. Almost all of the action in 1:5–4:13 takes place in Jerusalem or Judea (1:26–38 is the only exception), the center of Jewish temple politics and economics. By

---

3. Robert Maldonado, "Passing Fancy: Postcolonial Esther: A God(less) Story of Sex, Violence and Identity" (paper presented at the annual meeting of the SBL, Toronto, Ontario, Canada, 23 Nov. 2002).

4. John Oliver Perry, "World Literature in Review: India," in *World Literature Today* (summer 1998; http://www.britannica.com/magazine/article?content_id=73095&query=brahman).

way of contrast, all the stories of 4:14–18:35 take place outside of Judea and away from the temple. Second, although Jesus will become the main character in the Gospel, he is not a very active character at the beginning — even when he is clearly the focus of attention (2:41–52; 3:21–4:13). However, in 4:14ff. Jesus' public actions begin to be the focus of attention as he becomes a productive participant in fulfilling his divine purpose.

In the opening narrative sequence, Jesus is the subject of nativist songs and prophecies, the object of his parents' frantic three-day search, the person baptized, the beginning point of a genealogy, and the person "led by the Spirit, . . . tested by the devil." His only original lines in the entire opening sequence are the two questions he asks of his parents in 2:49, and in 4:4–13 he simply quotes Scripture in a defensive posturing with the devil. In this opening sequence, minor characters like the angel Gabriel; old righteous Zechariah and Elizabeth, Simeon, and Anna; and a young Mary and John are much more active participants in the plotted events than is Jesus.

This opening sequence falls into three carefully plotted segments, each of which is composed of two finely paralleled subunits. These subunits are the appearances by an angel of the Lord (1:5–56); a series of fulfillments related to John's and Jesus' births (1:57–2:52); and a second series of fulfillments that confirm John as a prophet and Jesus as God's Son (3:1–4:13). Ironically, imperial power functions as the background against which these nativist fulfillments take place. For example, a Roman taxation is the circumstance that gets Mary and Joseph to Bethlehem, and John the Baptist has tax collectors and soldiers in his audience as he preaches repentance beside the Jordan.

Just prior to Jesus' decision to go to Jerusalem (9:51), the reader will find a cluster of scenes similar to those encountered toward the end of this first major plot sequence. Prayer (3:21; 9:18, 28), the disclosing of divine status (3:22; 9:20, 35), and the multiplication of loaves (4:3–4; 9:12–17) all reappear, as if to confirm the proximity of a new turn in the narrative's plot.

Unique to Luke-Acts among the four Gospels is the special attention given to the ancient Jewish temple and the royal city of Jerusalem as the proper center of God's renewed activity on behalf of Israel. Corresponding to this, the Gospel's opening scene overdetermines nativist purity and honor codes in a number of ways. It does so by describing Zechariah and Elizabeth's proper pedigree (priestly order of Abijah, descendant of Aaron); their moral status (righteous before God); the highly significant ritual time and action (incense offering); and a most holy place in Judaism (inside the temple, near the altar of incense). The role of the Jewish temple is accented further by the fact that Mary and Joseph bring the baby Jesus to Jerusalem for "their" purification (2:22), and by the family's subsequent journey to Jerusalem when Jesus is twelve (2:42–52).

Thus, the hybrid characters and distant lands that appear later in Acts (e.g., the Ethiopian eunuch, the Samaritans, the Greek-fathered Timothy, and assorted Gentile God-fearers) will stand in bold contrast to the nativist, priestly characters Zechariah, Elizabeth, and John, who begin the story. Do the characters and lands in Acts function as a critique of the nativist claims that open the two-volume work, or do they simply present the reader with an alternative, minority voice? Paul's closing words to the Jews living in Rome appear to answer this question unequivocally: "Let it be known to you then that this salvation of God (*sōtērion tou theou* [cf. Luke 2:30; 3:6]) has been sent to the Gentiles; they will listen" (Acts 28:28 NRSV).

Reading Luke-Acts in Cabo San Lucas, Baja Mexico

I tip the Mexican waiter at poolside for bringing me another drink without my asking. I turn a page in Luke's Gospel, shade my eyes from the bright sun, and wonder absentmindedly where the waiter learned his impeccable English, and where he goes at night, when his work at our resort is done.

This resort near Cabo San Lucas is built in the style of a seventeenth-century Spanish mission — faux adobe bell tower and all. And even though I have never spent any time in a real Catholic mission, I know that missions are not resorts. No matter how hard I try to imagine that I am somewhere else, I am reading Luke-Acts at a U.S.-owned resort in Mexico, not at a Catholic mission on the imperial Spanish frontier, nor at the Four Corners on the Navajo Reservation. I am not at a freedom-fighters' fortress in the Judean desert, nor at the Jerusalem temple with Simeon and Anna; and I am not with John, who in the Jordan baptizes soldiers, tax collectors, and a hodge-podge of representatives of imperial rule.

The sign above the resort swimming pool reads, LIFE HAS ITS REWARDS. But this is not a reference to rewards beyond this world. There are none of the "desert's indifference," none of its "lowered expectations" here in Cabo.[5] People flee to the tip of Baja California to get away from the self-imposed hardness and harshness of the workaday world. They come here to unwind in the sun, like mummi-fied monks discovered by unsuspecting Egyptian dirt farmers. "Life has its rewards." Unlike the fierce landscapes of the Judean wilder-ness that John inhabits, Cabo San Lucas offers a "private therapeutic place for solace and rejuvenation."[6] "Life has its rewards." Here, what you see is what you get — right here, right now — if you have stored up enough stuff in your barns to last awhile (Luke 12:13–21; cf. 3:17) and don't have to worry about a snoopy apostle discovering your secret financial transactions (Acts 5:1–11; cf. Luke 3:13).

Reading in My Study,
in Bothell, Washington, Looking East —
the Genealogy of Jesus, Luke 3:23–38

Unlike the Matthean genealogy of Jesus, Luke's rendering of Jesus' pedigree is pure and undefiled. It runs backward from Jesus, to David, Judah, Jacob, and Abraham, and finally to Adam, who is "son of God." There are no women's names in this list, no outsiders, no worrisome borderland characters (cf. Matt 1:2–17).

While colonialism is founded upon the principles of radical dif-ference and unequal power relations, postcolonialism speaks to the

---

5. Belden C. Lane, *The Solace of Fierce Landscapes: Exploring Desert and Mountain Spirituality* (New York: Oxford University Press, 1998), 227.

6. Ibid., 165.

hybrid realism of imperial power. And thus Luke's genealogy mimics the very colonial power it challenges elsewhere (cf. 2:10–11; Acts 4:12). Here there is no genetic creolization marking the borders of Jesus' prophetic career. In Luke-Acts, the border between Jesus' childhood and public life is marked by a genealogical perfection that will not appear again until Jesus' apostles seek the ideal replacement for the traitor, Judas (Acts 1:15–26). So why the perfection of pedigreed borders here? Why should the author care so much about Jesus' ancestral purity when the Baptizer's God can turn desert stones into children of Abraham (Luke 3:8), or when Gentiles can participate in the new community apart from certain purity taboos (Acts 10:1–48; 15:1–22)? Ultimately, the test of God's perfect son (Luke 4:1–13) appears as an unnecessary footnote to his pristine parentage; a pandering to the very imperial hero stories that are destabilized elsewhere by Jesus' crucifixion and Paul's imprisonments.

Reading Luke-Acts in Cabo San Lucas, Baja Mexico

This resort makes no sense. Or should I say, the sense that it makes is a farcical exaggeration of Luke's "passing" interest. The social and economic gains from passing can be enormous. Take my creolized children, for example. Half Chinese, half your basic English-Swedish-Scotch-mongrel European-American. Most of the time they pass for Chinese — or here in Cabo, they could pass as Mexican. But if they were living in San Francisco at the beginning of the twentieth century, as their great-grandmother was, I know they would more likely pass as Caucasian. Jesus, in Luke's rendering, passes as an upper-class Jew: born in a *polis*, he can read; he is known in king's courts, has wealthy patrons, and frequents banquets where he tells entertaining stories about big money (15:1–2; 16:1–13; 19:1–27). Passing can be made easier by creolization, or cultural hybridity, or in Jesus' case, by hiring Luke the spin doctor.

Unlike Luke's desert locales where only Jesus, God, or the devil are present (1:80; 3:2–4; 4:1–13, 42; 5:16; 8:29), Cabo San Lucas passes itself off as a desert place. But there is nothing here of the stark, Zen-like emptiness of the Judean wilderness, or the bizarre perpendicular angularity of the American Southwest, where I grew up. This is a resort that exists solely for the sun. It turns burnt stone into thick-crusted panier. Mud into chocolate. "Life has its rewards."

There is an ocean beach nearby, forty feet from the resort property. But hardly anyone goes there to explore its sensuous curves. The waves are crunchers, and the beach slopes down steeply toward them, giving physical evidence of fierce undertows and demonic baptisms. Only the local Mexican peddlers venture out onto the blazing beach sand and pass near the water, ambling from resort to resort and selling their colorful wares just beyond the roped-off border signs that warn, NO UNAUTHORIZED SALES ON THE PREMISES. Step across the line, and someone is sure to be strung up, Jesus-like. Trespassers. Dead meat.

Reasonable pilgrims like me lounge at poolside; or, barely moving, sip margaritas at the swim-up bar. The pool is cruciform-shaped, and the bar is at one end of its transept. At the opposite end of the transept is a spirit-stirred Jacuzzi. The faithful can swim leisurely from one sacrament to the other: Holy Communion at one end, baptism at the other. No deadly crunchers here, no demand for "fruits worthy of repentance" (3:8) — unless you count the cool slices of mangoes and tart, ripe pineapples that are brought to us at poolside. Here, anyone can "take up their cross daily, and doggie-paddle after me," says the San Lucas Jesus (9:23). And if you want to learn to fish, you can learn that, too (5:1–11). Deep-sea fishing boats can be chartered by the half day for about fifty dollars a person. Catches are almost guaranteed.

Reading in My Study, in Bothell, Washington, Looking East — Jesus' First of Three Imperial Proclamations and the Plot of Luke 4:14–9:62

Luke's second narrative sequence (4:14–9:62) can be divided into three segments that are distinguished from the preceding sequence by the ways in which it develops Jesus' prophetic activity in new directions. Jesus' inaugural proclamation in Nazareth (Luke 4:16–30) mimics the grand imperial edicts of Rome (Luke 2:1; Acts 17:7), ancient Babylon (Dan 2:13; 3:10), and Persia (Esth 4:8; 9:1; Dan 6:8–10). It generates three narrative sequences (Luke 4:14–6:11; 6:12–7:50; 8:1–9:62), each of which also begins by mimicking imperial proclamations. The first of the three proclamations (4:16–30) is most like an imperial edict, since Jesus begins by reading from a written document and then interprets it for his audience. It is also a purely Lukan construction. The second proclamation (6:20–49) is formed from Q material, and the third (8:4–21) is a shortened version of Mark 4. But neither of these latter two proclamations by Jesus begins with Jesus reading a text (cf. Acts 15:22–33). Has he forgotten how to read? Or is he just less tied to his notes as he becomes more comfortable with working the crowds (9:12–17)?

The three proclamations and their introductory frames (4:14–15; 6:12–19; 8:1–3) summarize early plot developments by describing Jesus' ever-expanding spheres of influence and by introducing new emphases in his activity. A similar programmatic strategy structures the early part of Acts, where a series of narrative summaries describe the geographic expansion of the early Christian communities (Acts 2:43–47; 8:1b–8; 11:19–26). There, however, the mimicry of imperial power is more obvious since the expansion takes place on a grand territorial scale, not just in terms of movements from city to countryside as here in Luke.

By tracing the ways in which the "imperial edicts" of Jesus bear immediate fruit in his powerful deeds, one can see how they are interconnected with the powerful deeds that follow them. These interconnections allow the author's ideology to function covertly, working to convince the reader that Jesus is truly "a prophet mighty in deed and word," a divinely chosen emissary who has the authority to announce God's imperial rule (Luke 24:19, 21; Acts 2:22; 13:24–26). However, the opening proclamations in Acts function differently. There, only one powerful deed follows a proclamation (Acts 3:1–10), and there — as elsewhere — Jesus' name itself becomes the good news; a powerful agent of healing and the source of provocation (cf. Acts 3:6; 4:7; 5:28, 40; 8:12).

Say the name "Homi K. Bhabha" or "Gayatri C. Spivak" and you will get into high places around the University district of Seattle. But the names won't help in Cabo San Lucas. Just before we left the resort, I passed our maid in the hall. I thought she had a subaltern look about her, so I tried asking her if she had read Homi or Gayatri. She looked at me peculiarly and asked me what kind of guitar I had left at home. Did I want to buy another? I thanked her for her help, gave her a big tip, and hurried on down the hall.

"Adios, Baja."

Status Mimicry, "Passing," and Jesus as a Literary Character in Luke 4:16–30

Mimicking the grand style of imperial emissaries, Jesus and I have returned to our "cities" (*poleis*) of Nazareth and Bothell, Washington, where we are well-known (Luke 4:16, 22; cf. 1:26; 2:4, 39, 51), after having defeated our desert demons (4:1–13). Curiously, the word *polis* seems to function more as a rhetorical term in the narrative world of Luke-Acts than as a specific historical reference. Somewhat like Bothell, Washington, and Cabo San Lucas in this essay.

The apostle Paul, for example, is from Tarsus, "an important city" (Acts 21:39), and so Jesus, a much more important person than Paul, becomes a city person in the prequel to Acts l. Bethlehem and Nazareth are also cities in Luke, apparently because Jesus is from them. Likewise, Bethsaida, Capernaum, Chorazin, and Nain are cities primarily because Jesus visits them (just as Paul visits cities, as in Acts 13:50; 14:19). Cabo, the Four Corners, and Bothell are not particularly important places on the map of the world. But because I have been in all three places, they have for me become symbols of empire and neocolonial displacement; places of politically intertwined interdependency.

Jesus' public activity begins in a "city" with a public speech in a synagogue. And so Paul and I, later followers of Jesus, will mimic

Jesus' prophetic actions by beginning our own emissary-like activity — Paul, in the synagogues of Asia's cities, near his own native territory (Acts 13:14–44; 14:1); and I in Pacific Northwest regional SBL meetings. But unlike Jesus or Paul, no one has chased me out of a professional meeting for something I have read or said. Thankfully, prophets of postcolonialism are still accepted in their hometowns. I think most biblical scholars hope we are just a passing fancy, and believe that if they don't object too strenuously to anything we say, we will quietly leave town under our own power.

Of all the four Gospels, only Luke portrays Jesus as able to read. Only Luke refuses to call Jesus a carpenter or the son of a carpenter. He is a full-time prophet and emissary of God's imperial rule. Not an adjunct, part-time professor like me. Coupled with Jesus' status of being "city born and bred," he seems to mimic the social position of Luke's implied audience. Like second-generation immigrants today (for example, my Chinese-American wife's father) who assimilate and try to pass in the dominant colonial or neocolonial culture, Luke's Jesus is a model for upper-class, late-first-century Christians. Like me, Luke's audience can read and write, and may even be patrons or patronesses (cf. Luke 1:1–4; 8:1–3; Act 1:1). Like me, they have the means to care for the poor (Luke 11:39–41; 12:13–21; 14:13, 21; 16:19–26; 18:22–30; 19:8; 21:1–5; Acts 3:1–6; 4:34–5:2; 6:1; 9:36; 16:14; 19:23–27; 20:33–35). And like me, they encourage women to serve with grace and decorum in the patriarchal structures of their Christian communities (Luke 4:38–39; 8:47; 10:38–42; 21:1–5; 23:55–24:13; Acts 1:14; 9:36; 12:13–15; 16:14; 21:9), biding their time (*kairos*, Luke 21:8, 24, 36; Acts 1:7; 3:20).

After reading Isaiah 61:1–2 (Luke 4:18–19), Jesus and I roll up our scrolls, hand them back to the subalterns, and sit down. We look at each other, waiting for the other to speak. Then we both blurt out, "Let the postcolonial displacement begin!" He yells, "Salmaaaaan Rushdieeeeeee!" I shriek, "Sheeeerrrrman Aleeeeeeexie!" And both of us hightail it out of town.

Conclusion

While there is much I like about Luke's retelling of the Jesus story, the more I read it, the more I am conflicted by its own conflictions. Today, I am not so sure that Luke-Acts is particularly good news for a postcolonial or neocolonial world. For my tastes, there is in it too much staged mimicry, too much unreflected passing, and too much fawning to forms of imperialism. Too little space is left open for serious postcolonial critique. It is not without reason that Luke-Acts became the model for imperial mission movements of the nineteenth and early-twentieth centuries.

Nevertheless, I believe that reading Luke-Acts from multiple places — social, political, economic, and geographical — can open up spaces for postcolonial and neocolonial conversation. But the challenge for the postcolonial and neocolonial New Testament critic will be to find dialogue partners within Luke-Acts and without, in the broader diasporic Christian community, who will challenge and undermine Luke-Acts' imperial passing. Perhaps my reading from Cabo San Lucas, from the Four Corners overlooking the San Juan River, and from my study in Bothell, Washington, can be an impetus to that undermining venture.

19

The End of the Bible as We Know It

The Metamorphosis of the Biblical Traditions in the Electronic Age

Robert M. Fowler*

Introduction

As my tribute to Bob Tannehill, I survey briefly a new frontier that has recently come into our consciousness. We are beginning to catch the first glimmers of a metamorphosis of the biblical traditions in the dawn of the Electronic Age. It is hardly a novel thesis these days to suggest that the world is changing all around us, in large part because of a ubiquitous, global revolution in electronic, digital, communication media. However, the question of how this electronic revolution might transform the experience of scripture in the world's

---

*I am delighted to have the opportunity to contribute to this Festschrift in honor of Bob Tannehill. Through the years I have had many enjoyable and productive contacts with Bob. We both taught in Ohio and would see each other at the annual meetings of the Eastern Great Lakes Biblical Society. We were both active in the Literary Aspects of the Gospels and Acts Section of SBL, which, especially in the 1980s, was a lively forum for new literary criticism of the Gospels. Many of the groundbreaking books and articles on the literary criticism of the Gospels in the 1980s and early 1990s were first floated as trial balloons in boisterous sessions of the Literary Aspects Section. But Bob's contributions to the literary criticism of the Gospels go back even further than that.

When I arrived at the University of Chicago in 1974, prepared to do life-of-Jesus research and redaction criticism with the late Norman Perrin, I was surprised to hear Perrin declare, with his typical bravado, "We are all literary critics now!" That was more than a little hyperbolic, but it was a shrewd, prophetic utterance about things to come (Robert M. Fowler, "Using Literary Criticism on the Gospels," Christian Century [May 26, 1982]: 626–29). I vividly remember that one of the first books I read on the literary criticism of the Gospels was Bob Tannehill's The Sword of His Mouth (Semeia Supplements 1; Philadelphia: Fortress; Missoula, Mont.: Scholars, 1975). Bob was a trail-blazing pioneer in the practice of the literary criticism of the Gospels, and all of us who have toiled in that field in the years since owe him a great debt of gratitude. In what I hope is a similar pioneering spirit of openness to the new and largely unexplored, I offer my tribute to Bob Tannehill by surveying briefly another new frontier.

great religious traditions has only begun to receive attention. This is the question I would like to begin to explore in this essay.

Living in Cyberspace

It is a truism that those of us living in postmodern, postindustrial societies are spending more and more of our everyday lives in cyberspace. We are enmeshed in webs of digital, electronic communication, often without being aware of it. As one pundit has observed, "Cyberspace is where you are when you're talking on the telephone."[1] With the proliferation of cell phones around the world, our species seems destined to be able to telephone just about anyone on the planet, from anywhere on the planet, at any time. Cyberspace is also where our money is and where we conduct our financial affairs. For instance, last summer I stood at an ATM machine outside a bank in Jedburgh, Scotland. I pushed a few buttons, and the machine spat out crisp, new, Bank of Scotland pound sterling notes. Somewhere back in the United States, presumably, the electronic bits and bytes that are my bank account instantaneously recorded a corresponding debit in U.S. dollars. The transformation of U.S. dollars into pounds sterling did not exactly take place on the terra firma of Scotland, nor really even in the USA, but somewhere else. That "somewhere else" was cyberspace.

If our treasure has already moved into cyberspace, can our hearts be far behind? So much of our everyday lives is lived in cyberspace — as I sit here tapping on the keyboard of my Macintosh, keeping an eye open for incoming e-mail messages, hoping not to be interrupted by the telephone — that our religious lives cannot help but follow along. But what does it mean to be religious in cyberspace? And in particular, for the purposes of this essay, what might it mean to have scripture in cyberspace?

---

1. John Perry Barlow, in *Mondo 2000: A User's Guide to the New Edge* (ed. Rudy Rucker, R. U. Sirius, and Queen Mu; New York: HarperPerennial, 1992), 78.

Trusty Scouts on the New Media Frontier

There is no shortage of scouts on the new media frontier that we are now beginning to explore. My own thinking on media and media history has been shaped mostly by the pioneering theories of media ecology developed first by Harold Innis and Marshall McLuhan, and later consolidated and expanded by Walter Ong.[2] The biblical traditions are remarkable for being *the* paradigm in Western culture of a long-lived tradition that has seen every era in media history, from ancient, primary orality to chirographic (manuscript) culture, to typographic (print) culture, to the Electronic Age of digital communication media. Long ago Ong observed that one of the characteristics of the media ecology of our time is a resurgence of many of the characteristics of ancient orality, but now in a secondary (literate, electronic) mode.[3]

Ong offered valuable insights into the "secondary orality" of the Electronic Age, but his career was winding down in the 1980s, just before a multitude of new electronic technologies began to mushroom. The revolution in desktop computers, computer-mediated communication, the World Wide Web, virtual reality, cyberspace, hypertext, multimedia, cell phones — all of these and more came along too late for Ong to probe and to ponder. By now, those of us who are intrigued by what the new media are doing to culture have collected at least a shelfful of books, too numerous to mention, on the emerging cyberculture. A smaller, but growing, number of titles are available on the practice of religion in cyberspace.[4] There are

---

2. Walter J. Ong, SJ, *Orality and Literacy: The Technologizing of the Word* (London/New York: Methuen, 1982).

3. Ibid., 136–38.

4. Brenda E. Brasher, *Give Me That Online Religion* (San Francisco: Jossey-Bass, 2001); Jennifer Cobb, *Cybergrace: The Search for God in the Digital World* (New York: Crown Publishers, 1998); Erik Davis, *Techgnosis: Myth, Magic and Mysticism in the Age of Information* (New York: Harmony Books, 1998); Charles M. Ess, " 'Revolution? What Revolution?' Successes and Limits of Computing Technologies in Philosophy and Religion," in *Blackwell Companion to Digital Humanities* (ed. Susan Schreibman and John Unsworth; London: Blackwell, forthcoming); Bruce B. Lawrence, *The Complete Idiot's Guide to Religions Online* (Indianapolis: Alpha Books, 2000); Stephen D. O'Leary, "Cyberspace as Sacred Space: Communicating Religion on Computer Networks," *JAAR* 64 (1996): 781–808; Stephen D. O'Leary and Brenda E. Brasher, "The Unknown God of the Internet: Religious Communication from the Ancient Agora to the Virtual Forum," in *Philosophical Perspectives on Computer-Mediated*

even a few titles pondering what might become of the Bible in the
Electronic Age.[5]

The First Step: Transmediazation

By now it is a truism (often credited to Marshall McLuhan) that
when a dominant, new communication medium arrives on the scene,
its content is initially the prior dominant medium. This is the process of "transmediazation"[6] or "remediation,"[7] the leap "from one
medium to another."[8] For example, ancient Greek New Testament
manuscripts were written in *scriptura continua* — no spaces between
words — which is not helpful to the reader's eye but ably represents the continuous flow of sound in oral performance. The earliest
printed books were made to look like the finest hand-lettered and
illuminated manuscripts of the late medieval era. The first motion
pictures turned to the printed novel and stage plays for material.

Communication (ed. Charles Ess; Albany, N.Y.: SUNY Press, 1996), 233–69; Richard Thieme,
"Entering Sacred Digital Space: Seeking to Distinguish the Dreamer and the Dream," in *New
Paradigms for Bible Study: The Bible in the Third Millennium* (ed. Robert M. Fowler, Edith
Blumhofer, and Fernando F. Segovia; Harrisburg, Pa.: T. & T. Clark International, forth-
coming); Jeff Zaleski, *The Soul of Cyberspace: How New Technology Is Changing Our Spiritual
Lives* (New York: HarperEdge, 1997).
    5. A. K. M. Adam, "This Is Not a Bible: Dispelling the Mystique of Words for the
Future of Biblical Interpretation," in *New Paradigms for Bible Study* (ed. Fowler et al.);
Thomas E. Boomershine, "Biblical Megatrends: Towards a Paradigm for the Interpreta-
tion of the Bible in Electronic Media," in *The Bible in the Twenty-first Century* (ed.
Howard Clark Kee; Philadelphia: Trinity Press International, 1993), 109–30; Robert M.
Fowler, "How the Secondary Orality of the Electronic Age Can Awaken Us to the Primary
Orality of Antiquity, or What Hypertext Can Teach Us About the Bible, with Reflec-
tions on the Ethical and Political Issues of the Electronic Frontier," available online at
http://www.bw.edu/ rfowler/pubs/secondoral/index.html; last accessed on 9/5/03; idem, "The
Fate of the Notion of Canon in the Electronic Age," *Forum* 9 (1993): 151–72; Phil Mullins,
"Sacred Text in an Electronic Age," *BTB* 20 (fall 1990): 99–106; idem, "Sacred Texts in a
Sea of Texts: The Bible in North American Electronic Culture," in *Philosophical Perspectives*
(ed. Ess), 271–302; Paul A. Soukup and Robert Hodgson, eds., *From One Medium to Another:
Communicating the Bible through Multimedia* (Kansas City, Mo.: Sheed & Ward, 1997); idem,
eds., *Fidelity and Translation: Communicating the Bible in New Media* (Franklin, Wis.: Sheed
& Ward; New York: American Bible Society, 1999).
    6. Boomershine, "Biblical Megatrends," 221.
    7. Jay David Bolter, *Writing Space: Computers, Hypertext, and the Remediation of Print*
(Mahwah, N.J.: Lawrence Erlbaum Associates, 1991); Jay David Bolter and Richard Grusin,
Remediation: Understanding New Media (Cambridge/London: MIT, 1999).
    8. Soukup and Hodgson, eds., *From One Medium to Another*; idem, eds., *Fidelity and
Translation*.

Early television reprised radio and the movies. Similarly, in spite of the extraordinary multimedia that one can now create with a desktop computer, often these expensive information appliances are still used to produce pages that might just as well have been printed on a printing press. Paradoxically, armies prepare to fight the previous war, and the early participants in a media revolution do their utmost to mimic the prior dominant medium. Marshall McLuhan called this living in the rearview mirror.[9]

So, first we transmediate, using the new medium to mimic the old (e.g., Bibles, grammars, lexica on CD-ROM, appearing on the computer screen just like they do in print). But that rearview mirror behavior sooner or later gives way to a media meltdown, in which the old media are radically reconfigured under the aegis of the new, dominant medium, and genuinely new, unanticipated media expressions are given birth.

Learning from Past Media Revolutions

Past experience suggests that we cannot anticipate what lies ahead — it is surely beyond our imagining. From the perspective of the ancient oral bard, who could have imagined the magic of the written word, which allows the memory of sound to be transmitted over time and space, even between two people who have never stood in each other's presence? From the vantage point of the medieval monk, laboriously producing a single manuscript copy of a book over the course of a year, who could have imagined thousands of printed copies of thousands of different books, pouring out of Gutenberg's printing press? In the stillness of the libraries and bookshops of print culture, those temples of the Age of Print to which seekers of knowledge made pilgrimage, who could have imagined that the information of the world might one day come *to us*, via the telegraph, telephone, radio, television, and now the desktop computer networked on the World Wide Web?

---

9. Paul Benedetti and Nancy DeHart, eds., *Forward through the Rearview Mirror: Reflections on and by Marshall McLuhan* (Scarborough, Ont.: Prentice-Hall Canada, 1996).

The ramifications of past media revolutions were not anticipated, and I assume it will be the same for us. No one has a crystal ball that will tell us what lies ahead. The only safe prediction is that the media ecology of the future is likely to be unimaginably different from what has preceded.

What might happen to the Bible in a new media age is therefore anyone's guess. Unfortunately, we are so far removed from past media transformations of the biblical traditions — from orality to manuscript, from manuscript to print, and so on — that we have blissfully forgotten how wrenching such a transformation can be. Scripture hasn't always been "scripture," something "written." The Bible has not always been *The Bible*, dozens of books conveniently collected, translated into a vernacular language, and printed between two covers. In an age of new media, as all of the old media are caught up into a new media ecology dominated by electronic media, what will become of "scripture"? What will be become of *The Bible?*

As we move beyond mere transmediazation into an unforeseeable new media ecology, surely fundamental questions beg to be asked. Surely persons for whom the biblical traditions matter need to return to square 1 and ask the most basic questions imaginable, not only of the familiar printed Bible, but of all the biblical traditions that are now known to us, in all their vast, bewildering, historical variety. What are these traditions about? To what uses have they been put, and what good have they done for people? By the same token, to what misuses have they been put, how have they hurt people, and how might that be rectified? And who within the traditions will have the audacity to pursue such questions?!

The Traditioning Process

I am hardly alone in suspecting that the biblical traditions are now in travail, straining to give birth to lively new versions of themselves. Poignantly, the more old media that are in hand, waiting to be taken up and reconfigured into a new media ecology, the more difficult the (re)birth. Walter Ong and others have described how primary oral cultures adroitly slough off old memories that no longer serve useful purposes, thus maintaining homeostasis within the culture.[10] Sloughing off traditions that are no longer relevant or useable is much more difficult, however, once everything is in writing. Writing is a blessing, because it preserves words forever. Writing is also a curse, because it preserves words forever! The biblical traditions have been in written form for two to three thousand years, and it is probably time for a good housecleaning, with the introduction of some new greatest-hits material. Of course, such a suggestion will be taken as blasphemy by anyone who identifies the biblical traditions only with the media form in which these traditions have been expressed (manuscript and print) over the past three thousand years.[11] A person at home in primary oral culture might well look upon the written word with suspicion and distrust; at the other end of history, persons whose native habitat is cyberculture are also likely not to bow before the product of the quill pen or the printing press.

How does a tradition turn itself over and metamorphose into a healthy, viable, new manifestation of itself? Of course, any living tradition is constantly mutating and changing, but often with little self-conscious awareness by those participating within it. Happily, in our time there are many who are consumed by the question of how the biblical traditions might be creatively and responsibly born again. I think here especially of feminist and liberation theologians, who are passionately committed to sloughing off the injustices and oppressions of the past, so that a healthy new form of the tradition might be (re)born.[12]

---

10. Ong, *Orality and Literacy*, 46–49.

11. I am not being entirely fair here to biblical manuscript cultures, which, like primary oral cultures, were quite capable of jettisoning the old and embracing the new. For example, as far as we can tell, every biblical manuscript ever produced varied from its exemplar. Variation and change, both accidental and intentional, were the norm in manuscript culture, and as a result, no two biblical manuscripts are identical.

12. Kwok Pui-lan, "Finding a Home for Ruth: Gender, Sexuality, and the Politics of Otherness," in *New Paradigms for Bible Study* (ed. Fowler et al.); Elisabeth Schüssler Fiorenza, "Preface: Rethinking *The Women's Bible*," and "Introduction: Transforming the Legacy of *The Women's Bible*," in *A Feminist Introduction* (vol. 1 of *Searching the Scriptures*; ed. E. Schüssler Fiorenza; New York: Continuum, 1993), ix-24; idem, "Preface and Introduction: Transgressing Canonical Boundaries," in *A Feminist Commentary* (vol. 2 of *Searching*

Among the many ironies of our time, one of the more delicious is that people who care about the Bible, stereotypically a Protestant concern, might do well to learn about how tradition renews itself from those who stereotypically are less concerned about the Bible: Roman Catholics.[13]

A Revival of Ritual

Many people have discovered in cyberspace a rich new arena for human interaction, and it is only natural that religious people would want to use this new realm for religious practices. By now the popular press, as well as academe, has discovered the curiosity of online prayer groups, meditation (whether Buddhist contemplation of mandalas or Christian *lectio divina*), rituals, pilgrimages, and so on.[14] At the same time that this is happening online, a host of academic disciplines have discovered the interdisciplinary value of "ritual theory" or "performance theory" to make sense of the new forms of ritualized behavior that seem to confront us at every turn in everyday life.[15] It isn't just in cyberspace that new forms of ritual are emerging.

If cyberspace is not one's cup of tea, one might still stumble upon ritual and performance in an extraordinary, new, electronic mode by wandering into the neighborhood church just down the street. There is a revolution taking place in worship practices: churches are using electronic music instead of the pipe organ; popular, contemporary

---

the Scriptures; ed. E. Schüssler Fiorenza; New York: Continuum, 1994), ix-14; Rosemary Radford Ruether, *Womanguides: Readings toward a Feminist Theology* (Boston: Beacon, 1985); Abraham Smith, " 'Hidden in Plain View': Postcolonial Interrogations, a Poetics of Location, and African American Biblical Scholarship," in *New Paradigms for Bible Study* (ed. Fowler et al.).

13. Terrence W. Tilley, *Inventing Catholic Tradition* (Maryknoll, N.Y.: Orbis, 2000).

14. Brasher, *Give Me That Online Religion;* O'Leary, "Cyberspace as Sacred Space"; Basil Pennington, OCSO, *Lectio Divina: Renewing the Ancient Practice of Praying the Scriptures* (New York: Crossroad, 1998); Zaleski, *The Soul of Cyberspace.*

15. Catherine Bell, *Ritual Theory, Ritual Practice* (New York/Oxford: Oxford University Press, 1992); Ronald L. Grimes, *Deeply into the Bone: Re-Inventing Rites of Passage* (Berkeley: University of California Press, 2000); idem, *Readings in Ritual Studies* (Upper Saddle River, N.J.: Prentice-Hall, 1996); Richard Schechner, *Performance Theory* (rev., expanded ed.; New York: Routledge, 1988).

music, instead of classical; an exuberant, participatory style of worship, instead of quiet spectatorship; and so on.[16]

Presumably the Scriptures of Israel and the early Christian Church emerged out of the worship life of these ancient communities. For example, the Psalms in the Hebrew Scriptures and the letters of Paul in the New Testament signal unmistakably their origin in performances conducted in ancient communal gatherings. However, although the written scripts from those performances have survived, we have long since lost sight and sound of what the performances themselves must have been like. Is it any wonder that there are signs everywhere that as the biblical traditions are mutating into new media versions of themselves, persons of biblical faith are reinventing their rituals? If the written biblical traditions emerged out of ritual, is it not likely that new electronic forms of these traditions will also emerge from ritual?

For the past several years, prior to the annual meeting of the American Academy of Religion and the Society of Biblical Literature, a workshop on Religion and Media has been conducted. At the 2002 workshop, in Toronto, one of the presenters was Angela Zito, a professor in the Anthropology Department and the Program in Religious Studies at New York University. Professor Zito reported on The Virtual Casebook Project at NYU, which has created a powerful and moving website on the 9/11 disaster, rich with personal testimonials from New Yorkers.[17] She said that the two aims of the Virtual Casebook Project are "performance and archive." This struck me as a perfect description of the original function of the written traditions of the Bible. What are now the books of the Bible were probably once oral performances. By being written down, these performances were archived for future generations. Thus I would now rephrase the question that runs throughout this essay: where and how are the biblical

---

16. Tex Sample, *The Spectacle of Worship in a Wired World: Electronic Culture and the Gathered People of God* (Nashville: Abingdon, 1998); Len Wilson and Jason Moore, *Digital Storytellers: The Art of Communicating the Gospel in Worship* (Nashville: Abingdon, 2002).

17. Virtual Casebook Project, *9/11 and After* (New York University, 2002; available at http://www.nyu.edu/fas/projects/vcb/tactical.html; last accessed on 9/5/03).

traditions being "performed and archived" today, exploiting the new electronic media?

The Emergence of Secondary Orality and Rediscovery of Primary Orality

As noted above, Walter Ong deserves much credit for the shrewd insight that in myriad ways the Electronic Age has plunged us back into orality. Indeed, one might hypothesize that the experience of secondary orality has equipped us psychologically to carry out the rediscovery of primary orality that took place in the twentieth century.[18] It is probably a hopeless "chicken or egg?" argument to try to determine which mode of orality is prior. What is clear is that the last half of the twentieth century, a time of growing secondary orality, saw an explosion of research into ancient oral traditions,[19] including the biblical traditions, at the same that the practice of oral performance of ancient traditions was rediscovered.

Milman Parry and Albert Lord are justly famous for having discovered the oral formulaic performance of epic poetry, practiced not only by Homer in the *Iliad* and *Odyssey,* but practiced as well by generations of later bards, up to the twentieth century.[20] To Werner Kelber goes credit for having introduced this research into biblical studies.[21] In a series of important studies, William A. Graham has explored

---

18. Fowler, "Secondary Orality." One token only: Milman Parry and Albert Lord did not carry out their fieldwork on Yugoslav oral bards solely with the tools of print culture; they employed what today would be regarded as primitive recording equipment (aluminum phonographs) to record oral performances in the field, and thus they could document conclusively the variability of oral, bardic performance (Albert B. Lord, *The Singer of Tales* [ed. Stephen Mitchell and Gregory Nagy; 2d ed., with audio and video CD; Cambridge/London: Harvard University Press, 2000], x-xi, 279 n. 2).

19. John Miles Foley, *Oral-Formulaic Theory and Research: An Introduction and Annotated Bibliography* (New York: Garland, 1985); idem, *The Theory of Oral Composition: History and Methodology* (Bloomington: Indiana University Press, 1988); idem, *The Singer of Tales in Performance* (Bloomington: Indiana University Press, 1995); idem, ed., *Teaching Oral Traditions* (New York: Modern Language Association, 1998).

20. Lord, *Singer of Tales;* Foley, *Oral-Formulaic Theory;* idem, *Theory of Oral Composition;* idem, *Tales in Performance.*

21. Werner H. Kelber, *The Oral and the Written Gospel: The Hermeneutics of Speaking and Writing in the Synoptic Tradition, Mark, Paul, and Q* (Philadelphia: Fortress, 1983; repr. [with foreword by Walter J. Ong, SJ], Bloomington/Indianapolis: Indiana University Press, 1997).

the pervasive orality that has always undergirded and has sometimes dominated many of the world's great scriptural traditions.[22]

Besides the academic study of oral tradition and performance, recent years have seen an explosion in the practice of oral performance itself. Thomas Boomershine has long advocated the oral performance of biblical narrative, both as a worship practice of the church and as an investigative tool of biblical scholarship.[23] He was instrumental in founding the Network of Biblical Storytellers,[24] and he was deeply involved in founding the Bible in Ancient and Modern Media Section of the Society of Biblical Literature, which has explored all manner of media issues related to the Bible for the past twenty years.

There is such interest today in biblical storytelling that even professional actors have gotten into the act. The most famous of these is Alec McCowen, who started performing the Gospel of Mark as a one-man stage production in the late 1970s. McCowen describes what was surely the most unexpected success of his professional acting career in his revealing book *Personal Mark*.[25] By now it is commonplace to find professional actors as well as passionately committed amateurs who have taken it upon themselves to memorize and perform Scripture passages, both short and long.

Today there is such intense interest in the practice of oral performance, as well as in the academic study thereof, that I venture to say that the "scripture" of the future may be more like the "scripture" of the distant past. That is, the "scripture" that emerges in our Electronic Age of secondary orality may be more oral than written.

22. William A. Graham, "Scripture," in *Encyclopedia of Religion* (ed. Mircea Eliade et al.; New York: Macmillan, 1987), 13:133–45; idem, *Beyond the Written Word: Oral Aspects of Scripture in the History of Religion* (New York: Cambridge University Press, 1988); idem, "Scripture as Spoken Word," in *Rethinking Scripture: Essays from a Comparative Perspective* (ed. Miriam Levering; Albany, N.Y.: SUNY Press, 1989), 129–69. For example, the "sacred scripture" of Islam is the Qur'an, but the word *qur'an* means "recitation," something spoken. Although the revelations of the Qur'an were recorded in writing very early, the revelations came to the prophet Muhammad as spoken language, and the Qur'an has remained primarily an oral/aural phenomenon ever since. It is common for Muslims, even children, to memorize the Qur'an, to be able to recite it from memory.

23. Thomas E. Boomershine, *Story Journey: An Invitation to the Gospel as Storytelling* (Nashville: Abingdon, 1988).

24. Network of Biblical Storytellers (http://www.nobs.org/index.htm; last accessed on 9/5/03).

25. Alec McCowen, *Personal Mark* (New York: Crossroad, 1985).

The Undoing of the Canon
and the Authority of the Bible

Finally, I need to acknowledge a multitude of ways in which the notions of the canon and the authority of Scripture within the Christian traditions have come undone. Of course, there never has been a time in Christian history when there was unanimity on such matters. But today the contentiousness that has always driven decisions about canon and authority stares us in the face. We see now, more clearly than ever before, that such decisions have always been exercises of power and ideology. These issues are so immense and so tangled that I can, again, only gesture toward some of the relevant aspects, underscoring again that the current media revolution is deeply implicated within these issues, as well as the others I have already mentioned above. What are some of the ways in which the canon and the authority of Scripture have come undone in our own time?

First, notions of canon and authority have been undone by the resurgence of orality in our time. Canon and authority were ideals that emerged historically within manuscript and especially print culture, and the move to a digital culture may portend the end of the canon and authority of Scripture, as understood in earlier media eras. John Miles Foley has argued that the concept of a fixed canon is fundamentally "impossible" in the ebb and flow of oral culture.[26] Analogously, I have argued that, at the other end of history, the evanescence of digital electronic media also undermines print-culture notions of a fixed and static canon.[27]

Second, our understandings of the canon and authority of Scripture have been shattered forever by the rediscovery of submerged, lost, or marginalized traditions. The archaeological discoveries of the Dead Sea Scrolls and the Nag Hammadi gnostic texts have confronted us with the multiplicity and fluidity of ancient forms of both Judaism and Christianity. Movements to reclaim voices for the marginalized persons (e.g., liberation, feminist, and postcolonial theologies) have

---

26. Foley, *Theory of Oral Composition*, 13–33.
27. Fowler, "Notion of Canon."

knowingly practiced a "transgressive" critique of the old canonical boundaries.[28] Such radical reinterpretation of the biblical traditions gives pride of place to voices that have been muted within the canon, as well as voices that have been excluded from it.[29]

Third, along with transgressive readings of the received traditions, the liberation movements mentioned above are producing new expressions, in the multitude of media available today, of contemporary spiritual and political visions. For example, Rosemary Radford Ruether's *Womanguides*, while predominately a transgressive rereading of the existing canon, also contains some marvelous new contemporary texts.[30] Although Ruether does not claim to be proposing a new canon for feminists, clearly the hard shell of the traditional biblical canon has been cracked wide open by the appearance of powerful new texts whose voices will not be muted.

Fourth, in an increasingly global culture, it is no longer possible to embrace one's own scriptural traditions without also coming to terms with the scriptural traditions of other religious traditions. Wilfred Cantwell Smith has given us a series of important studies that grapple with the notion of scripture across all of the world's major religious traditions. Whereas once it might have been possible to live within one's own scriptural tradition in blissful ignorance of other religions and their scriptures, it is increasingly more difficult to remain in such isolation. Smith observes that, once upon a time, Christians projected their understanding of the Bible onto other scriptural traditions, but now the time has come to reverse directions and allow our encounter with other religions and their scriptures to reshape our understanding of the Bible.[31]

Fifth, as I and many others have argued, in a world dominated by fluid, everchanging, hyperlinked multimedia, the old notion of a fixed, static canon evaporates:

---

28. Schüssler Fiorenza, *Feminist Commentary,* 1:ix-24; 2:ix-14.
29. Kwok, "Finding a Home"; A. Smith, " 'Hidden in Plain View.' "
30. Ruether, *Womanguides*.
31. Wilfred Cantwell Smith, "Scripture as Form and Concept: Their Emergence for the Western World," in *Rethinking Scripture: Essays from a Comparative Perspective* (ed. Miriam Levering; Albany, N.Y.: SUNY Press, 1989), 29–57; idem, *What Is Scripture? A Comparative Approach* (Minneapolis: Fortress, 1993).

What happens when text moves from page to screen? First, the digital text becomes unfixed and interactive. The reader can change it, become writer. The center of Western culture since the Renaissance — really since the great Alexandrian editors of Homer — the fixed, authoritative, canonical text, simply explodes into the ether.[32]

In the world of electronic writing, there will be no texts that everyone must read. There will only be texts that more or fewer readers choose to examine in more or less detail. The idea of the great, inescapable book belongs to the age of print that is now passing.[33]

The canon and authority of the Bible are undermined in cyberspace because of the following considerations:

- Electronic media encompass the written word, but qualify and relativize it by positioning it alongside audio, video, and graphical expressions.

- Digital media are fluid, multiple, changing; not fixed or single.

- Every electronic "text" is potentially connected to any other text; thus no text is at the center, and no text is at the margin.

- Since in theory one can jump from anywhere to anywhere in cyberspace, digital documents have no real beginning or ending, no center or margin, no inside or outside.

- The distinction between the reader and writer vanishes: if you can "read" a piece of digital coding, you can also "write" your own (re)coding of it.

- Digital media are unruly: they are fundamentally antihierarchical and democratic, resistant to censorship and control.[34]

---

32. Richard A. Lanham, *The Electronic Word: Democracy, Technology, and the Arts* (Chicago/London: University of Chicago Press, 1993).
33. Bolter, *Writing Space*, 240.
34. Fowler, "Notion of Canon."

Whatever canon and authority might once have meant to persons living within the biblical traditions, these fundamental concepts have to be reconsidered and reinvented for a new media age.

Conclusion

Awhile back I fell into an e-mail conversation with a professional colleague whom I have never met face to face. Somehow we began chatting about the future of the Bible in the Electronic Age. My e-mail friend asked me, "So, what do you think will happen to the Bible in the Electronic Age?" I replied:

One, no one knows, certainly not I.

Two, ancient oral people could not anticipate the invention of writing and the scribal culture engendered thereby. Manuscript culture folk could not imagine the coming of the printing press and its ramifications for culture. Similarly, the results of the mutation of the printed Bible into digital electronic media are unimaginable to us now. Whatever will happen will be a surprise.

Three, still there are some early indications of what might result. One strong suspicion many people have is that "secondary orality" (Walter Ong) has already emerged vigorously. I.e., there seems to be a return to many of the psychological and sociological characteristics of oral cultures.

Four, old familiar notions associated with the Bible, such as canon and authority, have disintegrated. People of biblical faith will need to return to square one to reinvent the faith. Another thought: As the chrysalis of the printed Bible gives way to a now unimaginable electronic biblical butterfly, what will secular biblical scholars — now objectively distanced from the life of the church (in good Enlightenment fashion) and utterly committed to the Gutenberg Galaxy of print culture — do? There will be a lot of people, both in the church and in academe, who will cling to the shell of the chrysalis, while shooing away the butterfly.

The mention of church and academy brings up yet another topic that will need to be reinvented from the ground up in the Electronic Age. In an age in which so many things are mutating into new versions of themselves, what will the church and academy relationship mutate into?

To conclude, I offer some comments on my title and subtitle. For many reasons, I try to avoid speaking of "The Bible," unless I am referring to the printed, bound volume. More typically, if I am speaking of the media history of the Bible, in all its rich variety, I will speak of the "biblical traditions." We tend to think of "The Bible" as something single and fixed, but the "biblical traditions" have in fact always been multiple and fluid, evergrowing and everchanging. There were biblical traditions (plural) before there was a printed Bible (singular), and I imagine there will be biblical traditions galore long after the printed Bible loosens its grip upon the Christian imagination. We are not *at the end of the Bible,* merely at the end of the Bible *as we know it.* At the end (terminus) of the Bible as we know it, people of biblical faith must rediscover the ends (purposes or aims) of the Bible as we know it, and thus help to midwife the (re)birth of the biblical traditions into the new media forms of the Electronic Age.

The Writings of
Robert C. Tannehill

Compiled by Kevin L. Smith, Assistant Librarian,
Methodist Theological School in Ohio

1961

"A Study in the Theology of Luke-Acts." *AThR* 43 (Apr. 1961): 195–203.

1965

"Preparation for Biblical Preaching" (eight short articles). *Methodist Theological School Journal*, 1965–72.

1966

Review of *"Our Father": An Introduction to the Lord's Prayer*, by Ernst Lohmeyer, translated by John Bowden. *Religion in Life* 36 (winter 1966–67): 150–51.

1967

Dying and Rising with Christ: A Study in Pauline Theology. Berlin: Alfred Töpelmann, 1967.

1968

"Church Leadership and the Christ Event." *United Theological Seminary Bulletin* 67 (1968): 25–36.
Review of *Taufe und Ethik: Studien zu Römer 6*, by Niklaus Gäumann. *JBL* 87 (Dec. 1968): 470–72.

1970

"The Sword of His Mouth: The Significance of the Form of Synoptic Sayings." *Methodist Theological School Journal* 9 (1970): 1–9.
"The 'Focal Instance' as a Form of New Testament Speech: A Study of Matthew 5:39b–42." *JR* 50 (Oct. 1970): 372–85.

1971

Review of *The Resurrection of Jesus of Nazareth*, by Willi Marxsen. *Enc* 32 (summer 1971): 244–46.

1972

"The Mission of Jesus according to Luke 4:16–30." In *Jesus in Nazareth*. Edited by Walther Eltester. New York: Walter de Gruyter, 1972, 51–75.

Review of *The Obedience of Faith: The Purposes of Paul in the Epistle to the Romans*, by Paul S. Minear. *JBL* 91 (Sept. 1972): 426–28.

1973

Review of *The Meaning of Righteousness in Paul: A Linguistic and Theological Inquiry,* by J. A. Ziesler. *JBL* 92 (Sept. 1973): 457–59.

1974

"Comments on the Articles of Daniel Patte and John Dominic Crossan." *Semeia* 2 (1974): 113–16.

"The Magnificat as Poem." *JBL* 93 (June 1974): 263–75.

Review of *An die Römer*, by Ernst Käsemann. *JBL* 93 (Sept. 1974): 473–76.

1975

The Sword of His Mouth: Forceful and Imaginative Language in Synoptic Sayings. Semeia Supplements 1. Philadelphia: Fortress; Missoula, Mont.: Scholars, 1975.

1977

A Mirror for Disciples: Following Jesus through Mark. Nashville: Discipleship Resources, 1977.

"The Disciples in Mark: The Function of a Narrative Role." *JR* 57 (Oct. 1977): 386–405. German version published in *Der Erzähler des Evangeliums*. Edited by Ferdinand Hahn. Stuttgart: Katholisches Bibelwerk, 1985, 37–66.

Review of *Das Ego Jesu in den synoptischen Evangelien*, by Virgil Howard. *Perkins Journal* 30 (Sept. 1977): 39–40.

1979

"The Gospel of Mark as Narrative Christology." *Semeia* 16 (1979): 57–95.

1980

"Attitudinal Shift in Synoptic Pronouncement Stories." In *Orientation by Disorientation: Studies in Literary Criticism and Biblical Literary Criticism, Presented in Honor of William A Beardslee*. Edited by Richard A. Spencer. Pittsburgh: Pickwick, 1980, 183–97.

"Synoptic Pronouncement Stories: Form and Function." *SBLSP* 19 (1980): 51–56.

"Tension in Synoptic Sayings and Stories." *Int* 34 (Apr. 1980): 138–50.

Review of *Jesus and His Adversaries: The Form and Function of the Conflict Stories in the Synoptic Tradition*, by Arland J. Hultgren. *Religion in Life* 49 (winter 1980): 503–5.

Review of *Mark's Story of Jesus*, by Werner H. Kelber. *Int* 34 (Apr. 1980): 213–14.

1981

"Pronouncement Stories." *Semeia*. Vol. 20. Edited by Robert C. Tannehill. Chico, Calif.: SBL, Scholars, 1981.

"Introduction: The Pronouncement Story and Its Types." *Semeia* 20 (1981): 1–13.

"Varieties of Synoptic Pronouncement Stories." *Semeia* 20 (1981): 101–19.

Review of *The Genesis of Secrecy*, by Frank Kermode. *AThR* 63 (July 1981): 323–26.

1982

"Homiletical Resources: Gospel Lections for Advent." *QR* 2 (fall 1982): 9–42.

"Reading It Whole: The Function of Mark 8:34–35 in Mark's Story." *QR* 2 (summer 1982): 67–78.

1983

"Response to John Dominic Crossan and Vernon K. Robbins." *Semeia* 29 (1983): 103–7.

1984

"The Composition of Acts 3–5: Narrative Development and Echo Effect." *SBLSP* 23 (1984): 217–40.

"Types and Functions of Apophthegms in the Synoptic Gospels." In *ANRW* II.25.2. Berlin: Walter de Gruyter, 1984, 1792–1829.

Excerpts from previous writings quoted in *The New Testament in Literary Criticism*. Edited by Leland Ryken. New York: Frederick Ungar, 1984, 81, 96–97, 98–99, 116–17, 226–27, 232–33, 299–300.

1985

"Israel in Luke-Acts: A Tragic Story." *JBL* 104 (Mar. 1985): 69–85.

"Die Jünger im Markusevangelium — die Funktion einer Erzählfigur." In *Der Erzähler des Evangeliums.* Edited by Ferdinand Hahn. Stuttgart: Katholisches Bibelwerk, 1985, 37–66. English version published in *JR* 57 (1977): 386–405.

"Literature, the NT as." In *Harper's Bible Dictionary.* Edited by Paul J. Achtemeier. San Francisco: Harper & Row, 1985, 564–67.

Review of *Luke and the Law,* by Stephen G. Wilson. *Int* 39 (Oct. 1985): 428–30.

1986

The Gospel according to Luke Vol. 1 of *The Narrative Unity of Luke-Acts: A Literary Interpretation.* Philadelphia: Fortress, 1986.

"Rejection by Jews and Turning to Gentiles: The Pattern of Paul's Mission in Acts." *SBLSP* 25 (1986): 130–41. Revised version in *Luke-Acts and the Jewish People.* Edited by Joseph B. Tyson. Minneapolis: Augsburg, 1988, 83–101.

1987

Review of *Rediscovering Paul: Philemon and the Sociology of Paul's Narrative World,* by Norman R. Petersen. *Int* 41 (Jan. 1987): 76–78.

1988

"Aphorism and Narrative: A Response to John Dominic Crossan." *Semeia* 43 (1988): 141–44.

"Rejection by Jews and Turning to Gentiles: The Pattern of Paul's Mission in Acts." In *Luke-Acts and the Jewish People.* Edited by Joseph B. Tyson. Minneapolis: Augsburg, 1988, 83–101. Reprinted from *SBLSP* 25 (1986).

Review of *Word and Sign in the Acts of the Apostles,* by Leo O'Reilly. *JBL* 107 (Dec. 1988): 762–63.

1989

Review of *Luke-Acts and the Jews: Conflict, Apology and Conciliation,* by Robert L. Brawley. *Bib* 70 (1989): 278–82.

Review of *L'évangile selon Saint Luc: Analyse rhétorique,* by Roland Meynet. *Bib* 70 (1989): 561–64.

1990

The Acts of the Apostles Vol. 2 of *The Narrative Unity of Luke-Acts: A Literary Interpretation*. Minneapolis: Fortress, 1990.

"Beginning to Study 'How Gospels Begin.'" *Semeia* 52 (1990): 185–92.

"Mission in the 1990s: Reflections on the Easter Lections from Acts." *QR* 10 (spring 1990): 84–97.

"Narrative Criticism." In *A Dictionary of Biblical Interpretation*. Edited by Richard Coggins and Leslie Houlden. London: SCM; Philadelphia: Trinity Press International, 1990, 488–89.

"Paul outside the Christian Ghetto: Stories of Intercultural Conflict and Co-operation in Acts." In *Text and Logos: The Humanistic Interpretation of the New Testament*. Edited by Theodore Jennings Jr. Atlanta: Scholars, 1990, 247–63.

Review of *What Are They Saying about Luke*, by Mark Allen Powell. *Trinity Seminary Review* 12 (fall 1990): 103–4.

Review of *Literary Criticism and the Gospels: The Theoretical Challenge*, by Stephen D. Moore. *ThTo* 47 (Oct. 1990): 337–38.

1991

"The Functions of Peter's Mission Speeches in the Narrative of Acts." *NTS* 37 (July 1991): 400–414.

"Scripture and Spirit: Reflections on the 1988 General Conference Statement on 'Theological Guidelines.'" *QR* 11 (fall 1991): 20–32.

Review of *L'art de raconter Jesus Christ: L'écriture narrative de l'évangile de Luc*, by Jean Noel Aletti. *CRBR* (1991): 163–65.

1992

"The Lukan Discourse on Invitations (Luke 14, 7–24)." In *The Four Gospels, 1992: Festschrift Frans Neirynck*. 3 vols. Edited by Frans van Segbroeck et al. BETL 100. Leuven: Leuven University Press/Peeters, 1992, 2:1603–1616.

"What Kind of King? What Kind of Kingdom? A Study of Luke." *WW* 12 (winter 1992): 17–22.

"The Narrator's Strategy in the Scenes of Paul's Defense: Acts 21:27–26:32." *Foundations and Facets Forum* 8 (1992): 255–69.

Review of *A Theology of the Cross: The Death of Jesus in the Pauline Letters*, by Charles B. Cousar. *Int* 46 (Jan. 1992): 73.

1993

"The Story of Zacchaeus as Rhetoric: Luke 19:1–10." *Semeia* 64 (1993): 201–21.

"Visions and Vocation in Acts." *Haelan* 12/1 (1993): 5–9.

Review of *Metaphorik, Erzählstruktur und szenisch-dramatische Gestaltung in den Sondergutgleichnissen bei Lukas,* by Bernhard Heininger. *JBL* 112 (spring 1993): 148–50.

1994

" 'Cornelius' and 'Tabitha' Encounter Luke's Jesus." *Int* 48 (Oct. 1994): 347–56. Reprinted in *Gospel Interpretation.* Edited by Jack Dean Kingsbury. Harrisburg, Pa.: Trinity Press International, 1997, 132–41.

"Should We Love Simon the Pharisee? Hermeneutical Reflections on the Pharisees in Luke." *CurTM* 21 (Nov. 1994): 424–33.

Review of *Luke's Portrait of Paul,* by John C. Lentz. *CRBR* (1994): 218–20.

Review of *The Gospel according to Mark,* by Morna Hooker; and *The Gospel of Mark as a Model for Action: A Reader-Response Commentary,* by John Paul Heil. *Int* 48 (Oct. 1994): 414–18.

Review of *The Plan of God in Luke-Acts,* by John T. Squires. *Bib* 75 (1994): 425–28.

1995

"The Gospels and Narrative Literature." In *The New Interpreter's Bible.* Vol. 8. Nashville: Abingdon, 1995, 56–70.

1996

Luke. ANTC. Nashville: Abingdon, 1996.

"Literature, the NT as." In *The HarperCollins Bible Dictionary.* Edited by Paul J. Achtemeier. San Francisco: HarperSanFrancisco, 1996, 611–14.

Review of *Feasting and Social Rhetoric in Luke 14*, by Willi Braun. *Bib* 77 (1996): 564–67.

1997

" 'Cornelius' and 'Tabitha' Encounter Luke's Jesus." In *Gospel Interpretation: Narrative-Critical and Social-Scientific Approaches.* Edited by Jack Dean Kingsbury. Harrisburg, Pa.: Trinity Press International, 1997, 132–41. Previously published in *Int* 48 (1994): 347–56.

1998

"Freedom and Responsibility in Scripture Interpretation, with Application to Luke." In *Literary Studies in Luke-Acts: Essays in Honor of Joseph B. Tyson.* Edited by Richard Thompson and Thomas E. Phillips. Macon, Ga.: Mercer University Press, 1998, 265–78.

Review of *The Theology of the Acts of the Apostles*, by Jacob Jervell. *JBL* 117 (spring 1998): 147–49.

1999

"The Story of Israel within the Lukan Narrative." In *Jesus and the Heritage of Israel: Luke's Narrative Claim upon Israel's Legacy*. Edited by David P. Moessner. Harrisburg, Pa.: Trinity Press International, 1999, 325–39.

2000

Review of *The Acts of the Apostles: A New Translation and Commentary*, by Joseph A. Fitzmyer. AB, vol. 31. *JBL* 119 (spring 2000): 144–46.

2001

Review of *The Past as Legacy: Luke-Acts and Ancient Epic*, by Marianne Palmer Bonz. *JR* 81 (Jan. 2001): 110–12.

2002

Review of *New Light on Luke*, by Barbara Shellard. *Bib* 83 (2002): 586–89.

Forthcoming

"Repentance in the Context of Lukan Soteriology." In *God's Word for Our World: Theological and Cultural Studies in Honor of Simon John De Vries*. Vol. 2. Edited by Jay Harold Ellens. Sheffield: Sheffield-Continuum.

"Paul as Liberator and Oppressor: How Should We Evaluate Diverse Views of First Corinthians?" In *The Meanings We Choose: Hermeneutical Ethics, Indeterminacy, and the Conflict of Interpretations*. Edited by Charles H. Cosgrove. Sheffield: Sheffield Academic Press.

Contributors

Janice Capel Anderson, Professor of Philosophy and Religious Studies, University of Idaho; author of *Matthew's Narrative Web* (Sheffield Academic Press, 1994); coeditor with Stephen D. Moore of *Mark and Method* (Fortress, 1992) and of *New Testament Masculinities* (Society of Biblical Literature and Brill, 2003)

Robert L. Brawley, Albert G. McGaw Professor of New Testament, McCormick Theological Seminary; author of *Text to Text Pours Forth Speech: Voices of Scripture in Luke-Acts* (Indiana University Press, 1995); and *Centering on God: Method and Message in Luke-Acts* (Westminster John Knox, 1990)

Fred W. Burnett, Department of Religious Studies, Anderson (Ind.) University; coauthor of *The Postmodern Bible* (Yale University Press, 1995); and book review editor for *Religious Studies Review* in the area of Christian Origins

Simon J. De Vries, Professor Emeritus of Old Testament, Methodist Theological School in Ohio; author of *From Old Revelation to New: A Tradition-Historical and Redaction-Critical Study of Temporal Transitions in Prophetic Prediction* (Eerdmans, 1995); and *1 and 2 Chronicles* (FOTL 11; Eerdmans, 1985)

Sharyn Dowd, Associate Professor of Religion, Baylor University; author of *Prayer, Power, and the Problem of Suffering: Mark 11:22-25 in the Context of Markan Theology* (Atlanta: Scholars, 1988); and *Reading Mark: A Literary and Theological Commentary on the Second Gospel* (Macon, Ga.: Smyth & Helwys, 2000)

Robert M. Fowler, Chairperson and Professor of Religion, Baldwin-Wallace College; author of *Let the Reader Understand: Reader-Response Criticism and the Gospel of Mark* (Trinity Press International, 2001); and member of "The Bible and Culture Collective" (George Aichele, Fred Burnett, Elizabeth Castelli, Bob Fowler, David Jobling, Stephen Moore, Gary Phillips, Tina Pippin, Regina Schwartz, and Wilhelm Wuellner), collaborator in *The Postmodern Bible* (Yale University Press, 1995)

Hyun Chul Paul Kim, Assistant Professor of Hebrew Bible, Methodist Theological School in Ohio; author of *Ambiguity, Tension, and Multiplicity in Deutero-Isaiah* (Peter Lang, 2003)

Elizabeth Struthers Malbon, Professor of Religious Studies in the Department of Interdisciplinary Studies, Virginia Polytechnic Institute and State University; author of *In the Company of Jesus: Characters in Mark's Gospel* (Westminster John Knox, 2000); and *Hearing Mark: A Listener's Guide* (Trinity Press International, 2002)

Edgar V. McKnight, Research Professor and William R. Kenan Jr. Professor of Religion Emeritus, Furman University; author of *Meaning in Texts: The Historical Shaping of a Narrative Hermeneutics* (Fortress, 1978); and *Jesus Christ in History and Scripture: A Poetic and Sectarian Perspective* (Mercer University Press, 1999)

David P. Moessner, Professor of Biblical Theology, University of Dubuque Theological Seminary; author of *Lord of the Banquet* (Trinity Press International, 1998); editor of *Jesus and the Heritage of Israel: Luke's Narrative Claim upon Israel's Legacy* (vol. 1 of *Luke the Interpreter of Israel*; Trinity Press International, 1999)

Gail R. O'Day, A. H. Shatford Professor of New Testament and Preaching, Candler School of Theology, Emory University; author of "John," in *The New Interpreter's Bible*, vol. 9 (Abingdon, 1995); and *The Word Disclosed: Preaching the Gospel of John* (Chalice, 2002)

Mikeal C. Parsons, Professor of New Testament and Macon Chair in Religion, Baylor University; author with Heidi J. Hornik of *Illuminating Luke: The Infancy Narrative in Italian Renaissance Painting* (Trinity Press International, 2003); and with Richard I. Pervo of *Rethinking the Unity of Luke and Acts* (Fortress, 1993).

Mark Allan Powell, Professor of New Testament, Trinity Lutheran Seminary; author of *Chasing the Eastern Star: Adventures in Biblical Reader-Response Criticism* (Westminster John Knox Press, 2001); and *A Fortress Introduction to the Gospels* (Fortress, 1998)

David M. Rhoads, Professor of New Testament, Lutheran School of Theology at Chicago; author of *The Challenge of Diversity: The Witness of Paul and the Gospels* (Fortress, 1996); and coauthor with Joanna Dewey and Donald Michie of *Mark as Story: An Introduction to the Narrative of a Gospel* (2d ed.; Fortress, 1999)

Sharon H. Ringe, Professor of New Testament, Wesley Theological Seminary; author of *Wisdom's Friends: Community and Christology in the Fourth Gospel* (Westminster John Knox, 1999); and *Luke* (Westminster Bible Companion; Westminster John Knox, 1995)

Vernon K. Robbins, Winship Distinguished Research Professor of New Testament and Comparative Sacred Texts in the Humanities, Emory University; author of *The Tapestry of Early Christian Discourse: Rhetoric, Society and Ideology* (Routledge: 1996); and *Exploring the Texture of Texts: A Guide to Socio-Rhetorical Interpretation* (Trinity Press International, 1996)

Whitney Shiner, Assistant Professor of Christian Origins, George Mason University; author of *Proclaiming the Gospel: First-Century Performance of Mark* (Trinity Press International, 2003); and *Follow Me! Disciples in Markan Rhetoric* (SBLDS 145; Atlanta: Scholars, 1995)

Jeffrey L. Staley, Adjunct Professor of New Testament, Department of Theology and Religious Studies, Seattle University; author of *Reading with a Passion: Rhetoric, Autobiography, and the American West* *in the Gospel of John* (Continuum Publishing Group, 1995); and coeditor with Musa Dube of *John and Postcolonialism: Travel, Space, and Power* (Continuum International, 2002)

Charles H. Talbert, Distinguished Professor of Religion, Baylor University; author of *Reading Luke-Acts in Its Mediterranean Milieu* (NovTSup 106; Brill, 2003); and *Smyth and Helwys Bible Commentary: Romans* (Smyth & Helwys, 2002)

Carolyn Thomas, SCN, Professor of Biblical Studies, Pontifical College Josephinum; author of *Reading the Letters of Saint Paul* (Paulist, 2002); and *Gift and Response: A Biblical Spirituality for Contemporary Christians* (Paulist, 1994)